Reader Comments

What People are Saying About the *Cherrypickers' Guide*

The *Cherrypickers' Guide* is a standard reference in the hobby, a popular book that has been used and enjoyed by countless thousands of readers. Here are some sample comments from our mailbag:

"Bill Fivaz and J.T. Stanton have produced the **ultimate reference for variety collectors:** the *Cherrypickers' Guide.* The title suggests that it's all about money, but that misses the point. Variety collecting has become increasingly popular over the last several years, with new discoveries constantly turning up. Without the latest information, such as that presented by Bill and J.T., the collector cannot possibly know if a new variety has been found. As a cataloger, I keep a copy of the *Cherrypickers' Guide* on my desk, and refer to it constantly. When I travel to conventions, I never leave home without it."

Mark Borckardt
Numismatic researcher

"We received the *Cherrypickers' Guide* today. You know it's a special book when the graders let out a cheer of joy for having their very own copy on their desk!"

Mike Ellis
Grader and chief attributor, ICG
Past president, CONECA

"I purchased a copy of the third edition of the *Cherrypickers' Guide* from my local dealer. I immediately starting looking through my collection and found a few of the lesser varieties listed. However, the biggest surprise was finding a 1971-S Proof Lincoln cent, doubled-die obverse in my own collection! The value was listed at $1,000, but **I never expected to get that kind of money for my $1.50 investment.** Several coin shows later, a dealer actually offered me $1,200 for my 1971-S doubled die obverse. **I was elated!** The money from the sale of that coin enabled me to purchase a nice, high grade 1922 'Plain' Lincoln to finally complete my collection."

Jamie Giello
Collector

"Fivaz and Stanton—they're the ones who **almost singlehandedly brought *fun* back to coin collecting,** along with, incidentally, a horde of new and enthusiastic collectors."

James Taylor
President, ANACS

"Treasure hunting **makes this hobby fun.** The *Cherrypickers' Guide* is your map."

Bob Grellman
Copper coin specialist

"The *Cherrypickers' Guide* illustrates vividly, with sharp photos and descriptive text, the importance of die varieties. . . . This book is for both the novice and experienced collector, and **definitely belongs in your numismatic library."**

Remy Bourne
Numismatic literature specialist and dealer

"It just gets **better and better and better."**

Ed Hesse
Owner, The Reeded Edge

"The *Cherrypickers' Guide* is **one of those great ideas** that seem to revive the hobby every generation or so. Its impact on the collecting of varieties has already been profound, and this newest edition is filled with fascinating varieties that until now have been known only to a handful of specialists. The team of Fivaz and Stanton have produced a **handy and fun book** that will always be within arm's reach of my desk."

David W. Lange
Research director, NGC

"There are always special moments that stand out in a columnist's memory. I recall the first time I mentioned the *Cherrypickers' Guide* in my weekly coin column distributed by the Los Angeles Times Syndicate. I made note of a few listings and offered a free list to any reader submitting a self-addressed stamped envelope. Anticipating no more than a few requests, local editors were inundated with letters. I can well imagine the collector response to volume one (half cents through nickels), comprising some 450 pages. It should be **a hobby best-seller."**

Ed Rochette
Numismatic author

"With all the current interest in errors and varieties, this new edition has to be your first purchase—it will answer all your questions about 'what's different' on that coin you found. For the advanced specialist, the long wait for the updated edition is now over. This is the **most anticipated numismatic book of the year!"**

Fred Weinberg
Specialist and dealer in errors and varieties

CHERRYPICKERS' GUIDE

to Rare Die Varieties of United States Coins

Fifth Edition • Volume I
Half Cents Through Nickel Five-Cent Pieces

1936-D 3-1/2-Legged Buffalo Nickel
Regular 1936-D value, MS-60: $42.
1936-D 3-1/2-Legged variety value, MS-60: $18,500.

Bill Fivaz · J.T. Stanton
foreword by Q. David Bowers

Atlanta, Georgia

CHERRYPICKERS' GUIDE
to Rare Die Varieties of United States Coins
Fifth Edition • Volume I

© 2009 Whitman Publishing, LLC
3101 Clairmont Road · Suite C · Atlanta, GA 30329

The WCG™ grid used throughout this publication is patent pending.

Correspondence concerning this book may be directed to the publisher, Attn: CPG, at the address above.

ISBN: 0794822851
Printed in China

Disclaimer: Expert opinion should be sought in any significant numismatic purchase. This book is presented as a guide only. No warranty or representation of any kind is made concerning the completeness of the information presented. The authors are professional numismatists who regularly buy, trade, and sometimes hold certain of the items discussed in this book.

Caveat: The price estimates given are subject to variation and differences of opinion. Before making decisions to buy or sell, consult the latest information. Past performance of the rare coin market or any coin or series within that market is not necessarily an indication of future performance, as the future is unknown. Such factors as changing demand, popularity, grading interpretations, strength of the overall coin market, and economic conditions will continue to be influences.

Advertisements within this book: Whitman Publishing, LLC, does not endorse, warrant, or guarantee any of the products or services of its advertisers. All warranties and guarantees are the sole responsibility of the advertiser.

About the Cover: The featured coins are two legendary classics of American coinage. The "Three-Legged" variety of Buffalo nickel (1937, minted in Denver) was caused when a careless Mint worker polished the die too much—perhaps to remove a clash mark or defect—and polished off an entire Buffalo leg. This created one of the most eagerly sought curiosities in the hobby! The 1955 Doubled Die is the most famous variety in the Lincoln cent series. By the time the Mint's coin inspector noticed these dramatic oddities, thousands of them had already been mixed in with normal coins from other presses. They were allowed to be released, and today they are hot collectibles. Both the "Three-Legged" Buffalo and the 1955 Doubled Die are popular enough to be listed in the *Guide Book of United States Coins* (the hobby's famous "Red Book").

If you enjoy the *Cherrypickers' Guide*, you'll also enjoy these books (in Whitman's Bowers Series of numismatic references): *A Guide Book of Morgan Silver Dollars; A Guide Book of Double Eagle Gold Coins; A Guide Book of United States Type Coins; A Guide Book of Modern United States Proof Coin Sets; A Guide Book of Shield and Liberty Head Nickels; A Guide Book of Buffalo and Jefferson Nickels; A Guide Book of Flying Eagle and Indian Head Cents; A Guide Book of Washington and State Quarters; A Guide Book of United States Commemorative Coins; A Guide Book of United States Tokens and Medals; A Guide Book of Gold Dollars;* and *A Guide Book of Peace Dollars.*

For a complete catalog of numismatic reference books, supplies, and storage products, visit Whitman Publishing online at www.whitman**books**.com.

CONTENTS

ABOUT THE AUTHORS

J.T. Stanton began collecting coins in 1959 and began to specialize in the error/variety segment of the hobby in 1982. He has received numerous hobby recognitions and awards including the American Numismatic Association's Medal of Merit. Other ANA recognition includes the Glenn Smedley Memorial Award, the Outstanding Adult Advisor Award, and two ANA Presidential Awards. He was an ANA Summer Seminar instructor for 11 years and initiated the annual "Errors and Varieties and Modern Minting Process" class.

J.T. Stanton

J.T. has served on the board of governors of the ANA (1995 to 1997), on the board of directors of CONECA (Combined Organizations of Numismatic Error Collectors of America), and as president of CONECA from 1987 to 1990.

Other awards J.T. has received include CONECA's Dr. Lyndon M. King Jr. Award, Krause Publications' Numismatic Ambassador Award, and the A.J. Vinci Memorial Excellence in Numismatic Education Award (#6) of Florida United Numismatists (FUN). The fourth edition, volume II, of the *Cherrypickers' Guide* won the 2007 Numismatic Literary Guild's "Extraordinary Merit" award. J.T. has also been elected to CONECA's Hall of Fame.

He lives with his wife Susan in Savannah, has two sons, Jamie and Jeffery, and two grandsons, Thomas (J.T. III) and Henry.

Bill Fivaz has been collecting coins since 1950, and along with J.T. Stanton is one of the country's most respected authorities on numismatic errors and varieties. His numerous awards include the most prestigious recognition of the American Numismatic Association—the Farran Zerbe Award, presented in 1995. Bill is also a recipient of the ANA Medal of Merit (1984, 1989). He was named a Krause Publications Numismatic Ambassador in 1982, and was recognized with the ANA Adult Advisor Award (for Young Numismatists) in 1991. He was selected as the ANA Numismatist of the Year in 2001 and elected to the ANA Hall of Fame in 2002.

Bill Fivaz

Bill has been an Educational Forum speaker at FUN conventions since 1979, and an instructor for the ANA's Summer Seminar for more than 25 years. He has written hundreds of articles on a wide array of topics and is a consultant to ANACS, SEGS, and several other authentication services. Bill's contributions are noted in many of today's most popular and respected hobby books, including the *Guide Book of United States Coins* (the "Red Book"). He is the author of the award-winning *United States Gold Counterfeit Detection Guide*.

Bill is a former member of the board of governors of the ANA, and a former member of the board of directors of CONECA.

He has been married to his wife Marilyn for 50-plus years, and has a son, Bill, a daughter, Diane, two grandchildren, Erin and Jake, and a great-granddaughter, Ella.

FOREWORD

Q. David Bowers

Some numismatic books are interesting to have, perhaps for glancing through, setting aside, and possibly reading at a later time. Other books are a bit more useful, with listings, prices, and historical information that are very helpful to collecting endeavors. Then there are books that are *essential* (make that *absolutely essential*)—of which this is one.

In the years since the *Cherrypickers' Guide to Rare Die Varieties* first came out, the book has grown from interesting, to important, to now essential. I cannot imagine collecting or understanding the coins covered here—half cents through large and small cents, two-cent and three-cent pieces, and nickels—without a copy of this book near at hand. I refer to my older editions regularly, and this most recent volume will certainly be used even more—with its many new listings, photographs, and other improvements.

The preface describes how the *Cherrypickers' Guide* became a hobby best-seller. As but a quick perusal of the contents will suggest, excellent sales alone could not make up for the countless hours spent in perfecting each of the book's listings, one by one. As if this were not enough, the appendices include a bounty of useful information, along with tips on etiquette, common sense, and hints on how to collect more effectively. In fact, it is hard to envision that anything necessary is absent from the pages to follow—though, surely, when the sixth edition eventually comes out, there will be plenty of new content. If the field of die varieties is anything, it is *dynamic*, and scarcely a month goes by without new discoveries coming to light, including for current Mint products.

For a long time the team of Bill Fivaz and J.T. Stanton has been the focal point of verifying new varieties and finessing information (such as concerning rarity and value) of overdates, repunched mintmarks, die doublings, and other departures from the standard. As interest in die varieties increases—as it has been doing steadily for years—their books have become increasingly important.

A visual treat, a feast of information, and a delightful read, all come together in this latest edition of the *Cherrypickers' Guide*. Congratulations once again to Bill and J.T. for a job well done.

Q. David Bowers
Wolfeboro, New Hampshire

PREFACE

Around June of 1989, J. Woodside of Scotsman's Coins in St. Louis had a suggestion for numismatist Bill Fivaz. He thought Bill should produce a book studying all the neat coin varieties he was always searching for. Bill called a friend and fellow variety enthusiast, printer J.T. Stanton, to discuss the idea. They agreed that the hobby community needed such a reference. While Bill and J.T. were very experienced in numismatics, they both were novices when it came to publishing—and certainly not prepared for what they were about to undertake.

At first they decided to include only about 100 of the most significant varieties—those that any collector would certainly want. Those 100 varieties quickly turned into more than 160. With that, a format for the book was decided upon, and the *Cherry-pickers' Guide* became a reality.

Being in the printing business, J.T. handled the production. The U.S. Postal Service was very busy for a while as copy was going back and forth between Bill in Dunwoody, Georgia, and J.T. in Savannah. (Many readers don't realize there are about 275 miles between the coauthors.)

The final copy went to press in November 1989, with hopes of having the book finished and ready for distribution in time for the Florida United Numismatists (FUN) convention the first weekend of January 1990. J.T. stopped at the bindery in Jacksonville, Florida, on his way to Tampa for that show. His plan was to pick up a quantity they felt would be sufficient (about 500 copies); they were not sure how well the book would be received. When they left Tampa on Sunday, all 500 copies had been sold, with orders for more to be shipped and mailed as soon as possible.

The first edition was a great learning experience for both Bill and J.T. An initial printing of 3,000 copies was produced, which was more than they had anticipated selling. They actually felt lucky when all the copies were sold in less than 10 months.

A second edition was planned, which would increase the number of listings and add values for the varieties listed, along with some other improvements. Thanks to the numismatic press and many variety enthusiasts, word of the new edition spread. Dealers and wholesalers wanted the book to offer to their customers. The print run of 5,000 was sold in about six months.

Bill and J.T. were very pleased with the overall acceptance of the book—and the fact that grading services were using the Fivaz-Stanton (FS) attribution numbers on their slabs. (To the best of the authors' knowledge, ANACS was the first to recognize a coin with a Fivaz-Stanton designation.) It seems that Bill and J.T. had luckily stumbled onto a book with the right topic at the right time.

They offered the second edition in a spiral-bound format. "This might well have been the first numismatic book to be offered with the spiral or coil binding," says Stanton. This format makes perfect sense: it is easy to lay the book open to a particular variety and examine a coin for comparison without having to prop or hold the book open.

For the third edition, the entire print run was published in the spiral format.

When it was time for that third edition, one big hurdle needed to be overcome. J.T. simply didn't have time to handle the production. Therefore, the coauthors set out to find a willing publisher. Several were contacted, and several were interested. Bowers and Merena was the authors' choice, and they set out to provide what would become their best effort yet. The third edition, with about five times as many varieties as the first, went to six printings and more than 28,000 copies before volume one of the fourth edition finally came out.

Since J.T. was in the business of printing (and by this time some publishing), the authors asked famous numismatist Q. David Bowers (a principal of Bowers and Merena) if they could produce the fourth edition themselves. Being the gentleman everyone knows, Bowers immediately agreed—if that's what they wanted, that's what he wanted.

The fourth edition became by far the largest effort to that date, so large in fact that it had to be divided into two volumes so the spiral binding could be used. Volume 1 included half cents through nickels. Volume 2 (published by Whitman Publishing in 2006) picked up with half dimes and larger denominations. The division was a natural one. Volume 1 contained all minor coinage, and there are a lot of people who are only concerned with cents and nickels. Volume 2 includes other popular series comprising silver half dimes through dollars (including Bust and Liberty Seated series), gold coinage, and commemoratives.

The *Cherrypickers' Guide* proves that there are times when someone can get lucky, and tackle the right subject at the right time. Bill and J.T. have enjoyed the experience of creating the *Cherrypickers' Guide*, and hope its readers have learned a lot from the contributions of all the people who have made the book possible—those who have provided varieties and information, and who have made other contributions, including values, rarity data, and other vital details.

CREDITS AND ACKNOWLEDGMENTS

> Traditionally each volume of the *Cherrypickers' Guide* has included a dedication to an individual from the error-variety segment of the hobby community, for outstanding contributions to numismatics, especially from an educational standpoint. This entry, the fifth edition, volume I, is dedicated not to an individual but collectively to the thousands of everyday enthusiasts who have been bitten by the variety bug—those who carefully study their pocket change and their coin collections, report their unusual findings to their fellow collectors, and thereby make this one of the most vibrant and active areas of numismatics today.

The *Cherrypickers' Guide* lists Bill Fivaz and J.T. Stanton as its authors, but the fact is the contributions of hundreds of collectors, dealers, and specialists over the years are the backbone of the book. Without those very important people offering new listings, detailed descriptions, rarity information, values (updated on a constant basis), and basic knowledge of a variety or series, this book (and the entire set of *Cherrypickers'* volumes) would not have become the popular reference that it is today.

All the recognition possible cannot adequately express the gratitude appropriately due these individuals, companies, and groups. Yet there are several key people and organizations that must be mentioned for their tremendous contributions.

We have kept and maintained documentation of the people who have submitted various varieties for inclusion in the *Cherrypickers' Guide* over the years. The primary purpose of maintaining these records is to adequately acknowledge those who have submitted varieties. In a very few instances we may have missed one, but for the most part these records have been well maintained since 1991. In a few cases more than one person has contributed the same variety.

Special thanks must begin with **David W. Lange**. Dave examines thousands of varieties each year, and shares information and photographs of new discoveries. He is always willing to examine manuscripts before printing, helping to find mistakes and offer corrections. Dave has always been a strong supporter of, but more importantly a very good friend to, all numismatists. Thanks, Dave, for your help and support over the years.

Rick Snow generously shared his time and talents on this volume in particular. Rick is a specialist in early small cents, and is the author of numerous standard references, including Whitman's *Guide Book of Flying Eagle and Indian Head Cents*.

Ed Fletcher was instrumental in reviewing several sections of this volume, most notably the nickel five-cent pieces, in which series his expertise is well known.

There is a special collector who seems to have a new, previously undiscovered variety every time he is seen at a coin show. **Lee Day** has contributed new varieties for several years.

Chris Pilliod has contributed to every edition produced so far. Chris is very knowledgeable in virtually every series, but is best known for his enthusiasm for Flying Eagle and Indian Head cents and all Liberty Seated coinage. His contributions to the *Cherrypickers' Guide* and the hobby in general are too numerous to list. His help and friendship over the years are greatly appreciated.

Well-known and respected dealer **Larry Briggs** is one of the greatest contributors to this series of books. He always has new varieties to share, and gladly shares his coins for study and photos. Dealers such as Larry have really helped to make our work much easier.

Matt Allman has worked tirelessly to help with the compilation of values, recording results from online and traditional auctions. It is with his help that so many of the listed values are from actual sales.

There are numerous collectors, dealers, and specialists who have contributed greatly since the inception of the *Cherrypickers' Guide*. We wish to thank all those variety enthusiasts who are willing to share their coins, photographs, knowledge, and experience. Those who have contributed to this and previous editions are noted here. If we have missed anyone it is with our most sincere apologies.

Bill Affanato	Terry Campbell*
Leonard Albrecht	Donald Cantrell
Roger Alexander	Rick Carpenter
Brian Allen	Ken Chylinski
Matt Allman	Ted Clark
Gary Alt	Clem Clement
ANACS	Mark Clewell
Walter Anderson	*Coin World*
Guy Araby	Lou Coles
Richard Austin	Frank Colletti
Richard Bateson	CONECA
Frank Baumann	Bert Corkhill
Ed Becker	José Cortez
Jack Beymer	Billy Crawford
David Biglow	David Crawford
Dick Bland	Whaden Curtis
Al Blythe	Charles Daughtrey
Don Bonser	Dave's DCW Collection
Charlie Boyd	Ray Davis
Mike Bozovich	Lee Day
Dan Brady	Tom DeLorey
Jym Braun	George Derwart
Kenneth Bressett	Rick DeSanctis
Larry Briggs	Daniel Dodge
David Brody	J.T. Donahue
Robert Bruce	David Druzisky
Gene Bruder	Elliott Durann
Mike Bruggeman	Edgewood Coin Co.
Paul Bucerel	Brian Edwards
B. Buholtz	Harry Ellis*
Ty Buxton	Mike Ellis
Cameo Coin Gallery	Larry Emard
David J. Camire	Bill Erdokos
Will Camp	Richard Evans

* deceased

Michael "Skip" Fazzari
Joe Feld
Ron Fern
Michael Fey
Ed Fletcher
Kevin Flynn
Geoffrey Fults
Paul Funaiole
Bill Gase
Paul Geiserbach
Ray Gelewski
Jamie Giello
Jack Gorby*
Don Gordon*
Rudy Gos
Mike Gourley
Jane Gray
David Greenfelder
Brian Greer
Bob Grellman
Robert Griffiths
Richard Hana
Joe Haney
Rob Hanks Jr.
B.D. Harding
Tom Hart
Donald Hauser
James W. Hay
Dennis Heard
Doug Heisler
John Hemphill
Alan Herbert
Ronald Hickman
Lee Hiemke
Doug Hill
Ken Hill
ICG
Jim Jones
Martin Jordan
Matt Juppo
Mike Jurek
Carl Kanoff
Jonathan Kern
Jeff Kierstead
Derry King
Joe Kirchgessner

Keith Klopfenstein*
Gerald Kochel
Bud Kolanda
Martin Krashoc
Howard Kuykendall
Jim Lafferty
David W. Lange
Frank Leone
Akio Li
Fred Lindsey
Don Lommler
Carl R. Loyd
Aimee McCabe
Steve McCabe
Mark McWherter
Roy Maines
Ross Manning
Arnold Margolis
J.P. Martin
R.A. Medina
Tom Mendonca
Anthony Mesaros
Michael Mesaros
Michael Michel
Ed Miller
Joe Miller
Tom Miller
Ward Miller
Warren Mills
Michael Morris
Wali Motorwalla
Allan C. Murphy
Dan Murray
NGC
Gene Nichols
Neil Niederman
P. Nilson
John Nogosek
Charlie Nowack
Numismatic News
Numismedia.com
Jim O'Donnell
Old Pueblo Coin Exchange
Lynn Ourso
Jeff Oxman
Dick Painter

* deceased

Mike Paradis
Dennis Paulsen
George Pauwells
Richard Pawley
Daniel Pazsint
PCGS
PCI
Karen Peterson
Larry Philbrick*
Bob Piazza
Chris Pilliod
Denny Polly
Ron Pope
Ken Potter
Wayne Rattray
RCNH
Roger Reiner
Paul Reitmeir
Doug Riley
Mike Ringo
Joe Rizdy
Emory Robinson
Rogers' Coins
Del Romines
Lee Roschen
Gary Rosner
P. Scott Rubin
Bob Ryan
Rick Rybicki
Jerry Sajbel
Charles Schaefer
Steve Schmidt
Terry Searcy
SEGS
Mark Serafine
Gary Shaffstall
Blaise Sidor
Rich Sisti
Sue Sisti
E.O. Smith
Jim Smith
Les Leroy Smith
Ruben Smith
Richard Snow
Art Snyder
Terry Souder

Howard Spindel
Jeff Stahl
John Starr
Larry Steve
Bob Stimax
Tom Stott
Jim Stoutjesdyk
Eric Striegel
Dave Stutzman
Norm Talbert*
Sol Taylor
David Thacker
Dave Thomas
Carson Torpey
Lee Tucker
Leroy Van Allen
Marilyn Van Allen
John L. Veach
Michael Volz
Gary Wagnon
Dan Walker
Mike Wallace
J.R. Walters
Jonathan Warren
Richard Watts
Val Webb
David Welch
Dave Welsh
Michael Werda
John Wexler
Paul Wheeler
Bill White
Bob White
C.C. Whitaker
John Whitworth
James Wiles
Dave Wilson
Al Windholtz
Chuck Wishon
Andy Wong
Jay Woodward
Hank Woods
C.L. Wyatt
Jerry Wysong
Vicken Yegparian
Dan Zaporra
Anthony Zito

* deceased

HOW TO USE THIS BOOK

Like most technical reference books (especially those involving numismatics), the *Cherrypickers' Guide* frequently uses abbreviations, acronyms, and numbering systems to identify and attribute its listings as clearly as possible. Most experienced collectors will recognize and understand the format used herein. However, novices will find this section very helpful.

SYMBOLS USED IN THIS BOOK

The *Pocket Change* symbol indicates a variety that may reasonably be expected to be found in circulation today.

Pocket Change varieties typically are cents dated after 1959, Jefferson nickels (other than silver wartime issues), dimes and quarters minted after 1964, half dollars minted after 1970, and some circulation-strike modern dollars.

The *Red Book* symbol indicates a variety that is listed in the most recent edition of the *Guide Book of United States Coins* (popularly known as the "Red Book"), the best-selling annual price guide of U.S. coins.

The *Young Numismatists* symbol indicates a variety that young and/or emerging collectors might want to focus on. Many of these fall into the Pocket Change category as well.

In most cases, coins marked with the YN symbol are varieties of coins that are very inexpensive when found in their "normal" format, either in Mint State or high circulated grades. They usually can be sold for significant premiums through private sale or through auctions (such as those held periodically by CONECA, the Combined Organizations of Numismatic Error Collectors of America). Finding these varieties can help finance the collection of a numismatist with modest funds.

ABBREVIATIONS USED IN THIS BOOK

DDO	doubled-die obverse	PUP	Pick-Up Point *(see text)*
DDR	doubled-die reverse	R	rarity
I	Interest Factor	RPD	repunched date
L	Liquidity Factor	RPM	repunched mintmark
LD	large date	SD	small date
MPD	misplaced date	TDO	tripled-die obverse
NA	No Arrows	TDR	tripled-die reverse
ND	No Drapery	URS	Universal Rarity Scale
N/L	not listed	WA	With Arrows
OMM	over mintmark	WD	With Drapery
PF	Proof		

KOLIT POSITIONS (K-)

Locations of various coin characteristics are sometimes denoted by their *Kolit* positions (so named for Kolman and Litman, the two numismatists who devised this identification system). This is a shorthand reference based on the numbers on the face of a clock, expressed as K-3 (3 o'clock), K-7 (7 o'clock), and so on. Past editions of the *Cherrypickers' Guide* use this system.

PICK-UP POINTS (PUPS)

A variety's *Pick-Up Point* is its area most prone to exhibit whatever characteristic(s) makes the variety unique. In most cases, this will be the date, the mintmark, or legends. Other PUPs include denticles, stars, designer's initials, and various design elements.

VARIETY VALUE AND NORMAL VALUE

Throughout the guide we offer values for varieties in several grades of preservation. (For more information on grading, refer to *Grading Coins by Photographs* and the *Official American Numismatic Association Grading Standards for United States Coins*.)

Sources for the values of varieties include the following:

- actual sales reported to us, with the most recent sales bearing the most weight;
- our assessments comparing one variety to another similar in rarity, collectibility, interest, and other factors; and
- recommendation by those who specialize in particular series or denominations.

Also included in this volume are fair-market values for each variety's *normal*-version coin. These values are derived from the *Guide Book of United States Coins* (the "Red Book"), www.numismedia.com (a Web site that offers values for U.S. coins), and other sources. They reflect actual retail sales and offers from some of the most respected dealers across the country. These "normal coin" values provide an easy comparison for the amount or percentage of premium each variety can command.

As with any price guide, the values listed should be used strictly as a reference. Although great pains are taken to ensure as much accuracy as possible, values can and do change, especially among varieties that trade frequently.

Factors Affecting Value

Always keep in mind the two major factors affecting the value of any item: supply and demand. That advice has never been proven faulty. If 12 people want a particular variety and only 6 examples are available, the value will be far greater than a similar variety desired by 12 people with 20 examples available.

With numismatic varieties especially, add to those two factors a very important third: *eye appeal!* As a general rule (there may be very few exceptions), the more visually dramatic a variety, the greater its value. For instance, compare two different repunched dates, with similar rarity and in similar grade, on two 1868 Shield nickels—one with a wide degree of separation and one with a very close separation. The variety with the wide separation will always command a greater price.

Values are subject to change whenever a variety becomes more readily available or more desirable. Variety values certainly change with the normal fluctuations of the numismatic market. Remember that, generally speaking, the higher the *numismatic* value of a particular coin, the lower the premium associated with its varieties. For example, a nice doubled die on an Uncirculated Liberty Head $20 gold coin will (generally) command little, if any, premium for the knowledgeable collector.

Values for Actively Traded Varieties

Some of the varieties listed in the *Cherrypickers' Guide* are also noted in other hobby price guides that are updated on a regular basis. The values for these varieties, such as the 1955 Doubled-Die Lincoln cent, fluctuate quite often as a result of market trends. In these instances, we highly recommend that you refer to other *current* price guides to obtain an up-to-date value for the variety. Values for these varieties are included in the *Cherrypickers' Guide* for reference only. Collectors and dealers can compare the prices noted with current prices and use the difference as a guide for possibly adjusting other similar varieties.

THE FIVAZ-STANTON (FS) NUMBERING SYSTEM

The Fivaz-Stanton (FS) numbering system dramatically changed in the fourth edition, volume 2 (published in 2006).

In the older system, adding new listings was problematic as additional decimal places were required in many instances. Furthermore, an attribution number such as FS-05-003.752, or even FS-10c-0.008 would be very complicated, and not within the normal thought processes of most collectors. The older system simply left no room for additions. The newer system allows for additions to the listings on an ongoing basis, and *without any limitation!*

Reading the Fivaz-Stanton Number

With the Fivaz-Stanton numbering system, the complete listing number includes

- the denomination, followed by
- the date and mintmark (if there is a mintmark), and finally
- the sequential "identifier" number.

The identifiers essentially denote the type of variety, and/or the location of its point of interest. This number is usually three digits, but can be four digits.

A four-digit identifier is used for dates that include two or more major types. For instance, a date variety on an 1867 With Rays Shield nickel might be FS-05-1867-301, yet a date variety on an 1867 No Rays Shield nickel might be FS-05-1867-1301. There are a few instances when there are three or more distinctive types, such as the 1864 Indian Head cent (copper-nickel, bronze No L, and bronze With L). In these cases the first type will be three digits, with the second and third types will be four digits, such as 1301 and 2301.

With two major types, such as the 1867 With Rays and 1867 No Rays nickels, the With Rays varieties would have three digits, such as 301. The No Rays varieties would have four digits, such as 1301, with the last three digits always the same. The 1 at the beginning of the No Rays varieties differentiates the second type from the first.

There is one major exception in the identifier number system. The Morgan and Peace dollar series use their Van Allen–Mallis (VAM) numbers (when available) as the identifier. For instance, with an 1878 VAM 44, the FS number is FS-S1-1878-044. This is more convenient for VAM enthusiasts and for the grading services. (Dollar coins are covered in volume 2 of the *Cherrypickers' Guide*.)

Most third-party grading services will gladly change an existing slab with the old FS number for a new slab with the newer FS numbering system. A fee for this service can be expected, but it is usually lower than for a regular submission. Check with the grading service of your choice first.

Identifiers for Fivaz-Stanton Numbers

The following are the identifiers for the Fivaz-Stanton numbers and their related meanings:

101–299	obverse doubled die and/or obverse die variety
301–399	obverse date variety
401–499	obverse variety, miscellaneous
501–699	mintmark variety
701–799	miscellaneous variety
801–899	reverse doubled die
901–999	reverse variety, miscellaneous

Note: As mentioned, Morgan and Peace dollar varieties will have Van Allen–Mallis (VAM) numbers as the primary number sequence of their identifiers.

Old Fivaz-Stanton Numbers Included in the Listings

For this volume the old FS numbers are included as a cross-reference. The new FS number is primary, and the old FS number (when available) is listed in parentheses.

Abbreviations for Denominations

HC	half cent		50	half dollar
LC	large cent		S1	silver dollar
01	small cent		T1	trade dollar
02	two-cent piece		C1	clad dollar
3S	three-cent piece (silver)		G1	gold dollar
3N	three-cent piece (nickel)		G2.5	$2.50 gold piece
05	nickel five-cent piece		G5	$5 gold piece
H10	half dime		G10	$10 gold piece
10	dime		G20	$20 gold piece
20	twenty-cent piece		C50	commemorative half dollar
25	quarter dollar			

RARITY FACTOR

The rarity factors used in the *Cherrypickers' Guide* are based upon the Universal Rarity Scale developed by Q. David Bowers. This is the only rarity scale available that is reasonably accurate for die varieties of the late-19th and 20th centuries. Following you will find a background of the older Sheldon rarity scale, and details of Bowers's Universal Rarity Scale.

The Sheldon Scale

For many years, the only method of reasonably identifying rarity was with the use of the Sheldon scale, designed by numismatic author William H. Sheldon to identify the rarity of large-cent varieties. Applied to those coins, the Sheldon scale worked very well, as their mintage figures were relatively low. The Sheldon scale was further adapted for use with many other coin series and denominations, as it was the only common scale in existence. However, it was not quite appropriate for most series, most varieties, or even most errors.

The Sheldon scale was simply a progression of eight levels into which the populations of all large-cent varieties were to fall. Each level was prefaced with the letter R, for Rarity:

R-1   common

R-2   not so common

R-3   scarce

R-4   very scarce (est. 76–200 pieces in existence)

R-5   rare (31–75 pieces)

R-6   very rare (13–30 pieces)

R-7   extremely rare (4–12 pieces)

R-8   unique, or nearly so (1–3 pieces)

Numismatic writers adopted this scale to represent coins that were considered scarce or rare. However, as one can imagine, the scale is not appropriate for many coins, especially those of the late 19th and 20th centuries, with their high mintages. For instance, using this scale, the 1955 Doubled-Die Lincoln cent would be considered "common" or "not so common." Yet we know it is in fact scarce or rare.

Bowers's Universal Rarity Scale (URS)

Clearly, another scale was needed by the hobby community for indicating rarity of all coins. Leave it to numismatic historian Q. David Bowers to recognize the need and develop a method that could be used for any series, and any rarity. (In fact, it can be used not only for coins, but for virtually anything whose rarity, scarcity, or availability is important.) Bowers developed the Universal Rarity Scale (URS), which, as its name implies, is universal for any coin or item. He outlined this scale in the June 1992 issue of *The Numismatist,* and further popularized it in the *Expert's Guide to Collecting and Investing in Rare Coins.* The URS has already been adopted by many writers and catalogers and is used throughout the *Cherrypickers' Guide.*

The URS is simple and reasonable in its mathematical progression:

URS-0	none	URS-12	1,001 to 2,000
URS-1	1; unique	URS-13	2,001–4,000
URS-2	2	URS-14	4,001–8,000
URS-3	3 or 4	URS-15	8,001–16,000
URS-4	5–8	URS-16	16,001–32,000
URS-5	9–16	URS-17	32,001–65,000
URS-6	17–32	URS-18	65,001–125,000
URS-7	33–64	URS-19	125,001–250,000
URS-8	65–125	URS-20	250,001–500,000
URS-9	126–250	URS-21	500,001–1,000,000
URS-10	251–500	URS-22	1,000,001–2,000,000
URS-11	501–1,000	(etc.)	

When using rarity numbers with coins, there are a couple important factors to remember:

1. Rarity generally differs from one grade to another. If a coin is listed as URS-13 (2,001 to 4,000 known) it might be relatively common. However, if there are only two pieces known in grades above About Uncirculated, it would be a true rarity (URS-2) in MS-63. Such is the case with the 1888-O Morgan dollar, Hot Lips variety. These are fairly common in Very Good and Fine, but virtually unknown above About Uncirculated. Such a coin is often referred to as a *condition rarity*.

2. Rarity and value are not always as closely related as one might suspect. If there are nine known examples of a particular variety, but only six or seven collectors are interested in it, the coin would certainly be rare, but because of a relatively low interest factor (low demand), it would not command much of a premium. Conversely, there could be 10,000 pieces known of a variety, but if 11,000 collectors are interested in obtaining one, the premium over the normal value of the coin would be much greater, due to the high interest factor (high demand). This brings us back to the age-old law of supply and demand.

INTEREST FACTOR

Interest Factor is a term we use to indicate just how much demand a particular coin or variety has.

- A variety with a very high Interest Factor is in high demand, with several thousands of collectors desiring it.
- A medium Interest Factor may indicate that the variety is desired by hundreds or a few thousand people.
- A low Interest Factor might indicate that the coin is sought by just a handful of collectors.

In this guide, we rate each variety's Interest Factor as follows:

I-5   very high interest (most general collectors interested)

I-4   high interest (most variety collectors interested)

I-3   moderate interest (most series collectors interested)

I-2   minimal interest (some collectors interested)

I-1   very low interest (only very specialized collectors interested)

The Interest Factor, combined with the rarity, helps to determine the value of a variety or error. However, eye appeal is also a very important factor and must be considered in the final evaluation. A critical part of eye appeal for a variety or error is the relative strength or visibility of its defining characteristic—how easily can it be seen?

As a variety receives more publicity within the numismatic press, its Interest Factor might rise as demand increases. This can cause the price or value to increase without any change in the estimated quantity available.

LIQUIDITY FACTOR

The Liquidity Factor indicates how quickly or how easily a coin or variety *should* sell at auction, given normal market conditions.

- A coin with a high Liquidity Factor would be expected to sell right away, generally commanding full or inflated values.
- A coin with a low Liquidity Factor would not normally sell very easily or quickly, and then usually at a discount from suggested values.

Hot or highly active market conditions can inflate the Liquidity Factor of any coin, with a cold market having the opposite effect.

Our Liquidity Factor scale is as follows:

L-5   will sell easily, and often above listed value

L-4   will usually sell quickly at listed value (for variety enthusiasts)

L-3   will often sell in a reasonable time period, often to specialists

L-2   might sell in time, maybe at a discounted price

L-1   might sell provided the right buyer is available, but at a discount

OTHER NUMBERS AND ABBREVIATIONS

Identification numbers and abbreviations appear more frequently in the study of mint errors (and especially die varieties) than within the regular segment of the hobby. Some are easy methods of precisely identifying different varieties. Others are used to describe rarity, or even a certain class or type of variety. The important fact is with the use of these numbers, most specialists will know right away exactly which variety is being discussed. At the very least, a dealer or collector can consult a reference and find the corresponding number along with photos or detailed descriptions, which can easily and accurately identify a certain variety.

Most of these identification systems are simply numbers listed after the date and denomination. Some are more complex identification listings and include letters or symbols to further identify the variety or error.

RPM and OMM Listing Numbers

These are the original RPM (repunched mintmark) and OMM (over mintmark) listing numbers compiled by CONECA (Combined Organizations of Numismatic Error Collectors of America). You will notice most RPMs and OMMs are identified simply, such as 1949-D/S 5c, OMM-001. These numbers indicate that the coin is a 1949-D nickel, with an over mintmark (D Over S), and is over mintmark #1. This indicates that it was the first OMM listed for that particular date by John Wexler and Tom Miller when they originally began to catalog these varieties in the early 1980s. This cataloging system soon became the *RPM Book*, published in 1982.

Just because a variety is listed as #1 in no way should suggest it is the strongest, the most desirable, or the most valuable (although this is often the case).

Other publications listing all known varieties for a series will normally include newer listings for that series. These newer listings are being cataloged by James Wiles for CONECA.

Doubled-Die-Listing Numbers

As with the RPMs and OMMs, doubled dies are also assigned numbers that correspond to the listing numbers in CONECA's files. This numbering system was originally developed by Alan Herbert and John Wexler. These numbers can be confusing to the beginner, but they have a very logical and important sequence for serious collectors, so a brief explanation is included herewith.

There are eight basic classes of doubled dies. These classes generally have little to do with the strength of the doubling. Rather, they indicate how the particular doubling occurred. (Because of the complexity, the "how" of the doubling is not covered in this general overview.) To collectors, the strength of a doubling is generally more important than how it came about.

For example, there is a Lincoln cent listed as 1971-S PF 1c 1-O-II. These numbers indicate that the coin is a 1971-S Proof cent, listed as die #1, with the doubling on the obverse, and it is a Class II doubled die. As with the RPMs, if the coin is listed as die #1, it does not necessarily mean that it is the strongest doubled die for that date, only the first one listed. In this instance, die #2 for the 1971-S Proof cent is actually stronger, more valuable, and certainly in greater demand.

The sequence for these doubled-die listing numbers will always be the same. Following the date of the coin will be the indication of a Proof (if it is a Proof), then the denomination, the die number (indicated by Arabic numerals), an O or R signifying the doubled die is on the obverse or reverse, and finally the class of doubled die (indicated by Roman numerals). There are some doubled dies that were made as a result of a combination of more than one class of doubled die, such as 1971-S PF 1c 2-O-II+V-CW. The CW at the end indicates the spread of the doubling (from the Class V) is in a clockwise direction. Class I and Class V doubled dies use this CW or CCW direction indicator, meaning either a clockwise or counterclockwise spread. There are also cases in which a coin will have a doubled die on the obverse *and* reverse, such as 1963 25c 7-O-II+1-R-I. As mentioned above, these identification numbers should become easy to understand.

A more detailed description of each doubled die, by class, is published in *The Lincoln Cent Doubled Die*, by John Wexler, a book highly recommended for all variety enthusiasts. Although published in 1984, it is still a valuable source of information, and a must for variety collectors. These classes are also included in the *Cherrypickers' Guide* (third edition, and volume I of the fourth and fifth editions).

OTHER IDENTIFICATION NUMBERS

Other numbers are used from time to time in this book to indicate how a variety is cataloged in another reference book. The list below might not be comprehensive, as new books and reference works are being produced constantly.

Breen	*Walter Breen's Complete Encyclopedia of U.S. and Colonial Coins*
F (Fletcher)	Edward Fletcher, *Shield Five Cent Piece*
FF	Kevin Flynn and Edward Fletcher, *The Authoritative Reference on Three Cent Nickels*
FS (Fivaz-Stanton)	The *Cherrypickers' Guide*
Greer	Brian Greer, *Complete Guide to Liberty Seated Dimes*
L	David Lawrence's books on Barber coinage (as mentioned in the text)
Leone	Frank Leone, *Longacre's Two-Cent Piece—An Attribution Guide*
S (Snow)	Rick Snow, *Flying Eagle and Indian Cents*
VAM (Van Allen–Mallis)	*Comprehensive Catalog and Encyclopedia of Morgan and Peace Dollars*
WB (Wiley-Bugert)	*Complete Guide to Liberty Seated Half Dollars*

AVERAGE DIE LIFE

This chart indicates the average number of strikes that each obverse and reverse die for current coin designs are expected to produce. These figures are simply averages and expectations for circulation strikes. Dies can and do last longer, or may be retired from service earlier due to damage.

Damage can and does occur early in the life of a die. Depending on the severity of the damage, Mint technicians might repair the die, or (often) retire it early. Retirement can also occur if an abnormality—such as doubling or another inaccuracy—is discovered on a die. The following list shows the average number of strikes for each type and denomination:

Lincoln cent	1,400,000
Jefferson nickel	200,000 (This figure is for the 2006 Monticello design.)
Roosevelt dime	300,000 (At the time of publication, Denver was averaging about 400,000; Philadelphia, about 230,000.)
Washington quarter	752,000
statehood quarter	275,000
Kennedy half dollar	160,000
Sacagawea dollar	250,000

Half Cents, 1793–1857

The half-cent section is primarily the work of copper specialist J.R. "Bob" Grellman. Bob has provided the text, the rarity information, the detailed descriptions, and the photos.

Most of the specialists in this area are already very familiar with these varieties. However, we hope by including these a spark of interest may develop for some of you readers.

There are a couple of books that are well worth adding to your numismatic library for further study of the series:

> *The Half Cent Die State Book, 1793–1857*, by Ronald P. Manley, is one of the best books available today. Edited by Bob Grellman, the book contains hundreds of excellent photographs, very detailed descriptions, die-state census information, and much more. Well worth the retail price for a large, hardbound reference.

> *Walter Breen's Encyclopedia of United States Half Cents, 1793–1857*, by Walter Breen, is another excellent reference for the specialists. Like the Manley book, hundreds of photos are included with very detailed information on die marriages, die states, and even some pedigree information for some of the rarer varieties. With more than 500 pages and many color plates, this again is well worth the retail price for a deluxe, hardbound edition.

For specialty clubs there is none better than Early American Coppers (EAC), a group of the most devoted numismatists studying the early copper coins of the United States. Founded in 1967, EAC is dedicated to the advancement and study of U.S. colonial coins, half cents, large cents, and Hard Times tokens. More information and a membership application can be obtained at www.eacs.org.

1804 — FS-HC-1804-301 (001)

VARIETY: Date Orientation
PUP: Date
URS-5 · I-5 · L-5

COHEN-2

Description: *Obverse*—Same as Cohen-4. The 4 of the date is low and tilted slightly to the left. Digits are closely spaced, especially the 0 and 4. *Reverse*—Zeroes on the denominator are very close. The left side is always weakly struck.

	G-5	VG-8
VARIETY	$5,000	$10,000
NORMAL	$50	$65

1804 — FS-HC-1804-302 (002)

VARIETY: Date Orientation
PUP: Date
URS-5 · I-5 · L-5

COHEN-4

Description: *Obverse*—Same as Cohen-2. The 4 of the date is low and tilted slightly to the left. Digits are closely spaced, especially the 0 and 4. *Reverse*—Digits in the denominator are widely spaced.

	G-5	F-12
VARIETY	$500	$2,000
NORMAL	$50	$65

1805 — FS-HC-1805-301 (003)

VARIETY: Date Orientation   **COHEN-2**

PUP: Date and T of LIBERTY

URS-4 · I-5 · L-5

Description: *Obverse*—Same as Cohen-3. Small 5 in date. T in LIBERTY has no feet. *Reverse*—Stems on the reverse. Leaf tip is under the center of the O in OF. (On the more common Stems reverse, this leaf tip is under the right side of the O in OF.)

	G-5	VG-8
VARIETY	$3,000	$5,000
NORMAL	$50	$65

1806 — FS-HC-1806-301 (004)

VARIETY: Date Orientation   **COHEN-3**

PUP: Date

URS-4 · I-5 · L-5

Description: *Obverse*—The 6 of the date is small and high. The space between the 0 and 6 is equal to the space between the 8 and 0. (On the more common "Small 6 with Stems" variety, the 0 and 6 are closely spaced.) *Reverse*—No stems on the wreath. A few are known with a cud die break on the rim at ICA in AMERICA.

	G-5	VG-8
VARIETY	$3,000	$5,000
NORMAL	$50	$65

1808 — FS-HC-1808-301 (005)

VARIETY: Overdate

PUP: Date

URS-4 · I-5 · L-5

COHEN-1

Description: *Obverse*—Same as Cohen-2. Overdate, 8 over 7. *Reverse*—Leaf tip is close under the upright of the D in UNITED. (On the common reverse, this leaf tip is distant and left of the upright.) Usually cracked through tops of TED and STATES.

	AG-3	G-5
VARIETY	$8,000	$14,000
NORMAL	$50	$65

1809 — FS-HC-1809-301 (006)

VARIETY: Date Orientation

PUP: Date and T of LIBERTY

URS-4 · I-5 · L-5

COHEN-1

Description: *Obverse*—Same as Cohen-2. Close, straight date without any digits recut. *Reverse*—Berry is centered under the upright of the T in UNITED. The tip of the leaf is under the right edge of the second S in STATES. Two are well known for a cud die break joining MERI to the rim above.

	G-5	VG-8
VARIETY	$700	$1,400
NORMAL	$50	$65

HERITAGE

Large Cents, 1793–1857

The section on large cents was added originally to the second edition. As with the half cent section, the data and photos for this section are provided by J.R. "Bob" Grellman.

As with the half cent section, most of the specialists in this area are already very familiar with these varieties. However, we hope by including these a spark of interest may develop for new collectors.

Unlike for some of the other coin types listed, varieties are the primary focus for most serious copper specialists. As a result, some of the rarest varieties will bring huge premiums, often within an hour of their discovery. During the 1992 American Numismatic Association convention in Orlando, a rare large-cent variety was spotted and quietly purchased by a knowledgeable collector. The coin was subsequently sold within just an hour for a tidy $12,000—not bad for a $12 purchase!

Note that many of the diagnostics listed for this series are difficult to see except on very high-grade circulated, and/or Mint State, coins.

There are several excellent books highly recommended for further study of the series. The most detailed and easiest to use is *U.S. Cents, 1840–1857*, by J.R. "Bob" Grellman.

The "must have" and the foundation for variety collecting is *Penny Whimsy*, by William H. Sheldon. Originally published in 1958, updated versions are currently available for $60 or less.

Other excellent books for the series are also available. The dates covered and authors are noted as follows: for the years 1793 to 1814, a book by Bill Noyes and another by Walter Breen and Mark Borckardt have been published; and for the years 1816 to 1839, a book by Bill Noyes and another by John Wright have been published.

For specialty clubs there is none better than Early American Coppers (EAC). This group includes the most dedicated numismatists studying the early copper coins of the United States. Founded in 1967, it promotes the advancement and study of U.S. colonial coins, half cents, large cents, and Hard Time tokens. More information and a membership application can be obtained at: www.eacs.org.

1843 — FS-LC-1843-301 (001)

VARIETY: Date Orientation   NEWCOMB-17

PUP: Date

URS-6 · I-5 · L-5

Description: *Obverse*—Head of 1844. The point of the lowest curl is slightly to the right of the inner right curve of the 8 in the date. The 1 is closer to the denticles than to the bust. *Reverse*—Reverse of 1844. There are two points down to the right from the base of the N in ONE; and another up to the left at the same angle from the left top of that N.

	F-12	VF-20
VARIETY	$400	$1,500
NORMAL	$25	$40

1846

FS-LC-1846-301 (002)

VARIETY: Date Orientation

NEWCOMB-23

PUP: Date

URS-6 · I-5 · L-5

Description: *Obverse*—Tall date. There is a horizontal line through center of the 1, strongest on left side of the upright. *Note:* This obverse die comes matched with four different reverse dies, two of which resulted in rare pairings. *Reverse*—There are points down and slightly to the right from ONE and ENT, with some rough lines on the same angle between the N and E of ONE and the N of CENT. There are heavy, rough lines from the denticles to the T in UNITED, the second T in STATES, and the R in AMERICA.

Comments: A single example is known with a strong rim break over TES.

	F-12	VF-20
VARIETY	$450	$1,700
NORMAL	$25	$40

1846 — FS-LC-1846-302 (002.5)

VARIETY: Date Orientation

PUP: Date

URS-7 · I-5 · L-5

NEWCOMB-25

Description: *Obverse*—Same as N-23. Tall date. There is a horizontal line through the center of the 1, strongest on the left side. Points down from the inner bun, main curl, neck, throat, and jaw (strongest from the main curl). There is a coarse vertical line moving up from between the denticles to the right of the 6 in the date. *Reverse*—Early examples have fine lapping lines, pointing down and very slightly to the right, over most of the die, strongest on the right side. The tops of CE are connected by shallow crumbling, and minor crumbling is visible on the underside of the crossbar on the N in UNITED. There is a strong line from the denticles to the top left of the N in UNITED and a strong, short, dull line up from the top right of the first T in STATES. Another fine line moves down to the right from the denticles and passes into the E of AMERICA; another, wider line, at a different angle, goes from the denticles down to the top of that letter. Denticles below the point of the stem are crumbling at their bases.

	F-12	VF-20
VARIETY	$500	$1,500
NORMAL	$25	$40

1847

VARIETY: Date Orientation

NEWCOMB-36

PUP: Date

URS-6 · I-5 · L-5

Description: *Obverse*—The points of the lowest curl are slightly to the left of the right edge of the 8. The field is rough, especially in the area in front of the face, down to the bottom of the neck. Additional roughness is evident in the field from the 18 to star five (strongest around star four). The date is rather weak, especially the 84. The top of the 1 does not touch the base. *Reverse*—There are many points up slightly to the left around ONE CENT; another up from the berry left of the C in CENT. Additional points down and slightly to the right from ONE CENT (strongest from the right top of N in CENT). The points up from CENT reach nearly halfway up to the bases of ON in ONE. *Note:* This reverse die also comes matched to a common obverse on which the 1 touches the bust.

	F-12	VF-20
VARIETY	$400	$1,600
NORMAL	$25	$40

1847 — FS-LC-1847-302 (004)

VARIETY: Date Orientation   **NEWCOMB-43**
PUP: Date
URS-1 · I-5 · L-5

Description: *Obverse*—The point of the lowest curl is slightly to the right of the inner right curve of the 8 in the date. The base of the 1 is strongly repunched below. *Note:* This obverse die also comes mated with a common reverse without the fine lines at NE in ONE. *Reverse*—Many nearly horizontal lines and points are behind ONE CENT, strongest at NE, with some lines reaching the leaf and berry to the right of the T. A few lines on the same angle connect the wreath to the N and E of UNITED.

	F-12	VF-20
VARIETY	Speculative	
NORMAL	$25	$40

1849

VARIETY: Date Orientation

NEWCOMB-25

PUP: Date

URS-3 · I-5 · L-5

Description: *Obverse*—The point of the lowest curl is slightly to the right side of the 8 in the date. Lines point up to the left from the denticles below star 12 to below the date; others point down slightly to the left from the denticles between stars seven and eight; and some weaker ones point down from the denticles right of star 10. There are short spikes to the right from the denticles at stars three, four, five, and six. Fine lines point up and to the right from the inner curl and main curl just below the inner bun. All stars show crumbling or swelling (strongest on the side closest to Miss Liberty). The edge and entire field are wavy and irregular, as if the die was improperly hardened. The denticles are sharp, indicating this is not a worn die. There is a rust lump on the center of Liberty's cheek. *Reverse*—A rough line points up and to the right from the top of the N in UNITED to the denticles. There are fine lines over AME (nearly horizontal to the top of the M), and lumps on the edges of ONE CENT (strongest on the tops of C and T, very similar to N-10). The fields are wavy and irregular, similar to the obverse. The field around ERICA, extending to the stem tip, is extremely rough. The reverse die is not double hubbed (as seen on N-10 and 27).

	F-12	VF-20
VARIETY	$3,000	$5,000
NORMAL	$25	$40

1850 — FS-LC-1850-301 (005.5)

VARIETY: Date Orientation
PUP: Date
URS-7 · I-5 · L-5

NEWCOMB-24

Description: *Obverse*—Same as N-23. Open 5. The date is now very weak, especially the top right of the 0. There is a curved line under the top right serif of the T. The top points up to the right from the inner curl, seen on N-18 and 23, are obscured by roughness around the inner curl. There is a small dot near the hair right of the eyebrow; another weaker one left of the Y, almost touching that letter; and one below the eye, even with the front edge of the eyeball. *Reverse*—Points up and slightly to the right from ONE and ENT; a few stronger ones point down to the left from the bases of NE. Lines point down to the left inside NE and EN. There is a long, strong, slightly curved line near the denticles over UNI (strongest over the top left of N). There are also other minor lines and points on the U and around the wreath in early die states.

	F-12	VF-20
VARIETY	$100	$250
NORMAL	$25	$40

1851

FS-LC-1851-301 (006)

VARIETY: Date Orientation

NEWCOMB-42

PUP: Date

URS-1 · I-5 · L-5

Description: *Obverse*—Point of the lowest curl sits slightly to the right of the inner right curve of the 8 in the date. Three heavy, nearly vertical lines point down from the denticles left of star four. Many lines point down and to the right at different angles over most of the die, strongest from the lowest curl to star thirteen. *Note:* This obverse die also comes mated with a common reverse die without the lines from E in ONE. *Reverse*—Four lines point up and to the left from the top of the E in ONE. There is a short point up from the top left of the E in CENT, and others up and to the right from the top of the ribbon below EN in CENT. The reverse die is buckled, with wavy fields from improper die preparation.

	F-12	VF-20
VARIETY	Speculative	
NORMAL	$25	$40

1851 FS-LC-1851-302 (006.5)

VARIETY: Date Orientation

PUP: Date

URS-4 · I-5 · L-5

NEWCOMB-44

Description: *Obverse*—The date is heavily punched into the die, with both 1s repunched several times. The most prominent evidence of repunching is a horizontal dash below the left half of the base of the first 1; two more dashes to the right from its upright; a dash to the left from the bottom of the base of the second 1; and a dash to the left of its upright. There are short points up to the right from the denticles below 51. A long, dull vertical line points down from the curls over the space between the 5 and 1; a similar line points up from the denticles to the right of the date. There is a strong point up from the hair on the forehead; and others up from the hair and coronet, below star six. Minor die scratches point up to the right at different angles from the inner curl. The die is sinking, causing the fields to "puff out" slightly, most likely the result of improper die hardening. *Reverse*—There are fine lines up and to the left on top of the E in ONE; others at the same angle from the left at the right of that E. There are short points up from the left top of the E in CENT; others move up from the top of the T in UNITED. There are two points up to the right from the top of the ribbon below EN in CENT; and another point up to the right from the stem close to the top. The die is sinking, causing the fields to "puff out" slightly, most likely the result of improper die hardening.

	VG-08	VF-20
VARIETY	$2,000	$4,000
NORMAL	$25	$53

1856

FS-LC-1856-301 (007)

VARIETY: Date Orientation

NEWCOMB-22

PUP: Date

URS-5 · I-5 · L-5

Description: *Obverse*—Italic 5. The point of the lowest curl sits slightly to the left of the right edge of the 8 in the date. Lapping lines down and to the right cover the entire field. There is a point up and to the left on the same angle as the lapping lines from the nose, even with the top of the eye. There are dull points, up and to the left from the hair curl just below the front edge of the coronet. There is a short line up to the left, inside the top of the Y. An engraver's scratch curves up to the left in the hair over the left side of the ear. There is a small lump on the forehead under the left edge of the 1. Stars are not doubled as on N-17. *Reverse*—Lapping lines down and to the right cover most of the die, strongest at NIT, E in STATES, and E in AMERICA.

	F-12	VF-20
VARIETY	$200	$500
NORMAL	$25	$40

Flying Eagle Cents, 1856–1858

Varieties within this series are many, despite the very short period for which they were produced. We have not included any varieties for the year 1856, due to the fact this was a "Proof only" year, and these are generally considered pattern coins. The remaining two years contain several very exciting varieties, especially the year of 1857.

We are very fortunate in that we now have several references for this short series, most notably the references by Rick Snow. The first is *A Guide Book of Flying Eagle and Indian Head Cents.* This excellent general-purpose reference details the history of the series and features its mainstream varieties. The second, and most important for variety enthusiasts, is the *Flying Eagle and Indian Cent Attribution Guide, Second Edition, Volume One: 1856–1858.* This reference features all the known die varieties for the series, complete with excellent photos and important information. Other good reference books have been published and are generally easy to locate through numismatic book and supply dealers.

In today's world, researchers generally turn first to the Internet for much of their information. Snow's commercial Web site offers almost as much information as one might want. Best of all, the URL is easy to remember: www.indiancent.com.

There is also a very active and educational specialty club available to enthusiasts of the series—the Fly-In Club. The name was obviously derived by combining portions of the names of both series. Membership forms, online newsgroups, and forums are available at www.fly-inclub.org.

The varieties in this volume of the *Cherrypickers' Guide* are the "best of the best," and the list should not be considered complete.

Our thanks go to Rick Snow for his generous and invaluable contributions to this section.

1857 — FS-01-1857-101 (002)

SNOW-4

VARIETY: Doubled-Die Obverse (DDO-002)
PUP: Beak, eye, last A of AMERICA, wing tip
URS-9 · I-4 · L-3

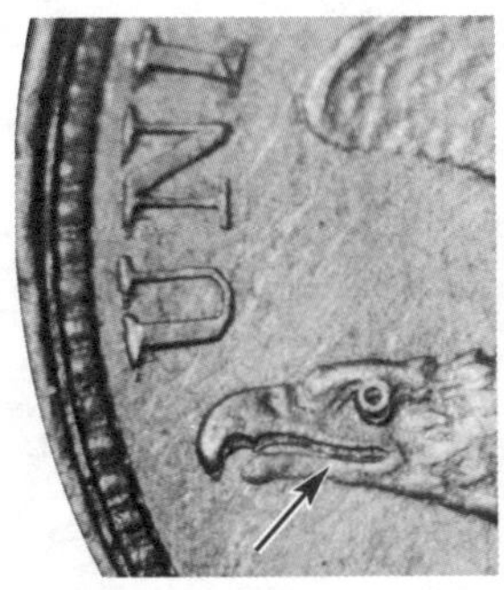 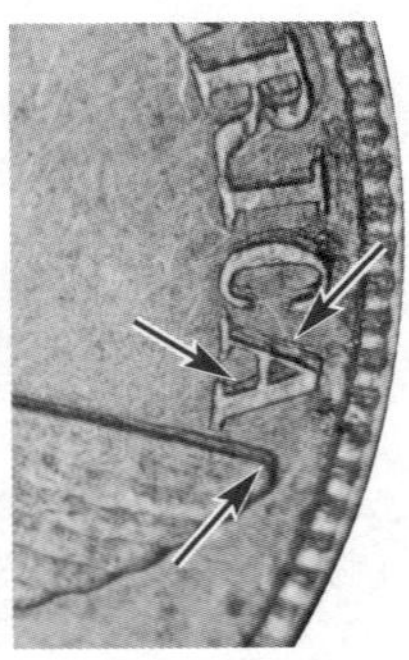

Description: There is doubling on the eagle's beak, eye, and tail feathers, and the letters of UNITED STATES OF AMERICA, with the spread increasing in strength from left to right. The eagle is missing a wing tip. This is a defect on the hub that is found on a few dies.

Comments: FS-105 and 101 are very similar, with 105 having a broken wing tip, while 101 has a missing wing tip.

	EF-40	AU-50	MS-60	MS-63	MS-65
VARIETY	$250	$500	$750	$1,000	$4,000
NORMAL	$150	$300	$500	$800	$3,500

1857 — FS-01-1857-102 (002.3)

SNOW-15

VARIETY: Doubled-Die Obverse (DDO-003)
PUP: Beak, eye, last A of AMERICA, wing tip
URS-8 · I-4 · L-3

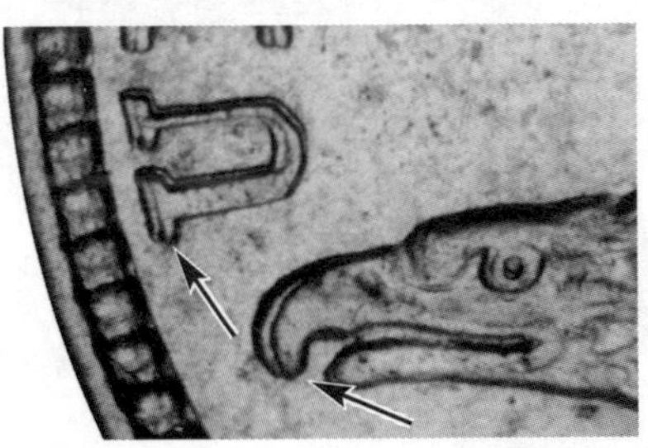 

Description: The doubling is evident on the eagle's eye and tail, and UNITED STATES OF AMERICA. Although not as strong as the other two listings, this variety is nonetheless exciting to locate.

Comments: This doubled die is very similar to FS-101 and 105. This one has the missing wing tip corrected by hand engraving of the die.

	EF-40	AU-50	MS-60	MS-63	MS-65
VARIETY	$200	$350	$600	$900	$4,000
NORMAL	$150	$300	$500	$800	$3,500

1857 — FS-01-1857-103 (002.7)

VARIETY: RPD + Doubled-Die Obverse (DDO-006)
SNOW-10
PUP: Beak, eye, last A of AMERICA, wing tip
URS-7 · I-4 · L-4

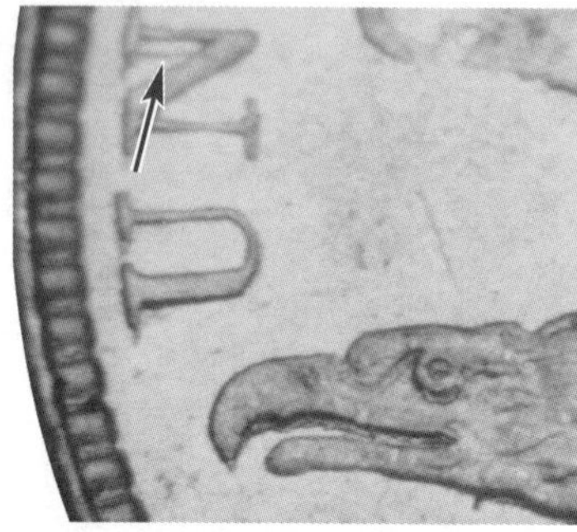
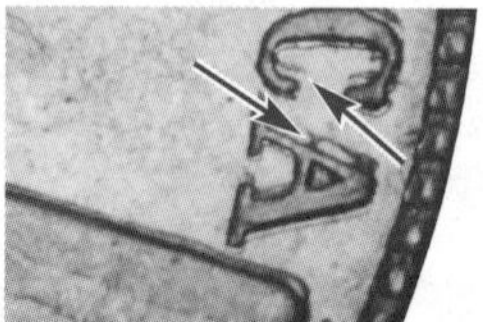
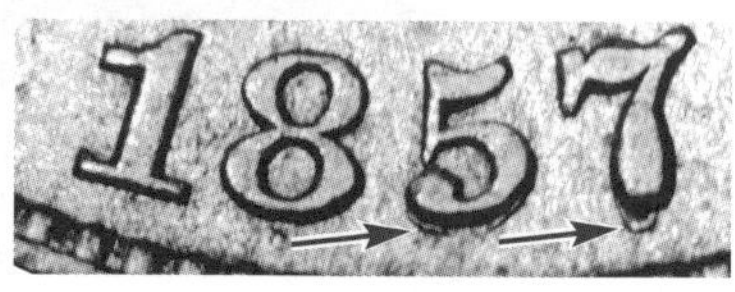

Description: Doubling is evident on UNITED STATES OF AMERICA and the eagle's eye and beak. A bold repunched date is evident as secondary digits below the primary digits of 5 and 7.

Comments: This is similar to many other doubled dies this year, but the repunched date makes it much more desirable! This is unusual, due to the few repunched dates found this year. Late-die-state specimens have a reverse cud from the left leaves to the rim, and are worth an additional premium.

	EF-40	AU-50	MS-60	MS-63	MS-65
VARIETY	$300	$700	$1,500	$2,500	$6,000
NORMAL	$150	$300	$500	$800	$3,500

1857 — FS-01-1857-104 (002.8)

VARIETY: Doubled-Die Obverse (DDO-005)
SNOW-5
PUP: Beak, UNITED STATES OF AMERICA
URS-5 · I-4 · L-4

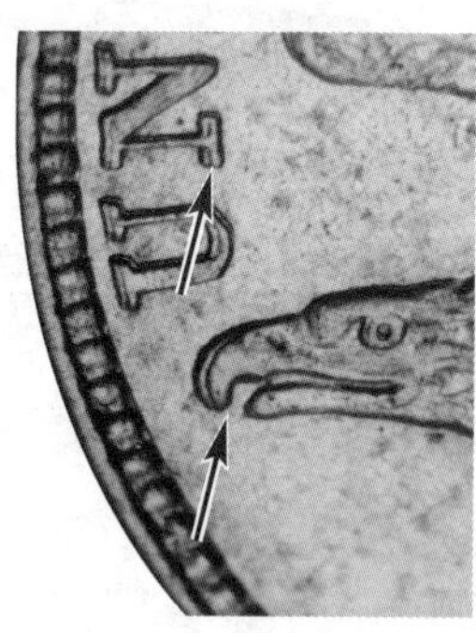

Description: Strong doubling is evident on UNITED STATES OF AMERICA and the eagle's eye, beak, and wing fold. Unlike the previous doubled dies for this date, the doubling on this variety is spread toward the center, away from the rim.

Comments: This doubled die is scarcer than others of the date.

	EF-40	AU-50	MS-60	MS-63	MS-65
VARIETY	$500	$1,000	$1,250	$2,000	$5,000
NORMAL	$150	$300	$500	$800	$3,500

1857 — FS-01-1857-105 (002)

VARIETY: Doubled-Die Obverse (DDO-008) — **SNOW-3**
PUP: Beak, eye, last A of AMERICA, wing tip
URS-9 · I-4 · L-3

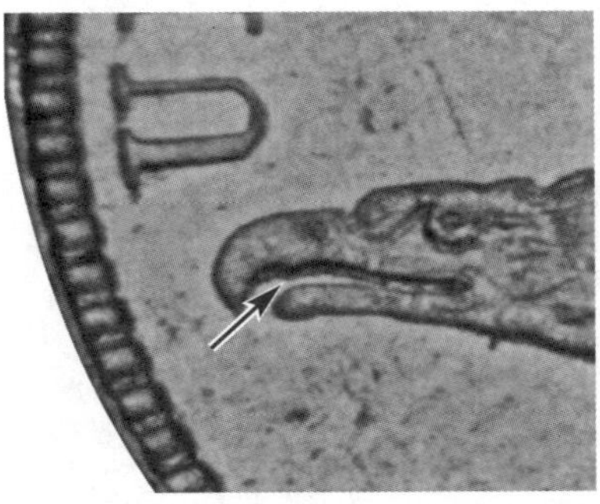 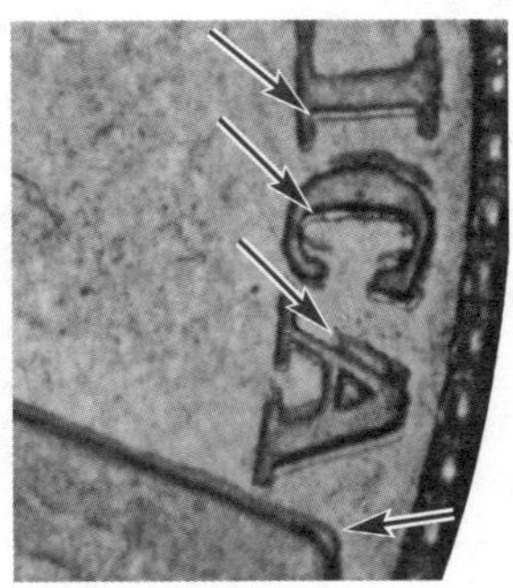

Description: There is doubling on the eagle's beak, eye, and tail feathers, and the letters of UNITED STATES OF AMERICA, with the spread increasing in strength from left to right. The obverse also has a broken wing tip—this is the same hub that produced the 1858/7 FS-301 (Snow-1).

Comments: FS-105 and 101 are very similar, with 105 having a broken wing tip, while 101 has a missing wing tip.

	EF-40	AU-50	MS-60	MS-63	MS-65
VARIETY	$250	$500	$750	$1,000	$4,000
NORMAL	$150	$300	$500	$800	$3,500

1857 — FS-01-1857-301 (001.5)

VARIETY: Repunched Date (RPD-003) — **SNOW-11**
PUP: Date
URS-8 · I-3 · L-3

Description: The digits from an initial date punch are evident south of the primary digits.

Comments: The weaker or secondary image is usually difficult to observe in specimens below EF-40, primarily due to the weakness of the initial date punch.

	EF-40	AU-50	MS-60	MS-63	MS-65
VARIETY	$250	$500	$900	$1,800	$5,500
NORMAL	$150	$300	$500	$800	$3,500

1857 — FS-01-1857-401a (001)

VARIETY: Type of 1856, Repunched Date (RPD-001)
SNOW-1
PUP: Date, letters of UNITED STATES OF AMERICA
URS-10 · I-5 · L-5

Description: Early die states show repunching on all of the digits in the date. Later dies states show repunching only on the 85. The obverse lettering (UNITED STATES OF AMERICA) of this variety is the same as that on the 1856 pattern cent. The opening of the letter O in OF is rectangular instead of round or oval, the serifs in the letters E and F are longer than on other 1857s, and the lower center point of the M is almost bulbous.

Comments: The early-die-state pieces are prooflike. An MS-66 prooflike example sold for $40,000 in 2007. At least five other obverse dies were made using the hub of 1856 (see next listing).

	EF-40	AU-50	MS-60	MS-63	MS-65
VARIETY	$400	$900	$1,500	$3,000	$8,000
NORMAL	$150	$300	$500	$800	$3,500

1857 — FS-01-1857-401b (001)

VARIETY: Type of 1856
SNOW-2
PUP: Letters of UNITED STATES OF AMERICA
URS-5 · I-5 · L-5

Description: The obverse lettering (UNITED STATES OF AMERICA) of this variety is the same as that on the 1856 pattern cent. The opening of the letter O in OF is rectangular instead of round or oval, the serifs in the letters E and F are longer than on other 1857s, and the lower center point of the M is almost bulbous.

Comments: At least five obverse dies were made using the hub of 1856. It is believed by Flying Eagle researcher Richard Snow that these dies were made at the same time as the other 1856 obverse dies, but were left undated until 1857.

	EF-40	AU-50	MS-60	MS-63	MS-65
VARIETY	$250	$500	$900	$1,500	$4,500
NORMAL	$150	$300	$500	$800	$3,500

1857

FS-01-1857-402 (003)

VARIETY: Obverse Clashed Die (with Liberty Seated 50¢) (MAD-003)

SNOW-9

PUP: Apparent retained cud through AMERICA

URS-10 · I-5 · L-5

Description: The obverse die of this 1857 Flying Eagle cent was clashed with the obverse die of a Liberty Seated half dollar. The clash is most evident through the word AMERICA.

Comments: Die researcher Chris Pilliod discovered that these clashes were probably caused while the dies in the press were being changed from half dollars to cents. In the process, the press was cycled through once and clashed the half dollar obverse die with the cent obverse die. Why are the dies head-to-head? Chris has shown through die cud research that the Flying Eagle dies were installed in the press with the obverse die in the anvil (lower) position, while Liberty Seated half dollars had their obverse die in the hammer (upper) position.

	EF-40	AU-50	MS-60	MS-63	MS-65
VARIETY	$250	$600	$1,200	$1,750	$6,000
NORMAL	$150	$300	$500	$800	$3,500

1857　　　　　　　　　　　　　　　　　　FS-01-1857-403 (004)

VARIETY: Obverse Clashed Die (with Liberty Head $20)　　　**SNOW-7**
　　　(MAD-001)
PUP: Profile of Liberty of the obverse right side
URS-8 · I-5 · L-5

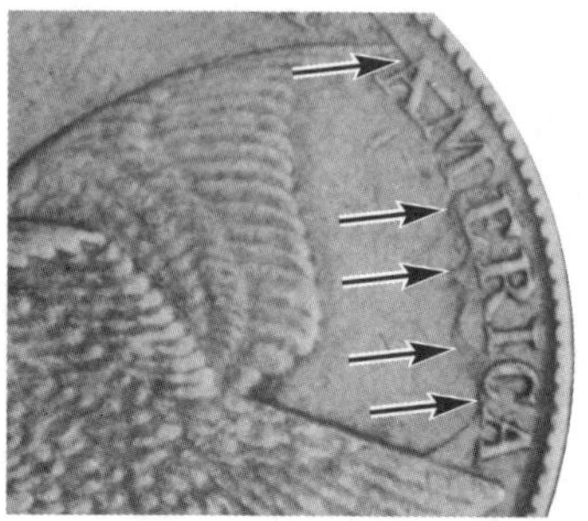

Description: The obverse die of this 1857 Flying Eagle cent was clashed with the obverse die of a Liberty Head double eagle.

Comments: No Mint State specimens of this variety are known as of 2008. These were caused the same way the half dollar clash of 1857 occurred. Many collectors actively search for the three multi-denominational die clashes of the 1857 cents. An AU-58 example sold for $15,000 in 2003. (See also FS-402 and 901.)

	EF-40	AU-50	MS-60	MS-63	MS-65
VARIETY	$3,000	$5,000	$15,000	–	–
NORMAL	$150	$300	$500	$800	$3,500

1857　　　　　　　　　　　　　　　　　　FS-01-1857-901 (005)

VARIETY: Reverse Clashed Die (with Liberty Seated 25¢)　　　**SNOW-8**
　　　(MAD-002)
PUP: Field on reverse above ONE
URS-9 · I-5 · L-5

Description: The reverse die of this 1857 Flying Eagle cent was clashed with the reverse die of a Liberty Seated quarter. The outline of the eagle's head is evident above the word ONE on the reverse.

Comments: Like FS-402 and 403, Chris Pilliod discovered that these clashes were probably caused during the die change from cents to quarter dollars. In this case, the Flying Eagle dies were installed in the press with the reverse die in the hammer position, while Liberty Seated quarter dollars had their reverse die in the anvil position in the press. The matching 1857 quarter with the reverse cent clash exists and is a very popular addition to the cent clash set. An MS-64 example sold for $12,500 in 2007.

	EF-40	AU-50	MS-60	MS-63	MS-65
VARIETY	$500	$800	$1,200	$3,000	$15,000
NORMAL	$150	$300	$500	$800	$3,500

1858, Large Letters — FS-01-1858-101 (005.5)

VARIETY: Doubled-Die Obverse (DDO-002)
SNOW-2
PUP: AMERICA
URS-6 · I-4 · L-3

Description: The doubling is evident on UNITED STATES OF AMERICA, with increasing strength of spread from left to right.

Comments: This doubled die is rarely encountered. The interest and liquidity might actually be higher than stated. These have been under-appreciated, as previous sales have not been at large premiums.

	EF-40	AU-50	MS-60	MS-63	MS-65
VARIETY	$200	$350	$550	$900	$4,000
NORMAL	$150	$300	$500	$800	$3,500

1858, Large Letters — FS-01-1858-301 (006)

VARIETY: Overdate [RPD(O)-001]
SNOW-1
PUP: Date
URS-10 · I-5 · L-5

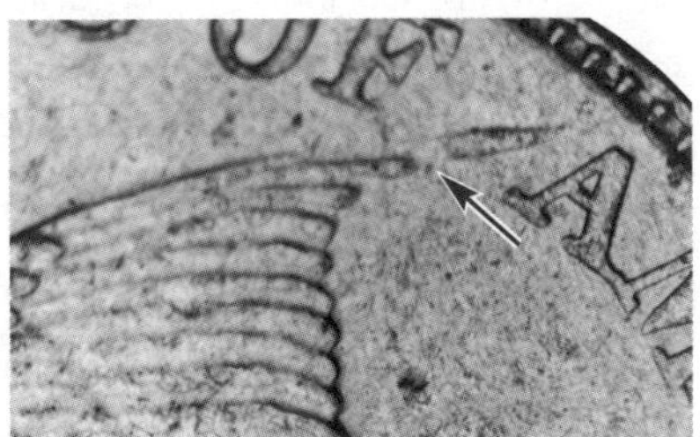

Description: The last 8 was punched over a 7. It is not known at this time whether a four-digit logo punch was used, or a three-digit logo punch in addition to a single digit punch. The flag of the upper right corner of a 7 can be seen above the second 8. There is a raised triangular-shaped dot in the field above the first 8. This die marker is the only confirming diagnostic. A secondary diagnostic for this variety is the "broken" right wing of the eagle. However, this diagnostic is also known for dies without the overdate, including other 1857s. The flag of the 7 may not be evident on later-die-state specimens, but the raised dot above the first 8 is virtually always visible.

Comments: Some specialists believe the triangular dot in the field is the remaining portion of an errantly punched 1. There is always weakness on the upper right area of the wreath on the reverse. An MS-65 specimen sold for $100,000 in 2006. Note that late-die-state specimens are always considered much less valuable than earlier die states.

	F-15	VF-20	EF-40	AU-50	MS-60	MS-63	MS-65
VARIETY	$500	$900	$1,500	$2,500	$4,000	$10,000	$100,000
LATE DIE STATE	$100	$150	$250	$400	$700	$1,000	$5,500
NORMAL	$38	$58	$150	$215	$350	$615	$3,325

1858, Large Letters — FS-01-1858-302 (006.1)

VARIETY: Overdate + Doubled-Die Obverse (DDO-007)   SNOW-7
PUP: Date and UNITED
URS-5 · I-5 · L-5

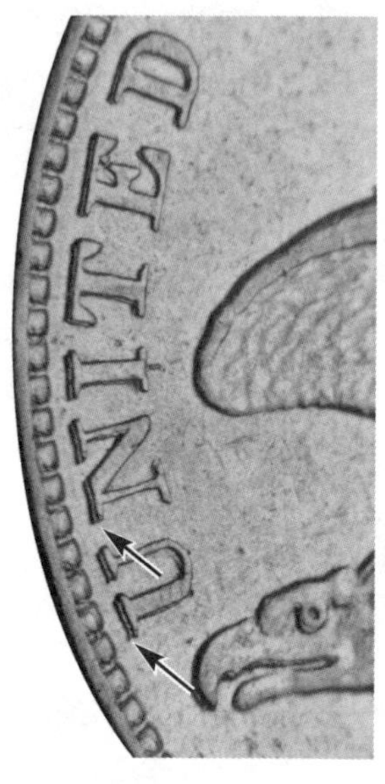

Description: This overdate is likely the result of two differently-dated four-digit logo punches: the first an 1857-dated punch and the second and primary date 1858. The flag of the upper right of a 7 is evident outside the top right of the second 8, and the flag of a secondary 1 is evident just left of the primary 1. Unlike FS-301, this variety is not found in die states. However, the overdate is rather light and difficult to spot without knowing what to look for. This overdate also exhibits a strong Class II doubled die, evident on UNITED STATES OF AMERICA.

Comments: This variety is much rarer than FS-301, but much less known. It was discovered by Mark McWherter. The lightness of the overdate and difficulty in detection present a great cherrypicking opportunity.

	F-15	VF-20	EF-40	AU-50	MS-60	MS-63	MS-65
VARIETY	$300	$500	$1,000	$2,000	$4,500	$7,500	$25,000
NORMAL	$38	$58	$150	$215	$350	$615	$3,325

Indian Head Cents, 1859–1909

Collectors of Indian Head cent varieties belong to one of the most active specialty groups in numismatics. Additionally, due primarily to the efforts of Rick Snow, many serious collectors of the series include most of the significant varieties in their collecting pursuits. Nice varieties are known for most of the dates within the series, beginning with 1859 and ending in 1909.

Indian Head cents will always be tied to the Flying Eagle cents, due in part to the fact that they comprise the first small cents, and both were designed by James B. Longacre. We are very fortunate in that there are several excellent references for this popular series, most notably the references by Rick Snow. The first is *A Guide Book of Flying Eagle and Indian Head Cents.* This excellent reference details the history of the series, and features its mainstream varieties. The second, and most important for variety enthusiasts, is the *Flying Eagle and Indian Cent Attribution Guide, Volume Two: 1859–1869, Volume Three: 1870–1889,* and *Volume Four: 1890–1909.* These books feature all the known die varieties for the series, complete with excellent photos and important information. Other good reference books have been published, and are generally easy to locate through numismatic book and supply dealers.

In today's world, researchers generally turn first to the Internet for much of their information. Snow's commercial Web site, www.indiancent.com, offers much information.

There is also a very active and educational specialty club open to enthusiasts of the series—the Fly-In Club. The name was derived by combined abbreviations of Flying Eagle and Indian Head. Membership forms, online newsgroups, and forums are available at www.fly-inclub.org.

The varieties illustrated in this volume of the *Cherrypickers' Guide* are considered to be the "best of the best." They do not make up a complete list.

We thank Rick Snow for contributing to this section.

1859 — FS-01-1859-301 (006.3)

VARIETY: Repunched Date (RPD-001)
SNOW-1
PUP: Date
URS-7 · I-4 · L-4

Description: This is a strong repunched date, with all secondary digits evident to the southwest of the primary digits. The flag of a secondary 1 is quite evident below the flag of the primary 1.

Comments: This RPD is considered to be rarer than the next listing, and due to the spread of the secondary digits should be considered worth a great premium.

	EF-40	AU-50	MS-60	MS-63	MS-65
VARIETY	$800	$1,250	$2,000	$4,000	$10,000
NORMAL	$80	$150	$250	$550	$3,000

1859 — FS-01-1859-302 (006.2)

VARIETY: Repunched Date (RPD-002)
SNOW-2
PUP: Date
URS-8 · I-4 · L-4

Description: This repunched date is evident with a secondary digit to the south on the 1 and 8, and very slightly on the 5.

Comments: Any repunched date on an 1859 cent is generally considered very scare to rare and is usually in reasonably high demand.

	EF-40	AU-50	MS-60	MS-63	MS-65
VARIETY	$165	$300	$500	$1,750	$5,000
NORMAL	$80	$150	$250	$550	$3,000

1859   FS-01-1859-303 (006.35)

VARIETY: Repunched Date (RPD-003)   **SNOW-3**
PUP: Date
URS-7 · I-3 · L-3

Description: This repunched date is evident with a secondary digit to the south of the 1 and very slightly on the 8.

Comments: This particular RPD is not as valuable, nor in such high demand, as the previous two listings, but it is scarcer.

	EF-40	AU-50	MS-60	MS-63	MS-65
VARIETY	$150	$250	$500	$800	$4,000
NORMAL	$80	$150	$250	$550	$3,000

1860   FS-01-1860-401 (006.4)

VARIETY: Transitional
PUP: Point of bust
URS-13 · I-4 · L-4

Description: This extremely important transitional obverse is evident from the pointed bust, typical of those dies of 1859. The bust of 1860 has a more rounded point than that of 1859. This is sometimes labeled as Type 1 (T1).

Comments: There are at last count six minutely different dies comprising this variety. It is getting more accepted as a regular member of the basic Indian Head cent collection. Presently it is priced similarly to the 1859, but it is much scarcer. A repunched date variety is known, with minute repunching on the 1. (Snow-T1-1)

	EF-40	AU-50	MS-60	MS-63	MS-65
VARIETY	$100	$200	$300	$750	$5,500
NORMAL	$65	$100	$175	$250	$1,300

1861   FS-01-1861-301 (006.45)

VARIETY: Repunched Date (RPD-001)   **SNOW-1**
PUP: Date
URS-11 · I-3 · L-3

Description: This RPD is evident with the second 1 having a weaker secondary digit slightly to the south of the primary 1.

Comments: This variety is quite scarce. Very few sales are noted.

	F-40	AU-50	MS-60	MS-63	MS-65
VARIETY	$200	$300	$400	$1,500	$3,000
NORMAL	$100	$150	$200	$250	$1,100

1862   FS-01-1862-301

VARIETY: Misplaced Date (MPD-002)   **SNOW-2**
PUP: Denticles below date
URS-4 · I-3 · L-3

Description: This MPD exhibits the remnants of two digits protruding from the denticles below the date.

Comments: This variety is relatively new and very few have been located.

	VF-20	EF-40	AU-50	MS-60	MS-63	MS-65
VARIETY	$40	$65	$120	$175	$300	$1,500
NORMAL	$20	$35	$75	$100	$175	$1,100

1862 — FS-01-1862-801

VARIETY: Doubled-Die Reverse (DDR-001)   **SNOW-5**
PUP: Arrow shafts
URS-3 · I-3 · L-3

Description: This is a very bold doubled die, with doubling on the arrow shafts.

Comments: Presently very rare. As more collectors turn over their coins, perhaps more will show up.

	VF-20	EF-40	AU-50	MS-60	MS-63	MS-65
VARIETY	$400	$750	$1,250	$2,000	$3,000	$5,500
NORMAL	$20	$35	$75	$100	$175	$1,100

1863 — FS-01-1863-301

VARIETY: Repunched Date (RPD-002)   **SNOW-2**
PUP: Date
URS-6 · I-3 · L-3

Description: Secondary digits are evident to the south on the last 3 digits. The secondary 8 is apparent within the upper loop of the primary 8, a secondary 6 within the upper loop of the 6, and the secondary 3 within the upper loop of the 3. Some collectors may feel this is an overdate (3/2) but the curve within the primary 3 too closely matches that of a 3.

Comments: This variety is very scarce.

	VF-20	EF-40	AU-50	MS-60	MS-63	MS-65
VARIETY	$50	$75	$150	$200	$300	$2,000
NORMAL	$20	$35	$75	$100	$175	$1,100

1863 — FS-01-1863-302

VARIETY: Misplaced Date

PUP: Neck at necklace

URS-4 · I-3 · L-3

SNOW: N/L

Description: A portion of a digit (likely a 1) is evident by the front of the neck at the necklace.

Comments: This is a new listing for the *Cherrypickers' Guide*.

	VF-20	EF-40	AU-50	MS-60	MS-63	MS-65
VARIETY	$25	$35	$75	$100	$200	$900
NORMAL	$13	$22	$48	$80	$150	$850

THE CHERRYPICKERS' GUIDE HELPFUL HINTS

Please read the information in the front of this book. It sets the tone for the material that follows and makes it easier to interpret the information for each listing.

1863

VARIETY: Doubled-Die Reverse (DDR-001)
PUP: Right leaves
URS-3 · I-3 · L-4

SNOW-10

Description: Strong doubling is evident on the right leaves of the wreath and to a lesser degree on the upper left leaves.

Comments: Discovered in 1999 (by Mike Ellis), this variety remains very scarce.

	F-40	AU-50	MS-60	MS-63	MS-65
VARIETY	$250	$500	$750	$1,000	$3,000
NORMAL	$35	$75	$100	$175	$1,100

1864, Copper-Nickel FS-01-1864-401

VARIETY: Polished Die   SNOW-5

PUP: Ear

URS-2 · I-2 · L-2

Description: Strong die polish is evident above and through the ear.

Comments: This is a recently discovered variety and a new listing for the *Cherrypickers' Guide*. Its true rarity is unknown and its value remains very subjective. Eventually its popularity may wane.

	VF-20	EF-40	AU-50	MS-60	MS-63	MS-65
VARIETY	$50	$100	$150	$175	$300	$1,200
NORMAL	$39	$56	$68	$120	$190	$1,025

Note: Values listed for MS-60 and higher are for RB (red and brown) specimens. Full red Uncirculated specimens command higher prices.

1864, Bronze FS-01-1864-1101 (006.47)

VARIETY: Doubled-Die Obverse + Repunched Date   SNOW-4
         (DDO-001, RPD-004)

PUP: LIBERTY

URS-5 · I-4 · L-4

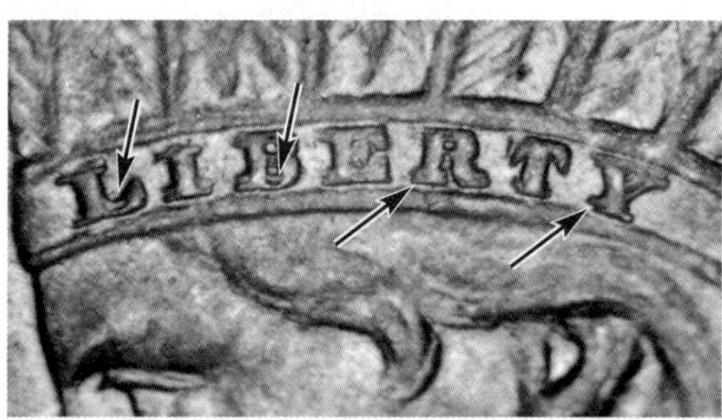

Description: Strong doubling is evident on LIBERTY and portions of the hair and headdress. Repunching on the 4.

Comments: This is an 1864 Bronze, No L cent. The variety was first reported by Bob Stimax in 1993. It is very scarce and desirable. Most examples are rather mushy, possibly due to improper hardening of the dies. Early die states are rare.

	VF-20	EF-40	AU-50	MS-60	MS-63	MS-65
VARIETY	$500	$800	$1,200	$2,000	$3,000	$15,000
NORMAL	$40	$60	$80	$100	$150	$300

Note: Values listed for MS-60 and higher are for RB (red and brown) specimens. Full red Uncirculated specimens command higher prices.

1864, Bronze   FS-01-1864-1301 (006.48)

VARIETY: Repunched Date (RPD-002)   **SNOW-2**
PUP: Date
URS-10 · I-3 · L-3

Description: Secondary digits of the 8, 6, and 4 are evident to the south of the primary digits.

Comments: This is not as strong as some other RPDs for this date. Many 1864, No L dies (both copper-nickel and bronze) show apparent repunching on the 4. This is due to a defect on the digit punch.

	VF-20	EF-40	AU-50	MS-60	MS-63	MS-65
VARIETY	$40	$75	$100	$150	$250	$400
NORMAL	$40	$60	$80	$100	$150	$300

Note: Values listed for MS-60 and higher are for RB (red and brown) specimens. Full red Uncirculated specimens command higher prices.

1864, With L   FS-01-1864-2301 (006.7)

VARIETY: Repunched Date (RPD-003)   **SNOW-1**
PUP: Date
URS-6 · I-4 · L-4

Description: The strongly repunched date, evident to the southwest, is possibly a tripled date. Secondary digits are most evident below the primary 1 and 8.

Comments: The savvy collector will look at all 1864-dated cents; there are numerous repunched dates.

	VF-20	EF-40	AU-50	MS-60	MS-63	MS-65
VARIETY	$200	$300	$400	$500	$750	$1,750
NORMAL	$150	$221	$242	$325	$575	$1,400

Note: Values listed for MS-60 and higher are for RB (red and brown) specimens. Full red Uncirculated specimens command higher prices.

1864, With L — FS-01-1864-2302 (006.71)

VARIETY: Repunched Date (RPD-003) **SNOW-3**
PUP: Date
URS-6 · I-4 · L-4

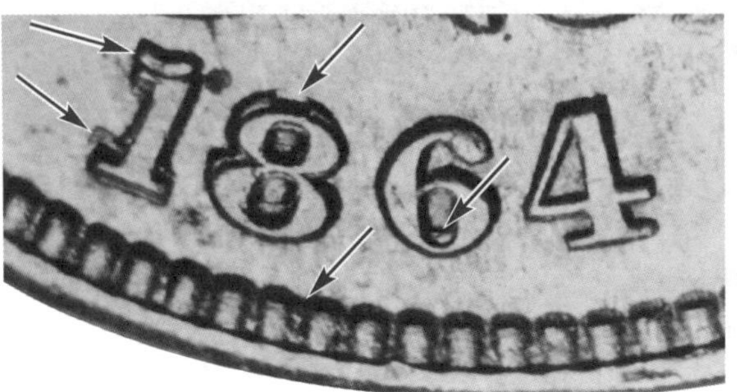

Description: Secondary images of the 1, 8, and 6 are evident to the northwest of the primary digits.

Comments: There is likely a digit in the denticles immediately below the 8, too.

	VF-20	EF-40	AU-50	MS-60	MS-63	MS-65
VARIETY	$200	$300	$400	$500	$750	$1,750
NORMAL	$150	$221	$242	$325	$575	$1,400

Note: Values listed for MS-60 and higher are for RB (red and brown) specimens. Full red Uncirculated specimens command higher prices.

1864, With L — FS-01-1864-2303 (006.72)

VARIETY: Repunched Date (RPD-004) **SNOW-4**
PUP: Date
URS-10 · I-4 · L-4

Description: Secondary digits are evident to the north on all four digits.

Comments: This is one of the more popular RPDs for this date.

	VF-20	EF-40	AU-50	MS-60	MS-63	MS-65
VARIETY	$200	$300	$400	$500	$750	$1,750
NORMAL	$150	$221	$242	$325	$575	$1,400

Note: Values listed for MS-60 and higher are for RB (red and brown) specimens. Full red Uncirculated specimens command higher prices.

1864, With L — FS-01-1864-2304 (006.5, 006.55)

VARIETY: Repunched Date

SNOW-5

PUP: Date

URS-10 · I-3 · L-3

Description: Secondary digits on the 1 and 8 are evident slightly to the north of the primary digits. The 1 is actually tripled, with yet another secondary digit evident slightly to the south of the primary.

Comments: This variety was at one time considered to be a "With L" type over a "Without L" type, but that is no longer considered plausible.

	VF-20	EF-40	AU-50	MS-60	MS-63	MS-65
VARIETY	$200	$300	$400	$500	$750	$1,750
NORMAL	$150	$221	$242	$325	$575	$1,400

Note: Values listed for MS-60 and higher are for RB (red and brown) specimens. Full red Uncirculated specimens command higher prices.

1864, With L — FS-01-1864-2305

VARIETY: Repunched Date (RPD-002)

SNOW-2

PUP: Date

URS-6 · I-4 · L-4

Description: The strongly repunched date, evident to the southwest, is possibly a tripled date. Secondary digits are most evident below the primary 1 and 8.

Comments: This variety is very similar to FS-2301.

	VF-20	EF-40	AU-50	MS-60	MS-63	MS-65
VARIETY	$200	$300	$400	$500	$750	$1,750
NORMAL	$150	$221	$242	$325	$575	$1,400

Note: Values listed for MS-60 and higher are for RB (red and brown) specimens. Full red Uncirculated specimens command higher prices.

1864, With L   FS-01-1864-2306 (006.73)

VARIETY: Repunched Date (RPD-009)   **SNOW-10**
PUP: Date
URS-10 · I-3 · L-3

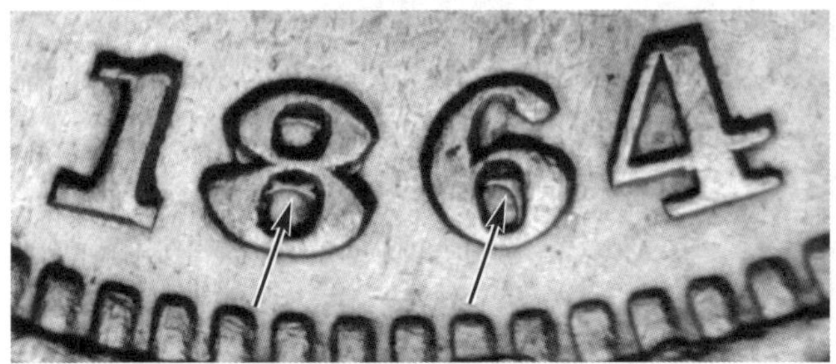

Description: Secondary digits are evident to the south of the primary date, but primarily within the lower loops of the 8 and the 6.

Comments: There are several other RPDs for this date, known on copper-nickel, bronze, and "With L" types.

	VF-20	EF-40	AU-50	MS-60	MS-63	MS-65
VARIETY	$200	$300	$400	$500	$750	$1,750
NORMAL	$150	$221	$242	$325	$575	$1,400

Note: Values listed for MS-60 and higher are for RB (red and brown) specimens. Full red Uncirculated specimens command higher prices.

1865, Plain 5   FS-01-1865-301 (007.4)

VARIETY: Repunched Date (RPD-001)   **SNOW-1**
PUP: Date
URS-9 · I-3 · L-3

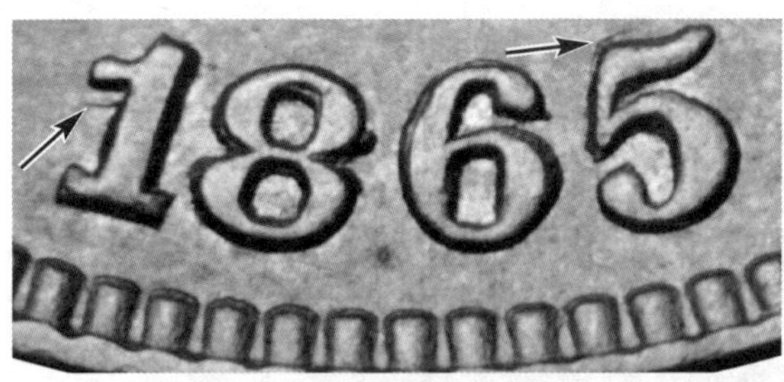 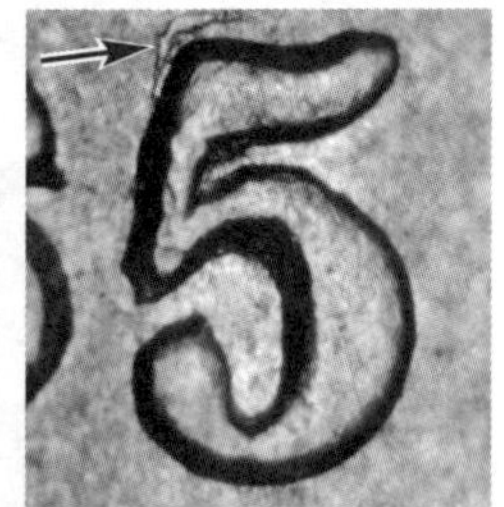

Description: Remnants of secondary digits are evident to the south on the 1 and 8, and to the north on the 5.

Comments: This variety was once considered to be a 5/4 overdate. However, during an Atlanta coin show in the mid-1990s, J.T. Stanton realized this is possibly a Plain 5 over Fancy 5 variety. This die is found on some copper-nickel pattern strikes (see J-406 in *United States Pattern Coins*).

	VF-20	EF-40	AU-50	MS-60	MS-63	MS-65
VARIETY	$75	$100	$200	$400	$600	$1,000
NORMAL	$25	$50	$70	$150	$200	$650

Note: Values listed for MS-60 and higher are for RB (red and brown) specimens. Full red Uncirculated specimens command higher prices.

1865, Plain 5 — FS-01-1865-302 (007.45)

Variety: Repunched Date

SNOW-4

PUP: Date

URS-9 · I-3 · L-3

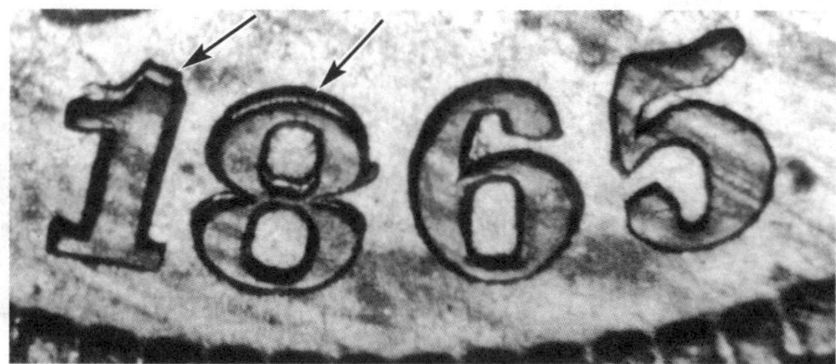

Description: Secondary digits are evident to the north of the 1 and 8, and very slightly within the upper loop of the 6.

Comments: This variety is primarily of interest to variety specialists and Indian Head cent collectors. On late-die-state pieces, a large cud forms above the shield. These are worth a significant premium.

	VF-20	EF-40	AU-50	MS-60	MS-63	MS-65
Variety	$40	$75	$100	$200	$250	$750
Normal	$25	$50	$70	$150	$200	$650

Note: Values listed for MS-60 and higher are for RB (red and brown) specimens. Full red Uncirculated specimens command higher prices.

1865, Plain 5 — FS-01-1865-303 (007.5)

Variety: Repunched Date + Misplaced Digit (RPD-003, MPD-002)

SNOW-3

PUP: Date

URS-9 · I-3 · L-3

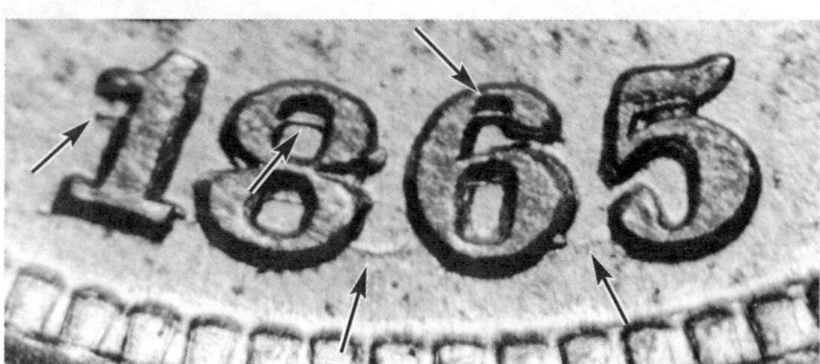

Description: Secondary digits are evident to the south of the 1, 8, and 6, with virtually no evidence of a secondary digit on the 5.

Comments: There are some slightly curved lines between the 8 and 6. These are widely misplaced digits with the base of either the 8 or 6 showing.

	VF-20	EF-40	AU-50	MS-60	MS-63	MS-65
Variety	$100	$150	$200	$400	$650	$1,500
Normal	$25	$50	$70	$150	$200	$650

Note: Values listed for MS-60 and higher are for RB (red and brown) specimens. Full red Uncirculated specimens command higher prices.

1865, Plain 5   FS-01-1865-304 (007.56)

VARIETY: Repunched Date + Misplaced Date   **SNOW-2**
(RPD-002, MPD-001)
PUP: Date
URS-9 · I-3 · L-3

 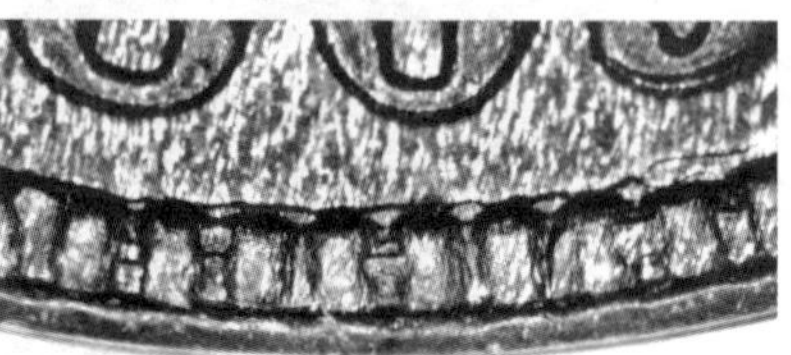

Description: A secondary 1 is evident under the right side of the 8, and the tops of four digits are evident protruding from the denticles below the date. Some specialists believe there are two sets of digits in the denticles.

Comments: This is a relatively new variety, first listed in the *Cherrypickers' Guide* in 2000.

	VF-20	EF-40	AU-50	MS-60	MS-63	MS-65
VARIETY	$100	$200	$300	$500	$1,000	$1,700
NORMAL	$25	$50	$70	$150	$200	$650

Note: Values listed for MS-60 and higher are for RB (red and brown) specimens. Full red Uncirculated specimens command higher prices.

1865, Fancy 5   FS-01-1865-1301 (007.3)

VARIETY: Digit Punch   **SNOW-1**
PUP: Date
URS-7 · I-3 · L-3

 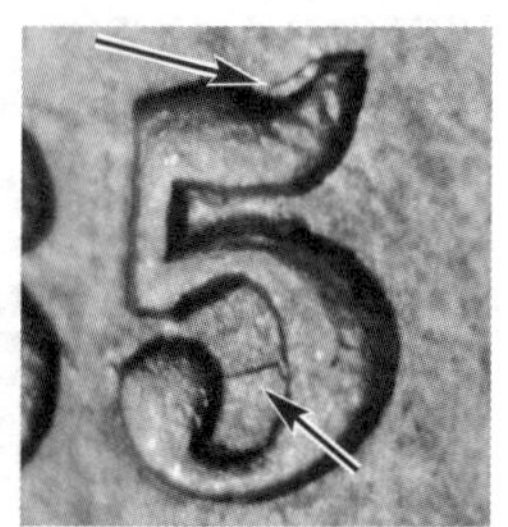

Description: A secondary 1 and 5 are visible, the 1 to the south of the primary 1, and the 5 very slightly to the north of the primary 5.

Comments: This variety was once considered to be a 5/4 overdate. However, photographic overlays disprove the theory, and show this to be a defective logo punch, similar to another known on an 1865 two-cent piece. Two different dies are known, with one of them having additional repunching on the 1.

	VF-20	EF-40	AU-50	MS-60	MS-63	MS-65
VARIETY	$50	$75	$100	$200	$300	$650
NORMAL	$25	$50	$70	$150	$200	$500

Note: Values listed for MS-60 and higher are for RB (red and brown) specimens. Full red Uncirculated specimens command higher prices.

1865, Fancy 5 — FS-01-1865-1302 (007.55)

VARIETY: Repunched Date (RPD-011)
PUP: Date
URS-3 · I-3 · L-3

SNOW-4

Description: Secondary digits are evident to the south of the 1, and slightly to the southwest of the 8 and 6.

Comments: This variety is very rare, although more may surface as collectors look more closely.

	VF-20	EF-40	AU-50	MS-60	MS-63	MS-65
VARIETY	$200	$500	$750	$1,250	$2,500	$3,500
NORMAL	$25	$50	$70	$150	$200	$500

Note: Values listed for MS-60 and higher are for RB (red and brown) specimens. Full red Uncirculated specimens command higher prices.

1865, Fancy 5 — FS-01-1865-1401 (007.2)

VARIETY: Die Gouge
PUP: Headdress
URS-4 · I-3 · L-4

SNOW-14

Description: There is a very strong die gouge through the Indian's headdress. The perfect arc of the die gouge makes this very interesting, although there is no known definitive cause for the aberration.

Comments: This variety was first reported by Bob Tagen many years ago. Subsequently it was publicized by J.P. Martin and the authentication staff of the American Numismatic Association.

	VF-20	EF-40	AU-50	MS-60	MS-63	MS-65
VARIETY	$100	$300	$500	$750	$1,200	$2,000
NORMAL	$25	$50	$70	$150	$200	$500

Note: Values listed for MS-60 and higher are for RB (red and brown) specimens. Full red Uncirculated specimens command higher prices.

1865, Fancy 5 — FS-01-1865-1801 (007)

VARIETY: Doubled-Die Reverse (DDR-001)
PUP: ONE CENT, left side of shield
URS-7 · I-5 · L-5

SNOW-2

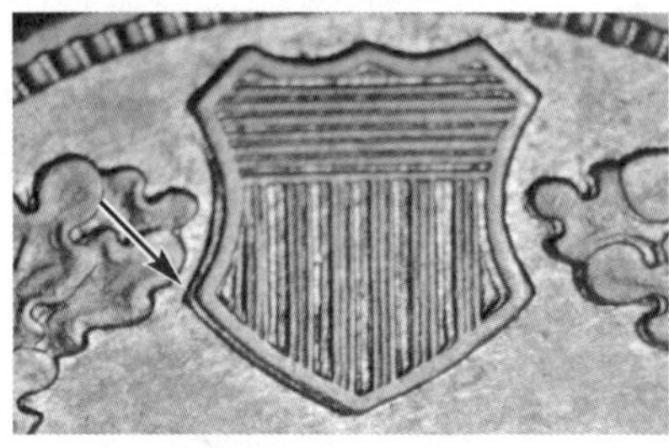 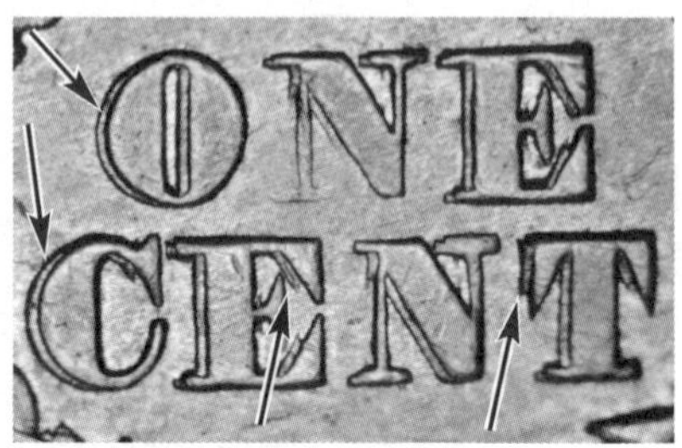

Description: This DDR is strongly doubled, primarily on the left side. The doubling is most evident on the letters of ONE CENT.

Comments: With relatively few known specimens, this is one of the more popular varieties of the entire series. An MS-64RB specimen sold for $12,000 in 2007.

	VF-20	EF-40	AU-50	MS-60	MS-63	MS-65
VARIETY	$750	$1,500	$2,000	$5,000	$7,500	–
NORMAL	$25	$50	$70	$150	$200	$500

Note: Values listed for MS-60 and higher are for RB (red and brown) specimens. Full red Uncirculated specimens command higher prices.

THE CHERRYPICKERS' GUIDE HELPFUL HINTS

Study and learn the Pick-Up-Points (PUPs) for each series so that you can focus your initial attention on these areas to find varieties. Don't forget the denticle area and the design above the date (especially on 19th-century coinage such as the Liberty Seated series) for misplaced numbers, etc. They hide, so use a good loupe and good light.

1866   FS-01-1866-101 (007.6)

VARIETY: Doubled Die + Misplaced Digit
(DDO-001, MPD-001)
PUP: Date, pearls, LIBERTY
URS-8 · I-2 · L-2

SNOW-1

Description: There is wide doubling on LIBERTY and elsewhere. The base of a 1 is visible in the necklace and there are digits in the denticles.

Comments: This is one of the top varieties in the Indian Head cent series. The multiple varieties are very interesting to collectors.

	VF-20	EF-40	AU-50	MS-60	MS-63	MS-65
VARIETY	$300	$500	$750	$1,000	$2,500	$6,000
NORMAL	$125	$200	$250	$350	$450	$1,400

Note: Values listed for MS-60 and higher are for RB (red and brown) specimens. Full red Uncirculated specimens command higher prices.

1866   FS-01-1866-301 (007.7)

VARIETY: Repunched Date (RPD-001)
PUP: Date
URS-8 · I-2 · L-2

SNOW-2

Description: A secondary 1 is visible to the south of the primary 1, with the flag evident below the primary flag. This is usually visible on higher-grade specimens. The top of a secondary 6 is evident to the north of the primary 6 and can be detected on lower grades.

Comments: This variety is in demand mostly from those trying to complete a variety set of the series.

	VF-20	EF-40	AU-50	MS-60	MS-63	MS-65
VARIETY	$150	$250	$300	$400	$550	$1,500
NORMAL	$125	$200	$250	$350	$450	$1,400

Note: Values listed for MS-60 and higher are for RB (red and brown) specimens. Full red Uncirculated specimens command higher prices.

1866 — FS-01-1866-302 (007.9)

VARIETY: Repunched Date (RPD-002) — SNOW-3
PUP: Date
URS-5 · I-2 · L-2

Description: A secondary 1 is evident to the left of the primary 1.

Comments: Early-die-state specimens may also show other digits repunched. On some examples, a reverse die cud shows between 8:00 and 9:00, from the wreath to the rim.

	VF-20	EF-40	AU-50	MS-60	MS-63	MS-65
VARIETY	$200	$300	$500	$750	$1,200	$2,500
NORMAL	$125	$200	$250	$350	$450	$1,400

Note: Values listed for MS-60 and higher are for RB (red and brown) specimens. Full red Uncirculated specimens command higher prices.

1866 — FS-01-1866-303 (007.8)

VARIETY: Repunched Date (RPD-008) — SNOW-9
PUP: Date
URS-7 · I-2 · L-2

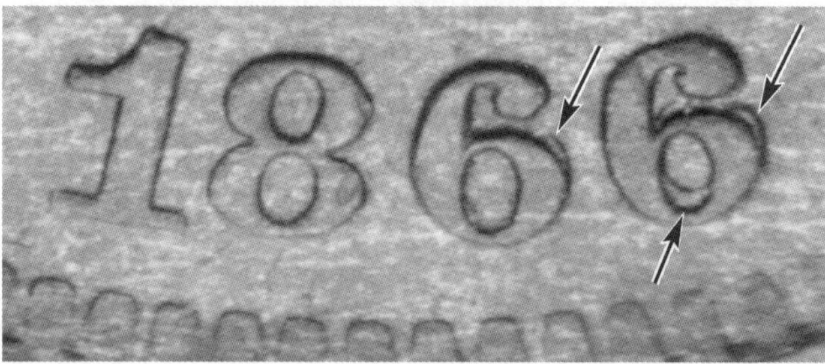

Description: Secondary 6s are evident to the east of the primary digits.

Comments: Although scarcer than FS-301, this variety is in demand mostly from those trying to complete a variety set of the series. Some coins seen have a bright, brassy look, probably due to different alloy content.

	VF-20	EF-40	AU-50	MS-60	MS-63	MS-65
VARIETY	$200	$275	$350	$500	$700	$1,600
NORMAL	$125	$200	$250	$350	$450	$1,400

Note: Values listed for MS-60 and higher are for RB (red and brown) specimens. Full red Uncirculated specimens command higher prices.

1867   FS-01-1867-301 (008)

VARIETY: Repunched Date (RPD-001)   **SNOW-1**
PUP: Date
URS-10 · I-4 · L-4

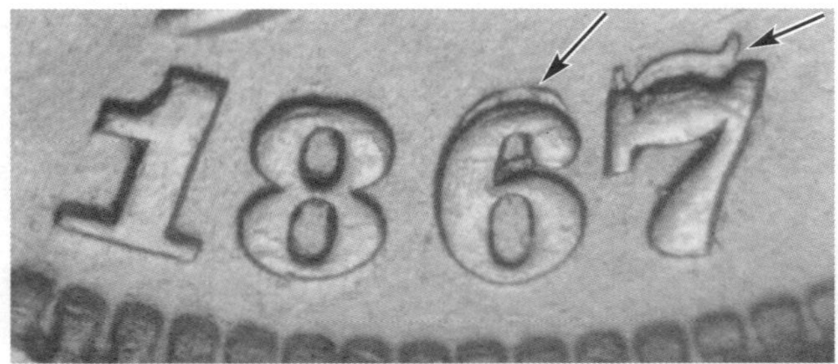

Description: Secondary digits are strongly evident to the north of the primary 6 and 7.

Comments: This is a very popular variety, but still can be cherrypicked. It is much easier to find in lower grades, which are less in demand.

	VF-20	EF-40	AU-50	MS-60	MS-63	MS-65
VARIETY	$500	$600	$800	$1,000	$1,500	$5,000
NORMAL	$125	$200	$250	$350	$450	$1,400

Note: Values listed for MS-60 and higher are for RB (red and brown) specimens. Full red Uncirculated specimens command higher prices.

1867   FS-01-1867-302 (008.1)

VARIETY: Repunched Date (RPD-004)   **SNOW-4**
PUP: Date
URS-6 · I-3 · L-3

Description: The 1 exhibits a secondary digit to the south of the primary digit, and the 8 exhibits a secondary digit slightly to the west of the primary.

Comments: This variety is primarily of interest to specialists and Indian Head cent collectors. It seems to be quite scarce.

	VF-20	EF-40	AU-50	MS-60	MS-63	MS-65
VARIETY	$200	$250	$300	$450	$600	$1,600
NORMAL	$125	$200	$250	$350	$450	$1,400

Note: Values listed for MS-60 and higher are for RB (red and brown) specimens. Full red Uncirculated specimens command higher prices.

1868 — FS-01-1868-101 (008.2)

VARIETY: Doubled-Die Obverse

PUP: LIBERTY

URS-7 · I-4 · L-4

SNOW-1

 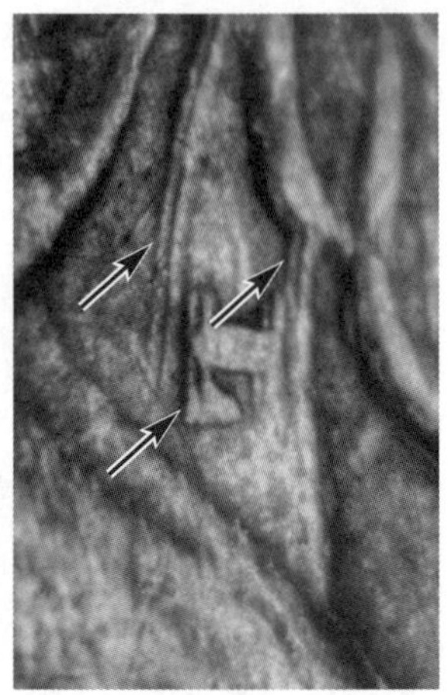

Description: Doubling is evident on the RTY of LIBERTY and on the ribbon, especially at the L.

Comments: This variety is very popular among specialists. It was discovered by Larry Steve.

	VF-20	EF-40	AU-50	MS-60	MS-63	MS-65
VARIETY	$200	$300	$350	$450	$600	$1,500
NORMAL	$125	$200	$250	$350	$450	$1,400

Note: Values listed for MS-60 and higher are for RB (red and brown) specimens. Full red Uncirculated specimens command higher prices.

THE CHERRYPICKERS' GUIDE HELPFUL HINTS

Strike doubling can often be confused with the more valuable die doubling, such as a doubled die or repunched mintmark. To help ensure you know the difference, take time to read, read, and re-read appendix A.

1868

VARIETY: Doubled-Die Obverse + Repunched Date
(DDO-002, RPD-004)

SNOW-4

PUP: LIBERTY, date

URS-6 · I-4 · L-4

Description: Doubling is evident on LIBERTY and other portions of the headdress. The repunched date exhibits secondary digits within the upper loops of both 8s, and just above the lower loop of the 6.

Comments: This variety is different from FS-103. It is one of those "it's got it all" varieties, and is very popular among collectors. Scarce.

	VF-20	EF-40	AU-50	MS-60	MS-63	MS-65
VARIETY	$125	$250	$300	$450	$650	$1,250
NORMAL	$85	$130	$167	$215	$300	$875

Note: Values listed for MS-60 and higher are for RB (red and brown) specimens. Full red Uncirculated specimens command higher prices.

1868 — FS-01-1868-103 (008.25)

VARIETY: Doubled-Die Obverse + Repunched Date +
Misplaced Date
(DDO-003, RPD-005, MPD-001)

SNOW-5

PUP: LIBERTY, date

URS-5 · I-4 · L-4

Description: The doubled die is evident on LIBERTY and is especially strong on the RTY. The repunched date is apparent with a secondary 8 slightly to the north of the primary 8. The MPD exhibits digits in the denticles below the 6—very likely a misplaced 6.

Comments: This variety is different from FS-102. It's another one of those "it's got it all" varieties. It is both very scarce and very popular among collectors.

	VF-20	EF-40	AU-50	MS-60	MS-63	MS-65
VARIETY	$200	$300	$400	$500	$800	$1,750
NORMAL	$125	$200	$250	$350	$450	$1,400

Note: Values listed for MS-60 and higher are for RB (red and brown) specimens. Full red Uncirculated specimens command higher prices.

1868 — FS-01-1868-301 (008.23)

VARIETY: Misplaced Date (MPD-002)   **SNOW-8**
PUP: Date
URS-4 · I-3 · L-3

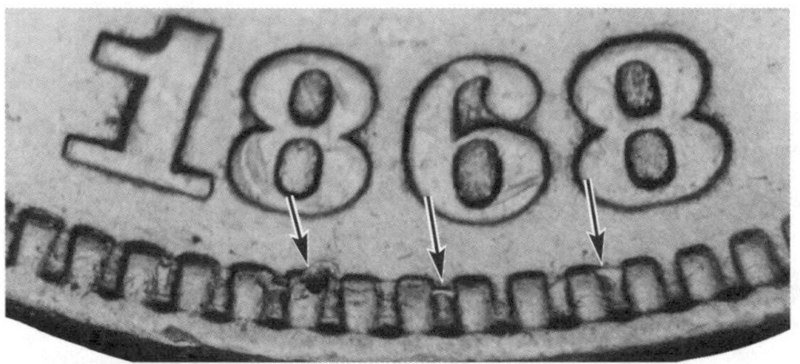

Description: There are three digits in the denticles below the date, very likely the 8, 6, and 8 of the primary date punch.

Comments: This variety is primarily of interest to specialists and Indian Head cent collectors. It is scarce.

	VF-20	EF-40	AU-50	MS-60	MS-63	MS-65
VARIETY	$200	$300	$350	$500	$600	$1,500
NORMAL	$125	$200	$250	$350	$450	$1,400

Note: Values listed for MS-60 and higher are for RB (red and brown) specimens. Full red Uncirculated specimens command higher prices.

1869 — FS-01-1869-301 (008.3)

VARIETY: Repunched Date (RPD-003)   **SNOW-3**
PUP: Date
URS-12 · I-5 · L-5

Description: Secondary digits are evident to the north of the 6 and 9, with a spread stronger on the 9 than the 6.

Comments: This variety was once considered an 1869/8 overdate, but the truth prevailed that it is simply a repunched date. Still, it is often listed in regular coin price guides, as is frequently considered a mainstay of the series. There is tremendous demand for circulated examples, especially because of the inclusion of this variety in popular coin albums. It is relatively common and found paired with eight different reverse dies!

	VF-20	EF-40	AU-50	MS-60	MS-63	MS-65
VARIETY	$500	$700	$800	$1,000	$1,200	$2,250
NORMAL	$300	$400	$500	$700	$900	$1,600

Note: Values listed for MS-60 and higher are for RB (red and brown) specimens. Full red Uncirculated specimens command higher prices.

1869 — FS-01-1869-302 (008.5)

VARIETY: Repunched Date (RPD-001)
PUP: Date
URS-8 · I-3 · L-3

SNOW-1

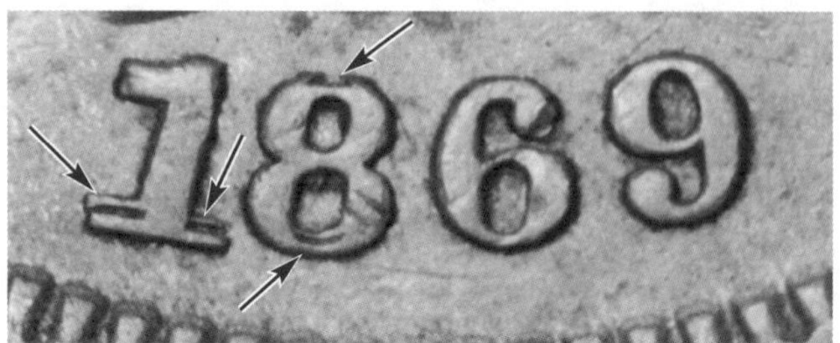

Description: Secondary digits are evident to the north of the 1 and 8, with a spread stronger on the 1 than the 8.

Comments: Generally speaking, die varieties of coins with a relatively high numismatic value rarely command much premium over the normal coin's value. This variety offers an exception. Only a single Mint State example is known. In circulated grades, too, it is very scarce.

	VF-20	EF-40	AU-50	MS-60	MS-63	MS-65
VARIETY	$500	$750	$800	$1,200	$2,000	$5,000
NORMAL	$300	$400	$500	$700	$900	$1,600

Note: Values listed for MS-60 and higher are for RB (red and brown) specimens. Full red Uncirculated specimens command higher prices.

1870 — FS-01-1870-101 (008.6)

VARIETY: Doubled-Die Obverse
(DDO-001, RPD-001)
PUP: TY of LIBERTY
URS-8 · I-3 · L-3

SNOW-1, S-2, S-13, S-22, S-28, S-33

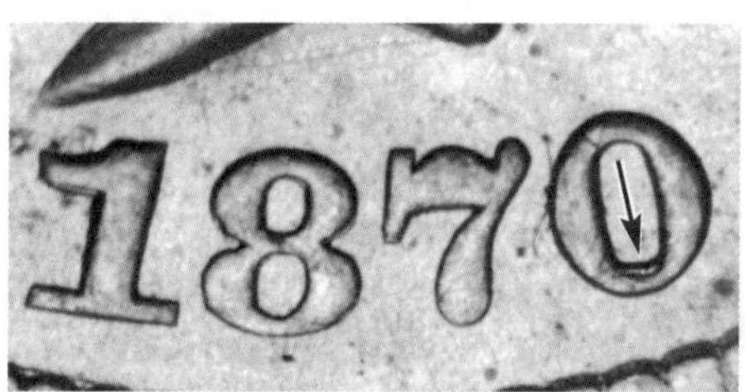
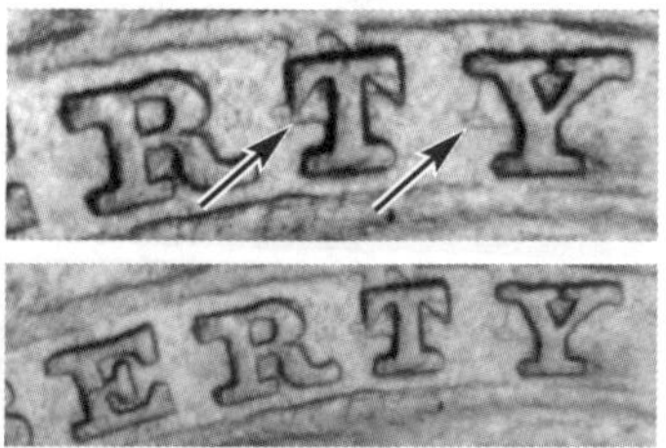

Description: Doubling is evident on the TY of LIBERTY, with a huge spread. The TY has a spread of half a letter's height. The top of the secondary T and Y are well into the ribbon. The coin also exhibits a minor repunched date, with a secondary 0 to the north, evidenced at the lower portion of the inside loop.

Comments: This obverse doubled die is paired with several different reverse dies, some of which are themselves major doubled dies.

	VF-20	EF-40	AU-50	MS-60	MS-63	MS-65
VARIETY	$400	$500	$600	$750	$1,000	$2,000
NORMAL	$300	$400	$500	$650	$800	$1,800

Note: Values listed for MS-60 and higher are for RB (red and brown) specimens. Full red Uncirculated specimens command higher prices.

1870 — FS-01-1870-102 (008.82)

VARIETY: Doubled-Die Obverse + Repunched Date + Misplaced Date
(DDO-003, RPD-003, MPD-001)

SNOW-5

PUP: LIBERTY, date
URS-7 · I-2 · L-2

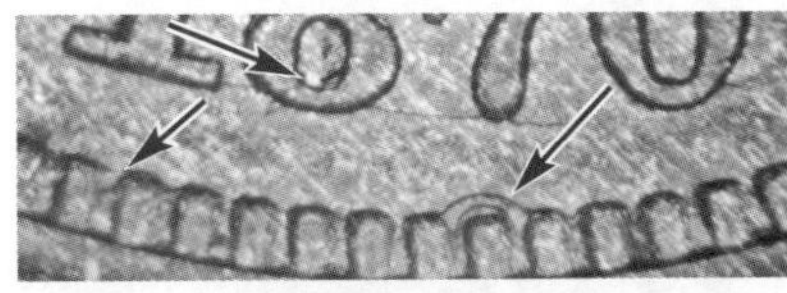

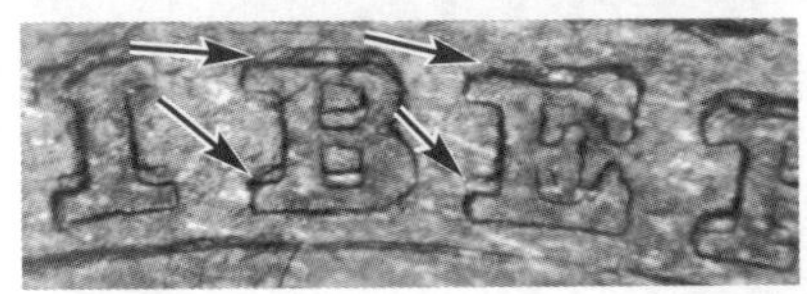

Description: Doubling is evident on LIBERTY, with the secondary letters to the north of the primary letters. A portion of a 0 is evident protruding from the denticles below the 7, and there are possibly portions of other digits protruding from the denticles below the primary 1. A secondary 8 is visible within the loops of the primary 8.

Comments: This variety is highly sought after by collectors of the series.

	VF-20	EF-40	AU-50	MS-60	MS-63	MS-65
VARIETY	$1,500	$2,000	$2,500	$4,000	$6,000	–
NORMAL	$300	$400	$500	$650	$800	$1,800

Note: Values listed for MS-60 and higher are for RB (red and brown) specimens. Full red Uncirculated specimens command higher prices.

1870 — FS-01-1870-301 (008.81)

VARIETY: Repunched Date (RPD-002)

SNOW-4

PUP: Date
URS-5 · I-2 · L-2

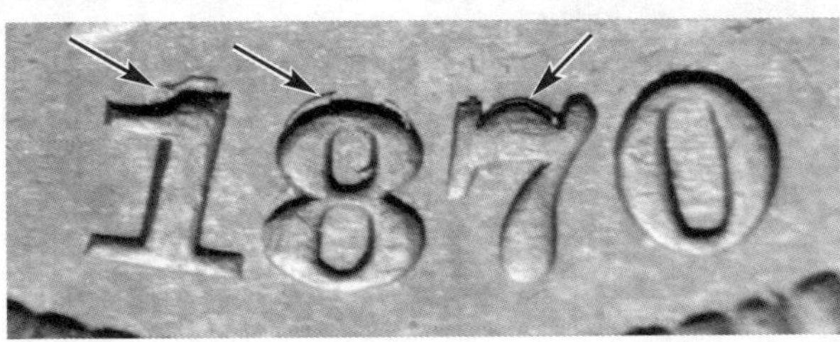

Description: Secondary digits are evident to the north of the primary 1 and 8.

Comments: This coin is primarily of interest to variety specialists and Indian Head cent collectors. Very scarce.

	VF-20	EF-40	AU-50	MS-60	MS-63	MS-65
VARIETY	$500	$600	$800	$1,100	$1,500	$2,500
NORMAL	$300	$400	$500	$650	$800	$1,800

Note: Values listed for MS-60 and higher are for RB (red and brown) specimens. Full red Uncirculated specimens command higher prices.

1870 FS-01-1870-302 (008.8)

VARIETY: Misplaced Date + Doubled-Die Reverse
    (MPD-002, DDR-011) SNOW-8

PUP: Denticles below date

URS-5 · I-4 · L-5

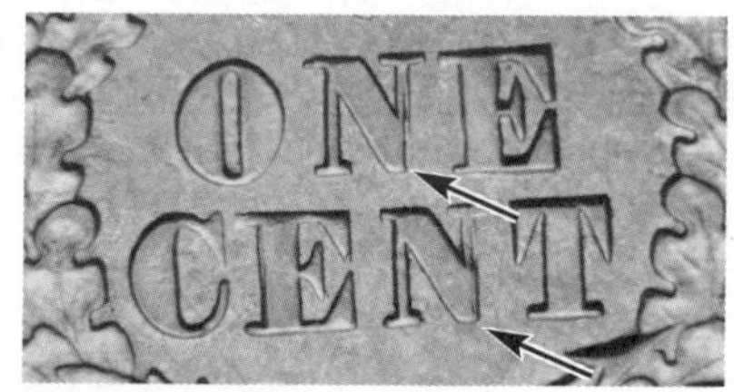

Description: Portions of several numbers are evident within the denticles below the date. Some specialists believe there are as many as 12 numbers present. The doubled-die reverse is evident to the right of the letters NE of ONE and EN of CENT.

Comments: This is one of the wildest misplaced dates known in the Indian Head cent series and likely one of the wildest of any series. This variety is fairly easily detected in lower grades.

	VF-20	EF-40	AU-50	MS-60	MS-63	MS-65
VARIETY	$500	$700	$1,000	$1,250	$2,000	–
NORMAL	$300	$400	$500	$650	$800	$1,800

Note: Values listed for MS-60 and higher are for RB (red and brown) specimens. Full red Uncirculated specimens command higher prices.

1870 — FS-01-1870-801 (008.7)

VARIETY: Doubled-Die Reverse
PUP: ONE CENT
URS-9 · I-4 · L-5

SNOW-2, S-3, S-14

Description: This is a very popular doubled die, with the doubling evident on ONE CENT, both sides of the wreath, and the top of the shield.

Comments: This variety is known paired with a doubled-die obverse (FS-101), and with a normal obverse. Some specimens exhibit a small die crack from 11:30 to the wreath at 2:00. One of the obverse dies paired with this reverse is also listed as FS-101 (Snow-2), making that variety a double find!

	VF-20	EF-40	AU-50	MS-60	MS-63	MS-65
VARIETY	$500	$700	$1,000	$1,200	$1,500	$2,500
NORMAL	$300	$400	$500	$650	$800	$1,800

Note: Values listed for MS-60 and higher are for RB (red and brown) specimens. Full red Uncirculated specimens command higher prices.

1870 — FS-01-1870-901

VARIETY: Reverse of 1869 (Shallow N)
PUP: ONE CENT
URS-14 · I-4 · L-5

Description: Reverse design from 1869 with a shallow N in ONE. The E's in ONE CENT have T-shaped centers.

Comments: William Barber redesigned the reverse die in 1870. The new version has a bold N in ONE and trumpet-shaped centers of the E's in ONE CENT. These are slightly scarce, but no premium is presently due them. This may change as demand increases.

	VF-20	EF-40	AU-50	MS-60	MS-63	MS-65
VARIETY	$300	$400	$500	$650	$800	$1,800
NORMAL	$300	$400	$500	$650	$800	$1,800

Note: Values listed for MS-60 and higher are for RB (red and brown) specimens. Full red Uncirculated specimens command higher prices.

1871 — FS-01-1871-901

VARIETY: Reverse of 1869 (Shallow N)
PUP: ONE CENT
URS-7 · I-4 · L-5

SNOW-4, S-5

Description: Reverse design from 1869 with a shallow N in ONE. The E's in ONE CENT have T-shaped centers.

Comments: William Barber redesigned the reverse die in 1870. The new version has a bold N in ONE and trumpet-shaped centers of the E's in ONE CENT. The shallow N's are quite rare for this date, and as more collectors desire to add them to their sets they will become even rarer. An MS-65RB sold for $13,000 in 2005. Proofs do not command these premiums.

	VF-20	EF-40	AU-50	MS-60	MS-63	MS-65
VARIETY	$650	$850	$1,300	$2,000	$3,000	$10,000
NORMAL	$400	$500	$600	$700	$900	$2,500

Note: Values listed for MS60 and higher are for RB (red and brown) specimens. Full red Uncirculated specimens command higher prices.

1872 — FS-01-1872-301 (008.9)

VARIETY: Repunched Date
PUP: Date
URS-7 · I-3 · L-3

SNOW-1

Description: A secondary image is evident to the north of the primary 1 and 2. There is no visible doubling evident on the 8 or 7.

Comments: This variety is highly sought by collectors of the series. Premiums are small, due to the high value of the date.

	VF-20	EF-40	AU-50	MS-60	MS-63	MS-65
VARIETY	$500	$600	$750	$850	$1,100	$3,800
NORMAL	$400	$500	$650	$800	$1,000	$3,700

Note: Values listed for MS-60 and higher are for RB (red and brown) specimens. Full red Uncirculated specimens command higher prices.

1872

FS-01-1872-901

SNOW-10, S-13, S-14

VARIETY: Reverse of 1869 (Shallow N)
PUP: ONE CENT
URS-9 · I-4 · L-5

Description: Reverse design from 1869 with a shallow N in ONE. The E's in ONE CENT have T-shaped centers.

Comments: William Barber redesigned the reverse die in 1870. The new version has a bold N in ONE and trumpet-shaped centers of the E's in ONE CENT. These are quite scarce and as more collectors desire to add them to their sets they will become even rarer. No Proofs were struck with the Shallow N reverse. An MS-65RB sold for $6,500 in 2005.

	VF-20	EF-40	AU-50	MS-60	MS-63	MS-65
VARIETY	$550	$750	$1,000	$1,500	$2,200	$5,000
NORMAL	$400	$500	$650	$800	$1,000	$3,700

Note: Values listed for MS-60 and higher are for RB (red and brown) specimens. Full red Uncirculated specimens command higher prices.

1873, Close 3

FS-01-1873-101 (009)

SNOW-1

VARIETY: Doubled-Die Obverse (DDO-001)
PUP: LIBERTY
URS-9 · I-5 · L-5

Description: This strong doubled die is evident by the doubling on LIBERTY, the entire headdress, the feather spines, and even the eye. This is a Close 3 variety.

Comments: This variety, considered the "chief" of all Indian Head cent varieties, is in very high demand. It is always sought by collectors, in all grades. An MS-65RB sold in 2005 for $69,000. An MS-64RD sold for more than $100,000 in 1998.

	VF-20	EF-40	AU-50	MS-60	MS-63	MS-65
VARIETY	$2,000	$3,000	$4,000	$7,500	$14,000	$70,000
NORMAL	$150	$200	$250	$400	$600	$2,500

Note: Values listed for MS-60 and higher are for RB (red and brown) specimens. Full red Uncirculated specimens command higher prices.

1873, Close 3 — FS-01-1873-102 (009.1)

VARIETY: Doubled-Die Obverse (DDO-002)

SNOW-2

PUP: LIBERTY

URS-8 · I-4 · L-4

 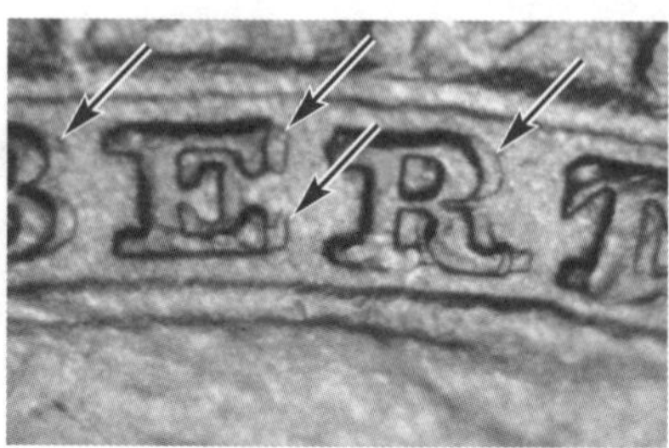

Description: This is another strong doubled die; the letters of LIBERTY show a secondary image slightly to the right of the primary image.

Comments: This variety is well known among Indian Head cent specialists and die-variety enthusiasts, but is often confused as the "biggie" (FS-101) by novice variety collectors. Prices have declined since publication of the fourth edition of the *Cherrypickers' Guide*, due to more examples surfacing.

	VF-20	EF-40	AU-50	MS-60	MS-63	MS-65
VARIETY	$500	$800	$1,000	$1,500	$2,000	$5,000
NORMAL	$150	$200	$250	$400	$600	$2,500

Note: Values listed for MS-60 and higher are for RB (red and brown) specimens. Full red Uncirculated specimens command higher prices.

1873, Open 3 — FS-01-1873-1301 (009.3)

VARIETY: Repunched Date (RPD-001)

SNOW-1

PUP: Date

URS-5 · I-5 · L-4

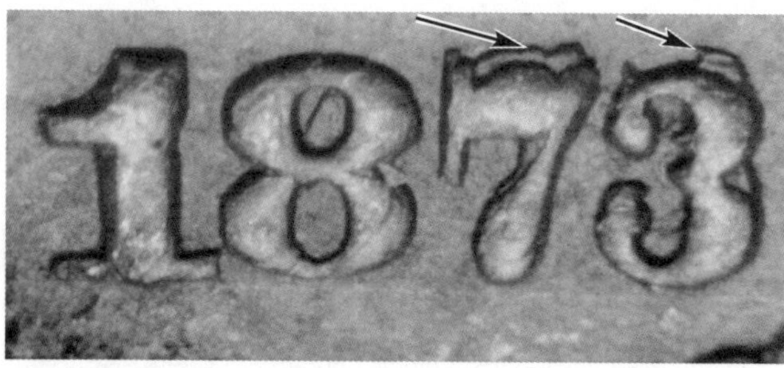

Description: This is a strong repunched date to the north of the 73.

Comments: Due to the repunching on the 3, it appears to be a Close 3 rather than an Open 3. This variety is very scarce.

	VF-20	EF-40	AU-50	MS-60	MS-63	MS-65
VARIETY	$200	$300	$600	$800	$1,200	–
NORMAL	$75	$150	$200	$275	$550	$1,700

Note: Values listed for MS-60 and higher are for RB (red and brown) specimens. Full red Uncirculated specimens command higher prices.

1874

VARIETY: Doubled-Die Obverse (DDO-001)

PUP: LIBERTY

URS-5 · I-4 · L-3

SNOW-1

 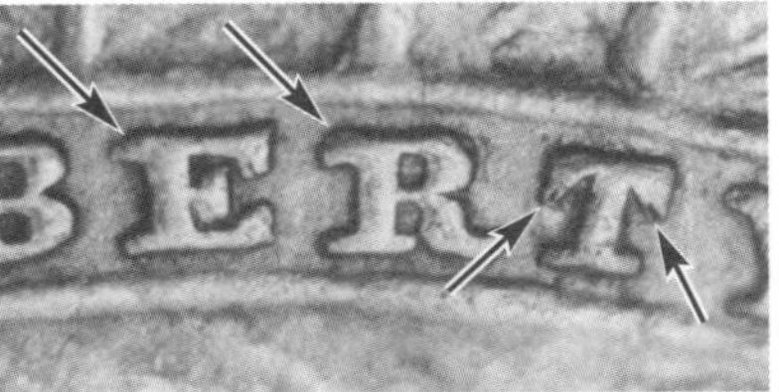

Description: Doubling is evident on LIBERTY, the designer's initials, the feathers, and the eye. The secondary image of LIBERTY is spread to the left of the primary image.

Comments: This variety is well known among Indian Head cent specialists and die-variety enthusiasts. It is considered by most to be highly collectible.

	VF-20	EF-40	AU-50	MS-60	MS-63	MS-65
VARIETY	$250	$400	$600	$800	$1,000	$3,500
NORMAL	$60	$100	$150	$200	$300	$750

Note: Values listed for MS-60 and higher are for RB (red and brown) specimens. Full red Uncirculated specimens command higher prices.

1875

VARIETY: Repunched Date (RPD-001)

PUP: Date

URS-7 · I-4 · L-3

SNOW-1

Description: Repunching is evident on the base of the 1.

Comments: This is a fairly bold repunched date. The variety is very similar to FS-303.

	VF-20	EF-40	AU-50	MS-60	MS-63	MS-65
VARIETY	$100	$150	$200	$300	$450	$850
NORMAL	$60	$100	$150	$200	$300	$750

Note: Values listed for MS-60 and higher are for RB (red and brown) specimens. Full red Uncirculated specimens command higher prices.

1875   FS-01-1875-302

VARIETY: Repunched Date (RPD-002)   **SNOW-2**
PUP: Date
URS-7 · I-4 · L-3

Description: The date is repunched far to the left of the primary 1. The initial date was started with the base of the 1 into the denticles. It was then corrected.

Comments: This is a dramatic repunched date.

	VF-20	EF-40	AU-50	MS-60	MS-63	MS-65
VARIETY	$100	$150	$200	$300	$450	$850
NORMAL	$60	$100	$150	$200	$300	$750

Note: Values listed for MS-60 and higher are for RB (red and brown) specimens. Full red Uncirculated specimens command higher prices.

1875   FS-01-1875-303

VARIETY: Repunched Date (RPD-003)   **SNOW-3**
PUP: Date
URS-7 · I-4 · L-3

Description: Repunching is evident on the base of the 1.

Comments: This is a fairly bold repunched date, very similar to FS-301.

	VF-20	EF-40	AU-50	MS-60	MS-63	MS-65
VARIETY	$100	$150	$200	$300	$450	$850
NORMAL	$60	$100	$150	$200	$300	$750

Note: Values listed for MS-60 and higher are for RB (red and brown) specimens. Full red Uncirculated specimens command higher prices.

1875

FS-01-1875-801

VARIETY: Intentional Die Alteration

PUP: N in ONE

URS-1 · I-4 · L-5

SNOW-16

Description: A crude dot is raised at the top of the diagonal of the N in ONE.

Comments: This is a great "story coin" within the Indian Head cent series. In 1875, Mint officials secretly modified a reverse die by gouging a small dot into the N in ONE. The die was put into production one morning in order to catch an employee of 50-plus years' standing, who was suspected of stealing coins. Late that morning the employee was called aside and asked to empty his pockets, which contained 33 of the marked cents. At first he insisted his pocket change was from his son, but when confronted with the secretly marked die, he admitted his guilt, and tendered his resignation in disgrace. The market value for this variety is not yet reliably established.

	VF-20	EF-40	AU-50	MS-60	MS-63	MS-65
VARIETY	–	–	–	–	–	–
NORMAL	$60	$100	$150	$200	$300	$750

Note: Values listed for MS-60 and higher are for RB (red and brown) specimens. Full red Uncirculated specimens command higher prices.

1878

FS-01-1878-301 (009.4)

VARIETY: Misplaced Date (MPD-001)

PUP: Denticles below date

URS-5 · I-3 · L-2

SNOW-2

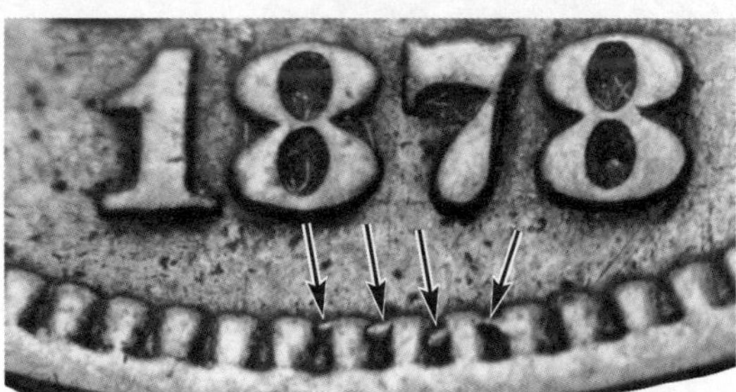

Description: The tops of three numbers (likely all 8s) are evident protruding from the denticles below the 87 of the date.

Comments: This misplaced date is fairly bold. Very few specimens have been found.

	VF-20	EF-40	AU-50	MS-60	MS-63	MS-65
VARIETY	$300	$400	$550	$750	$1,000	$2,000
NORMAL	$150	$200	$300	$400	$500	$850

Note: Values listed for MS-60 and higher are for RB (red and brown) specimens. Full red Uncirculated specimens command higher prices.

1880 — FS-01-1880-101 (009.41)

VARIETY: Doubled-Die Obverse + Reverse Clash (DDO-001, MAD-001)   SNOW-1

PUP: Reverse field above E of ONE

URS-10 · I-5 · L-5

Description: The primary variety is the misaligned die clash evident on the reverse, with obvious reeding running from the upper-right leaf tip, through the E of ONE, and down to the very top of the N of CENT. Doubling is visible on the obverse in higher grades, as a very close spread on LIBERTY.

Comments: This has become one of the most desirable Indian Head cent varieties, but mainly for the misaligned clashed die. The clash of this depth is difficult to visualize in a hardened die. Perhaps the clash marks were created before the dies were hardened.

	VF-20	EF-40	AU-50	MS-60	MS-63	MS-65
VARIETY	$150	$250	$400	$750	$1,500	$3,500
NORMAL	$10	$25	$50	$75	$120	$400

Note: Values listed for MS-60 and higher are for RB (red and brown) specimens. Full red Uncirculated specimens command higher prices.

1882

VARIETY: Misplaced Date (MPD-001)
PUP: Necklace
URS-6 · I-4 · L-4

SNOW-6

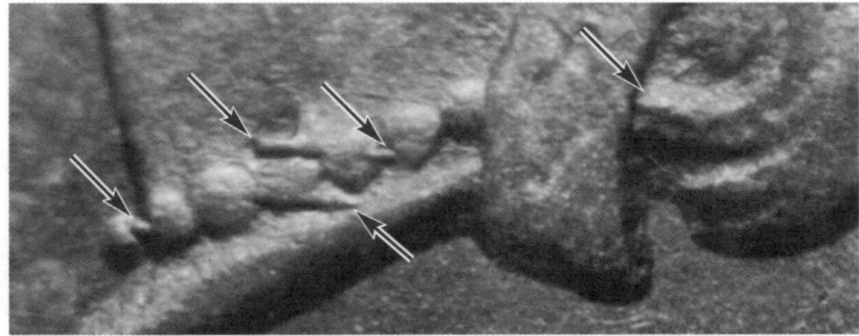

Description: The bases of at least four 1s are evident within the beads of the necklace.

Comments: This is one of the most popular MPDs of the series. It was first reported by W.O. Walker and has since proven to be very rare, with very few examples coming to light.

	VF-20	EF-40	AU-50	MS-60	MS-63	MS-65
VARIETY	$200	$300	$500	$1,000	$2,500	$6,000
NORMAL	$10	$25	$50	$75	$120	$350

Note: Values listed for MS-60 and higher are for RB (red and brown) specimens. Full red Uncirculated specimens command higher prices.

1883

VARIETY: Misplaced Date (MPD-002)
PUP: Denticles below date
URS-6 · I-3 · L-3

SNOW-8

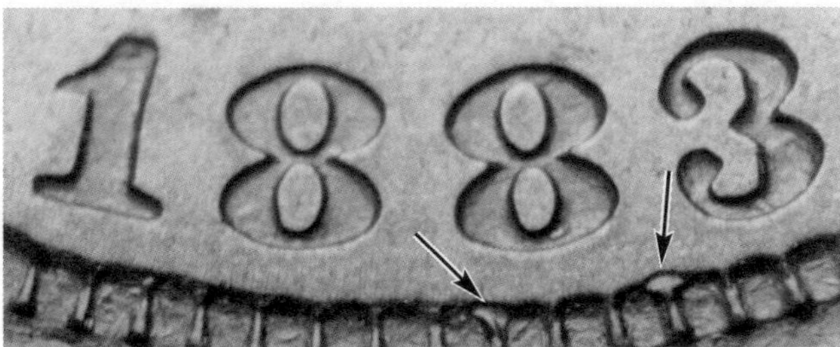

Description: The tops of two digits (likely an 8 and a 3) are evident protruding from the denticles below the date.

Comments: The misplaced digit in this variety is very obvious and therefore quite popular.

	VF-20	EF-40	AU-50	MS-60	MS-63	MS-65
VARIETY	$75	$100	$200	$350	$500	$1,250
NORMAL	$10	$25	$50	$75	$120	$350

Note: Values listed for MS-60 and higher are for RB (red and brown) specimens. Full red Uncirculated specimens command higher prices.

1883   FS-01-1883-402

VARIETY: Misplaced Date (MPD-003)   **SNOW-7**
PUP: Pearls
URS-5 · I-4 · L-4

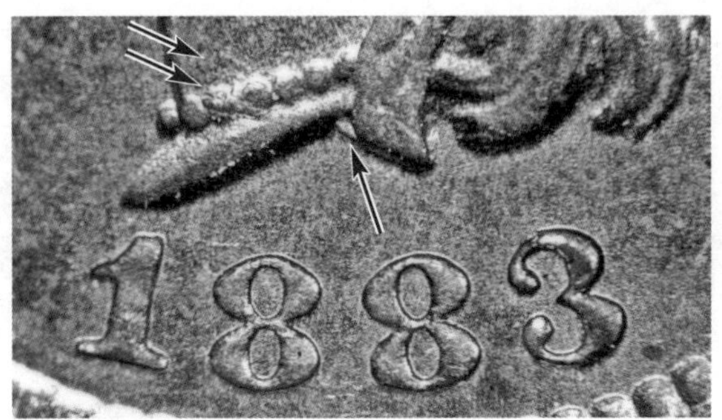

Description: The base of a 1 digit is sticking out of the neck, below the pearls.

Comments: Collector interest in misplaced digits increases when they are very visible, such as this one.

	VF-20	EF-40	AU-50	MS-60	MS-63	MS-65
VARIETY	$100	$150	$250	$400	$750	$1,500
NORMAL	$10	$25	$50	$75	$120	$350

Note: Values listed for MS-60 and higher are for RB (red and brown) specimens. Full red Uncirculated specimens command higher prices.

1883   FS-01-1883-403

VARIETY: Misplaced Date (MPD-001)   **SNOW-1**
PUP: Neck
URS-8 · I-4 · L-4

Description: The base of a 1 digit is sticking out of the neck, below the pearls.

Comments: Collector interest in misplaced digits increases when they are easily visible, such as this one.

	VF-20	EF-40	AU-50	MS-60	MS-63	MS-65
VARIETY	$100	$200	$300	$500	$1,000	$1,750
NORMAL	$10	$25	$50	$75	$120	$350

Note: Values listed for MS-60 and higher are for RB (red and brown) specimens. Full red Uncirculated specimens command higher prices.

1883

FS-01-1883-801 (009.46)

VARIETY: Doubled-Die Reverse (DDR-002)

SNOW-6

PUP: Ribbon ends and arrowheads

URS-4 · I-3 · L-3

Description: The doubling is evident on the wreath veins, leaves, arrowheads, and ribbon ends.

Comments: Very few examples of this variety have been reported. As more collectors look at the reverse dies, perhaps more will show up.

	VF-20	EF-40	AU-50	MS-60	MS-63	MS-65
VARIETY	$100	$150	$250	$300	$400	$700
NORMAL	$10	$25	$50	$75	$120	$350

Note: Values listed for MS-60 and higher are for RB (red and brown) specimens. Full red Uncirculated specimens command higher prices.

1884 — FS-01-1884-401 (009.48)

VARIETY: Misplaced Date (MPD-001) SNOW-1
PUP: Denticles below date
URS-6 · I-2 · L-2

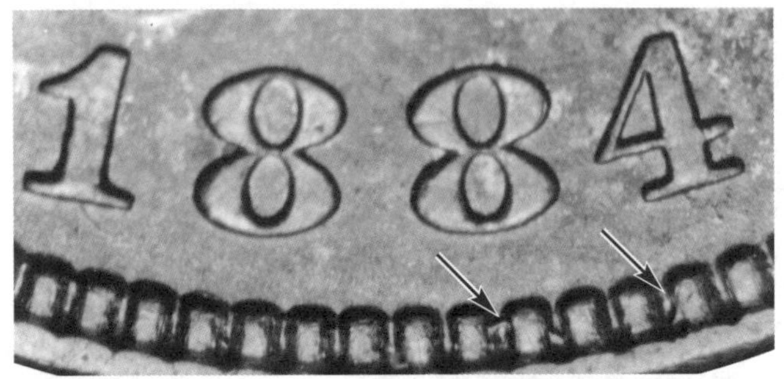

Description: The tops of an 8 and 4 are evident protruding from the denticles below the date.

Comments: This coin is primarily of interest to variety specialists and Indian Head cent collectors.

	VF-20	EF-40	AU-50	MS-60	MS-63	MS-65
VARIETY	$25	$50	$75	$100	$150	$350
NORMAL	$10	$25	$50	$75	$120	$350

Note: Values listed for MS-60 and higher are for RB (red and brown) specimens. Full red Uncirculated specimens command higher prices.

1887 — FS-01-1887-101 (009.5)

VARIETY: Doubled-Die Obverse (DDO-001) SNOW-1
PUP: AMERICA
URS-9 · I-5 · L-5

Description: Very strong doubling is evident on UNITED STATES OF AMERICA, with the doubling increasing from left to right.

Comments: This is easily one of the strongest doubled dies in the Indian Head cent series. It's a very impressive variety, especially in high grade.

	VF-20	EF-40	AU-50	MS-60	MS-63	MS-65
VARIETY	$150	$300	$500	$1,000	$2,500	$8,000
NORMAL	$8	$20	$30	$70	$120	$550

Note: Values listed for MS-60 and higher are for RB (red and brown) specimens. Full red Uncirculated specimens command higher prices.

1888 — FS-01-1888-301 (010)

VARIETY: Overdate (RPD-001)
PUP: Date
URS-7 · I-5 · L-5

SNOW-1

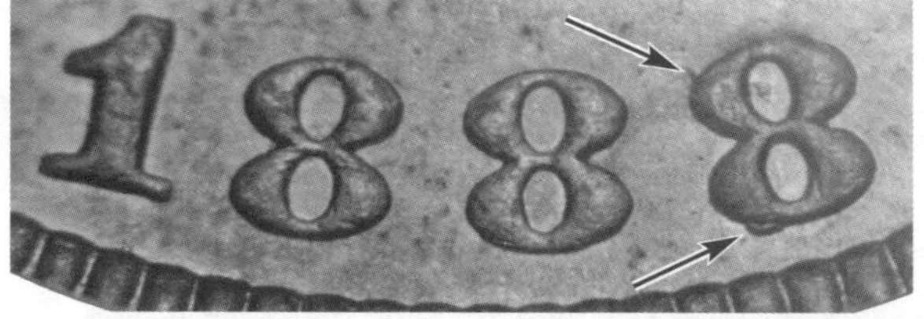
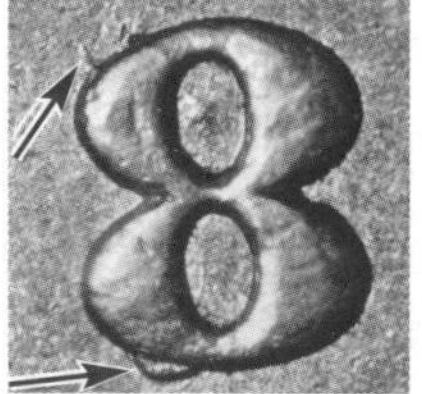

Description: The upper left portion of a 7 is evident protruding from the upper left of the last 8, and the base of that 7 protrudes from the lower left. A portion of the upper-left crossbar may be seen inside the upper loop of the 8 on high-grade specimens.

Comments: Most specimens have a small cud (die break) over UNITED. No coins above Very Good have been seen without this cud. This variety is the #1 cherrypick among Indian Head cents. About 30 examples are known and demand is very high. An MS-63BN example sold for $74,750 in 2007.

	VF-20	EF-40	AU-50	MS-60	MS-63	MS-65
VARIETY	$10,000	$17,000	$25,000	$35,000	$80,000	–
NORMAL	$7	$20	$30	$85	$170	$850

Note: Values listed for MS-60 and higher are for RB (red and brown) specimens. Full red Uncirculated specimens command higher prices.

1888 — FS-01-1888-302 (010.7)

VARIETY: Repunched Date (Possible Overdate) (RPD-002)
PUP: Date
URS-6 · I-5 · L-5

SNOW-2

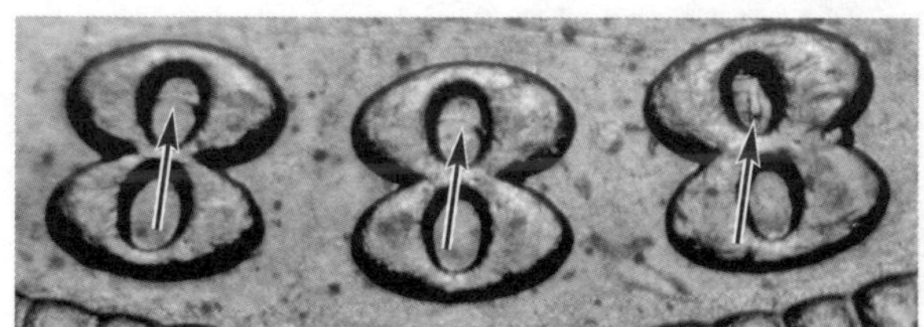
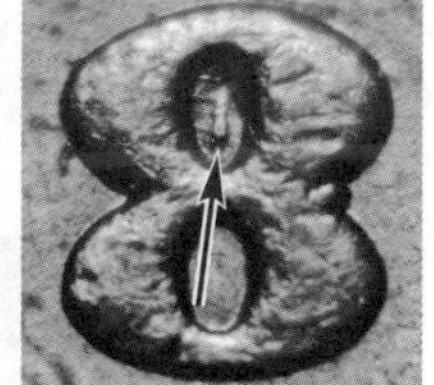

Description: This possible overdate, discovered by Bill Fivaz in July 1990, was initially confirmed by overlay photos, but has been questioned by some collectors who opine that it is only a repunched date. (See Tim Larson, "1888/7 S2, Is it Really an Overdate?" *Longacre's Ledger*, June 2000.) Apparent remnants of the underlying 7 are evident inside the upper loop of the last 8 and outside the left and right top of the last 8. The second and third 8 also show evidence of repunching. There is also the base of a 1 sticking out of the first pearl.

Comments: On the reverse, there is a die break leading upward from the rim at 7:30 to a point in the wreath opposite the C of CENT. One example is struck in copper-nickel!

	VF-20	EF-40	AU-50	MS-60	MS-63	MS-65
VARIETY	$500	$750	$1,500	$2,500	$3,500	$5,000
NORMAL	$7	$20	$30	$85	$170	$850

Note: Values listed for MS-60 and higher are for RB (red and brown) specimens. Full red Uncirculated specimens command higher prices.

1888 — FS-01-1888-303 (010.73)

VARIETY: Misplaced Date — SNOW-27
PUP: Bottom of ribbon
URS-6 · I-2 · L-2

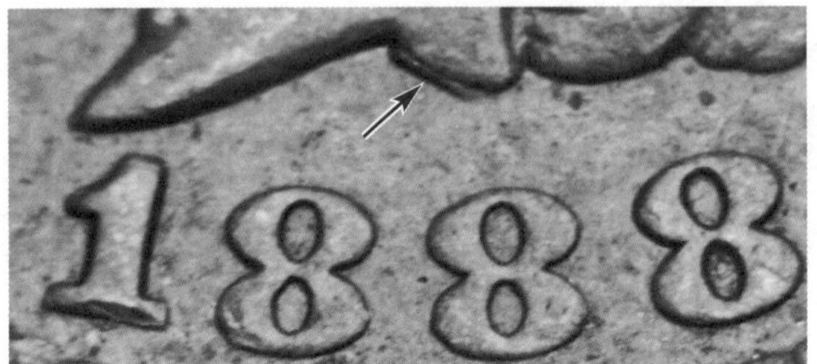

Description: What is believed to be the base of a 1 is evident protruding from the base of the ribbon.

Comments: It is now commonly believed that the misplaced digits are remnants of a quick hardness test employed by Mint die makers. This variety seems to be quite rare, although it is not well known.

	VF-20	EF-40	AU-50	MS-60	MS-63	MS-65
VARIETY	$40	$75	$100	$200	$400	$1,500
NORMAL	$7	$20	$30	$85	$170	$850

Note: Values listed for MS-60 and higher are for RB (red and brown) specimens. Full red Uncirculated specimens command higher prices.

1888 — FS-01-1888-305 (010.75)

VARIETY: Misplaced Date — SNOW-32
PUP: Lower hair curls
URS-4 · I-2 · L-2

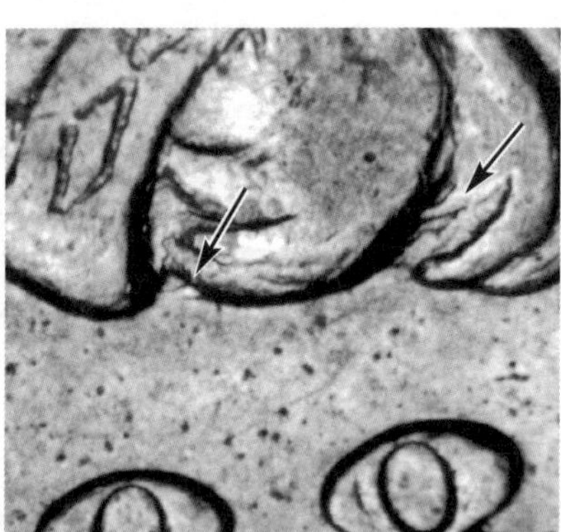

Description: What is believed to be the bases of two 8s are evident within the lower hair curls.

Comments: Many minor misplaced digits are known for this year.

	VF-20	EF-40	AU-50	MS-60	MS-63	MS-65
VARIETY	$15	$30	$40	$90	$175	$850
NORMAL	$7	$20	$30	$85	$170	$850

Note: Values listed for MS-60 and higher are for RB (red and brown) specimens. Full red Uncirculated specimens command higher prices.

1889 — FS-01-1889-301 (010.8)

VARIETY: Repunched Date (RPD-002) — **SNOW-3**
PUP: Date
URS-9 · I-2 · L-1

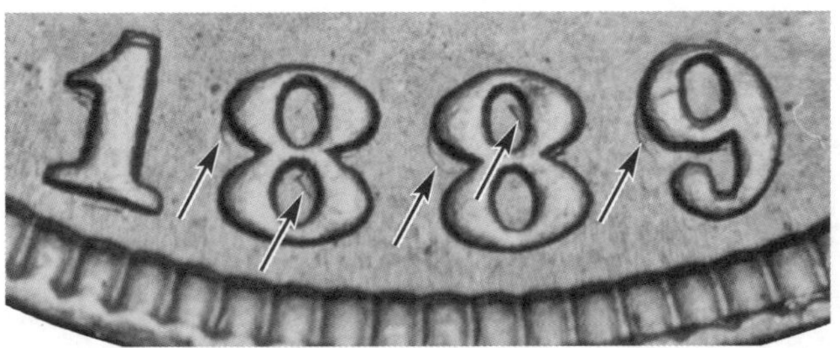

Description: Secondary digits are evident to the southwest of the primary digits on both of the 8s and the 9.

Comments: This has proven to be a relatively easy variety to locate.

	VF-20	EF-40	AU-50	MS-60	MS-63	MS-65
VARIETY	$10	$25	$50	$75	$150	$650
NORMAL	$5	$10	$30	$50	$100	$600

Note: Values listed for MS-60 and higher are for RB (red and brown) specimens. Full red Uncirculated specimens command higher prices.

1889 — FS-01-1889-801 (010.81)

VARIETY: Doubled-Die Reverse (DDR-001) — **SNOW-1**
PUP: Date
URS-8 · I-4 · L-3

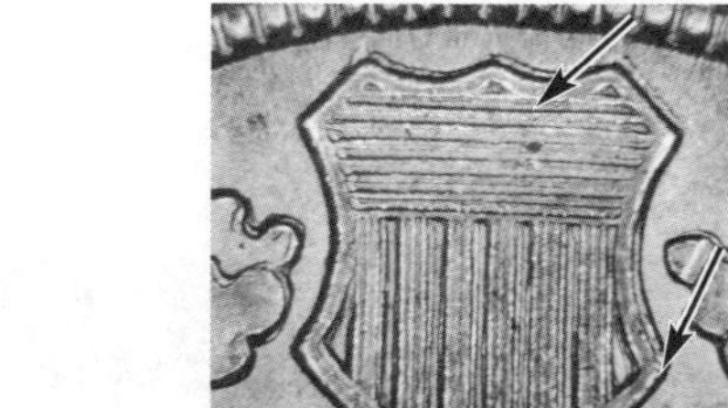 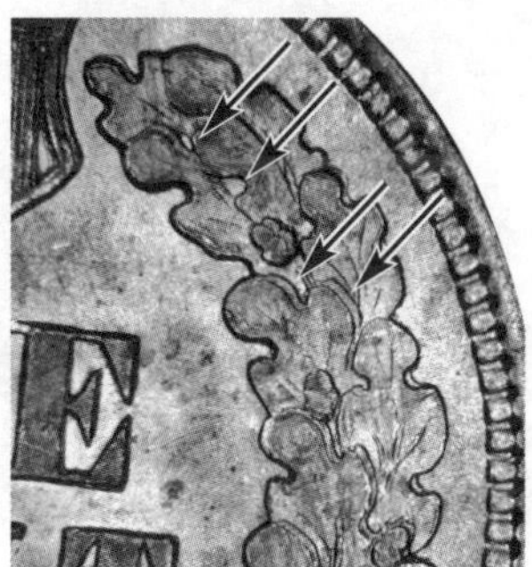

Description: There is strong doubling to the northwest on the shield, right wreath, and upper left wreath. The doubling is strongest in the upper-right wreath.

Comments: This is a very bold doubled die.

	VF-20	EF-40	AU-50	MS-60	MS-63	MS-65
VARIETY	$30	$50	$75	$100	$175	$1,000
NORMAL	$5	$10	$30	$50	$100	$600

Note: Values listed for MS-60 and higher are for RB (red and brown) specimens. Full red Uncirculated specimens command higher prices.

1889 FS-01-1889-802

VARIETY: Doubled-Die Reverse (DDR-002) **SNOW-11**
PUP: Date
URS-6 · I-4 · L-3

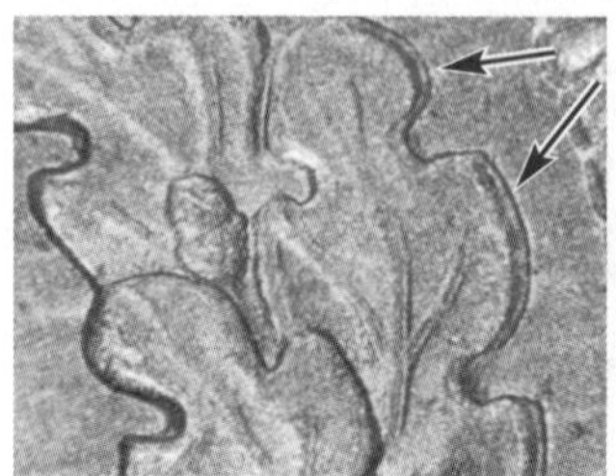 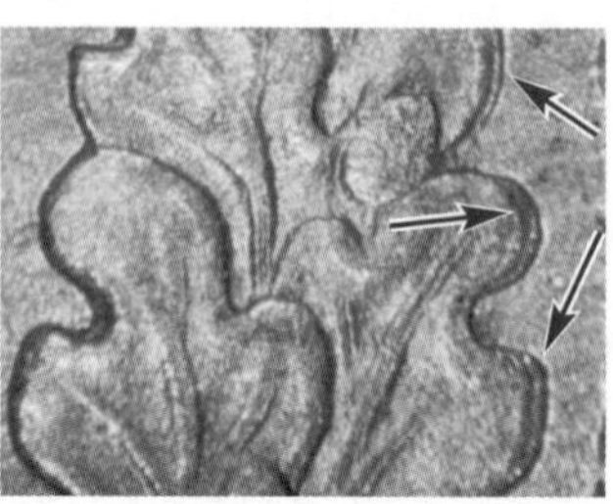

Description: Strong doubling on the right wreath.

Comments: This is another doubled-die reverse for this year—not as dramatic as FS-801, but scarcer.

	VF-20	EF-40	AU-50	MS-60	MS-63	MS-65
VARIETY	$30	$50	$75	$100	$175	$1,000
NORMAL	$5	$10	$30	$50	$100	$600

Note: Values listed for MS-60 and higher are for RB (red and brown) specimens. Full red Uncirculated specimens command higher prices.

1890 FS-01-1890-101 (010.85)

VARIETY: Tripled-Die Obverse (TDO-001) **SNOW-1**
PUP: United States of America
URS-7 · I-5 · L-5

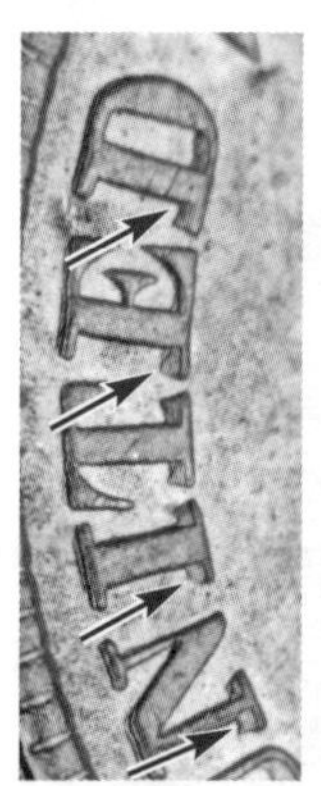  

Description: This is one of the more popular Indian Head cent varieties. A tripled image is evident, spread toward the center on all letters of UNITED STATES OF AMERICA.

Comments: This variety was caused by the design spreading with each successive impression of the hub.

	VF-20	EF-40	AU-50	MS-60	MS-63	MS-65
VARIETY	$100	$250	$350	$500	$1,200	$2,500
NORMAL	$5	$10	$30	$50	$100	$600

Note: Values listed for MS-60 and higher are for RB (red and brown) specimens. Full red Uncirculated specimens command higher prices.

1890

FS-01-1890-401 (010.82)

VARIETY: Misplaced Date (MPD-004)

SNOW-3

PUP: Neck

URS-7 · I-3 · L-3

Description: The flag of a 1 is evident protruding from the neck, just above the necklace.

Comments: The digit in the neck is quite prominent.

	VF-20	EF-40	AU-50	MS-60	MS-63	MS-65
VARIETY	$15	$30	$75	$100	$200	$750
NORMAL	$5	$10	$30	$50	$100	$600

Note: Values listed for MS-60 and higher are for RB (red and brown) specimens. Full red Uncirculated specimens command higher prices.

1890

FS-01-1890-402 (010.84)

VARIETY: Misplaced Date (MPD-001)

SNOW-6

PUP: Denticles below date

URS-7 · I-2 · L-2

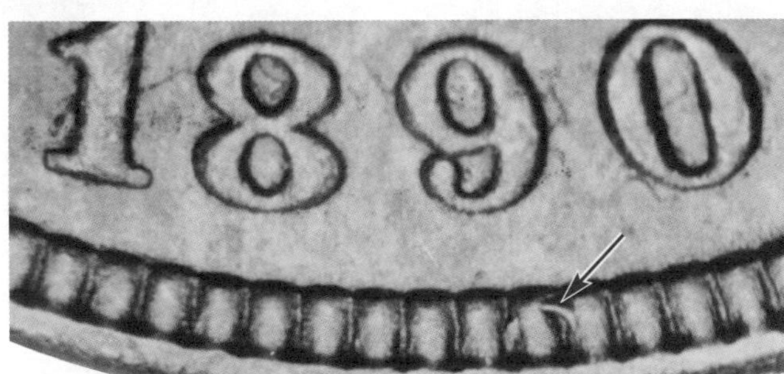

Description: A portion of a digit (likely a 0) can be seen within the denticles below the 9 of the date.

Comments: Misplaced digits get more interest the more prominent they are.

	VF-20	EF-40	AU-50	MS-60	MS-63	MS-65
VARIETY	$10	$20	$50	$70	$140	$600
NORMAL	$5	$10	$30	$50	$100	$600

Note: Values listed for MS-60 and higher are for RB (red and brown) specimens. Full red Uncirculated specimens command higher prices.

1891 — FS-01-1891-101 (010.88)

VARIETY: Doubled-Die Obverse (DDO-001) **SNOW-1**
PUP: Date
URS-7 · I-5 · L-5

Description: The doubling on this variety is evident on LIBERTY and the words STATES OF AMERICA, where the spread decreases from left to right.

Comments: This variety also exhibits a minor repunched date on some higher-grade specimens. It is one of the top Indian Head cent varieties.

	VF-20	EF-40	AU-50	MS-60	MS-63	MS-65
VARIETY	$150	$250	$500	$1,000	$1,750	$3,500
NORMAL	$5	$10	$30	$50	$100	$600

Note: Values listed for MS-60 and higher are for RB (red and brown) specimens. Full red Uncirculated specimens command higher prices.

1891 — FS-01-1891-301 (010.87)

VARIETY: Repunched Date (RPD-001) **SNOW-3**
PUP: Date
URS-9 · I-3 · L-3

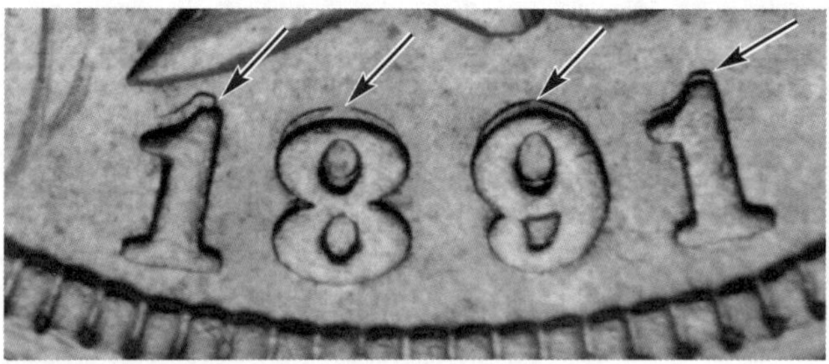

Description: Secondary digits are evident to the north of all four primary digits.

Comments: This variety exhibits wide repunching.

	VF-20	EF-40	AU-50	MS-60	MS-63	MS-65
VARIETY	$20	$30	$50	$100	$250	$750
NORMAL	$5	$10	$30	$50	$100	$600

Note: Values listed for MS-60 and higher are for RB (red and brown) specimens. Full red Uncirculated specimens command higher prices.

1892   FS-01-1892-301 (010.89)

VARIETY: Repunched Date (RPD-008)   **SNOW-8**
PUP: Date
URS-6 · I-4 · L-4

Description: Secondary digits are evident to the east of the 8 and 2 in the date. Earlier die states may exhibit secondary digits on the 1 and/or 9 as well.

Comments: This variety is quite popular, primarily due to the width of the spread of the secondary digits.

	VF-20	EF-40	AU-50	MS-60	MS-63	MS-65
VARIETY	$25	$50	$100	$150	$200	$800
NORMAL	$5	$10	$30	$50	$100	$600

Note: Values listed for MS-60 and higher are for RB (red and brown) specimens. Full red Uncirculated specimens command higher prices.

1892   FS-01-1892-302 (010.9)

VARIETY: Repunched Date + Doubled Die Reverse   **SNOW-1**
           (RPD-002, DDR-001)
PUP: Date
URS-6 · I-4 · L-4

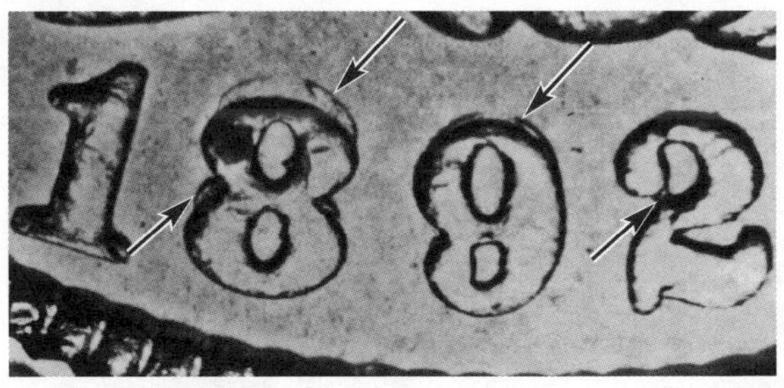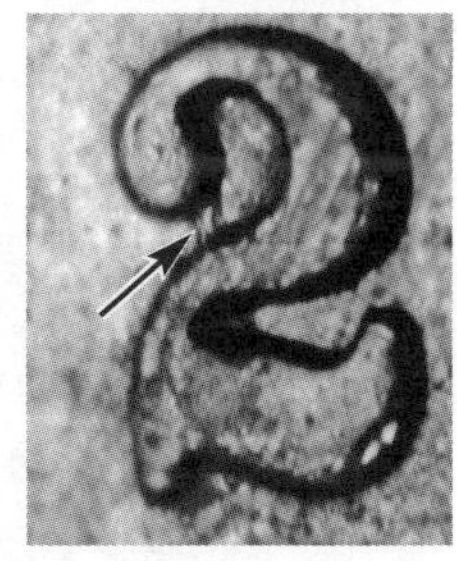

Description: Secondary digits are evident to the north of the 8 and 9. There is a vertical bar, within the opening of the 2, which some believe is a 1. However, most specialists believe this is nothing more than a damaged date punch. A very minor doubled-die reverse is paired with this obverse die.

Comments: This is a very dramatic repunched date and is very scarce.

	VF-20	EF-40	AU-50	MS-60	MS-63	MS-65
VARIETY	$30	$50	$100	$175	$250	$750
NORMAL	$5	$10	$30	$50	$100	$600

Note: Values listed for MS-60 and higher are for RB (red and brown) specimens. Full red Uncirculated specimens command higher prices.

1892 — FS-01-1892-401 (010.91)

VARIETY: Heavy Die Scratches
PUP: Cheek
URS-4 · I-4 · L-4

SNOW-14

Description: Heavy scratches and/or gouges are evident on the face, neck, and headdress, and slightly into the left field. One of the authors feels these scratches may have been a crude attempt to "cancel" the die.

Comments: This is affectionately referred to as the "Scarface" variety.

	VF-20	EF-40	AU-50	MS-60	MS-63	MS-65
VARIETY	$75	$150	$200	$300	$400	$1,000
NORMAL	$5	$10	$30	$50	$100	$600

Note: Values listed for MS-60 and higher are for RB (red and brown) specimens. Full red Uncirculated specimens command higher prices.

1893 — FS-01-1893-301 (010.95)

VARIETY: Repunched Date (RPD-002)
PUP: Date
URS-5 · I-3 · L-3

SNOW-2

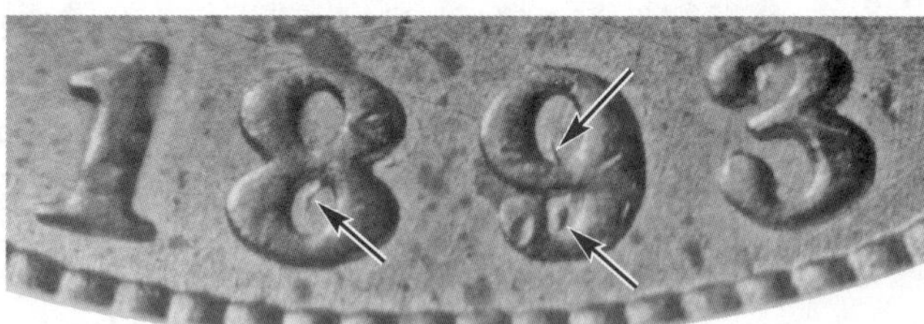

Description: Secondary digits are evident in the lower loop of the 8, in both loops of the 9, and within the upper loop of the 3.

Comments: Lower grades or late die states don't exhibit the secondary image of the 3. A partial roll of these coins was located in the late 1990s.

	VF-20	EF-40	AU-50	MS-60	MS-63	MS-65
VARIETY	$20	$30	$50	$75	$150	$650
NORMAL	$5	$10	$30	$50	$100	$600

Note: Values listed for MS-60 and higher are for RB (red and brown) specimens. Full red Uncirculated specimens command higher prices.

1894

FS-01-1894-301 (011)

VARIETY: Repunched Date (RPD-001)

SNOW-1

PUP: Date

URS-9 · I-5 · L-5

Description: This massive repunched date is one of the Top 5 varieties in the Indian Head cent series. Secondary digits are vividly evident to the east of the primary digits, with the secondary 4 to the north and east of the primary 4. The repunching can be detected in low grades, and is still saleable down to G-4.

Comments: Don't pass on this variety in any grade. Values have continued to rise over the years as popularity and demand increase.

	VF-20	EF-40	AU-50	MS-60	MS-63	MS-65
VARIETY	$150	$300	$600	$800	$1,000	$5,000
NORMAL	$20	$50	$60	$80	$100	$700

Note: Values listed for MS-60 and higher are for RB (red and brown) specimens. Full red Uncirculated specimens command higher prices.

1894

FS-01-1894-402 (011.2)

VARIETY: Misplaced Digits (MPD-001)

SNOW-2

PUP: Date

URS-6 · I-3 · L-3

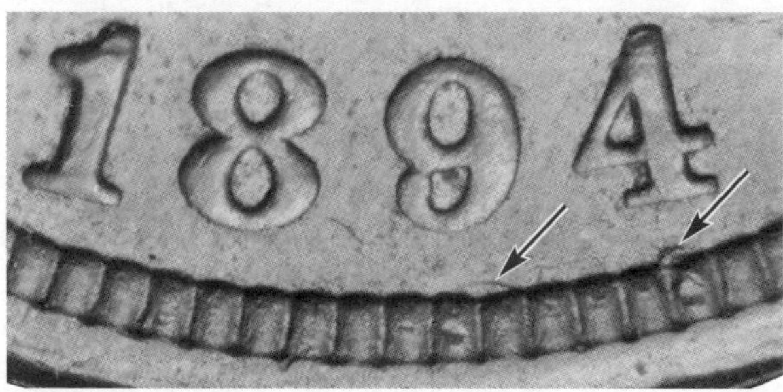

Description: The very top portions of a 9 and a 4 are evident protruding from the denticles below the primary numbers.

Comments: This variety has proven elusive for many years.

	VF-20	EF-40	AU-50	MS-60	MS-63	MS-65
VARIETY	$50	$80	$125	$250	$500	$1,250
NORMAL	$20	$50	$60	$80	$100	$700

Note: Values listed for MS-60 and higher are for RB (red and brown) specimens. Full red Uncirculated specimens command higher prices.

1895 — FS-01-1895-301 (011.3)

VARIETY: Repunched Date (RPD-001) — **SNOW-1**
PUP: Date
URS-8 · I-3 · L-3

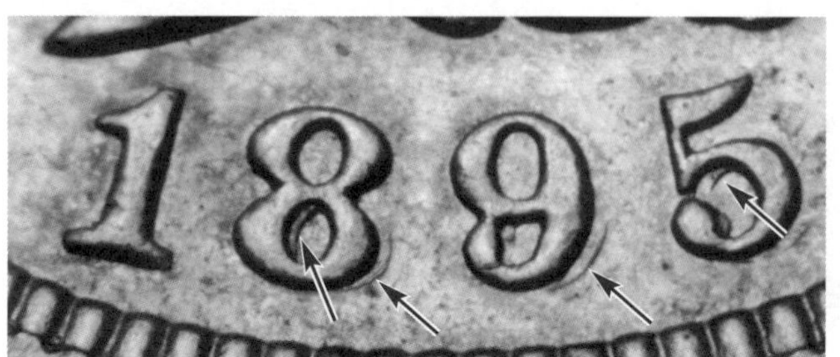

Description: Secondary digits are evident to the right of the primary digits on the 8, 9, and 5.

Comments: There are other, less obvious RPDs for this date.

	VF-20	EF-40	AU-50	MS-60	MS-63	MS-65
VARIETY	$15	$25	$50	$90	$150	$375
NORMAL	$5	$10	$25	$35	$60	$275

Note: Values listed for MS-60 and higher are for RB (red and brown) specimens. Full red Uncirculated specimens command higher prices.

1895 — FS-01-1895-302 (011.31)

VARIETY: Repunched Date (RPD-009) — **SNOW-9**
PUP: Date
URS-5 · I-3 · L-3

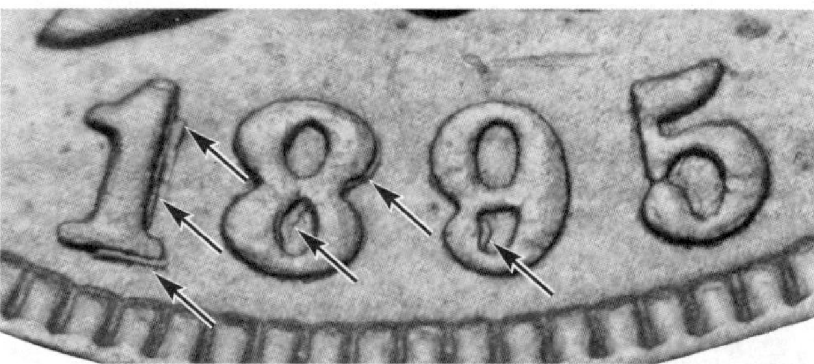

Description: The 1 of the date is tripled, with the two secondary images evident to the right of the primary 1. A secondary 8, 9, and 5 are also evident to the right of the primary.

Comments: This variety is interesting with the tripled 1. It is very rarely seen.

	VF-20	EF-40	AU-50	MS-60	MS-63	MS-65
VARIETY	$15	$25	$50	$75	$150	$350
NORMAL	$5	$10	$25	$35	$60	$275

Note: Values listed for MS-60 and higher are for RB (red and brown) specimens. Full red Uncirculated specimens command higher prices.

1896 — FS-01-1896-301 (011.4)

VARIETY: Repunched Date (RPD-001)   **SNOW-1**
PUP: Date
URS-8 · I-3 · L-3

Description: The top of a secondary 6 is evident fairly wide to the right.

Comments: Varieties such as this, wherein only a single digit shows evidence of repunching, are not that uncommon, especially from the 19th century.

	VF-20	EF-40	AU-50	MS-60	MS-63	MS-65
VARIETY	$30	$50	$100	$175	$250	$500
NORMAL	$5	$10	$25	$35	$60	$275

Note: Values listed for MS-60 and higher are for RB (red and brown) specimens. Full red Uncirculated specimens command higher prices.

1897 — FS-01-1897-401 (011.5)

VARIETY: Misplaced Date (MPD-001)   **SNOW-1**
PUP: Front of neck
URS-9 · I-5 · L-5

Description: The numeral 1 is evident protruding from the front of the neck.

Comments: This variety, although popular, is fairly easy to locate in lower grades. Mint State pieces, though, are very hard to locate. An MS-65RB example sold for $7,500 in 2007.

	VF-20	EF-40	AU-50	MS-60	MS-63	MS-65
VARIETY	$200	$350	$750	$1,000	$2,500	$7,000
NORMAL	$5	$10	$25	$35	$60	$275

Note: Values listed for MS-60 and higher are for RB (red and brown) specimens. Full red Uncirculated specimens command higher prices.

1897 — FS-01-1897-402 (011.6)

VARIETY: Repunched Date (RPD-008) — **SNOW-8**
PUP: Date
URS-6 · I-4 · L-3

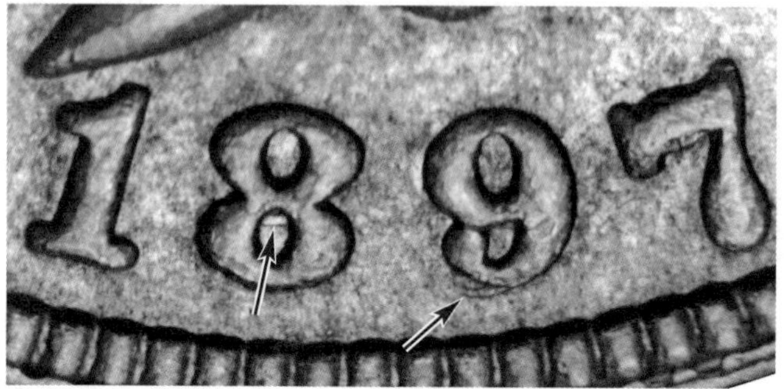

Description: A portion of a loop of the secondary 8 is evident just below the primary center bar, and the lower loop of a secondary 9 is evident just to the south of the primary 9.

Comments: This variety is scarce and dramatic but not as popular as many other RPDs of the Indian Head cent series.

	VF-20	EF-40	AU-50	MS-60	MS-63	MS-65
VARIETY	$15	$25	$40	$60	$90	$300
NORMAL	$5	$10	$25	$35	$60	$275

Note: Values listed for MS-60 and higher are for RB (red and brown) specimens. Full red Uncirculated specimens command higher prices.

1898 — FS-01-1898-401 (011.65)

VARIETY: Misplaced Date (MPD-012) — **SNOW-12**
PUP: Denticles below date
URS-6 · I-2 · L-2

Description: The top of a digit, likely an 8, is evident protruding from the denticles below the second 8.

Comments: This is just one of the many MPDs within the series. This one has turned out to be rather scarce in high grades.

	VF-20	EF-40	AU-50	MS-60	MS-63	MS-65
VARIETY	$10	$20	$40	$60	$150	$400
NORMAL	$5	$10	$25	$35	$60	$275

Note: Values listed for MS-60 and higher are for RB (red and brown) specimens. Full red Uncirculated specimens command higher prices.

1898 — FS-01-1898-402 (011.66)

VARIETY: Misplaced Date (MPD-003) **SNOW-5**
PUP: Denticles below date
URS-7 · I-3 · L-2

Description: The top of a digit, likely a 9, is evident protruding from the denticles below the primary 9.

Comments: This variety has slightly better eye appeal than the previous. When MPDs are visible without magnification, such as this one, they get more interest from collectors.

	VF-20	EF-40	AU-50	MS-60	MS-63	MS-65
VARIETY	$40	$75	$125	$200	$300	$750
NORMAL	$5	$10	$25	$35	$60	$275

Note: Values listed for MS-60 and higher are for RB (red and brown) specimens. Full red Uncirculated specimens command higher prices.

1899 — FS-01-1899-301 (011.7)

VARIETY: Repunched Date (RPD-001) **SNOW-1**
PUP: Date
URS-10 · I-2 · L-2

Description: A secondary 8 is evident to the east of the primary 8, and secondary 9s can be detected within the lower loops of both of the primary digits.

Comments: This RPD is primarily of interest to variety specialists and Indian Head cent collectors.

	VF-20	EF-40	AU-50	MS-60	MS-63	MS-65
VARIETY	$10	$15	$30	$50	$75	$250
NORMAL	$5	$10	$25	$35	$60	$200

Note: Values listed for MS-60 and higher are for RB (red and brown) specimens. Full red Uncirculated specimens command higher prices.

1899 — FS-01-1899-302 (011.75)

VARIETY: Repunched Date (RPD-013)
PUP: Date
URS-8 · I-3 · L-3

SNOW-13

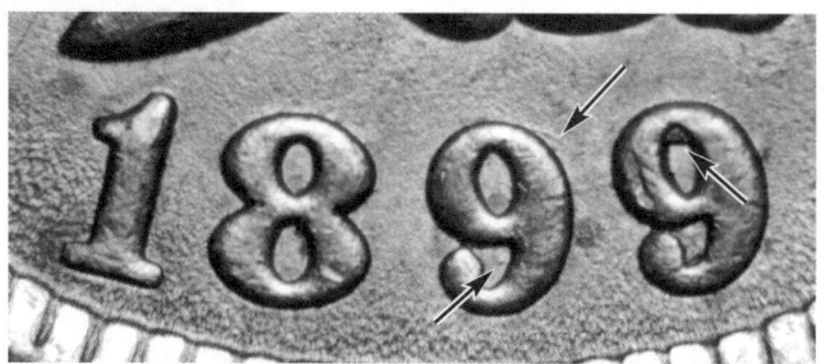

Description: The first 9 is lightly repunched, with the secondary digit visible to the right of the upper portion. There is also a metal fill in the top of the second 9.

Comments: This RPD is listed by Breen as an overdate, but there is not enough evidence to support that listing in the opinion of most specialists. The variety is primarily of interest to specialists and Indian Head cent collectors.

	VF-20	EF-40	AU-50	MS-60	MS-63	MS-65
VARIETY	$20	$30	$50	$100	$200	$500
NORMAL	$5	$10	$25	$35	$60	$200

Note: Values listed for MS-60 and higher are for RB (red and brown) specimens. Full red Uncirculated specimens command higher prices.

1899 — FS-01-1899-303

VARIETY: Repunched Date (RPD-009)
PUP: Date
URS-8 · I-3 · L-3

SNOW-9

Description: The 1 is repunched, with the secondary digit to the south. The final 9 is also repunched, with the secondary digit to the north.

Comments: This RPD is primarily of interest to variety specialists and Indian Head cent collectors.

	VF-20	EF-40	AU-50	MS-60	MS-63	MS-65
VARIETY	$20	$30	$35	$80	$150	$300
NORMAL	$5	$10	$25	$35	$60	$200

Note: Values listed for MS-60 and higher are for RB (red and brown) specimens. Full red Uncirculated specimens command higher prices.

1900   FS-01-1900-301 (011.751)

VARIETY: Repunched Date (RPD-001)   **SNOW-1**
PUP: Date
URS-8 · I-4 · L-2

Description: The primary second 0 exhibits a secondary 0 to the northeast.

Comments: Although a dramatic repunched date, few collectors are aware of this variety.

	VF-20	EF-40	AU-50	MS-60	MS-63	MS-65
VARIETY	$20	$30	$35	$80	$150	$300
NORMAL	$5	$10	$25	$35	$60	$200

Note: Values listed for MS-60 and higher are for RB (red and brown) specimens. Full red Uncirculated specimens command higher prices.

1900   FS-01-1900-302

VARIETY: Repunched Date (RPD-003)   **SNOW-3**
PUP: Date
URS-8 · I-4 · L-2

Description: Repunching is visible inside the 9 and to the south. There is also repunching on the 0, to the north.

Comments: This is an easy to spot variety—fairly scarce, though.

	VF-20	EF-40	AU-50	MS-60	MS-63	MS-65
VARIETY	$20	$30	$35	$80	$150	$300
NORMAL	$5	$10	$25	$35	$60	$200

Note: Values listed for MS-60 and higher are for RB (red and brown) specimens. Full red Uncirculated specimens command higher prices.

1901 — FS-01-1901-301

VARIETY: Repunched Date (RPD-019)   **SNOW-19**
PUP: Date
URS-8 · I-4 · L-2

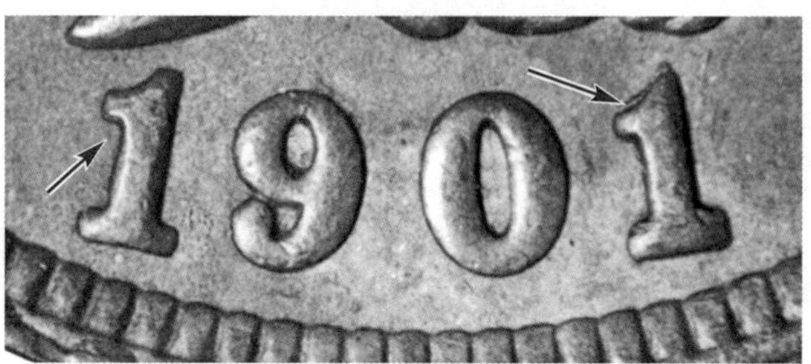

Description: The first 1 is repunched to the south. The second 1 is repunched to the north.

Comments: This is a fairly bold repunched date. It's easy to spot, but tough to find.

	VF-20	EF-40	AU-50	MS-60	MS-63	MS-65
VARIETY	$20	$30	$35	$80	$150	$300
NORMAL	$5	$10	$25	$35	$60	$200

Note: Values listed for MS-60 and higher are for RB (red and brown) specimens. Full red Uncirculated specimens command higher prices.

1902 — FS-01-1902-401

VARIETY: Die Gouge   **SNOW-4**
PUP: Eye
URS-6 · I-4 · L-3

Description: A bold die gouge is under the eye.

Comments: This is a very interesting die gouge. Like the 1870 "Pick-axe," collectors really like it.

	VF-20	EF-40	AU-50	MS-60	MS-63	MS-65
VARIETY	$20	$30	$35	$80	$150	$300
NORMAL	$5	$10	$25	$35	$60	$200

Note: Values listed for MS-60 and higher are for RB (red and brown) specimens. Full red Uncirculated specimens command higher prices.

1903
FS-01-1903-301 (011.76)

SNOW-10

VARIETY: Misplaced Date (MPD-002)
PUP: Denticles below date
URS-7 · I-3 · L-3

Description: The tops of three digits are evident within the denticles below the date.

Comments: This MPD is primarily of interest to variety specialists and Indian Head cent collectors.

	VF-20	EF-40	AU-50	MS-60	MS-63	MS-65
VARIETY	$10	$15	$35	$50	$80	$250
NORMAL	$5	$10	$25	$35	$60	$200

Note: Values listed for MS-60 and higher are for RB (red and brown) specimens. Full red Uncirculated specimens command higher prices.

1903
FS-01-1903-302 (011.765)

SNOW-6

VARIETY: Misplaced Date (MPD-007)
PUP: Denticles below date
URS-7 · I-3 · L-3

Description: The top of a digit (likely a 0) is evident within the denticles below and right of the primary 0.

Comments: This MPD is primarily of interest to variety specialists and Indian Head cent collectors.

	VF-20	EF-40	AU-50	MS-60	MS-63	MS-65
VARIETY	$10	$15	$35	$50	$80	$250
NORMAL	$5	$10	$25	$35	$60	$200

Note: Values listed for MS-60 and higher are for RB (red and brown) specimens. Full red Uncirculated specimens command higher prices.

1903 — FS-01-1903-303

VARIETY: Repunched Date (RPD-006) **SNOW-7**
PUP: Date
URS-7 · I-4 · L-2

Description: Repunching is evident to the right of the base of the 1, as well as above and to the left of the top of the 1.

Comments: This is a scarce repunched date, but easy to spot.

	VF-20	EF-40	AU-50	MS-60	MS-63	MS-65
VARIETY	$20	$30	$35	$80	$150	$300
NORMAL	$5	$10	$25	$35	$60	$200

Note: Values listed for MS-60 and higher are for RB (red and brown) specimens. Full red Uncirculated specimens command higher prices.

1903 — FS-01-1903-304

VARIETY: Repunched Date (RPD-003) **SNOW-3**
PUP: Date
URS-8 · I-4 · L-2

Description: Repunching is apparent on the base of all the digits, to the southeast.

Comments: This is a dramatic repunched date.

	VF-20	EF-40	AU-50	MS-60	MS-63	MS-65
VARIETY	$20	$30	$35	$80	$150	$300
NORMAL	$5	$10	$25	$35	$60	$200

Note: Values listed for MS-60 and higher are for RB (red and brown) specimens. Full red Uncirculated specimens command higher prices.

1904

VARIETY: Repunched Date (RPD-010)
PUP: Date
URS-8 · I-4 · L-3

SNOW-10

Description: Repunching is apparent on the tops of the 04.

Comments: This is a very noticeable variety.

	VF-20	EF-40	AU-50	MS-60	MS-63	MS-65
VARIETY	$20	$30	$50	$100	$175	$350
NORMAL	$5	$10	$25	$35	$60	$200

Note: Values listed for MS-60 and higher are for RB (red and brown) specimens. Full red Uncirculated specimens command higher prices.

1905
FS-01-1905-301

VARIETY: Repunched Date (RPD-301)
PUP: Date
URS-8 · I-4 · L-2

SNOW-1

Description: Repunching is evident below the 5.

Comments: This is an obvious variety—and very scarce.

	VF-20	EF-40	AU-50	MS-60	MS-63	MS-65
VARIETY	$20	$30	$35	$80	$150	$300
NORMAL	$5	$10	$25	$35	$60	$200

Note: Values listed for MS-60 and higher are for RB (red and brown) specimens. Full red Uncirculated specimens command higher prices.

1906 — FS-01-1906-301

VARIETY: Repunched Date (RPD-001) — **SNOW-7**
PUP: Date
URS-7 · I-4 · L-2

Description: Repunching is apparent below the 19 and inside the top of the 0.

Comments: There are many minor repunched dates among Indian Head cents of this year. This is one of the more pronounced varieties.

	VF-20	EF-40	AU-50	MS-60	MS-63	MS-65
VARIETY	$20	$30	$35	$80	$150	$300
NORMAL	$5	$10	$25	$35	$60	$200

Note: Values listed for MS-60 and higher are for RB (red and brown) specimens. Full red Uncirculated specimens command higher prices.

1906 — FS-01-1906-302

VARIETY: Misplaced Date + Repunched Date (MPD-002, RPD-014) — **SNOW-14**
PUP: Date, denticles
URS-8 · I-4 · L-2

Description: Repunching is evident inside the top of the 0. The tops of two digits in the denticles are also visible below and slightly left of the 06.

Comments: Multiple types add desirability to this variety.

	VF-20	EF-40	AU-50	MS-60	MS-63	MS-65
VARIETY	$20	$30	$35	$80	$150	$300
NORMAL	$5	$10	$25	$35	$60	$200

Note: Values listed for MS-60 and higher are for RB (red and brown) specimens. Full red Uncirculated specimens command higher prices.

1906   FS-01-1906-303

SNOW-20

VARIETY: Repunched Date (RPD-017)
PUP: Date
URS-7 · I-4 · L-2

Description: Bold repunching is evident in the lower loop of the 6, minor repunching on the 19 to the south.

Comments: This variety is easy to spot.

	VF-20	EF-40	AU-50	MS-60	MS-63	MS-65
VARIETY	$20	$30	$35	$80	$150	$300
NORMAL	$5	$10	$25	$35	$60	$200

Note: Values listed for MS-60 and higher are for RB (red and brown) specimens. Full red Uncirculated specimens command higher prices.

1907   FS-01-1907-301

SNOW-1

VARIETY: Repunched Date (RPD-001)
PUP: Date
URS-8 · I-4 · L-3

Description: Repunching is evident on the base of the 07 and inside the 9. A minor misplaced digit is visible in the denticles under the 0.

Comments: This is a bold and interesting repunched date.

	VF-20	EF-40	AU-50	MS-60	MS-63	MS-65
VARIETY	$20	$30	$50	$100	$175	$350
NORMAL	$5	$10	$25	$35	$60	$200

Note: Values listed for MS-60 and higher are for RB (red and brown) specimens. Full red Uncirculated specimens command higher prices.

1907 — FS-01-1907-302

SNOW-2

VARIETY: Repunched Date (RPD-002)
PUP: Date
URS-6 · I-4 · L-3

Description: Very bold repunching is visible inside the 90.

Comments: This is a very interesting repunched date, although rarely seen.

	VF-20	EF-40	AU-50	MS-60	MS-63	MS-65
VARIETY	$40	$65	$100	$150	$250	$400
NORMAL	$5	$10	$25	$35	$60	$200

Note: Values listed for MS-60 and higher are for RB (red and brown) specimens. Full red Uncirculated specimens command higher prices.

1907 — FS-01-1907-303

SNOW-27

VARIETY: Repunched Date (RPD-026)
PUP: Date
URS-6 · I-4 · L-2

Description: Wide repunching is apparent inside the bottom of the 90, to the east.

Comments: This is an obvious repunched date. The variety is tough to locate.

	VF-20	EF-40	AU-50	MS-60	MS-63	MS-65
VARIETY	$20	$30	$35	$80	$150	$300
NORMAL	$5	$10	$25	$35	$60	$200

Note: Values listed for MS-60 and higher are for RB (red and brown) specimens. Full red Uncirculated specimens command higher prices.

1908 — FS-01-1908-201

VARIETY: Repunched Mintmark (RPM-001) **SNOW-1**
PUP: Denticles below date
URS-10· I-5 · L-4

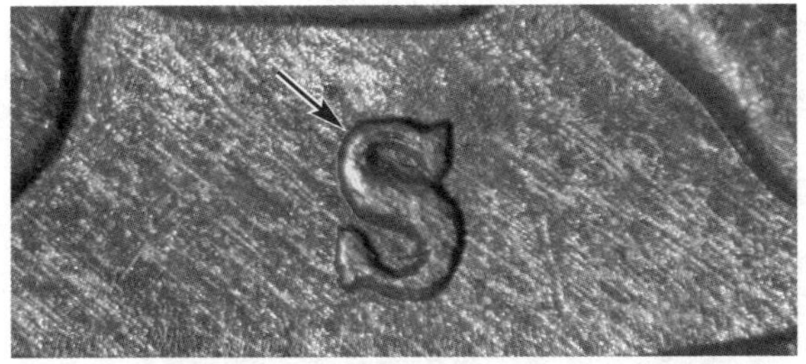

Description: Repunching is visible on the top portion of the mintmark.

Comments: As the only repunched mintmark of the Indian Head cent series, this is quite popular. One variety of 1908-S shows a straight die line in the upper loop of the S. This is not a repunched date. Regular 1908-S cents with strike doubling may show outlines on the mintmark as well as the base of the wreath.

	VF-20	EF-40	AU-50	MS-60	MS-63	MS-65
VARIETY	$150	$250	$375	$650	$800	$2,500
NORMAL	$85	$150	$200	$300	$400	$700

Note: Values listed for MS-60 and higher are for RB (red and brown) specimens. Full red Uncirculated specimens command higher prices.

1908 — FS-01-1908-301 (011.77)

VARIETY: Misplaced Date (MPD-002) **SNOW-4**
PUP: Denticles below date
URS-7 · I-3 · L-3

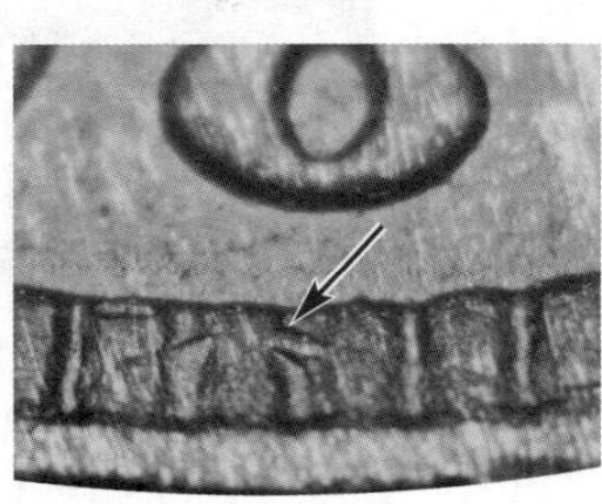

Description: The upper portion of a complete date is evident within the denticles below and slightly left the primary date. The MPD is most prominent under the 8.

Comments: This MPD is primarily of interest to variety specialists and Indian Head cent collectors.

	VF-20	EF-40	AU-50	MS-60	MS-63	MS-65
VARIETY	$10	$20	$35	$50	$75	$225
NORMAL	$5	$10	$25	$35	$60	$200

Note: Values listed for MS-60 and higher are for RB (red and brown) specimens. Full red Uncirculated specimens command higher prices.

1908 — FS-01-1908-302 (011.79)

VARIETY: Misplaced Date (MPD-003) **SNOW-9**
PUP: Denticles below date
URS-7 · I-3 · L-3

Description: The upper portions of two digits (likely a 9 and 0) are evident within the denticles below the primary 0 and 8.

Comments: This MPD is primarily of interest to variety specialists and Indian Head cent collectors.

	VF-20	EF-40	AU-50	MS-60	MS-63	MS-65
VARIETY	$10	$20	$35	$50	$75	$225
NORMAL	$5	$10	$25	$35	$60	$200

Note: Values listed for MS-60 and higher are for RB (red and brown) specimens. Full red Uncirculated specimens command higher prices.

1909 — FS-01-1909-101 (011.9)

VARIETY: Doubled-Die Obverse **SNOW-1**
PUP: Designer's initial
URS-12 · I-2 · L-2

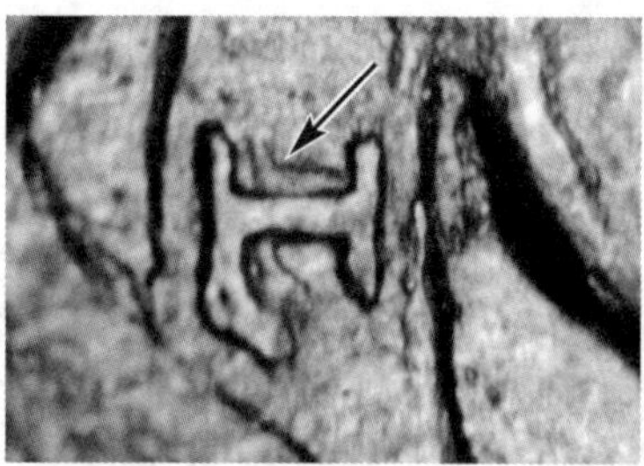

Description: The designer's initial, "L," is doubled, giving the illusion of a large L over a small L, though this is not the case. The doubling was apparently on a master die, as many of the working dies have been identified as having this abnormality.

Comments: This variety was once considered more collectible than it is now, due to the false belief that the doubling was, in fact, a "large L over small L." No premium should be expected for this variety today. About a quarter of the existing 1909 Indian Head cents show this effect.

	VF-20	EF-40	AU-50	MS-60	MS-63	MS-65
VARIETY	$5	$10	$25	$35	$60	$200
NORMAL	$5	$10	$25	$35	$60	$200

Note: Values listed for MS-60 and higher are for RB (red and brown) specimens. Full red Uncirculated specimens command higher prices.

Lincoln Cents, 1909 to Date

Lincoln cent varieties are, without a doubt, the most widely collected in today's numismatics. While some varieties in other series might be somewhat difficult to sell, that is not necessarily the case with the Lincoln cents. They are always popular, and always in demand.

A list of the books that we highly recommend for further study of varieties would have to begin with *The Authoritative Reference on Lincoln Cents,* by John A. Wexler and Kevin Flynn. Loaded with photos of varieties, this is a treasure trove for the enthusiast. Others include *The RPM Book, Second Edition: Lincoln Cents,* by James Wiles; *The Complete Price Guide and Cross Reference to Lincoln Cent Mint Mark Varieties,* by John A. Wexler and Brian Allen; and *A Quick Reference to the Top Lincoln Cent Die Varieties,* by Gary Wagnon, Karen Peterson, and Kevin Flynn.

If you're interested in more general books on the Lincoln cent, an excellent one is *The Complete Guide to the Lincoln Cent,* by David W. Lange. Sol Taylor's *Standard Guide to the Lincoln Cent,* fourth edition, and Q. David Bowers's *Guide Book of Lincoln Cents* are also both wonderful choices.

1909, V.D.B. — FS-01-1909-1101 (012)

VARIETY: Doubled-Die Obverse   **CONECA: DDO-001**
PUP: Date, RTY of LIBERTY
URS-13 · I-3 · L-3

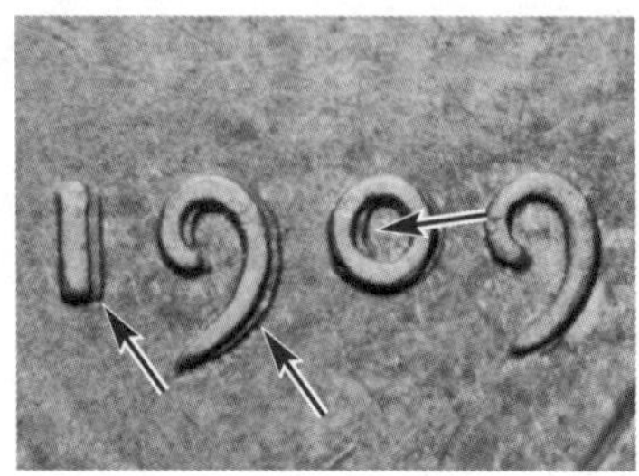

Description: Doubling is evident on the RTY of LIBERTY and on all four digits of the date, with the secondary image east of the primary image.

Comments: Though this variety can be located in Uncirculated grades with some looking, sales remain surprisingly high; unfortunately, prices are somewhat depressed.

	VF-20	EF-40	AU-50	MS-60	MS-63	MS-65
VARIETY	$10	$15	$20	$30	$35	$90
NORMAL	$7	$9	$11	$14	$23	$60

Note: Values listed for MS-60 and higher are for RB (red and brown) specimens. Full red Uncirculated specimens command higher prices.

1909, V.D.B. — FS-01-1909-1102 (012.1)

VARIETY: Doubled-Die Obverse   **CONECA: DDO-002**
PUP: Date, R of LIBERTY
URS-12 · I-2 · L-3

Description: The doubling on this variety is evident as extra thickness on all obverse letters and numbers, but it is most noticeable on the date. The upright strokes of the letters of LIBERTY are also thicker than normal, and there is a die chip within the upper loop of the R.

Comments: This variety is scarcer that FS-01-1909-1101, but less evident and usually more difficult to sell.

	VF-20	EF-40	AU-50	MS-60	MS-63	MS-65
VARIETY	$10	$15	$20	$25	$30	$75
NORMAL	$7	$9	$11	$14	$23	$60

Note: Values listed for MS-60 and higher are for RB (red and brown) specimens. Full red Uncirculated specimens command higher prices.

1909-S

FS-01-1909S-1501 (012.2)

VARIETY: Repunched Mintmark
PUP: Mintmark
URS-10 · I-3 · L-4

CONECA: RPM-001

 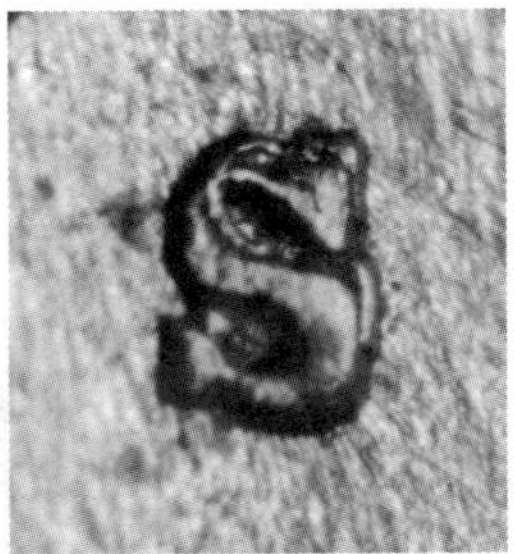

Description: A secondary S is evident slightly north of the primary S.

Comments: Though not as well known as the S Over Horizontal S variety (next listing), this RPM is scarcer and in much more demand by specialists than the well-known variety.

	VF-20	EF-40	AU-50	MS-60	MS-63	MS-65
VARIETY	$175	$225	$300	$350	$450	$650
NORMAL	$125	$165	$180	$230	$300	$500

Note: Values listed for MS-60 and higher are for RB (red and brown) specimens. Full red Uncirculated specimens command higher prices.

1909-S

FS-01-1909S-1502 (012.3)

VARIETY: Repunched Mintmark
PUP: Mintmark
URS-12 · I-4 · L-5

CONECA: RPM-002

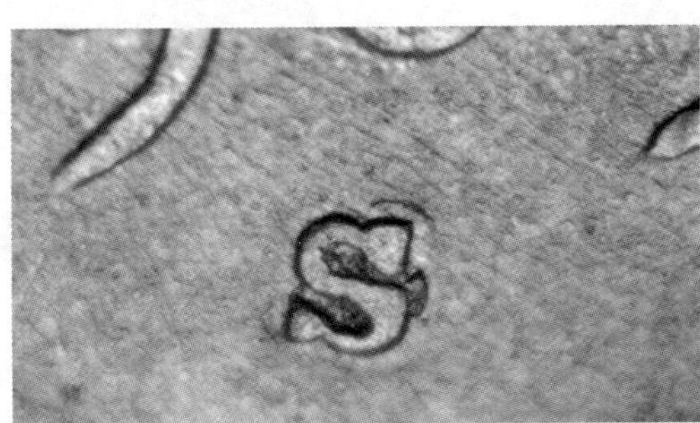

Description: A secondary S is evident north of the primary S, but orientated horizontally.

Comments: This is a relatively easy variety to purchase, as many examples have already been located and authenticated. Late die states make the horizontal orientation of the secondary S difficult to view, yet the fact that there is an RPM is still evident.

	VF-20	EF-40	AU-50	MS-60	MS-63	MS-65
VARIETY	$150	$200	$250	$300	$400	$650
NORMAL	$125	$160	$180	$230	$300	$500

Note: Values listed for MS-60 and higher are for RB (red and brown) specimens. Full red Uncirculated specimens command higher prices.

1910-S   FS-01-1910S-501

VARIETY: Repunched Mintmark
PUP: Mintmark   **CONECA: RPM-001**
URS-7 · I-2 · L-2

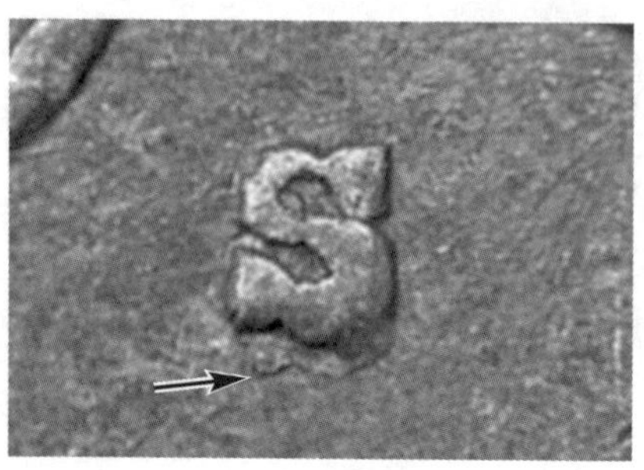

Description: A secondary S is evident south of the primary S.

Comments: Primarily due to the relatively high value of the normal coins, any premium associated with this variety will generally be minimal.

	VF-20	EF-40	AU-50	MS-60	MS-63	MS-65
VARIETY	$20	$35	$75	$100	$150	$350
NORMAL	$12	$27	$49	$67	$85	$250

Note: Values listed for MS-60 and higher are for RB (red and brown) specimens. Full red Uncirculated specimens command higher prices.

1910-S   FS-01-1910S-502 (012.7)

VARIETY: Repunched Mintmark
PUP: Mintmark   **CONECA: RPM-002**
URS-8 · I-3 · L-4

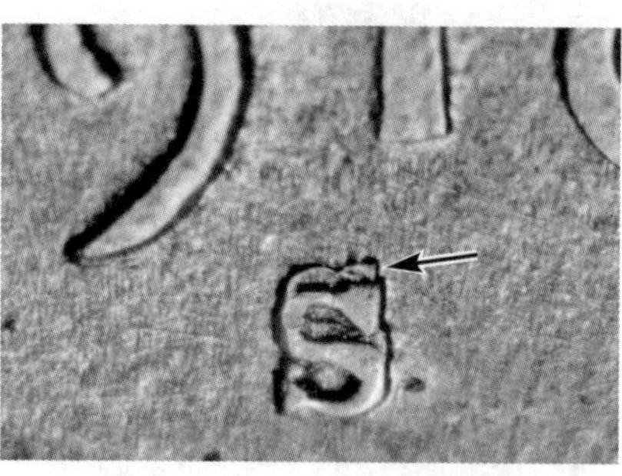

Description: A secondary S is evident north of the primary S.

Comments: This variety may be slightly easier to sell that the previous RPM, primarily due to its popularity.

	VF-20	EF-40	AU-50	MS-60	MS-63	MS-65
VARIETY	$25	$50	$95	$125	$175	$400
NORMAL	$12	$27	$49	$67	$85	$250

Note: Values listed for MS-60 and higher are for RB (red and brown) specimens. Full red Uncirculated specimens command higher prices.

1911-D · FS-01-1911D-501 (012.8)

Variety: Repunched Mintmark
PUP: Mintmark
URS-4 · I-3 · L-3

CONECA: RPM-001

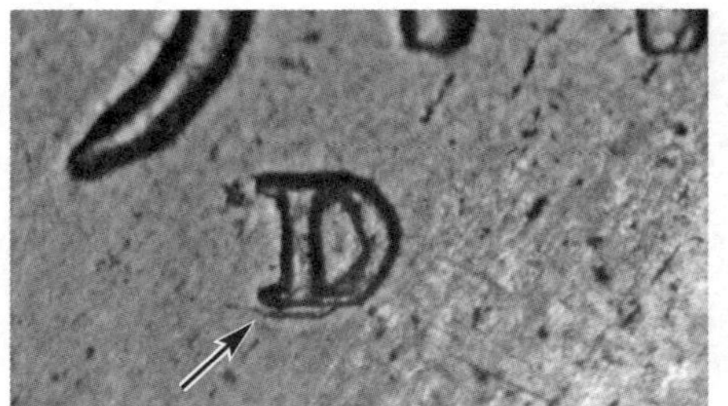

Description: A secondary D is evident southwest of the primary D.

Comments: Primarily due to the relatively high value of the regular coins, Extremely Fine and About Uncirculated specimens may be easier to sell than higher grades.

	VF-20	EF-40	AU-50	MS-60	MS-63	MS-65
Variety	$35	$50	$100	$150	$200	$650
Normal	$13	$35	$55	$75	$125	$500

Note: Values listed for MS-60 and higher are for RB (red and brown) specimens. Full red Uncirculated specimens command higher prices.

1911-D · FS-01-1911D-502 (012.81)

Variety: Repunched Mintmark
PUP: Mintmark
URS-3 · I-3 · L-4

CONECA: RPM-002

Description: A secondary D is evident to the southwest of the primary D. The vertical bar of the secondary D is evident slightly west of the primary D.

Comments: As of this writing, there are no known Mint State specimens. Primarily due to the relatively high value of the regular coins, Extremely Fine and About Uncirculated specimens may be easier to sell than higher grades.

	VF-20	EF-40	AU-50	MS-60	MS-63	MS-65
Variety	$35	$50	$100	$150	$200	$650
Normal	$13	$35	$55	$75	$125	$500

Note: Values listed for MS-60 and higher are for RB (red and brown) specimens. Full red Uncirculated specimens command higher prices.

1911-D   FS-01-1911D-503 (012.82)

VARIETY: Repunched Mintmark   **CONECA: RPM-003**
PUP: Mintmark
URS-1 · I-3 · L-4

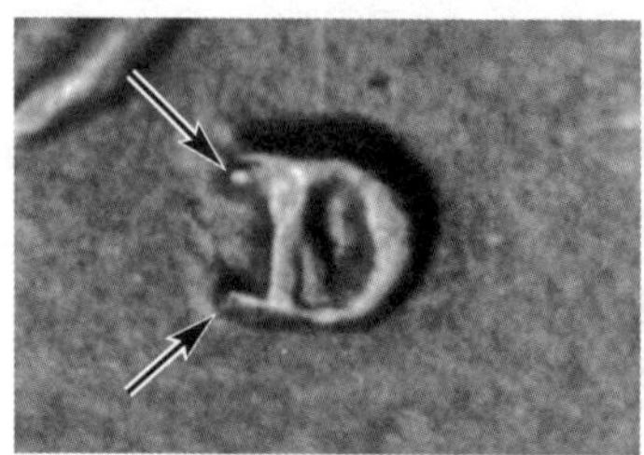

Description: The secondary D mintmark is rotated slightly counterclockwise in relation to the primary D. The top serif of the weaker D is evident just south of the primary upper serif, and a portion of the secondary D's vertical bar is evident within the loop of the primary D.

Comments: As of this writing, there is only one example known, a Mint State specimen.

	VF-20	EF-40	AU-50	MS-60	MS-63	MS-65
VARIETY	$35	$50	$100	$150	$200	$650
NORMAL	$13	$35	$55	$75	$125	$500

Note: Values listed for MS-60 and higher are for RB (red and brown) specimens. Full red Uncirculated specimens command higher prices.

1911-D   FS-01-1911D-504 (012.83)

VARIETY: Repunched Mintmark   **CONECA: RPM-004**
PUP: Mintmark
URS-3 · I-3 · L-4

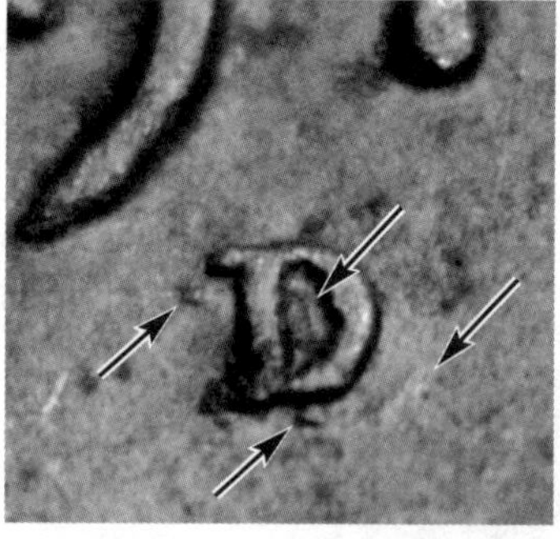

Description: This variety is actually a triple-punched mintmark, with portions of the secondary mintmarks evident south and southeast of the primary D.

Comments: Very few examples of this variety are known, with no Mint State examples reported.

	VF-20	EF-40	AU-50	MS-60	MS-63	MS-65
VARIETY	$35	$50	$100	$150	$200	$650
NORMAL	$13	$35	$55	$75	$125	$500

Note: Values listed for MS-60 and higher are for RB (red and brown) specimens. Full red Uncirculated specimens command higher prices.

1911-S

FS-01-1911S-501 (012.85)

VARIETY: Repunched Mintmark
PUP: Mintmark
URS-4 · I-3 · L-3

CONECA: RPM-001

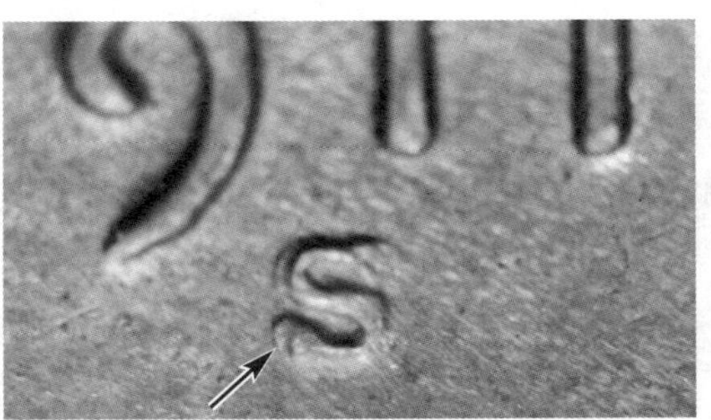

Description: A secondary S mintmark is evident to the west of the primary mintmark.

Comments: This variety is highly sought after by serious Lincoln cent collectors. RPM-002 is very similar, though positioned higher.

	VF-20	EF-40	AU-50	MS-60	MS-63	MS-65
VARIETY	$40	$75	$125	$200	$325	$750
NORMAL	$26	$43	$72	$145	$225	$660

Note: Values listed for MS-60 and higher are for RB (red and brown) specimens. Full red Uncirculated specimens command higher prices.

1917

FS-01-1917-101 (013)

VARIETY: Doubled-Die Obverse
PUP: Date, TRUST
URS-8 · I-5 · L-5

CONECA: DDO-001

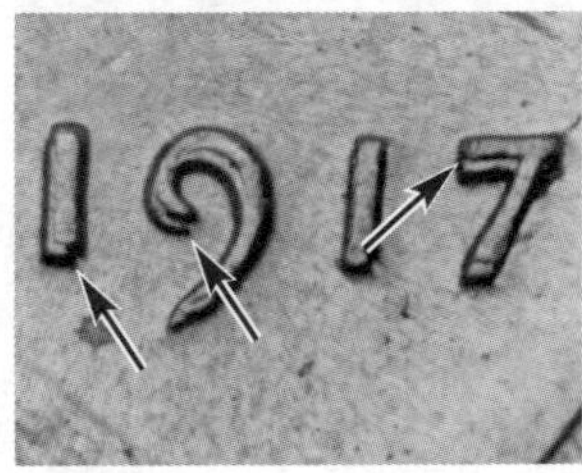

Description: The doubling on this very popular variety is evident on the date and GOD WE TRUST. The earliest die state specimens will exhibit slight doubling on the RTY of LIBERTY.

Comments: This variety has finally become arguably the most sought after of the early Lincoln cent varieties. Grades as low as G-4 are easily sold, and higher grade examples may command prices higher than those listed here.

	VF-20	EF-40	AU-50	MS-60	MS-63	MS-65
VARIETY	$10	$1,000	$2,000	$3,500	$7,000	$15,000
NORMAL	$7	$9	$11	$14	$23	$56

Note: Values listed for MS-60 and higher are for RB (red and brown) specimens. Full red Uncirculated specimens command higher prices.

1922 — FS-01-1922-401 (013.2)

VARIETY: "No D" Mintmark
CONECA: N/L
PUP: Mintmark area
URS-11 · I-5 · L-5

Die pair #1

Die pair #2

Die pair #3

Description: The mintmark from this working die was omitted.

Comments: There is only one die pair for this variety universally recognized, commonly referred to as die pair #2. While three die pairings have been referred to in the past as a "No D," only die pair #2 is believed to have *never* had a D mintmark. The other two die pairs (#1 and #3) are believed to have had a D mintmark at one time, with the D being obliterated either during heavy die polishing, or resulting from a filled die. Die pair #2 is identified by several markers: (1) the second 2 in the date is sharper than the first, (2) all letters of TRUST are very sharp, (3) WE is only slightly mushy, and (4) the reverse is very sharp. Die pairs #1 and #3 are known for their weak reverses, dates, and mottos. Any specimen should be authenticated by a reputable third-party service.

	VF-20	EF-40	AU-50	MS-60	MS-63	MS-65
VARIETY	$1,300	$2,650	$4,925	$10,500	$26,500	$72,500
NORMAL	$13	$22	$44	$68	$100	$360

Note: Values listed for MS-60 and higher are for RB (red and brown) specimens. Full red Uncirculated specimens command higher prices.

1925-S   FS-01-1925S-101 (013.3)

VARIETY: Doubled-Die Obverse
PUP: Date, LIBERTY, motto
URS-5 · I-3 · L-3

CONECA: 1-O-VI

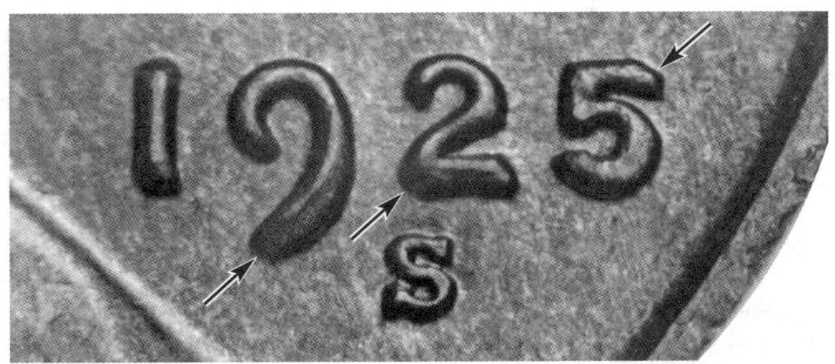

Description: Strong doubling is evident on all obverse letters and numbers. Most of the doubling is evident as extra thickness, though some separation can be detected on the digits of the date.

Comments: This variety was first published in the April 1988 issue of *ERRORSCOPE.*

	VF-20	EF-40	AU-50	MS-60	MS-63	MS-65
VARIETY	$10	$15	$50	$95	$175	$1,400
NORMAL	$2	$9	$24	$55	$150	$1,275

Note: Values listed for MS-60 and higher are for RB (red and brown) specimens. Full red Uncirculated specimens command higher prices.

1925-S   FS-01-1925S-501 (013.31)

VARIETY: Repunched Mintmark
PUP: Mintmark
URS-8 · I-3 · L-3

CONECA: RPM-001

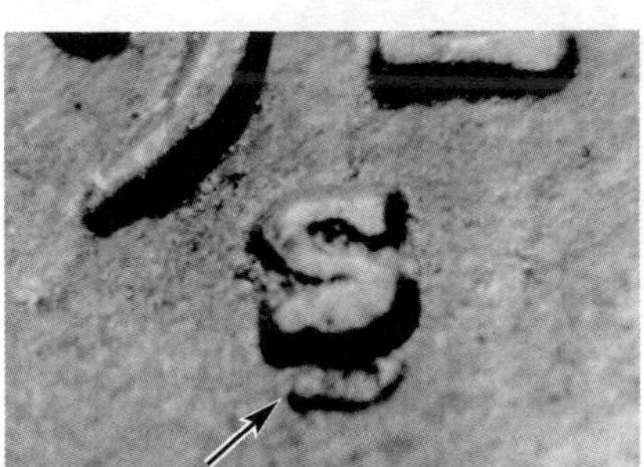

Description: The remains of a secondary S are evident to the south of the primary mintmark.

Comments: This is a fairly popular RPM, highly sought after by variety specialists and Lincoln cent collectors.

	VF-20	EF-40	AU-50	MS-60	MS-63	MS-65
VARIETY	$10	$15	$50	$95	$175	$1,400
NORMAL	$2	$9	$24	$55	$150	$1,275

Note: Values listed for MS-60 and higher are for RB (red and brown) specimens. Full red Uncirculated specimens command higher prices.

1927 — FS-01-1927-101 (013.5)

VARIETY: Doubled-Die Obverse
PUP: Motto, date, LIBERTY
URS-8 · I-3 · L-3

CONECA: 1-O-I

Description: Moderate doubling is evident on the LIBE of LIBERTY, IN GOD WE TRUST, and slightly on the date.

Comments: Although the doubling is not very evident on later die states, this variety is very collectible among Lincoln cent specialists.

	VF-20	EF-40	AU-50	MS-60	MS-63	MS-65
VARIETY	$5	$15	$25	$50	$75	$150
NORMAL	$1	$2	$4	$8	$15	$50

Note: Values listed for MS-60 and higher are for RB (red and brown) specimens. Full red Uncirculated specimens command higher prices.

1927-D — FS-01-1927D-501 (013.51)

VARIETY: Repunched Mintmark
PUP: Mintmark
URS-8 · I-4 · L-3

CONECA: RPM-001

Description: This strong RPM is evident with the secondary D visible to the north of the primary D.

Comments: This die also exhibits a very minor doubled-die obverse with a doubled eyelid, listed as CONECA 1-O-IV. This may appear to be a Large D Over Small D (or vice versa) by many, but it is simply a nice RPM.

	VF-20	EF-40	AU-50	MS-60	MS-63	MS-65
VARIETY	$5	$10	$35	$75	$125	$425
NORMAL	$1	$6	$19	$46	$80	$375

Note: Values listed for MS-60 and higher are for RB (red and brown) specimens. Full red Uncirculated specimens command higher prices.

1928-S
FS-01-1928S-501 (013.6)

VARIETY: Large S Mintmark
PUP: Mintmark
URS-14 · I-3 · L-3

CONECA: N/L

Small mintmark

Large mintmark

Description: The common mintmark for this date is relatively small. This large, trumpet-style S mintmark is very scarce and highly collectible.

Comments: All Lincoln cent mintmark varieties are growing rapidly in popularity. There is no doubt this will continue with the centennial of the Lincoln cent in 2009.

	VF-20	EF-40	AU-50	MS-60	MS-63	MS-65
VARIETY	$15	$25	$50	$95	$150	$750
NORMAL	$2	$7	$17	$52	$82	$575

Note: Values listed for MS-60 and higher are for RB (red and brown) specimens. Full red Uncirculated specimens command higher prices.

1929-S
FS-01-1929S-501 (013.65)

VARIETY: Repunched Mintmark
PUP: Mintmark
URS-6 · I-3 · L-3

CONECA: RPM-001

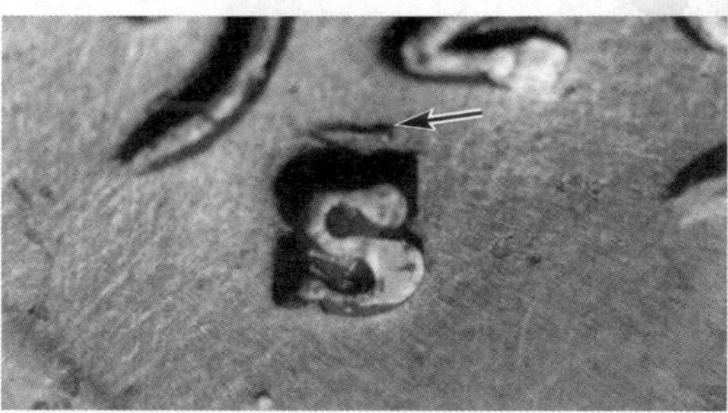

Description: The secondary S mintmark is evident north of the primary mintmark.

Comments: This RPM is considered rare, and is tough to locate in any grade.

	VF-20	EF-40	AU-50	MS-60	MS-63	MS-65
VARIETY	$5	$15	$25	$45	$75	$125
NORMAL	$1	$6	$10	$19	$26	$70

Note: Values listed for MS-60 and higher are for RB (red and brown) specimens. Full red Uncirculated specimens command higher prices.

1930-D — FS-01-1930D-501

VARIETY: Repunched Mintmark **CONECA: RPM-001**
PUP: Mintmark
URS-8 · I-3 · L-3

Description: The secondary mintmark is evident north of the primary D.

Comments: Another very popular RPM.

	VF-20	EF-40	AU-50	MS-60	MS-63	MS-65
VARIETY	$5	$15	$25	$45	$75	$100
NORMAL	$1	$2	$4	$11	$23	$38

Note: Values listed for MS-60 and higher are for RB (red and brown) specimens. Full red Uncirculated specimens command higher prices.

1930-D — FS-01-1930D-502 (013.7)

VARIETY: Repunched Mintmark **CONECA: RPM-002**
PUP: Mintmark
URS-8 · I-3 · L-3

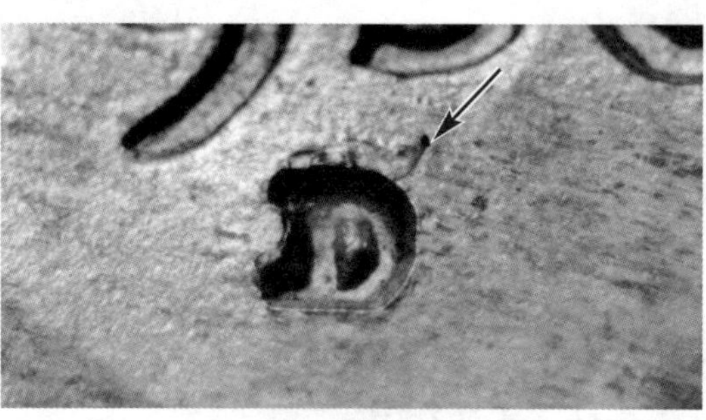

Description: The secondary mintmark is evident north of the primary D.

Comments: Another very popular RPM.

	VF-20	EF-40	AU-50	MS-60	MS-63	MS-65
VARIETY	$5	$15	$25	$45	$75	$100
NORMAL	$1	$2	$4	$11	$23	$38

Note: Values listed for MS-60 and higher are for RB (red and brown) specimens. Full red Uncirculated specimens command higher prices.

1930-S
FS-01-1930S-501 (013.73)

VARIETY: Repunched Mintmark
CONECA: RPM-001
PUP: Mintmark
URS-8 · I-3 · L-3

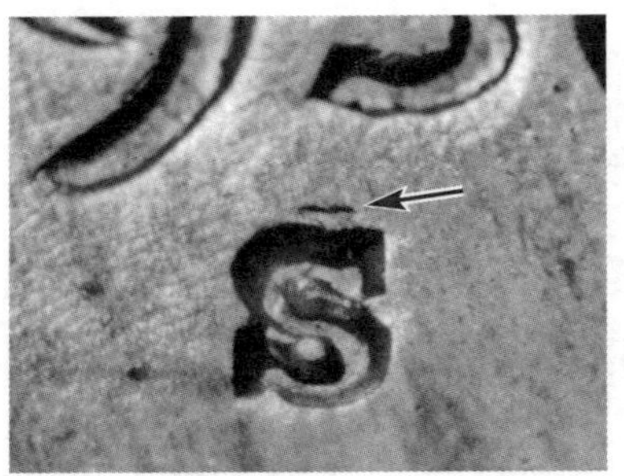

Description: The secondary S is evident north of the primary S.

Comments: This is a well known and highly collected RPM.

	VF-20	EF-40	AU-50	MS-60	MS-63	MS-65
VARIETY	$5	$10	$15	$25	$45	$75
NORMAL	$1	$2	$5	$8	$16	$34

Note: Values listed for MS-60 and higher are for RB (red and brown) specimens. Full red Uncirculated specimens command higher prices.

1934
FS-01-1934-101 (013.79)

VARIETY: Doubled-Die Obverse
CONECA: N/L
PUP: Field below date
URS-4 · I-4 · L-4

Description: The remains of a secondary 3 and 4 are evident below the primary digits.

Comments: Since this was first reported by Lee Day, very few additional specimens have been found.

	VF-20	EF-40	AU-50	MS-60	MS-63	MS-65
VARIETY	$50.00	$75.00	$100.00	$150	$250	$500
NORMAL	$0.50	$0.65	$1.35	$3	$10	$24

Note: Values listed for MS-60 and higher are for RB (red and brown) specimens. Full red Uncirculated specimens command higher prices.

1934-D   FS-01-1934D-503 (013.81)

VARIETY: Repunched Mintmark (D/D/D/D)   **CONECA: RPM-003**
PUP: Mintmark
URS-8 · I-3 · L-3

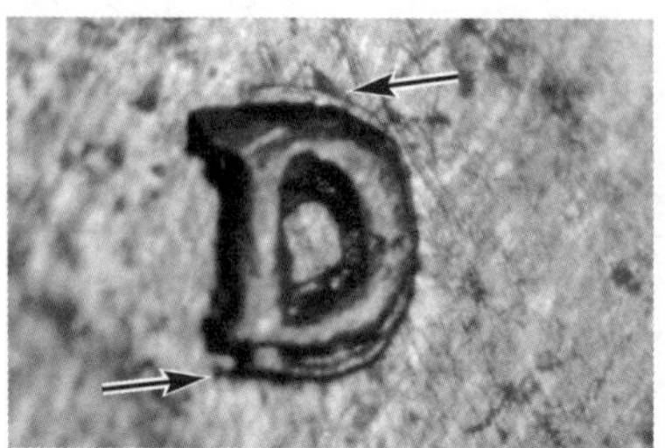

Description: This is a quadrupled-punched mintmark, with one secondary D evident to the northwest of the primary D, and two other secondary D's evident to the south of the primary D.

Comments: This RPM was long thought to be a triple-punched RPM, but a recent discovery of an early die state specimen expanded the known attributes.

	VF-20	EF-40	AU-50	MS-60	MS-63	MS-65
VARIETY	$5.00	$8.00	$15	$20	$25	$75
NORMAL	$0.50	$4.25	$6	$11	$15	$27

Note: Values listed for MS-60 and higher are for RB (red and brown) specimens. Full red Uncirculated specimens command higher prices.

1934-D   FS-01-1934D-504 (013.8)

VARIETY: Repunched Mintmark   **CONECA: RPM-004**
PUP: Mintmark
URS-8 · I-3 · L-3

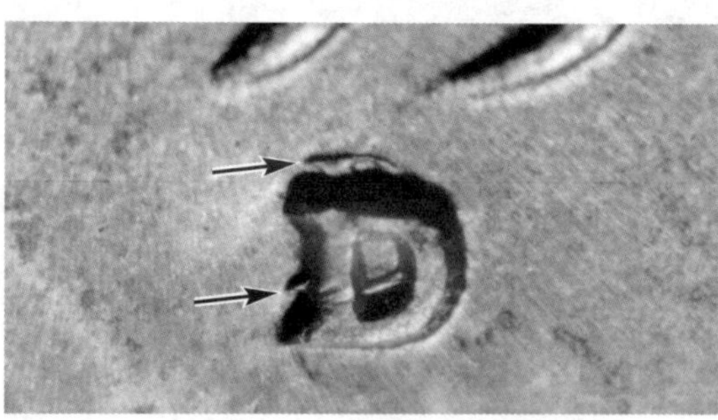

Description: The secondary mintmark is evident to the north of the primary D.

Comments: This variety may appear to be a large over small mintmark, but it is believed to be a normal RPM with the same-sized letter punches.

	VF-20	EF-40	AU-50	MS-60	MS-63	MS-65
VARIETY	$5.00	$8.00	$15	$20	$25	$75
NORMAL	$0.50	$4.25	$6	$11	$15	$27

Note: Values listed for MS-60 and higher are for RB (red and brown) specimens. Full red Uncirculated specimens command higher prices.

1935   FS-01-1935-101 (013.9)

VARIETY: Doubled-Die Obverse   **CONECA: 1-O-V**
PUP: Date
URS-6 · I-3 · L-3

Description: Moderate doubling is evident on the date and on IN GOD WE TRUST.

Comments: This variety is extremely scarce overall, and exceptionally rare in Mint State. It is well known to Lincoln cent and variety specialists, yet very few specimens have been located.

	VF-20	EF-40	AU-50	MS-60	MS-63	MS-65
VARIETY	$10.00	$20.00	$50.00	$75	$125	$250
NORMAL	$0.30	$0.50	$0.75	$2	$7	$18

Note: Values listed for MS-60 and higher are for RB (red and brown) specimens. Full red Uncirculated specimens command higher prices.

1936   FS-01-1936-101 (014)

VARIETY: Doubled-Die Obverse   **CONECA: 1-O-IV**
PUP: Date, LIBERTY
URS-10 · I-4 · L-5

Description: Very strong doubling is evident on the date, LIBERTY, and IN GOD WE TRUST.

Comments: This is the first of three significant doubled dies for this date. This listing, and the following (FS-102) are the strongest and most desirable. However, the third is no slouch, and in very high demand. Collectors like to assemble all three of the 1936-dated varieties. This variety is extremely rare in Mint State.

	VF-20	EF-40	AU-50	MS-60	MS-63	MS-65
VARIETY	$75.00	$100.00	$150.00	$200.00	$350.00	$1,250
NORMAL	$0.30	$0.50	$0.75	$1.10	$4.50	$10

Note: Values listed for MS-60 and higher are for RB (red and brown) specimens. Full red Uncirculated specimens command higher prices.

1936 — FS-01-1936-102 (015)

VARIETY: Doubled-Die Obverse
CONECA: 2-O-V
PUP: IN GOD WE TRUST
URS-10 · I-4 · L-4

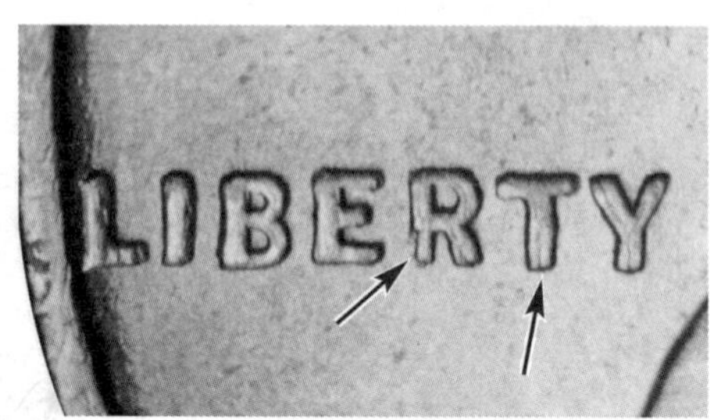

Description: Strong doubling is evident on the date, IN GOD WE TRUST, and LIBERTY.

Comments: One of the working hubs for the 1935 cents had a broken left leg of the R in LIBERTY. This listing was first hubbed by that broken-leg-R hub, then had a second hubbing with a normal R hub.

	VF-20	EF-40	AU-50	MS-60	MS-63	MS-65
VARIETY	$35.00	$75.00	$100.00	$150.00	$250.00	$450
NORMAL	$0.30	$0.50	$0.75	$1.10	$4.50	$10

Note: Values listed for MS-60 and higher are for RB (red and brown) specimens. Full red Uncirculated specimens command higher prices.

1936 — FS-01-1936-103 (016)

VARIETY: Doubled-Die Obverse
CONECA: 3-O-V
PUP: IN GOD WE TRUST
URS-7 · I-4 · L-4

Description: Strong doubling is evident on IN GOD WE TRUST and LIBERTY, with a slight rotation of the secondary image counterclockwise to the primary image.

Comments: This is the third of the major 1936 doubled dies.

	VF-20	EF-40	AU-50	MS-60	MS-63	MS-65
VARIETY	$25.00	$50.00	$75.00	$100.00	$150.00	$250
NORMAL	$0.30	$0.50	$0.75	$1.10	$4.50	$10

Note: Values listed for MS-60 and higher are for RB (red and brown) specimens. Full red Uncirculated specimens command higher prices.

1938-D — FS-01-1938D-501 (016.4)

VARIETY: Repunched Mintmark
CONECA: RPM-001
PUP: Mintmark
URS-10 · I-2 · L-2

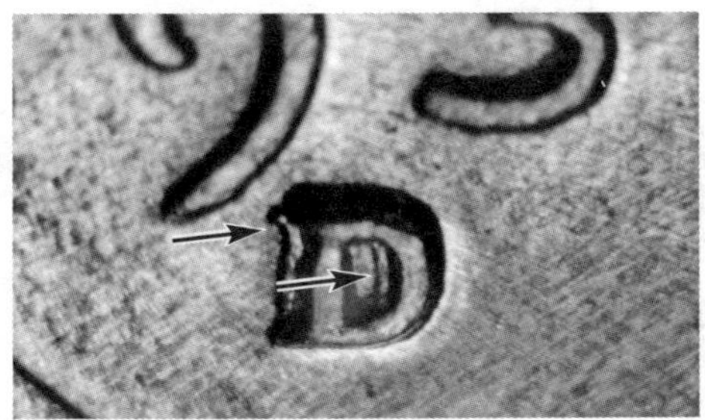

Description: The secondary mintmark is evident west of the primary D.

Comments: Although this RPM is obtainable and only scarce, demand remains fairly high.

	VF-20	EF-40	AU-50	MS-60	MS-63	MS-65
VARIETY	$1.00	$2.00	$5.00	$10.00	$15	$25
NORMAL	$0.65	$0.75	$0.85	$4.50	$6	$11

Note: Values listed for MS-60 and higher are for RB (red and brown) specimens. Full red Uncirculated specimens command higher prices.

1938-S — FS-01-1938S-501 (016.51)

VARIETY: Repunched Mintmark
CONECA: RPM-001
PUP: Mintmark
URS-10 · I-3 · L-3

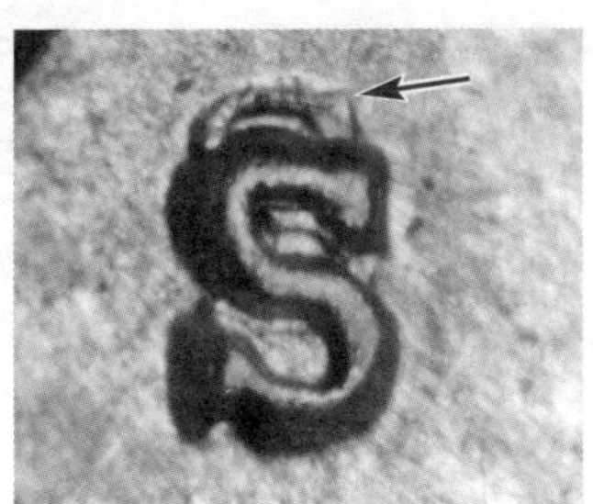

Description: The secondary S mintmark is evident north of the primary S.

Comments: This is one of the more popular RPMs in the Lincoln series—much scarcer than the next listing, which is better known. The EDS specimens (shown here) are very easy to sell.

	VF-20	EF-40	AU-50	MS-60	MS-63	MS-65
VARIETY	$1.00	$2.00	$5.00	$10.00	$15.00	$25
NORMAL	$0.30	$0.50	$0.75	$1.10	$4.50	$10

Note: Values listed for MS-60 and higher are for RB (red and brown) specimens. Full red Uncirculated specimens command higher prices.

1938-S
FS-01-1938S-502 (016.5)

VARIETY: Repunched Mintmark (S/S/S)
PUP: Mintmark
URS-11 · I-3 · L-3

CONECA: RPM-002

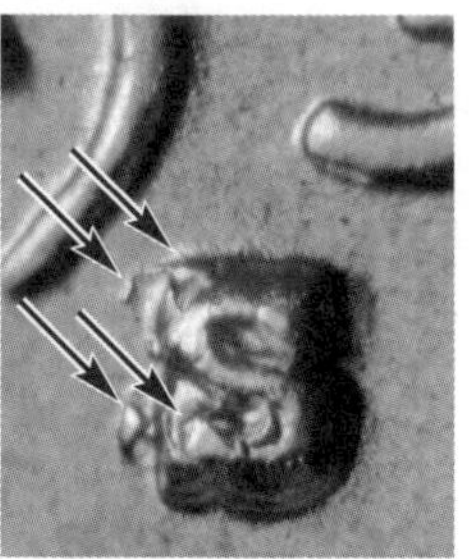

Description: This is a popular triple S mintmark, with both the secondary images northwest of the primary S. All three S mintmarks are clearly visible, especially on Mint State examples.

Comments: Though this is a very popular RPM, supply seems to at least equal demand.

	VF-20	EF-40	AU-50	MS-60	MS-63	MS-65
VARIETY	$1.00	$2.00	$5.00	$8.00	$12.00	$20
NORMAL	$0.30	$0.50	$0.75	$1.10	$4.50	$10

Note: Values listed for MS-60 and higher are for RB (red and brown) specimens. Full red Uncirculated specimens command higher prices.

1939
FS-01-1939-101 (017)

VARIETY: Doubled-Die Obverse
PUP: Date, LIBERTY
URS-8 · I-2 · L-2

CONECA: 1-O-I

Description: Although the first hubbing was weak, the spread of the doubling is strong on the 19 of the date, BERTY of LIBERTY, the eyelid, and the ear.

Comments: Although this variety proves to be fairly scarce and difficult to find, the popularity for the coin has not grown as expected.

	VF-20	EF-40	AU-50	MS-60	MS-63	MS-65
VARIETY	$8.00	$10.00	$12.00	$15.00	$25.00	$50
NORMAL	$0.20	$0.25	$0.85	$1.10	$4.25	$8

Note: Values listed for MS-60 and higher are for RB (red and brown) specimens. Full red Uncirculated specimens command higher prices.

1941 — FS-01-1941-101 (018)

VARIETY: Doubled-Die Obverse
PUP: LIBERTY, TRUST
URS-11 · I-4 · L-4

CONECA: 1-O-I

Description: The doubling is strongest on LIBERTY and IN GOD WE TRUST. The spread of the doubling is strong; however, the first hubbing was very weak in that the hub was set shallow in the die.

Comments: This is one of the "old school" doubled dies and has been known by specialists for decades. It can still be cherrypicked from time to time.

	VF-20	EF-40	AU-50	MS-60	MS-63	MS-65
VARIETY	$15.00	$25.00	$50.00	$75	$125.00	$200
NORMAL	$0.25	$0.35	$0.40	$1	$3.20	$12

Note: Values listed for MS-60 and MS-63 are for RB (red and brown) specimens; values listed for MS-65 specimens are for full red specimens.

1941 — FS-01-1941-102 (018.1)

VARIETY: Doubled-Die Obverse
PUP: IN GOD WE TRUST
URS-10 · I-4 · L-4

CONECA: 2-O-I

Description: This is similar to FS-01-1941-101; the doubling is evident on LIBERTY and IN GOD WE TRUST, and slightly on the date. The first hubbing was almost as strong as the second, which creates the primary difference between this listing and the previous.

Comments: This variety is in slightly greater demand than the previous listing.

	VF-20	EF-40	AU-50	MS-60	MS-63	MS-65
VARIETY	$25.00	$35.00	$75.00	$100	$150.00	$300
NORMAL	$0.25	$0.35	$0.40	$1	$3.20	$12

Note: Values listed for MS-60 and MS-63 are for RB (red and brown) specimens; values listed for MS-65 specimens are for full red specimens.

1941 — FS-01-1941-103 (018.3)

VARIETY: Doubled-Die Obverse
PUP: Ear, LIBERTY, 19 of the date
URS-9 · I-3 · L-3

CONECA: 5-O-IV

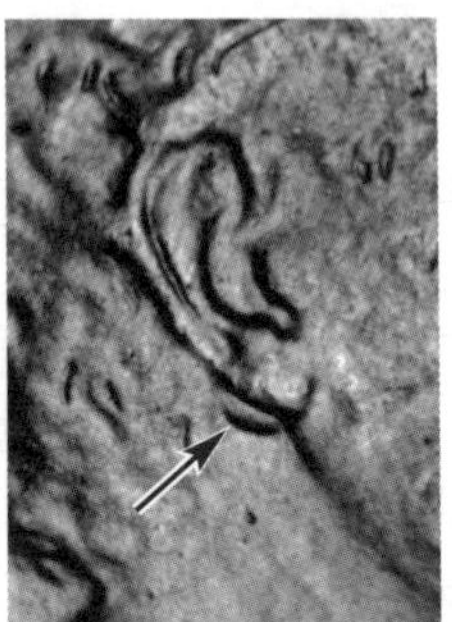

Description: The doubling is particularly evident as a second earlobe to the south, and also in the 19 of the date and the TY of LIBERTY.

Comments: The first hubbing was very weak and may be visible only on higher grade specimens.

	VF-20	EF-40	AU-50	MS-60	MS-63	MS-65
VARIETY	$10.00	$15.00	$35.00	$50	$100.00	$175
NORMAL	$0.25	$0.35	$0.40	$1	$3.20	$12

Note: Values listed for MS-60 and MS-63 are for RB (red and brown) specimens; values listed for MS-65 specimens are for full red specimens.

1942 — FS-01-1942-102 (018.7)

VARIETY: Doubled-Die Obverse
PUP: LIBERTY, 1 of the date
URS-4 · I-2 · L-3

CONECA: 4-O-V

Description: The first hubbing, although somewhat weak, is visible to the north on LIBERTY and the 1 of the date.

Comments: This variety was discovered years ago by Del Romines.

	VF-20	EF-40	AU-50	MS-60	MS-63	MS-65
VARIETY	$10.00	$15.00	$25.00	$35.00	$50.00	$75
NORMAL	$0.20	$0.30	$0.40	$0.90	$3.20	$13

Note: Values listed for MS-60 and MS-63 are for RB (red and brown) specimens; values listed for MS-65 specimens are for full red specimens.

1942
FS-01-1942-103 (018.9)

VARIETY: Doubled-Die Obverse
PUP: Eyelid, TRUST
URS-4 · I-3 · L-2

CONECA: 6-O-IV

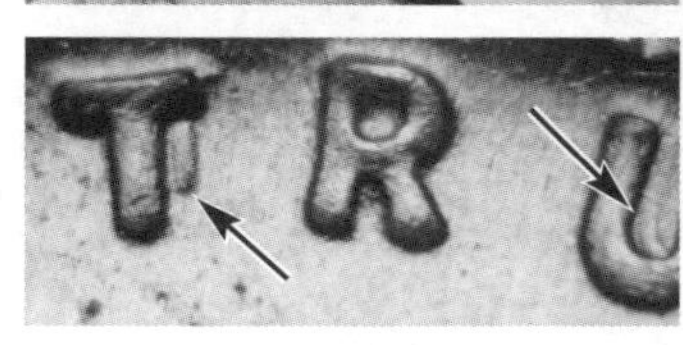
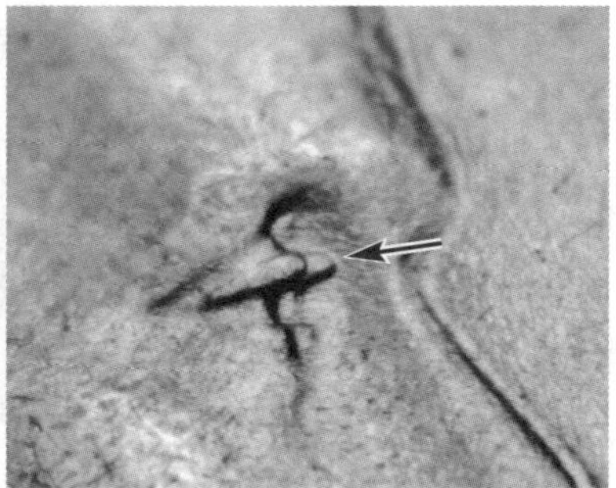

Description: Faint doubling is evident on IN GOD WE TRUST, LIBERTY, and the date, though a strong spread can be detected on high-grade specimens. Very strong doubling is evident on the eyelid.

Comments: Due to the weakness of the secondary image, look for the doubled eyelid. There are several known doubled dies for this date with a doubled eyelid, but only this variety also has strong doubling on TRUST.

	VF-20	EF-40	AU-50	MS-60	MS-63	MS-65
VARIETY	$10.00	$15.00	$25.00	$35.00	$50.00	$75
NORMAL	$0.20	$0.30	$0.40	$0.90	$3.20	$13

Note: Values listed for MS-60 and MS-63 are for RB (red and brown) specimens; values listed for MS-65 specimens are for full red specimens.

1942-D
FS-01-1942D-502 (018.91)

VARIETY: Repunched Mintmark
PUP: Mintmark
URS-8 · I-3 · L-3

CONECA: RPM-002

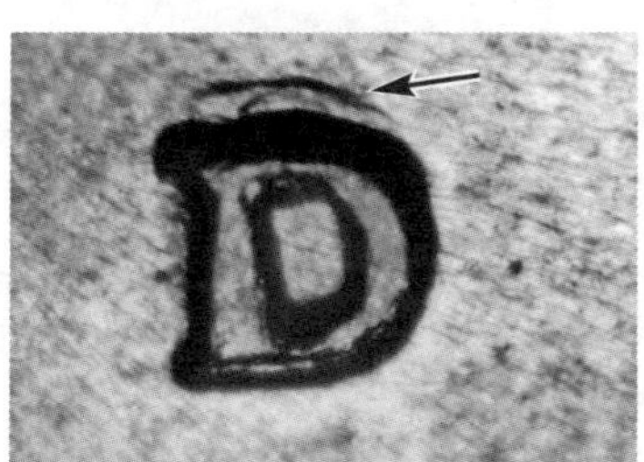

Description: The secondary D is evident to the north of the primary D.

Comments: There are several nice, collectible RPMs for this series in the 1940s.

	VF-20	EF-40	AU-50	MS-60	MS-63	MS-65
VARIETY	$5.00	$8.00	$10.00	$15.00	$20	$35
NORMAL	$0.30	$0.35	$0.40	$0.70	$6	$13

Note: Values listed for MS-60 and MS-63 are for RB (red and brown) specimens; values listed for MS-65 specimens are for full red specimens.

1942-D   FS-01-1942D-504 (018.92)

VARIETY: Repunched Mintmark   **CONECA: RPM-004**
PUP: Mintmark
URS-6 · I-3 · L-3

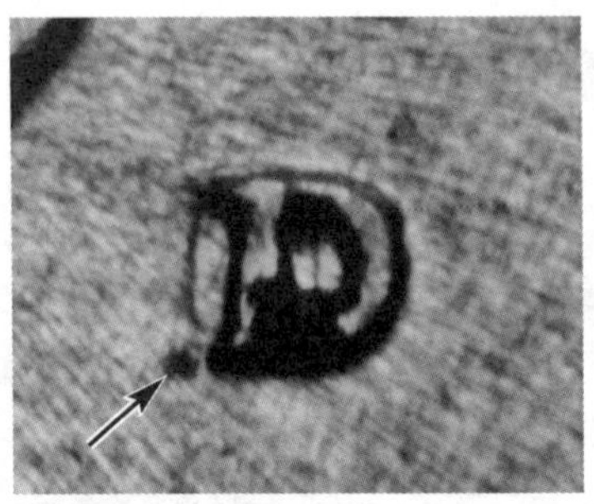

Description: The secondary D is evident to the west of the primary D.

Comments: There are several nice, collectible RPMs for this series in the 1940s.

	VF-20	EF-40	AU-50	MS-60	MS-63	MS-65
VARIETY	$5.00	$8.00	$10.00	$15.00	$20	$35
NORMAL	$0.30	$0.35	$0.40	$0.70	$6	$13

Note: Values listed for MS-60 and MS-63 are for RB (red and brown) specimens; values listed for MS-65 specimens are for full red specimens.

1942-S   FS-01-1942S-101 (018.94)

VARIETY: Doubled-Die Obverse + Repunched Mintmark   **CONECA: 1-O-IV**
PUP: LIBERTY, date, mintmark
URS-9 · I-3 · L-3

Description: The doubling on this variety is evident to the north on LIBERTY, IN GOD, the eyelid, and the 19. The mintmark is also repunched, with the secondary S evident to the west of the primary S.

Comments: This variety is extremely difficult to locate.

	VF-20	EF-40	AU-50	MS-60	MS-63	MS-65
VARIETY	$15.00	$35.00	$50	$60.00	$75	$150
NORMAL	$0.60	$0.80	$1	$3.50	$6	$18

Note: Values listed for MS-60 and MS-63 are for RB (red and brown) specimens; values listed for MS-65 specimens are for full red specimens.

1942-S

FS-01-1942S-512 (018.93)

VARIETY: Repunched Mintmark (S/S/S)
PUP: Mintmark
URS-4 · I-4 · L-3

CONECA: RPM-012

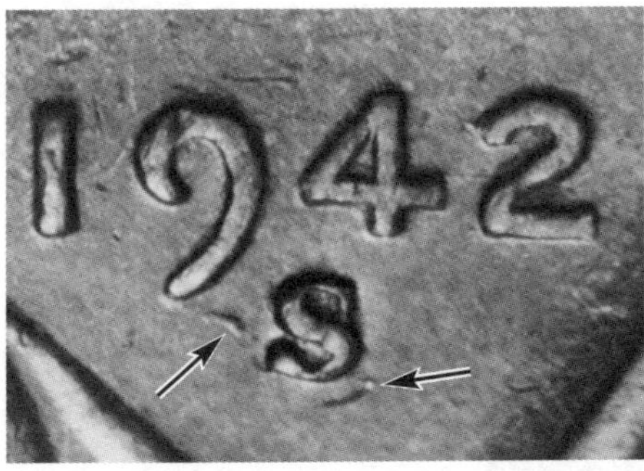
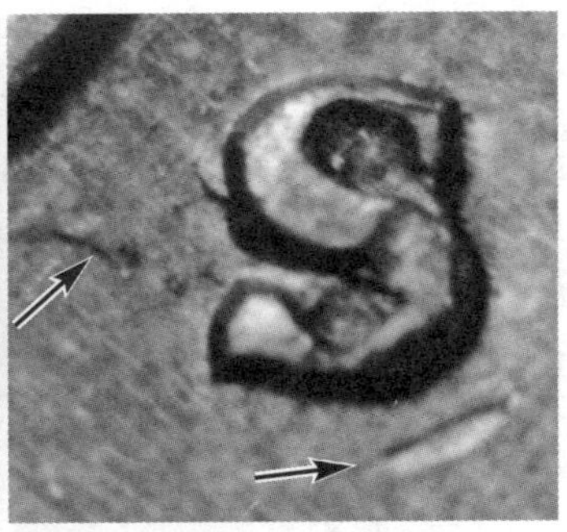

Description: This is a popular triple-punched mintmark, with secondary letters to the west and northwest of the primary S. The image to the west is totally separated from the primary S.

Comments: This is one of the very few RPMs with a totally separated mintmark.

	VF-20	EF-40	AU-50	MS-60	MS-63	MS-65
VARIETY	$5.00	$10.00	$20	$25.00	$35	$50
NORMAL	$0.60	$0.80	$1	$3.50	$6	$18

Note: Values listed for MS-60 and MS-63 are for RB (red and brown) specimens; values listed for MS-65 specimens are for full red specimens.

1943

FS-01-1943-101 (018.97)

VARIETY: Doubled-Die Obverse
PUP: Date, LIBERTY
URS-7 · I-4 · L-3

CONECA: 1-O-VI

Description: The doubling is evident as extremely thick letters on LIBERTY and IN GOD WE TRUST, and very thick digits on the date.

Comments: This is one of the strongest class VI doubled dies in the series, and it has always been very popular among Lincoln cent specialists.

	VF-20	EF-40	AU-50	MS-60	MS-63	MS-65
VARIETY	$5.00	$10.00	$20	$25.00	$35	$50
NORMAL	$0.60	$0.80	$1	$3.50	$6	$18

1943-D — FS-01-1943D-501 (019)

VARIETY: Repunched Mintmark
PUP: Mintmark
URS-9 · I-5 · L-5

CONECA: RPM-001

Description: The secondary D is evident to the southwest of the primary D.

Comments: This RPM is extremely tough to locate. This variety will be very easy to sell at a significant premium.

	VF-20	EF-40	AU-50	MS-60	MS-63	MS-65
VARIETY	$25.00	$40.00	$50.00	$75.00	$100	$250
NORMAL	$0.35	$0.50	$0.65	$1.25	$6	$17

1943-D — FS-01-1943D-513 (019.1)

VARIETY: Repunched Mintmark
PUP: Mintmark
URS-3 · I-3 · L-3

CONECA: RPM-013

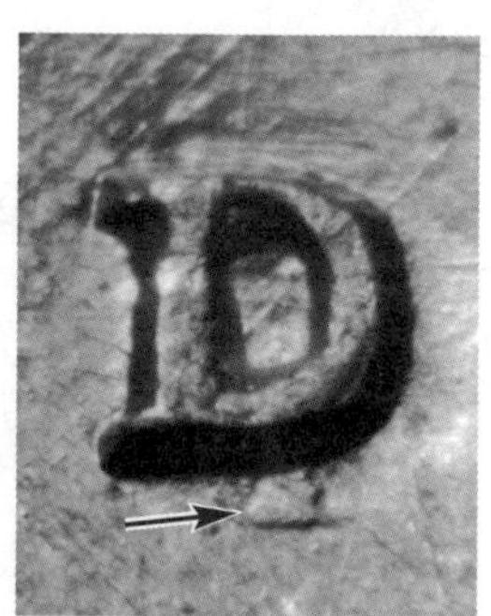

Description: The secondary D is evident to the southeast of the primary D.

Comments: This is a relatively new RPM. Very few specimens have been reported. High-grade examples will sell easily, especially to Lincoln cent variety enthusiasts. The values noted here are guides and do not represent actual sales.

	VF-20	EF-40	AU-50	MS-60	MS-63	MS-65
VARIETY	$25.00	$30.00	$40.00	$50.00	$75	$150
NORMAL	$0.35	$0.50	$0.65	$1.25	$6	$17

1943-S
FS-01-1943S-101 (019.5)

VARIETY: Doubled-Die Obverse
PUP: Date, eyelid
URS-9 · I-3 · L-3

CONECA: 1-O-IV

Description: Doubling is evident on the date, bowtie, eye, IN GOD WE TRUST, and LIBERTY.

Comments: Steel cent varieties are fast becoming very popular in their own right.

	VF-20	EF-40	AU-50	MS-60	MS-63	MS-65
VARIETY	$5.00	$15.00	$25.00	$35	$50.00	$95
NORMAL	$0.40	$0.55	$0.80	$3	$8.50	$18

1944-D
FS-01-1944D-502 (021.1)

VARIETY: Repunched Mintmark
PUP: Mintmark
URS-9 · I-2 · L-2

CONECA: RPM-002

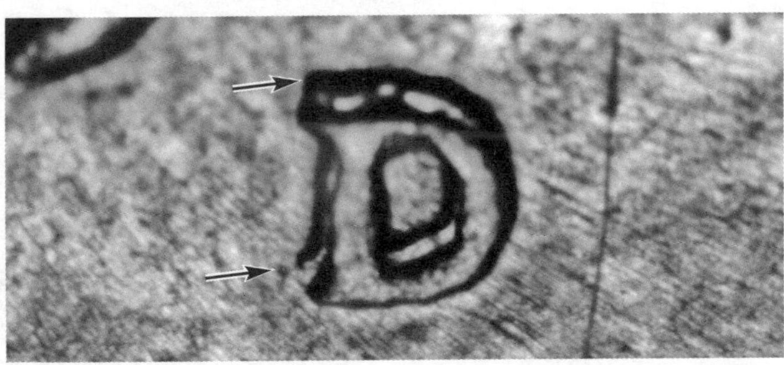

Description: The secondary D is evident to the north of the primary D.

Comments: There are several nice, collectible RPMs for this series in the 1940s.

	EF-40	AU-50	MS-60	MS-63	MS-65
VARIETY	$3.00	$5.00	$8.00	$15	$35
NORMAL	$0.25	$0.30	$0.40	$5	$14

Note: Values listed for MS-60 and MS-63 are for RB (red and brown) specimens; values listed for MS-65 specimens are for full red specimens.

1944-D

FS-01-1944D-507 (021.11)

VARIETY: Repunched Mintmark
PUP: Mintmark
URS-8 · I-3 · L-3

CONECA: RPM-007

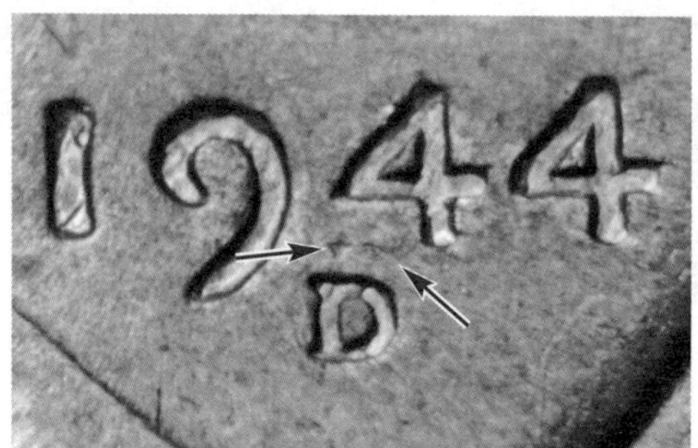 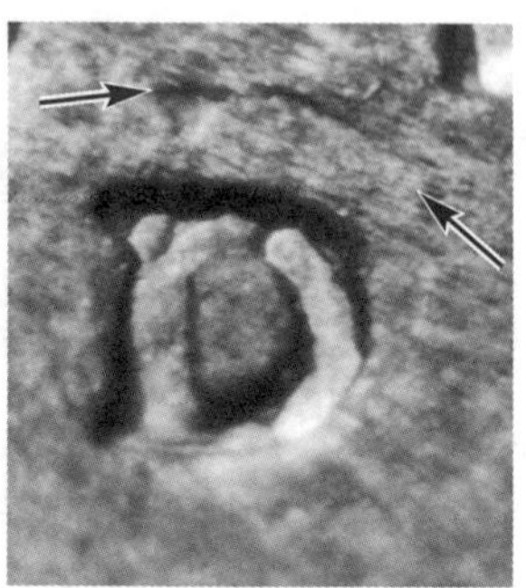

Description: The secondary D is evident to the northeast of the primary D.

Comments: This is the most popular RPM for the date.

	EF-40	AU-50	MS-60	MS-63	MS-65
VARIETY	$8.00	$10.00	$15.00	$25	$50
NORMAL	$0.25	$0.30	$0.40	$4	$14

Note: Values listed for MS-60 and MS-63 are for RB (red and brown) specimens; values listed for MS-65 specimens are for full red specimens.

1944-D

FS-01-1944D-511 (020)

VARIETY: Over Mintmark (D/S)
PUP: Mintmark
URS-12 · I-5 · L-5

CONECA: OMM-001

  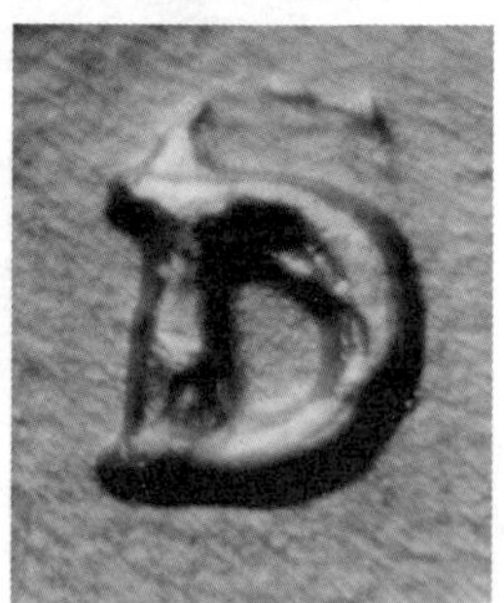

Description: This is a strong variety, listed by CONECA as OMM-001. The secondary S is evident clearly protruding from the top of the D.

Comments: This variety is the 1944-D/S that is generally quoted in various price guides. This variety is much rarer than the next listing.

	EF-40	AU-50	MS-60	MS-63	MS-65
VARIETY	$150.00	$165.00	$275.00	$375	$900
NORMAL	$0.25	$0.30	$0.40	$4	$14

Note: Values listed for MS-60 and MS-63 are for RB (red and brown) specimens; values listed for MS-65 specimens are for full red specimens.

1944-D

FS-01-1944D-512 (021)

VARIETY: Over Mintmark (D/S)
PUP: Mintmark
URS-12 · I-4 · L-4

CONECA: OMM-002

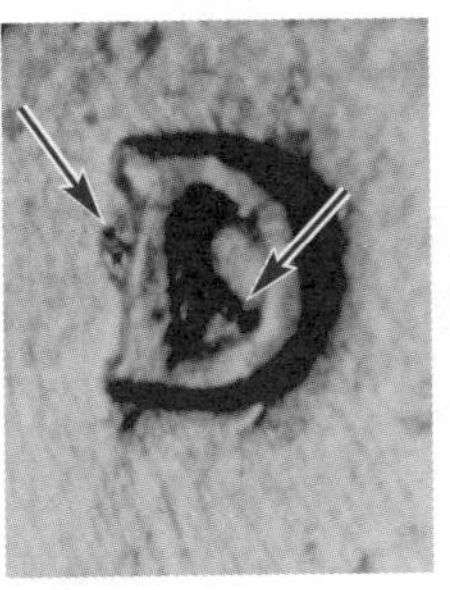

Description: The S is evident centered behind the primary D. On high grade specimens, the diagonal of the center S crossbar can be seen within the opening of the primary D. On lower grade specimens, the left curve of the upper loop of the S can be detected to the left of the upright of the D.

Comments: This variety is much more available than the previous listing and does not command the high premiums as the former.

	EF-40	AU-50	MS-60	MS-63	MS-65
VARIETY	$75.00	$95.00	$150.00	$300	$600
NORMAL	$0.25	$0.30	$0.40	$4	$14

Note: Values listed for MS-60 and MS-63 are for RB (red and brown) specimens; values listed for MS-65 specimens are for full red specimens.

1946-S

FS-01-1946S-511 (021.2)

VARIETY: Over Mintmark (S/D)
PUP: Mintmark
URS-9 · I-4 · L-5

CONECA: OMM-001

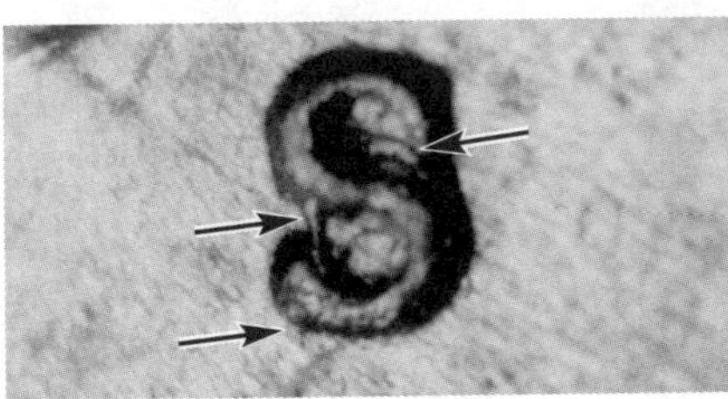

Description: The underlying D mintmark is evident centered below the primary S. The vertical bar of the D is visible in the lower opening of the S. The top curved bar of the D is visible within the upper opening of the S.

Comments: This excellent variety was discovered in the mid-1990s, which is evidence neat varieties are still out there yet to be discovered!

	EF-40	AU-50	MS-60	MS-63	MS-65
VARIETY	$75.00	$95.00	$150.00	$300.00	$500
NORMAL	$0.10	$0.15	$0.30	$1.25	$15

Note: Values listed for MS-60 and MS-63 are for RB (red and brown) specimens; values listed for MS-65 specimens are for full red specimens.

1947 — FS-01-1947-101 (021.3)

VARIETY: Doubled-Die Obverse
PUP: Date, TRUST
URS-6 · I-3 · L-3

CONECA: 1-O-I

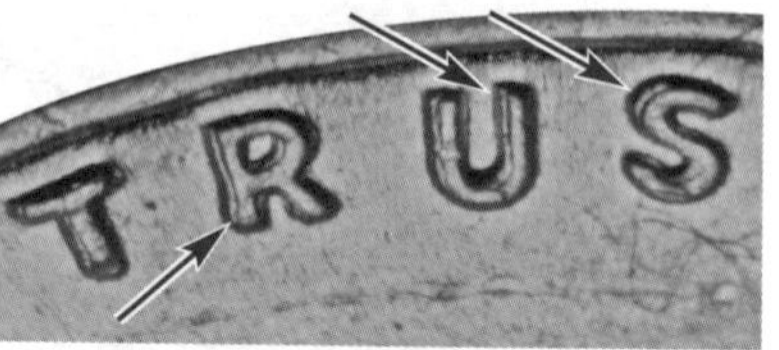

Description: Doubling is visible on LIBERTY, IN GOD WE TRUST, the date, eye, and vest.

Comments: This excellent variety was discovered in the mid-1990s, which is evidence neat varieties are still out there yet to be discovered!

	EF-40	AU-50	MS-60	MS-63	MS-65
VARIETY	$20.00	$25.00	$45	$75	$95
NORMAL	$0.10	$0.20	$1	$4	$17

Note: Values listed for MS-60 and MS-63 are for RB (red and brown) specimens; values listed for MS-65 specimens are for full red specimens.

1947-S — FS-01-1947S-504 (021.31)

VARIETY: Repunched Mintmark (Sans Over Serif)
PUP: Mintmark
URS-7 · I-4 · L-4

CONECA: RPM-004

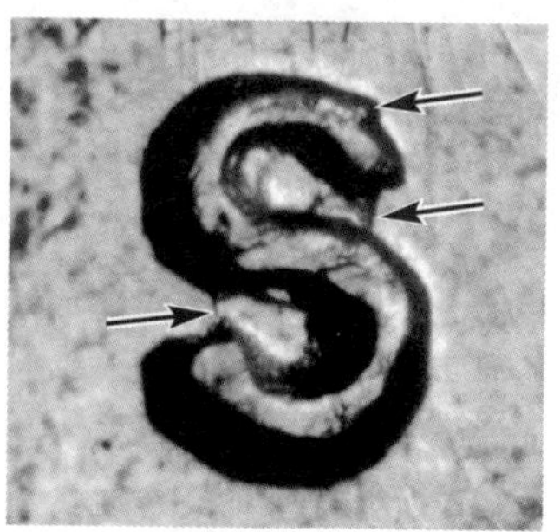

Description: The secondary S is evident squarely underneath the primary S mintmark. The significance of this RPM is that the first punch was with a trumpet tail S, and the primary S is the sans serif type.

Comments: This is a very popular RPM among specialists, primarily for the two different mintmark types. This is listed as a CONECA Top 100 variety.

	EF-40	AU-50	MS-60	MS-63	MS-65
VARIETY	$8.00	$10.00	$12.00	$15.00	$25
NORMAL	$0.10	$0.15	$0.35	$1.25	$14

Note: Values listed for MS-60 are for RB (red and brown) specimens; values listed for MS-63 and MS-65 specimens are for full red specimens.

1949-D   FS-01-1949D-501 (021.33)

CONECA: RPM-001

VARIETY: Repunched Mintmark
PUP: Mintmark
URS-7 · I-3 · L-3

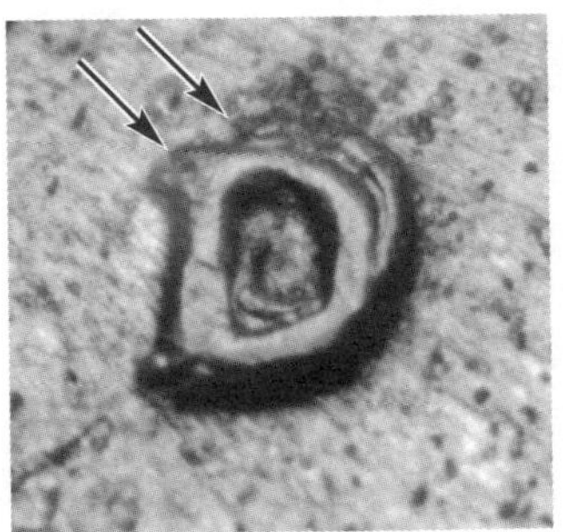

Description: The mintmark is triple-punched, with one of the weaker images to the northeast and one to the south of the primary mintmark.

Comments: This is another CONECA Top 100 variety.

	EF-40	AU-50	MS-60	MS-63	MS-65
VARIETY	$4.00	$7.00	$10.00	$15.00	$35
NORMAL	$0.10	$0.15	$0.40	$2.50	$14

Note: Values listed for MS-60 are for RB (red and brown) specimens; values listed for MS-63 and MS-65 specimens are for full red specimens.

1950-S   FS-01-1950S-504 (021.34)

CONECA: RPM-004

VARIETY: Repunched Mintmark
PUP: Mintmark
URS-7 · I-3 · L-3

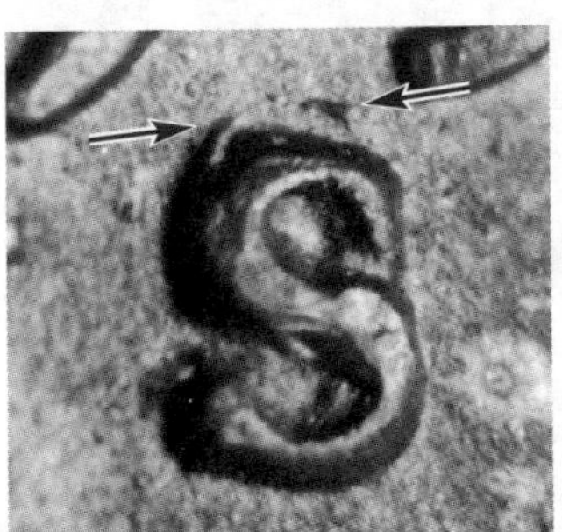

Description: The secondary S is clearly evident north of the primary S. This is actually a tripled S mintmark. Another S is visible to the north of, but very close to, the primary S.

Comments: Yet another CONECA Top 100 variety.

	EF-40	AU-50	MS-60	MS-63	MS-65
VARIETY	$4.00	$7.00	$10.00	$15.00	$35
NORMAL	$0.10	$0.15	$0.35	$1.25	$16

Note: Values listed for MS-60 are for RB (red and brown) specimens; values listed for MS-63 and MS-65 specimens are for full red specimens.

1951 Proof — FS-01-1951-101 (021.35)

VARIETY: Doubled-Die Obverse
PUP: IN GOD WE TRUST
URS-6 · I-3 · L-2

CONECA: 1-O-II

Description: There is a strong spread evident on IN GOD WE TRUST.

Comments: This variety can be located with some looking, but may be difficult to sell.

	PF-63	PF-65	PF-66
VARIETY	$50	$95	$150
NORMAL	$30	$56	$100

Note: Values listed for Proof Lincoln cents are for full red specimens. Red-and-brown and all-brown specimens command less. Cameo and deep cameo specimens should command much greater prices.

1951-D — FS-01-1951D-101 (021.4)

VARIETY: Doubled-Die Obverse
PUP: LIBERTY, IN GOD WE TRUST
URS-11 · I-3 · L-3

CONECA: 1-O-V

Description: Moderate doubling is evident on the motto and LIBERTY.

Comments: This is one of those varieties that is highly visible, yet seems to be difficult to sell as most who want a copy would prefer to cherrypick their own.

	EF-40	AU-50	MS-60	MS-63	MS-65
VARIETY	$8.00	$10.00	$15.00	$25.00	$50
NORMAL	$0.10	$0.15	$0.30	$1.25	$11

Note: Values listed for MS-60 and MS-63 are for RB (red and brown) specimens; values listed for MS-65 specimens are for full red specimens.

1951-D

FS-01-1951D-511 (021.5)

VARIETY: Over Mintmark (D/S)
PUP: Mintmark
URS-9 · I-4 · L-4

CONECA: OMM-001

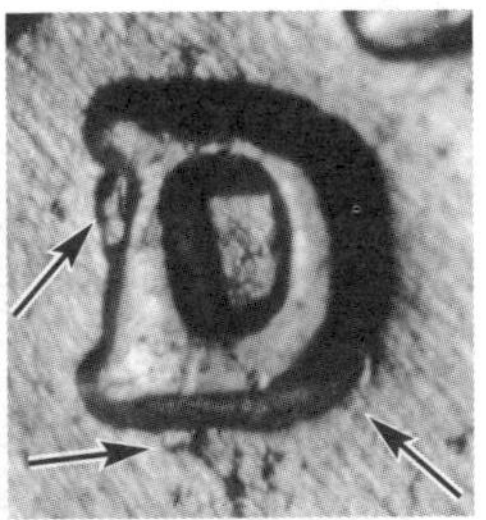

Description: The primary D mintmark was punched squarely over the secondary S. The upper left curve of the S is evident protruding from the upper left of the D's upright, and the lower loop of the S is evident slightly south of the primary D. A portion of the lower serif of the S is evident protruding from the D on earlier die state specimens.

Comments: This is a well known and very popular variety and will usually sell easily at fair prices.

	EF-40	AU-50	MS-60	MS-63	MS-65
VARIETY	$25.00	$40.00	$60.00	$100.00	$150
NORMAL	$0.10	$0.15	$0.30	$1.25	$11

Note: Values listed for MS-60 and MS-63 are for RB (red and brown) specimens; values listed for MS-65 specimens are for full red specimens.

1951-D

FS-01-1951D-512 (021.52)

VARIETY: Over Mintmark (D/S)
PUP: Mintmark
URS-9 · I-4 · L-4

CONECA: OMM-002

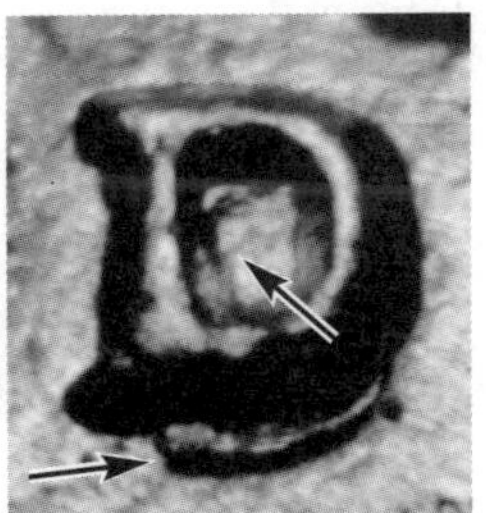

Description: The secondary, underlying S mintmark is evident protruding from the lower portion of the primary D. The lower serif of the underlying S is visible protruding from the lower portion of the primary D.

Comments: Another well known and very popular variety that will usually sell easily at fair prices. Values will usually be close to the previous listing.

	EF-40	AU-50	MS-60	MS-63	MS-65
VARIETY	$25.00	$40.00	$60.00	$100.00	$150
NORMAL	$0.10	$0.15	$0.30	$1.25	$11

Note: Values listed for MS-60 and MS-63 are for RB (red and brown) specimens; values listed for MS-65 specimens are for full red specimens.

1951-D   FS-01-1951D-521 (021.51)

VARIETY: Misplaced Mintmark   **CONECA: N/L**
PUP: 5 of date
URS-1 · I-2 · L-2

Description: What appears to be a misplaced D mintmark is evident within the loop of the 5 of the date.

Comments: To date only the discovery piece is known to us. This variety has yet to receive many accolades. Few other variety specialists have "blessed" the listing. However, the shape and size of the image in the 5 match exactly that of the appropriate D for the date. We would very much like to hear from others on their thoughts, and especially from anyone who has located additional examples.

	EF-40	AU-50	MS-60	MS-63	MS-65
VARIETY	$5.00	$10.00	$15.00	$20.00	$35
NORMAL	$0.10	$0.15	$0.30	$1.25	$11

Note: Values listed for MS-60 and MS-63 are for RB (red and brown) specimens; values listed for MS-65 specimens are for full red specimens.

1952-D   FS-01-1952D-511 (021.6)

VARIETY: Possible Over Mintmark (D/S)   **CONECA: OMM-001**
PUP: Mintmark
URS-9 · I-4 · L-4

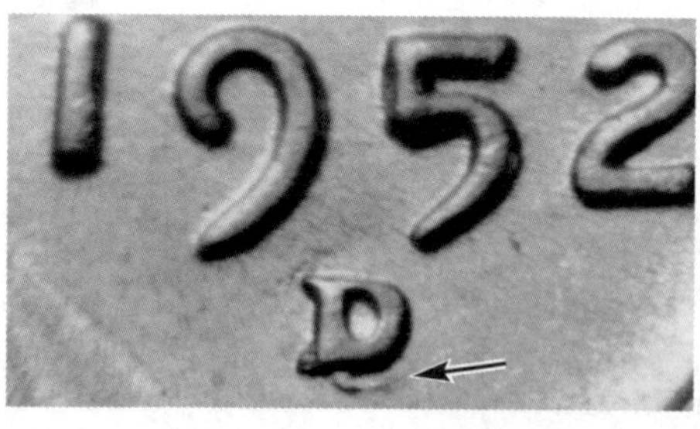 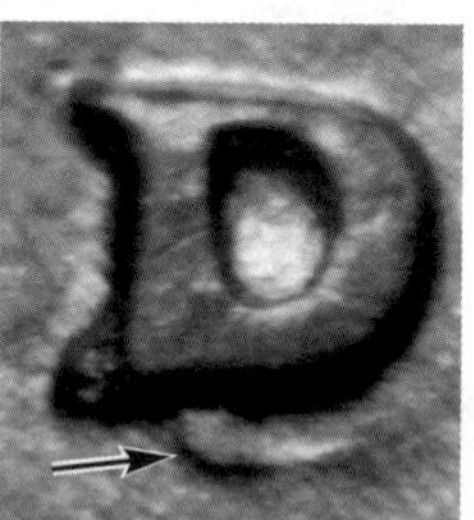

Description: The primary D mintmark was punched into the die over a previously punched S. The lower curve of the S is evident south of the D.

Comments: This OMM has received confirmation from all major variety specialists.

	EF-40	AU-50	MS-60	MS-63	MS-65
VARIETY	$25.00	$40.00	$60.00	$100	$150
NORMAL	$0.08	$0.10	$0.25	$4	$12

Note: Values listed for MS-60 and MS-63 are for RB (red and brown) specimens; values listed for MS-65 specimens re for full red specimens.

1953 Proof   FS-01-1953-101 (021.7)

VARIETY: Doubled-Die Obverse   **CONECA: 1-O-II**
PUP: Date
URS-6 · I-3 · L-3

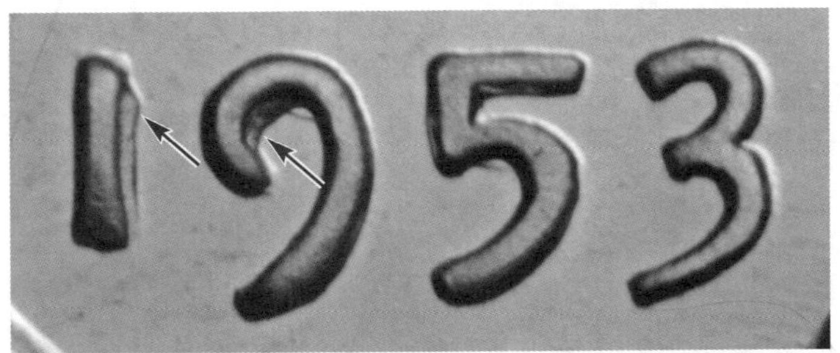

Description: There is a strong spread west on the date, and doubling is also evident on the RTY of LIBERTY. Extra thickness from the doubled die is evident on the remainder of the lettering.

Comments: Another nice doubled die on a Lincoln Proof.

	PF-63	PF-65	PF-66
VARIETY	$30	$65	$100
NORMAL	$11	$32	$41

Note: Values listed for Proof Lincoln cents are for full red specimens. Red-and-brown and full brown specimens command less. Cameo and deep cameo specimens should command much greater prices.

1953-D   FS-01-1953D-501 (021.73)

VARIETY: Repunched Mintmark   **CONECA: RPM-001**
PUP: Mintmark
URS-10 · I-3 · L-3

Description: The secondary D is evident west of the primary D. Portions of the underlying D are also evident inside the opening of the primary D.

Comments: Another CONECA Top 100 variety.

	EF-40	AU-50	MS-60	MS-63	MS-65
VARIETY	$5.00	$10.00	$15.00	$20.00	$35
NORMAL	$0.08	$0.10	$0.25	$1.25	$23

Note: Values listed for MS-60 and MS-63 are for RB (red and brown) specimens; values listed for MS-65 specimens are for full red specimens.

1954-D

FS-01-1954D-501 (021.76)

VARIETY: Repunched Mintmark (D/D/D)
PUP: Mintmark
URS-10 · I-3 · L-3

CONECA: RPM-001

Description: This is a tripled mintmark, with secondary D's evident to the north and south of the primary D.

Comments: This is a very popular RPM.

	EF-40	AU-50	MS-60	MS-63	MS-65
VARIETY	$3.00	$5.00	$8.00	$10	$15
NORMAL	$0.09	$0.10	$0.25	$1	$13

Note: Values listed for MS-60 and MS-63 are for RB (red and brown) specimens; values listed for MS-65 specimens are for full red specimens.

THE CHERRYPICKERS' GUIDE **HELPFUL HINTS**

Remember, if you can't see the characteristics of a coin clearly, you'll likely miss a variety on that coin. Don't take a chance. Always use a good, Hastings triplet magnifier (7x or 10x). The added expense will be more than offset by just one nice find. There are additional magnifying suggestions in appendix C.

1955 — FS-01-1955-101 (021.8)

VARIETY: Doubled-Die Obverse **CONECA: 1-O-I**
PUP: LIBERTY, date, motto
URS-15 · I-5 · L-5

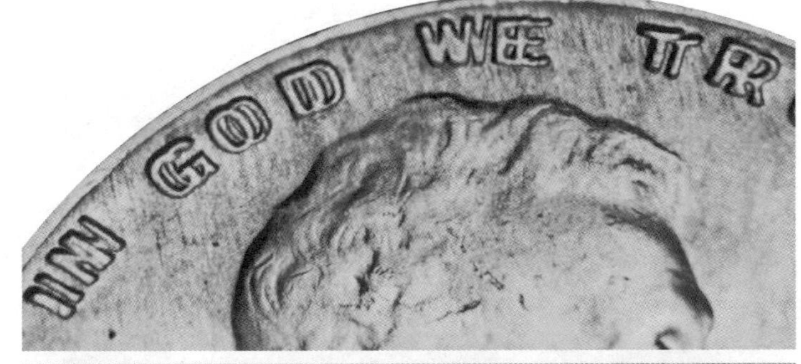

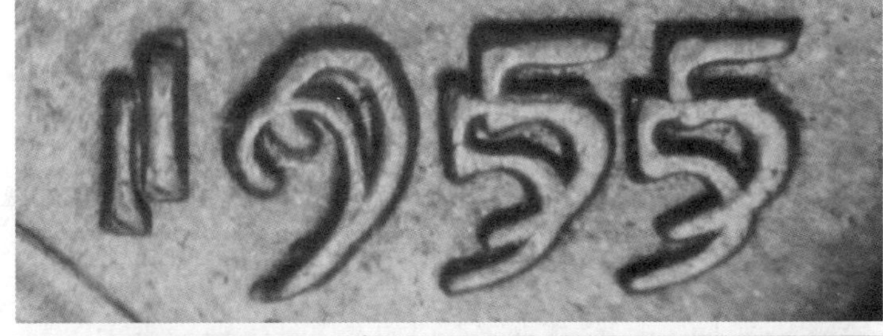

Description: There is very strong doubling on all lettering and the date.

Comments: Although very well known and not considered cherrypickable, this book would not be complete without this listing. Plus, it is helpful for all collectors to be very familiar with the die markers for the genuine coin, as there are many counterfeits available. Check for a faint die scratch under the left horizontal bar of the T of CENT to establish authenticity.

	EF-40	AU-50	MS-60	MS-63	MS-65RB	MS-65RD
VARIETY	$1,250.00	$1,350.00	$1,725.00	$2,250.00	$4,500	$30,000
NORMAL	$0.10	$0.15	$0.25	$0.65	$12	$15

Note: Values listed for MS-60 and MS-63 are for RB (red and brown) specimens; values listed for MS-65 are shown for full red and red-and-brown specimens. Check current price guides.

1955 — FS-01-1955-102 (021.9)

VARIETY: Doubled-Die Obverse
CONECA: 2-O-II+V
PUP: Motto, date, LIBERTY
URS-6 · I-4 · L-4

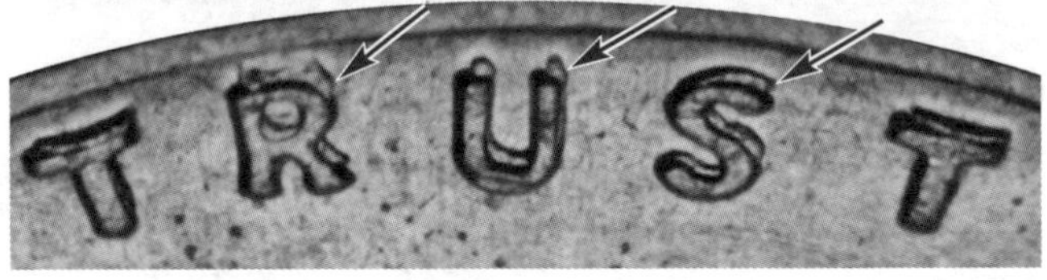

Description: Very strong doubling is evident on the motto and some slight doubling is visible on LIBERTY. The spread is strong, though the secondary hubbing was somewhat weak.

Comments: This is an extremely popular variety among Lincoln cent and variety specialists. Were it not for the previous listing, this would be considered a fantastic doubled die.

	EF-40	AU-50	MS-60	MS-63	MS-65RD
VARIETY	$75.00	$95.00	$175.00	$250.00	$500
NORMAL	$0.10	$0.15	$0.25	$0.65	$15

Note: Values listed for MS-60 and MS-63 are for RB (red and brown) specimens; values listed for MS-65 are for full red specimens. Check current price guides.

1955-D — FS-01-1955D-101 (021.93)

VARIETY: Doubled-Die Obverse
CONECA: 1-O-IV+VIII
PUP: Date, eye
URS-9 · I-3 · L-3

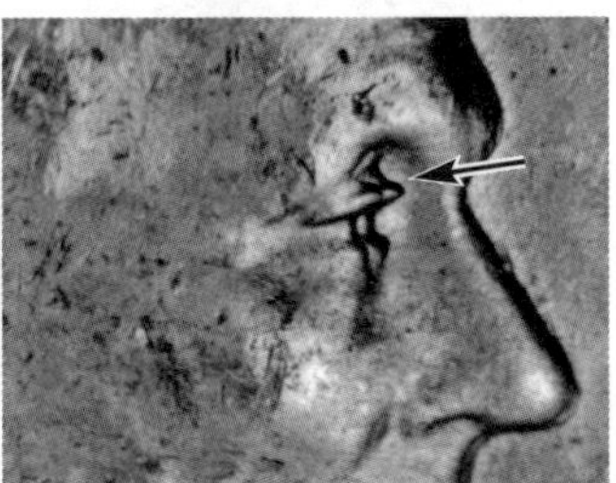

Description: Strong doubling is evident on the 19 of the date and Lincoln's eye.

Comments: Another well-known variety among specialists, this variety would be fairly easy to sell when located.

	EF-40	AU-50	MS-60	MS-63	MS-65RD
VARIETY	$8.00	$10.00	$15.00	$35	$50
NORMAL	$0.10	$0.15	$0.25	$2	$14

Note: Values listed for MS-60 and MS-63 are for RB (red and brown) specimens; values listed for MS-65 are for full red specimens. Check current price guides.

1955-D — FS-01-1955D-503 (021.94)

VARIETY: Repunched Mintmark
PUP: Mintmark
URS-9 · I-3 · L-3

CONECA: RPM-003

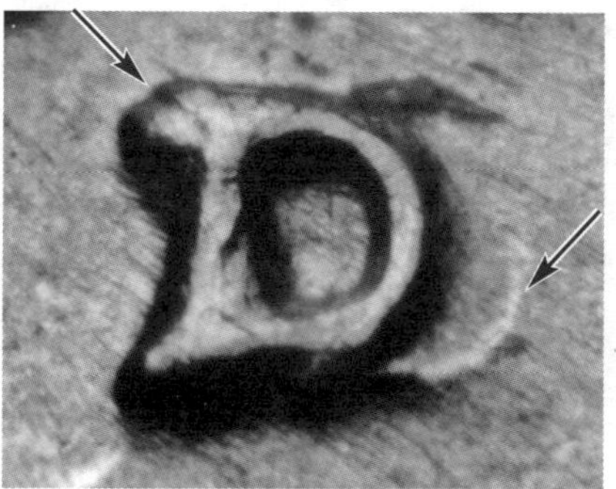

Description: The secondary D is evident widely to the east of the primary D.

Comments: This is a widely spaced RPM. This is still another CONECA Top 100.

	EF-40	AU-50	MS-60	MS-63	MS-65RD
VARIETY	$8.00	$10.00	$15.00	$35	$50
NORMAL	$0.10	$0.15	$0.25	$2	$14

Note: Values listed for MS-60 and MS-63 are for RB (red and brown) specimens; values listed for MS-65 are for full red specimens. Check current price guides.

1955-D — FS-01-1955D-511 (021.95)

VARIETY: Repunched Mintmark
PUP: Mintmark
URS-1 · I-4 · L-4

CONECA: N/L

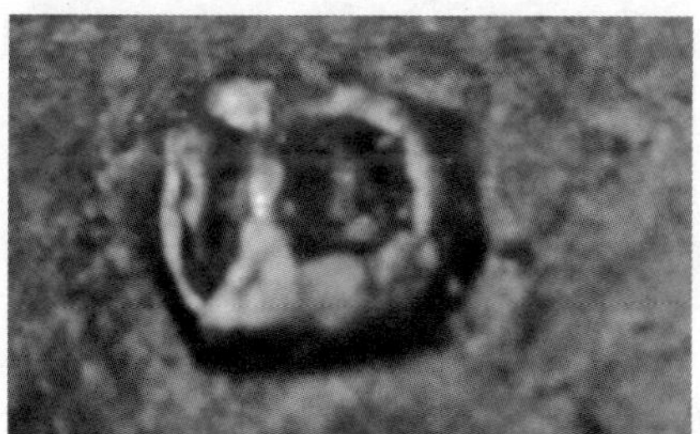

Description: The secondary mintmark was punched into the die in a horizontal orientation, with the primary mintmark punched afterward in the normal orientation. Prices noted below are estimates.

Comments: This variety was first reported in July 1992. To date, no additional specimens have been reported.

	EF-40	AU-50	MS-60	MS-63	MS-65RD
VARIETY	$150.00	$200.00	$250.00	$350	$750
NORMAL	$0.10	$0.15	$0.25	$2	$14

Note: Values listed for MS-60 and MS-63 are for RB (red and brown) specimens; values listed for MS-65 are for full red specimens. Check current price guides.

1955-S — FS-01-1955S-501 (021.97)

VARIETY: Repunched Mintmark (S/S/S)
CONECA: RPM-001
PUP: Mintmark
URS-8 · I-3 · L-3

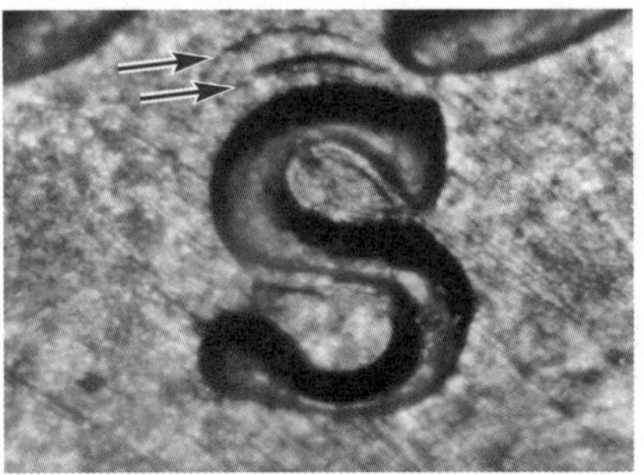

Description: This is a triple-punched mintmark—both secondary S's are evident to the north of the primary S.

Comments: This is a very popular RPM among specialists.

	EF-40	AU-50	MS-60	MS-63	MS-65RD
VARIETY	$8.00	$10.00	$15.00	$25.00	$50
NORMAL	$0.10	$0.15	$0.30	$0.65	$12

Note: Values listed for MS-60 and MS-63 are for RB (red and brown) specimens; values listed for MS-65 are for full red specimens. Check current price guides.

1956-D — FS-01-1956D-501 (022.1)

VARIETY: Repunched Mintmark
CONECA: RPM-001
PUP: Mintmark
URS-10 · I-3 · L-3

Description: This is a very strong RPM, with the secondary D evident to the west of the primary D.

Comments: Another of the CONECA Top 100.

	EF-40	AU-50	MS-60	MS-63	MS-65RD
VARIETY	$8.00	$10.00	$15.00	$20.00	$30
NORMAL	$0.10	$0.15	$0.25	$0.70	$12

Note: Values listed for MS-60 and MS-63 are for RB (red and brown) specimens; values listed for MS-65 are for full red specimens. Check current price guides.

1956-D

VARIETY: Repunched Mintmark

CONECA: RPM-008

PUP: Mintmark

URS-11 · I-4 · L-4

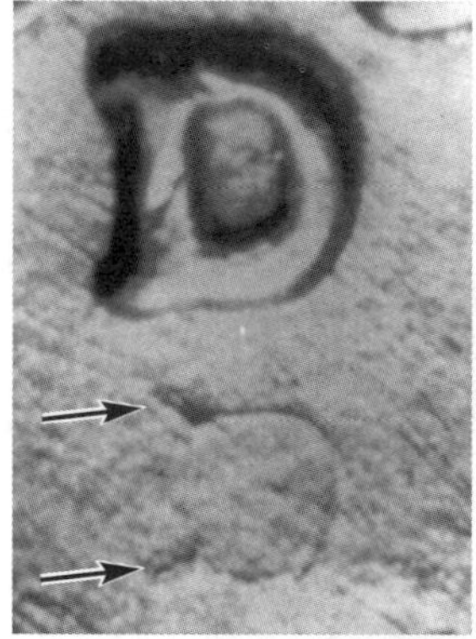

Description: This is a very well known and popular variety, with a totally separated mintmark; the remains of a secondary D are evident in the field below the primary D.

Comments: Another of the CONECA Top 100. Early die state specimens, which show a complete D, are very rare and will command a premium.

	EF-40	AU-50	MS-60	MS-63	MS-65RD
VARIETY	$20.00	$25.00	$50.00	$90.00	$150
NORMAL	$0.10	$0.15	$0.25	$0.70	$12

Note: Values listed for MS-60 and MS-63 are for RB (red and brown) specimens; values listed for MS-65 are for full red specimens. Check current price guides.

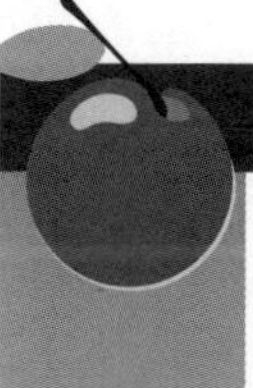

THE CHERRYPICKERS' GUIDE HELPFUL HINTS

Check all the coins in your 1960 and 1968 Proof sets. These are known to have nice doubled dies for each denomination, some on the obverse and some on the reverse. For a complete list of known Mint set and Proof set varieties, refer to appendix D.

1958 FS-01-1958-101 (022.15)

VARIETY: Doubled-Die Obverse **CONECA: 1-O-I**
PUP: All obverse lettering
URS-3 · I N/A · L N/A

Description: This is a very strong doubled-die obverse, with obvious separation on all letters and numbers. The weakest doubling is on the date.

Comments: The authors feel this variety has never reached the general population. To the best of our knowledge, the only known specimens came either directly or indirectly from an employee of the U.S. Mint in Philadelphia. The variety was first reported during ERRORAMA in Cherry Hill, New Jersey (suburban Philadelphia), in 1983 or 1984. No specimens have been reported being found in circulation, wheat cent bags, BU rolls, or other means that would lead to credibility of a true accidental release from the mint. We would caution the purchase of any specimen.

	EF-40	AU-50	MS-60	MS-63	MS-65
VARIETY				–	–
NORMAL	$0.10	$0.15	$0.25	$0.70	$12

1959 — FS-01-1959-101 (022.2)

VARIETY: Doubled-Die Obverse
CONECA: 1-O-II
PUP: Date
URS-9 · I-3 · L-3

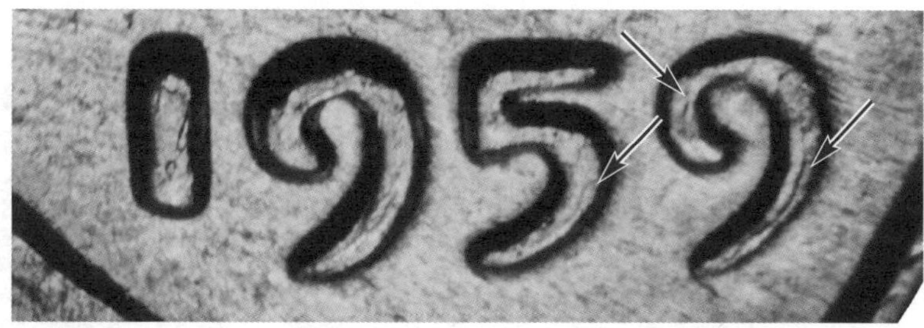

Description: The doubling is evident on the date as notable extra thickness. There are separation lines evident on the 59.

Comments: Early die state specimens show separation lines on the 959 and should command a slight premium.

	EF-40	AU-50	MS-60	MS-63	MS-65
VARIETY	$3.00	$5.00	$10.00	$15.00	$35
NORMAL	$0.03	$0.03	$0.05	$0.10	$11

Note: Values for MS-60 and MS-63 coins are for RB (red and brown) specimens; values for MS-65 are for full red specimens.

1959 — FS-01-1959-104 (022.3)

VARIETY: Doubled-Die Obverse
CONECA: 4-O-II
PUP: LIBERTY
URS-9 · I-2 · L-2

Description: Doubling is evident on LIBERTY, with slight notching evident on IN GOD WE TRUST.

Comments: Although not a big doubled die, variety specialists do have interest.

	EF-40	AU-50	MS-60	MS-63	MS-65
VARIETY	$3.00	$5.00	$8.00	$10.00	$25
NORMAL	$0.03	$0.03	$0.05	$0.10	$11

Note: Values for MS-60 and MS-63 coins are for RB (red and brown) specimens; values for MS-65 are for full red specimens.

1959-D

FS-01-1959D-501 (022.5)

VARIETY: Repunched Mintmark
PUP: Mintmark
URS-12 · I-4 · L-4

CONECA: RPM-001

Description: This is a very nice triple-punched mintmark, with secondary D's evident to the west and east of the primary D.

Comments: This variety is fairly easy to locate. Look for original rolls to search.

	EF-40	AU-50	MS-60	MS-63	MS-65
VARIETY	$3.00	$5.00	$8.00	$10.00	$20
NORMAL	$0.03	$0.03	$0.05	$0.10	$14

Note: Values for MS-60 and MS-63 coins are for RB (red and brown) specimens; values for MS-65 are for full red specimens.

1960 Proof

FS-01-1960-101 (025)

VARIETY: Doubled-Die Obverse
PUP: Date
URS-9 · I-5 · L-5

CONECA: 1-O-III

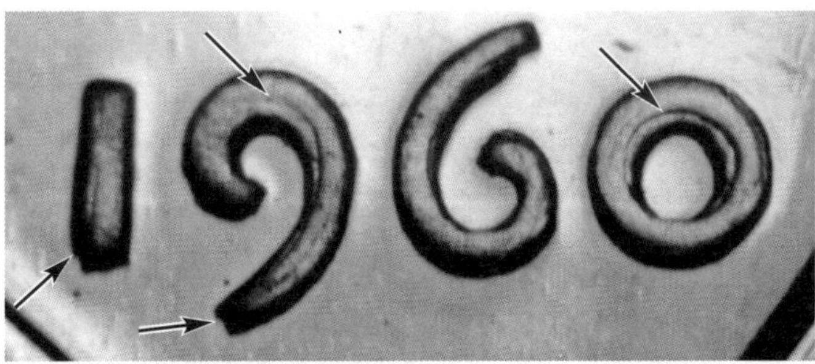

Description: This is best known for being a Large Date Over Small Date Proof. There is also doubling evident to the southwest on BERTY of LIBERTY.

Comments: This is the first of three known doubled dies for the Proof versions involving both sizes of the date.

	PF-63	PF-65	PF-66	PF-67
VARIETY	$250	$450	$600	$750
NORMAL	$3	$8	$17	$28

Note: Values listed for Proof Lincoln cents are for full red specimens. Red-and-brown and full brown specimens command less. Cameo and deep cameo specimens should command much greater prices.

1960 Proof — FS-01-1960-102 (024)

Variety: Doubled-Die Obverse
PUP: Date
URS-9 · I-5 · L-5

CONECA: 2-O-III

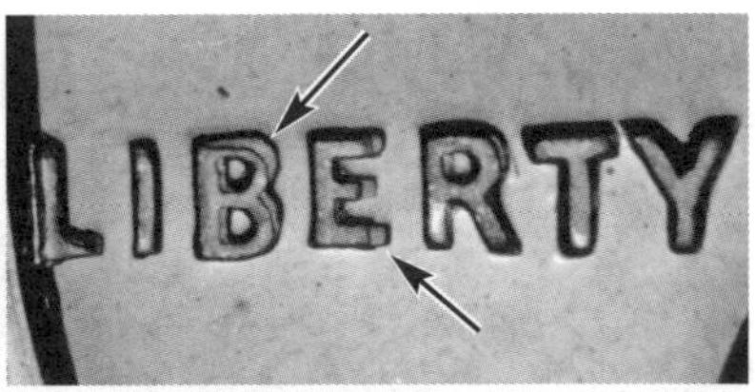

Description: This is best known for being a Small Date Over Large Date Proof. There is also doubling evident to the west on BER of LIBERTY and minor doubling evident on the tops of some letters of IN GOD WE TRUST.

Comments: This is the second of three known doubled dies for the Proof versions involving both sizes of the date.

	PF-63	PF-65	PF-66	PF-67
Variety	$250	$450	$600	$750
Normal	$3	$8	$17	$28

Note: Values listed for Proof Lincoln cents are for full red specimens. Red-and-brown and full brown specimens command less. Cameo and deep cameo specimens should command much greater prices.

1960 Proof — FS-01-1960-103 (023)

Variety: Tripled-Die Obverse
PUP: Date
URS-9 · I-5 · L-5

CONECA: 3-O-II+III

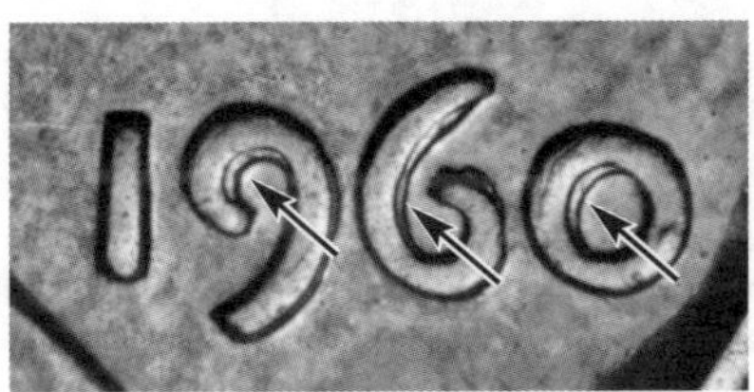

Description: This is best known for being a Large Date Over Large Date Over Small Date Proof. There is also doubling evident on LIBERTY and IN GOD WE TRUST.

Comments: This is the third of three known doubled dies for the Proof versions involving both sizes of the date. However, this one is distinguished by being a tripled date.

	PF-63	PF-65	PF-66	PF-67
Variety	$250	$450	$600	$750
Normal	$3	$8	$17	$28

Note: Values listed for Proof Lincoln cents are for full red specimens. Red-and-brown and full brown specimens command less. Cameo and deep cameo specimens should command much greater prices.

1960-D — FS-01-1960D-101 (025.5)

VARIETY: Doubled-Die Obverse
PUP: Date, mintmark
URS-9 · I-5 · L-5

CONECA: 1-O-III

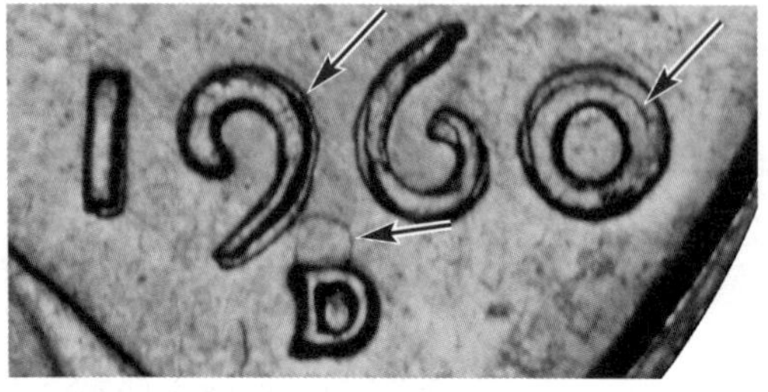

Description: The doubling is evident as a Small Date Over Large Date. There is also a very wide RPM, with the secondary D far north of the primary D, actually touching the 9 of the date.

Comments: In the not so distant past, this coin would sell for $25 in MS-63. Due to increased exposure and certain popularity added to fewer examples being found, prices have increased 10 times.

	AU-50	MS-60	MS-63	MS-65
VARIETY	$100.00	$150.00	$250.00	$500
NORMAL	$0.03	$0.05	$0.10	$11

Note: Values for MS-60 and MS-63 coins are for RB (red and brown) specimens; values for MS-65 are for full red specimens.

1961-D — FS-01-1961D-501

VARIETY: Repunched Mintmark
PUP: Mintmark
URS-14 · I-4 · L-4

CONECA: RPM-001

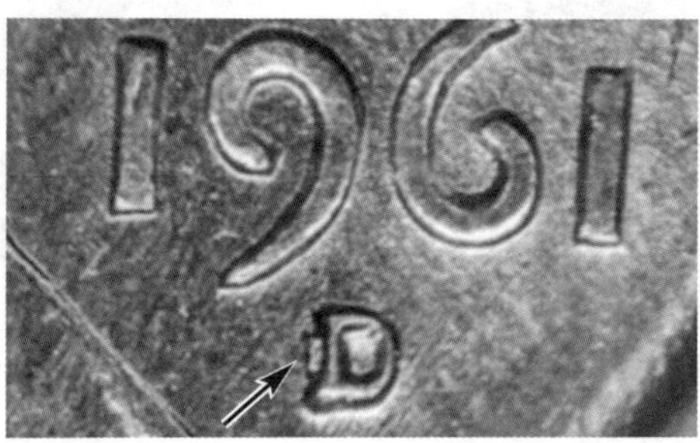

Description: The secondary D is evident in a horizontal orientation protruding left of the primary D.

Comments: This has long been a very popular variety and is well known. There are also enough specimens available to meet current demand, which is keeping the values down for a relatively neat variety.

	AU-50	MS-60	MS-63	MS-65
VARIETY	$2.00	$5.00	$10.00	$35
NORMAL	$0.03	$0.05	$0.10	$18

Note: Values for MS-60 and MS-63 coins are for RB (red and brown) specimens; values for MS-65 are for full red specimens.

1963-D

FS-01-1963D-101 (025.8)

Variety: Doubled-Die Obverse   **CONECA: 1-O-VII**

PUP: Date

URS-13 · I-3 · L-2

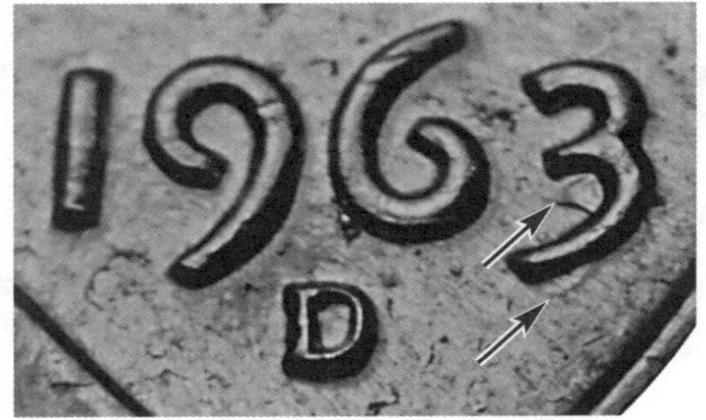

Description: The only significant marker for this doubled die is a secondary 3 evident inside the lower opening of the primary 3, and trailing slightly below the primary 3.

Comments: This doubled die is relatively common, in that it is readily available. Due to large numbers available, sales of any finds may be slow.

	AU-50	MS-60	MS-63	MS-65
Variety	$2.00	$5.00	$8.00	$45
Normal	$0.02	$0.05	$0.10	$23

Note: Values for MS-60 and MS-63 coins are for RB (red and brown) specimens; values for MS-65 are for full red specimens.

1964

FS-01-1964-801 (026)

Variety: Doubled-Die Reverse   **CONECA: 1-R-I**

PUP: UNITED STATES OF AMERICA

URS-12 · I-3 · L-3

Description: A very strong spread is evident on the letters lf UNITED STATES OF AMERICA, and E PLURIBUS UNUM, and to a lesser degree on ONE CENT and the designer's initials.

Comments: This doubled die has been known for many years, yet can still be cherrypicked.

	AU-50	MS-60	MS-63	MS-65
Variety	$20.00	$25.00	$35.00	$95
Normal	$0.02	$0.05	$0.10	$10

Note: Values for MS-60 and MS-63 coins are for RB (red and brown) specimens; values for MS-65 are for full red specimens.

1964 — FS-01-1964-802 (027)

VARIETY: Doubled-Die Reverse
PUP: AMERICA
URS-7 · I-2 · L-2

CONECA: 58-R-II

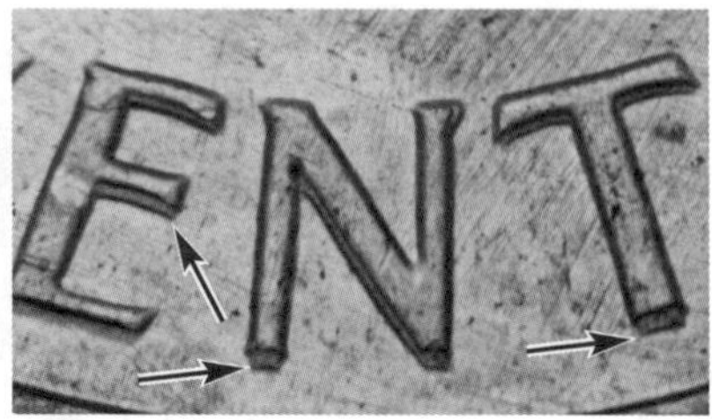

Description: Nice doubling evident on the upper portion of the reverse, especially STATES OF AMERICA.

Comments: Known in two distinct die states, the earlier being more desirable and rare.

	AU-50	MS-60	MS-63	MS-65
VARIETY	$25.00	$35.00	$50.00	$125
NORMAL	$0.02	$0.05	$0.10	$10

Note: Values for MS-60 and MS-63 coins are for RB (red and brown) specimens; values for MS-65 are for full red specimens.

1964 — FS-01-1964-803

VARIETY: Doubled-Die Reverse
PUP: AMERICA
URS-7 · I-2 · L-2

CONECA: 20-R-II

Description: A very strong spread is evident on UNITED STATES OF AMERICA and on ONE CENT, with slight doubling evident on the lower edges of the building.

Comments: This is a fairly strong doubled die.

	AU-50	MS-60	MS-63	MS-65
VARIETY	$25.00	$35.00	$50.00	$125
NORMAL	$0.02	$0.05	$0.10	$10

Note: Values for MS-60 and MS-63 coins are for RB (red and brown) specimens; values for MS-65 are for full red specimens.

1966 — FS-01-1966-101

VARIETY: Doubled-Die Obverse
PUP: Date, IN GOD WE TRUST
URS-4 · I-3 · L-3

CONECA: 20-R-II

Description: Moderate doubling is evident on IN GOD WE TRUST and the date.

Comments: This is another relatively unknown variety, yet an early die state specimen will really get your attention!

	AU-50	MS-60	MS-63	MS-65
VARIETY	$10.00	$15.00	$20.00	$35
NORMAL	$0.02	$0.05	$0.10	$4

Note: Values for MS-60 and MS-63 coins are for RB (red and brown) specimens; values for MS-65 are for full red specimens.

1968-D — FS-01-1968D-501 (027.3)

VARIETY: Repunched Mintmark
PUP: Mintmark
URS-7 · I-3 · L-3

CONECA: RPM-001

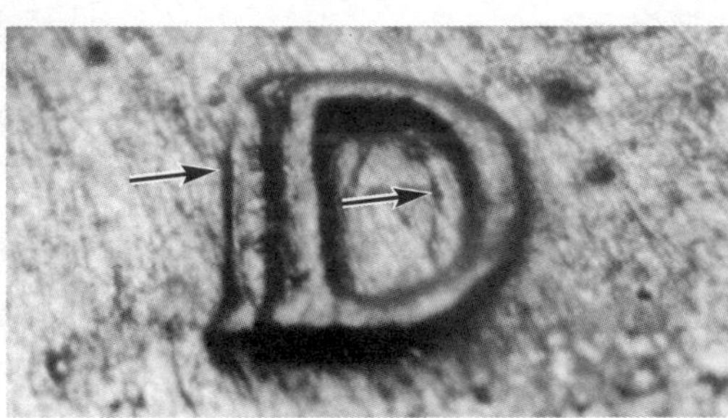

Description: The secondary D is evident to the west of the primary D.

Comments: This has long been a very popular variety and is well known. There are also enough specimens available to meet current demand, which is keeping the values down for a relatively neat variety.

	AU-50	MS-60	MS-63	MS-65
VARIETY	$2.00	$5.00	$10.00	$25
NORMAL	$0.03	$0.05	$0.10	$9

Note: Values for MS-60 and MS-63 coins are for RB (red and brown) specimens; values for MS-65 are for full red specimens.

1968-D   FS-01-1968D-801 (027.4)

VARIETY: Doubled-Die Reverse   **CONECA: 1-R-V**
PUP: AMERICA
URS-4 · I-3 · L-3

Description: Moderate doubling is evident on STATES OF AMERICA, E PLURIBUS UNUM, and the designer's initials.

Comments: This variety is really neat, yet has received very little publicity.

	AU-50	MS-60	MS-63	MS-65
VARIETY	$8.00	$10.00	$15.00	$25
NORMAL	$0.02	$0.05	$0.10	$4

Note: Values for MS-60 and MS-63 coins are for RB (red and brown) specimens; values for MS-65 are for full red specimens.

1968-S Proof   FS-01-1968S-101 (027.5)

VARIETY: Doubled-Die Obverse   **CONECA: 5-O-II**
PUP: Date, LIBERTY
URS-9 · I-3 · L-3

Description: Strong doubling is evident on the date, LIBERTY, and IN GOD WE TRUST.

Comments: This is another underrated variety.

	PF-63	PF-65	PF-66	PF-67
VARIETY	$10.00	$25	$35	$75
NORMAL	$1.50	$6	$8	$11

Note: Values listed for Proof Lincoln cents are for full red specimens. Red-and-brown and full brown specimens command less. Cameo and deep cameo specimens should command much greater prices.

1969-D FS-01-1969D-901

VARIETY: Missing Designer's Initials   **CONECA: N/L**
PUP: Right of memorial
URS-3 · I-3 · L-3

Description: The designer's initials on this die were obviously completely polished away.

Comments: This variety has received very little publicity. Certainly, other dates in the series exist with a similar aberration. Walking Liberty halves with missing initials are becoming very popular, and no doubt this series will follow.

	AU-50	MS-60	MS-63	MS-65
VARIETY	$15.00	$25.00	$35.00	$50
NORMAL	$0.02	$0.05	$0.10	$4

Note: Values for MS-60 and MS-63 coins are for RB (red and brown) specimens; values for MS-65 are for full red specimens.

THE CHERRYPICKERS' GUIDE **HELPFUL HINTS**

Generally speaking, varieties known in Mint and Proof sets are more difficult to sell or auction than other varieties. Obviously, exceptions are known. Many enthusiasts would prefer to locate their own varieties, thereby enjoying the hunt.

1969-S   FS-01-1969S-101 (028)

VARIETY: Doubled-Die Obverse   **CONECA: 1-O-I**
PUP: Date
URS-6 · I-5 · L-5

Description: Extremely strong doubling is evident on all obverse lettering and numbers.

Comments: The publicity this coin has received over its lifetime has been enormous, hence the very high values, which are well deserved. This is a very rare, strong doubled die. Beware of examples that are strike doubling, which are essentially worth face value. Compare the photos below with those of the true doubled die.

	EF-40	AU-50	MS-60	MS-63	MS-65RB
VARIETY	$65,000.00	$75,000.00	$85,000.00	$100,000.00	$150,000
NORMAL	$0.02	$0.03	$0.05	$0.10	$25

Note: A PCGS MS-64RB example recently (02/08) sold for $130,000. Values for MS-60 and MS-63 coins are for RB (red and brown) specimens; values for MS-65 are for full red specimens.

The photos below are NOT a 1969-S doubled die. Read below.

The photo on the left shows the date area of a 1969-S cent with strike doubling. On the right is a photo of LIBERTY on the same coin. Compare these photos with the photos above. This coin with strike doubling has no value above that of a normal coin. Do not be fooled into thinking this is the doubled die. Please read the section on page 322 comparing true die doubling with strike doubling.

1970-S, Large Date
FS-01-1970S-101 (029)

VARIETY: Doubled-Die Obverse

CONECA: 1-O-I

PUP: TRUST

URS-5 · I-5 · L-5

Description: Extremely strong doubling is evident on the date, LIBERTY, and IN GOD WE TRUST.

Comments: This very strong doubled die is extremely rare. To this point, fewer examples are known that the previous listing, the 1969-S. However, this variety has not received the publicity as the previous, thus the lower values.

	EF-40	AU-50	MS-60	MS-63	MS-65RB
VARIETY	$750.00	$1,250.00	$6,500.00	$10,000.00	$18,000
NORMAL	$0.02	$0.03	$0.05	$0.10	$18

Note: Values for MS-60 and MS-63 coins are for RB (red and brown) specimens; values for MS-65 are for full red specimens.

1970-S Proof, Large Date — FS-01-1970S-102 (030)

VARIETY: Doubled-Die Obverse

CONECA: 3-O-III

PUP: Date

URS-9 · I-4 · L-4

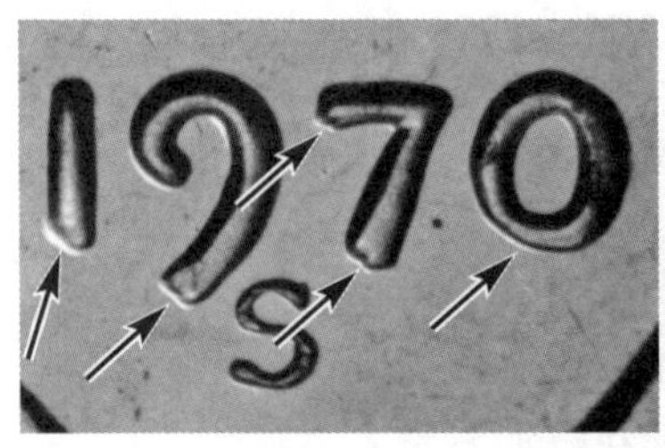

Description: Strong doubling is evident on the date, LIBERTY, and IN GOD WE TRUST. This is actually a large date over a small date.

Comments: This was long considered a typical class VI doubled die. In the late 1990s, eagle-eyed Mike Ellis realized (correctly) this was a doubled die created by the use of a small-dated hub and then a large-dated hub.

	PF-63	PF-65	PF-66	PF-67
VARIETY	$125.00	$300	$500	$650
NORMAL	$2.25	$5	$7	$12

Note: Values listed for Proof Lincoln cents are for full red specimens. Red-and-brown and full brown specimens command less. Cameo and deep cameo specimens should command much greater prices.

1970-S, Large Date — FS-01-1970S-103 (030.1)

VARIETY: Doubled-Die Obverse

CONECA: 5-O-V

PUP: Date

URS-13 · I-2 · L-2

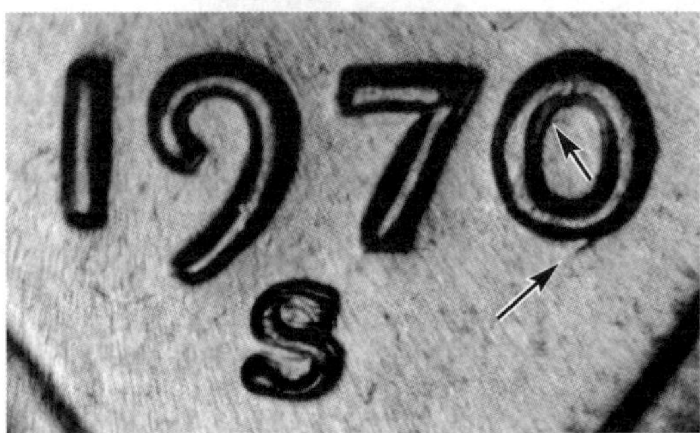

Description: This doubled die is evident only by the secondary bar visible below the primary 0. Similar doubling is also known on Philadelphia and Denver mint coins.

Comments: A relatively minor doubled die, this is interesting to many collectors.

	AU-50	MS-60	MS-63	MS-65RB
Variety	$3.00	$5.00	$10.00	$20
Normal	$0.03	$0.05	$0.10	$18

Note: Values for MS-60 and MS-63 coins are for RB (red and brown) specimens; values for MS-65 are for full red specimens.

1970-S Proof, Large Date   FS-01-1970S-107 (030.4)

VARIETY: Tripled-Die Obverse   **CONECA: 7-O-I**
PUP: Date, LIBERTY
URS-8 · I-3 · L-3

Description: The tripling is evident on all obverse lettering and numbers. It is stronger toward the rim on the date and LIBERTY.

Comments: This was first discovered by J.T. Stanton during the Blue Ridge convention in 1985.

	PF-63	PF-65	PF-66	PF-67
VARIETY	$35.00	$75.00	$125.00	$150
NORMAL	$0.02	$0.05	$0.10	$18

Note: Values listed for Proof Lincoln cents are for full red specimens. Red-and-brown and full brown specimens command less. Cameo and deep cameo specimens should command much greater prices.

1970-S Proof, Large Date   FS-01-1970S-113 (030.6)

VARIETY: Doubled-Die Obverse   **CONECA: 13-O-I**
PUP: Date, TRUST
URS-6 · I-3 · L-3

Description: Strong doubling is evident on the date, LIBERTY, and IN GOD WE TRUST.

Comments: This variety is at least as rare as previously thought, and is very difficult to locate.

	PF-63	PF-65	PF-66	PF-67
VARIETY	$75.00	$125.00	$175.00	$225
NORMAL	$0.02	$0.05	$0.10	$18

Note: Values listed for Proof Lincoln cents are for full red specimens. Red-and-brown and full brown specimens command less. Cameo and deep cameo specimens should command much greater prices.

1970-S, Small Date   FS-01-1970S-1401 (030.2)

VARIETY: Small Date   **CONECA: N/L**
PUP: Date
URS-18 · I-5 · L-5

Small Date

Large Date

Description: The date on some 1970-S–dated cents is smaller than the "normal" or large date coin. Compare the photos.

Comments: Many collectors miss this variety when looking only at the date. The easiest way to distinguish the small date cents of 1970 is actually the word LIBERTY, which weakens dramatically from left to right. Compare the photos above.

	AU-50	MS-60	MS-63	MS-65RB
VARIETY	$13.00	$17.00	$20.00	$28
NORMAL	$0.02	$0.05	$0.10	$2

Note: Values for MS-60 and MS-63 coins are for RB (red and brown) specimens; values for MS-65 are for full red specimens.

1970-S Proof, Small Date — FS-01-1970S-1402 (030.2)

VARIETY: Small Date

CONECA: N/L

PUP: Date

URS-18 · I-5 · L-5

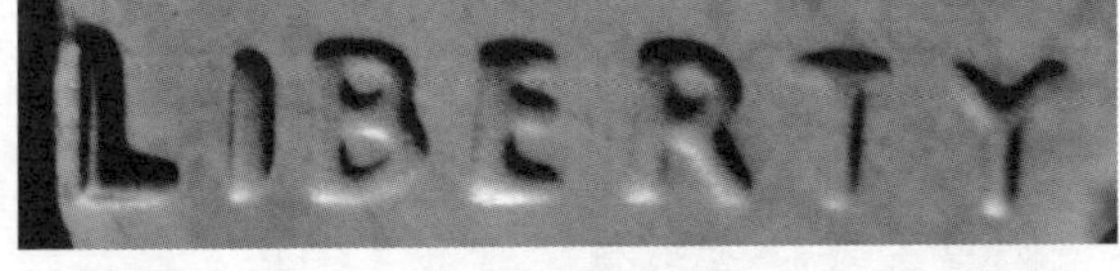

Small Date

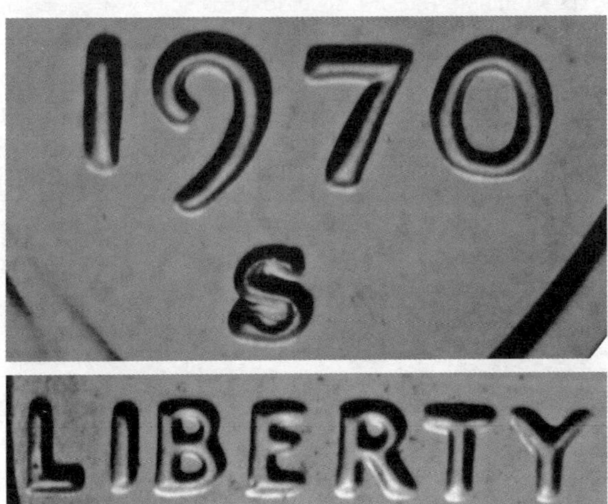

Large Date

Description: The date on some 1970-S–dated cents is smaller than the "normal" or large date coin. Compare the photos.

Comments: Many collectors miss this variety when looking only at the date. The easiest way to distinguish the small date cents of 1970 is actually the word LIBERTY, which weakens dramatically from left to right. Compare the photos above.

	PF-65	PF-66	PF-67
VARIETY	$75	$100	$125
NORMAL	$5	$7	$12

Note: Values listed for Proof Lincoln cents are for full red specimens. Red-and-brown and full brown specimens command less. Cameo and deep cameo specimens should command much greater prices.

1971 — FS-01-1971-101 (031)

VARIETY: Doubled-Die Obverse
CONECA: N/L
PUP: LIBERTY
URS-9 · I-4 · L-4

Description: Strong doubling is evident on LIBERTY, IN GOD WE TRUST, and slightly on the date.

Comments: This variety can be spotted in a dealer's case from 3 feet away! The obverse die was also slightly misaligned, which makes it appear slightly off center.

	AU-50	MS-60	MS-63	MS-65
VARIETY	$35.00	$50.00	$75.00	$150
NORMAL	$0.02	$0.05	$0.10	$29

Note: Values for MS-60 and MS-63 coins are for RB (red and brown) specimens; values for MS-65 are for full red specimens.

1971 — FS-01-1971-102 (030.7)

VARIETY: Doubled-Die Obverse (?)
CONECA: N/L
PUP: Date, LIBERTY
URS-5 · I-3 · L-3

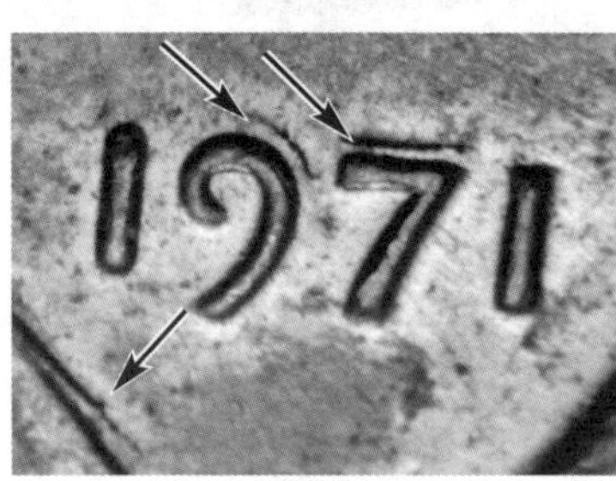
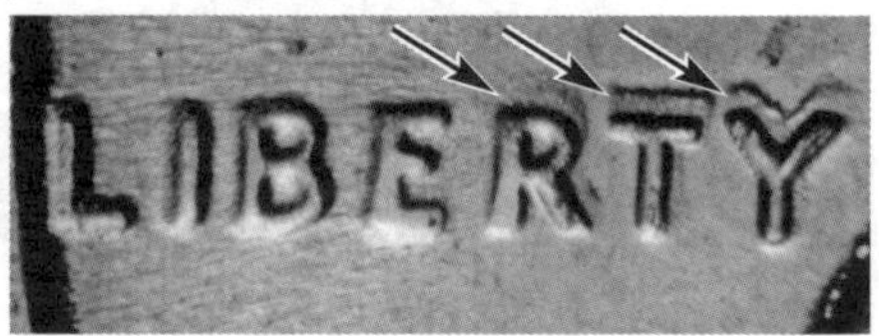

Description: Doubling is evident at the top of the RTY of LIBERTY and the 97 of the date.

Comments: This variety has been the topic of many discussions among several variety specialists. CONECA (among others) no longer considers this to be a doubled die, but rather die fatigue or some other aberration. In our opinion, the doubling is strong enough to have character. Either way you believe, this is a very interesting variety, and many specialists consider it collectible.

	AU-50	MS-60	MS-63	MS-65
VARIETY	$10.00	$15.00	$25.00	$50
NORMAL	$0.02	$0.05	$0.10	$29

Note: Values for MS-60 and MS-63 coins are for RB (red and brown) specimens; values for MS-65 are for full red specimens.

1971-S Proof — FS-01-1971S-101 (032)

VARIETY: Doubled-Die Obverse
CONECA: 1-O-II
PUP: LIBERTY
URS-8 · I-5 · L-5

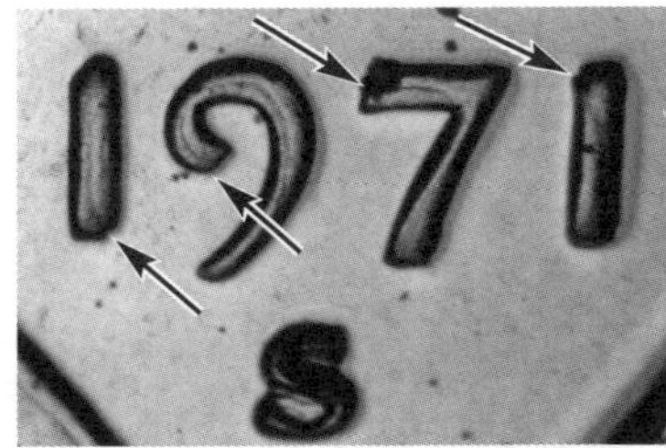

Description: Strong doubling is evident on IN GOD, TRUST, LIBERTY, and slightly on the date.

Comments: There is little, if any, doubling on WE. This is a popular doubled die, but not as rare as the next listing.

	PF-63	PF-65	PF-66	PF-67
VARIETY	$250	$450	$600	$750
NORMAL	$1	$5	$7	$10

Note: Values listed for Proof Lincoln cents are for full red specimens. Red-and-brown and full brown specimens command less. Cameo and deep cameo specimens should command much greater prices.

1971-S Proof — FS-01-1971S-102 (033)

VARIETY: Doubled-Die Obverse
CONECA: 2-O-II+V
PUP: LIBERTY
URS-6 · I-5 · L-5

Description: Strong doubling is evident on IN GOD WE TRUST and LIBERTY. There is no doubling on the date.

Comments: This is by far one of the rarest Proof doubled dies in the Lincoln cent series. While this and the previous listing are both strong in terms of the doubling, this variety commands far greater premiums.

	PF-63	PF-65	PF-66	PF-67
VARIETY	$500	$750	$1,100	$1,500
NORMAL	$1	$5	$7	$10

Note: Values listed for Proof Lincoln cents are for full red specimens. Red-and-brown and full brown specimens command less. Cameo and deep cameo specimens should command much greater prices.

1971-S Proof — FS-01-1971S-103 (033.1)

VARIETY: Doubled-Die Obverse
CONECA: 4-O-V
PUP: LIBERTY, GOD
URS-6 · I-3 · L-3

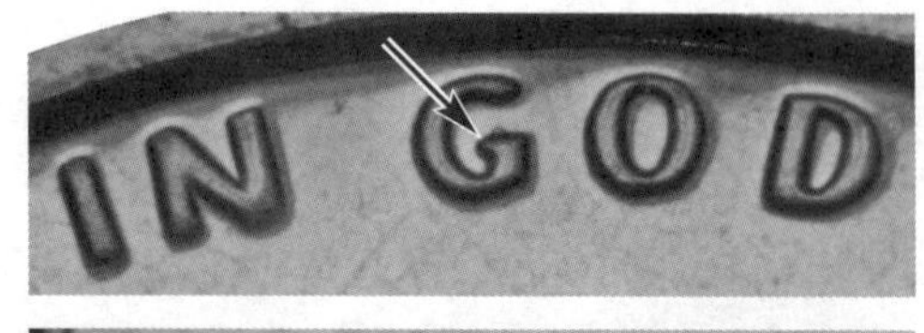

Description: Moderate doubling is evident on LIBERTY and IN GOD WE TRUST but only very slightly on the date.

Comments: Just another reason to check the 1971 Proof sets.

	PF-63	PF-65	PF-66	PF-67
VARIETY	$35	$75	$125	$150
NORMAL	$1	$5	$7	$10

Note: Values listed for Proof Lincoln cents are for full red specimens. Red-and-brown and full brown specimens command less. Cameo and deep cameo specimens should command much greater prices.

1972 — FS-01-1972-101 (033.3)

VARIETY: Doubled-Die Obverse
CONECA: 1-O-I
PUP: Date, lettering
URS-16 · I-5 · L-5

Description: Very strong doubling is evident on the date, LIBERTY, and IN GOD WE TRUST. The secondary image is spread clockwise to the primary image.

Comments: This is the popular doubled die for the year. Genuine examples exhibit a small die gouge on the reverse near the rim above the D of UNITED. This is the first of nine different obverse doubled dies for this date.

	AU-50	MS-60	MS-63	MS-65
VARIETY	$240.00	$300.00	$360.00	$400.00
NORMAL	$0.01	$0.03	$0.09	$6.50

Note: Values for MS-60 and MS-63 coins are for RB (red and brown) specimens; values for MS-65 are for full red specimens.

1972

FS-01-1972-102 (033.52)

VARIETY: Doubled-Die Obverse

CONECA: 2-O-I

PUP: LIBERTY

URS-14 · I-3 · L-3

Description: Very strong doubling is evident on the date, LIBERTY, and IN GOD WE TRUST. The secondary image is spread clockwise to the primary image.

Comments: This is the second of the nine obverse doubled dies for this year. Many people want to assemble a set of all nine examples.

	AU-50	MS-60	MS-63	MS-65
VARIETY	$10.00	$25.00	$35.00	$50.00
NORMAL	$0.01	$0.03	$0.09	$6.50

Note: Values for MS-60 and MS-63 coins are for RB (red and brown) specimens; values for MS-65 are for full red specimens.

1972 — FS-01-1972-103 (033.53)

VARIETY: Doubled-Die Obverse
PUP: LIBERTY
URS-15 · I-3 · L-3

CONECA: 3-O-I

Description: Very strong doubling is evident on the date, LIBERTY, and IN GOD WE TRUST. The secondary image is spread counterclockwise to the primary image.

Comments: This is the third of the nine obverse doubled dies for this year. Many people want to assemble a set of all nine examples.

	AU-50	MS-60	MS-63	MS-65
VARIETY	$3.00	$6.00	$10.00	$15.00
NORMAL	$0.01	$0.03	$0.09	$6.50

Note: Values for MS-60 and MS-63 coins are for RB (red and brown) specimens; values for MS-65 are for full red specimens.

1972 — FS-01-1972-104 (033.54)

VARIETY: Doubled-Die Obverse
PUP: LIBERTY
URS-6 · I-4 · L-5

CONECA: 4-O-I

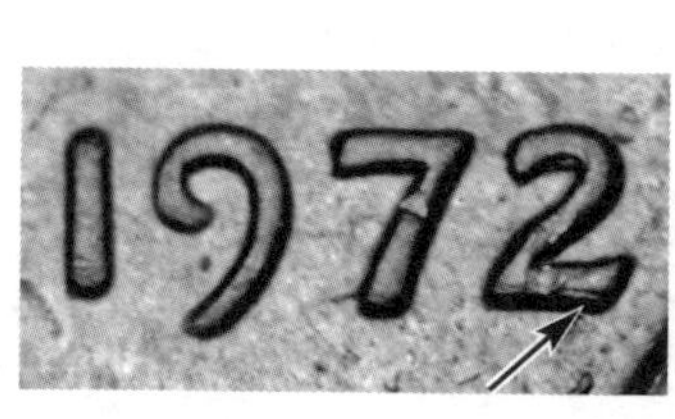

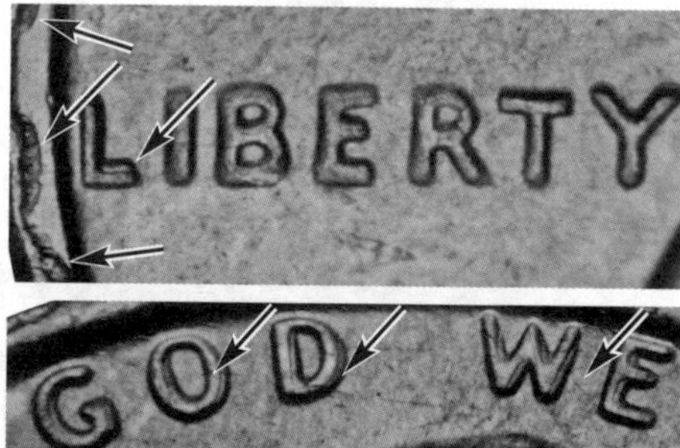

Description: Very strong doubling is evident on the date, LIBERTY, and IN GOD WE TRUST. The secondary image is spread clockwise to the primary image.

Comments: This is the fourth of the nine obverse doubled dies for this year. Many people want to assemble a set of all nine examples. This is by far the rarest of the 1972 doubled dies.

	AU-50	MS-60	MS-63	MS-65
VARIETY	$150.00	$275.00	$350.00	$500.00
NORMAL	$0.01	$0.03	$0.09	$6.50

Note: Values for MS-60 and MS-63 coins are for RB (red and brown) specimens; values for MS-65 are for full red specimens.

1972 — FS-01-1972-105 (033.55)

VARIETY: Doubled-Die Obverse
CONECA: 5-O-I
PUP: LIBERTY
URS-10 · I-1 · L-1

Description: Very strong doubling is evident on the date, LIBERTY, and IN GOD WE TRUST. The secondary image is spread counterclockwise to the primary image.

Comments: This is the fifth of the nine obverse doubled dies for this year. Many people want to assemble a set of all nine examples. This is the weakest and least desirable of the nine examples.

	AU-50	MS-60	MS-63	MS-65
VARIETY	$1.00	$2.00	$3.00	$10.00
NORMAL	$0.01	$0.03	$0.09	$6.50

Note: Values for MS-60 and MS-63 coins are for RB (red and brown) specimens; values for MS-65 are for full red specimens.

1972 — FS-01-1972-106 (033.56)

VARIETY: Doubled-Die Obverse
CONECA: 6-O-I
PUP: LIBERTY
URS-13 · I-3 · L-3

Description: Very strong doubling is evident on the date, LIBERTY, and IN GOD WE TRUST. The secondary image is spread counterclockwise to the primary image.

Comments: This is the sixth of the nine obverse doubled dies for this year. Many people want to assemble a set of all nine examples.

	AU-50	MS-60	MS-63	MS-65
VARIETY	$3.00	$5.00	$8.00	$10.00
NORMAL	$0.01	$0.03	$0.09	$6.50

Note: Values for MS-60 and MS-63 coins are for RB (red and brown) specimens; values for MS-65 are for full red specimens.

1972 — FS-01-1972-107 (033.57)

VARIETY: Doubled-Die Obverse
PUP: LIBERTY
URS-13 · I-2 · L-2

CONECA: 7-O-I

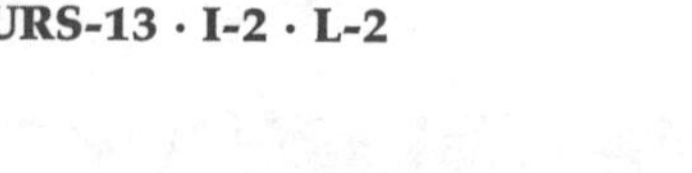

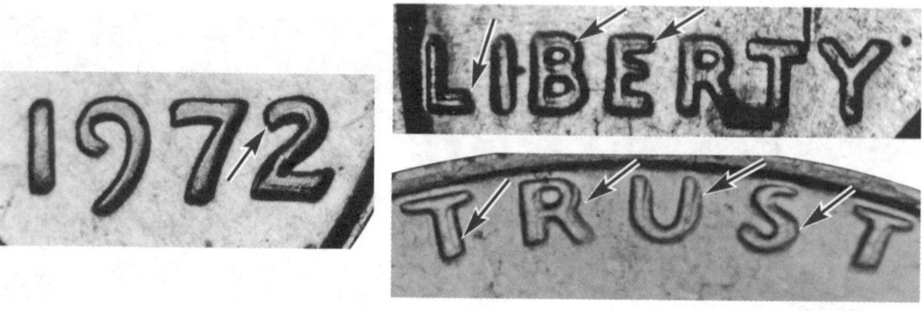

Description: Very strong doubling is evident on the date, LIBERTY, and IN GOD WE TRUST. The secondary image is spread clockwise to the primary image.

Comments: This is the seventh of the nine obverse doubled dies for this year. Many people want to assemble a set of all nine examples.

	AU-50	MS-60	MS-63	MS-65
VARIETY	$3.00	$5.00	$8.00	$10.00
NORMAL	$0.01	$0.03	$0.09	$6.50

Note: Values for MS-60 and MS-63 coins are for RB (red and brown) specimens; values for MS-65 are for full red specimens.

1972 — FS-01-1972-108 (033.58)

VARIETY: Doubled-Die Obverse
PUP: LIBERTY
URS-14 · I-2 · L-2

CONECA: 8-O-I

Description: Very strong doubling is evident on the date, LIBERTY, and IN GOD WE TRUST. The secondary image is spread counterclockwise to the primary image.

Comments: This is the eighth of the nine obverse doubled dies for this year. Many people want to assemble a set of all nine examples.

	AU-50	MS-60	MS-63	MS-65
VARIETY	$3.00	$5.00	$8.00	$25.00
NORMAL	$0.01	$0.03	$0.09	$6.50

Note: Values for MS-60 and MS-63 coins are for RB (red and brown) specimens; values for MS-65 are for full red specimens.

1972

FS-01-1972-109 (033.59)

VARIETY: Doubled-Die Obverse

CONECA: 9-O-VIII

PUP: Date

URS-11 · I-2 · L-2

Description: This variety is totally different from the others. The only doubling visible is on the tail of the 2, where a secondary tail is evident protruding.

Comments: This is the ninth of the nine obverse doubled dies for this year. Many people want to assemble a set of all nine examples.

	AU-50	MS-60	MS-63	MS-65
VARIETY	$3.00	$5.00	$8.00	$25.00
NORMAL	$0.01	$0.03	$0.09	$6.50

Note: Values for MS-60 and MS-63 coins are for RB (red and brown) specimens; values for MS-65 are for full red specimens.

1972-S Proof

FS-01-1972S-101 (033.7)

VARIETY: Doubled-Die Obverse

CONECA: 1-O-I

PUP: LIBERTY

URS-7 · I-3 · L-3

Description: Moderate doubling is evident on IN GOD WE TRUST and LIBERTY. Slight doubling is visible on the date.

Comments: This variety takes a back seat to the two major 1971-S doubled dies, but this is a very collectible variety nonetheless.

	PF-63	PF-65	PF-66	PF-67
VARIETY	$100	$195	$275	$350
NORMAL	$1	$5	$7	$10

Note: Values listed for Proof Lincoln cents are for full red specimens. Red-and-brown and full brown specimens command less. Cameo and deep cameo specimens should command much greater prices.

1980

FS-01-1980-101 (034)

VARIETY: Doubled-Die Obverse
PUP: Date
URS-11 · I-3 · L-3

CONECA: 1-O-V

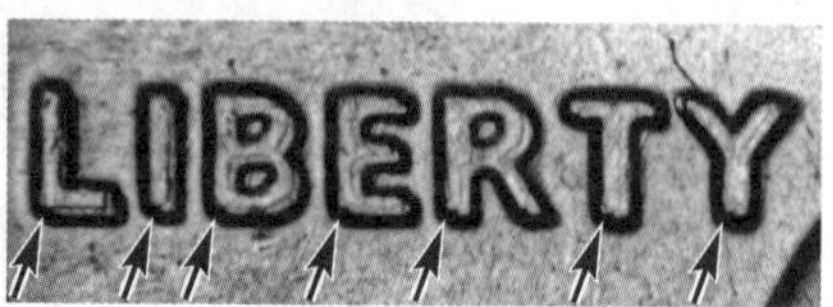

Description: Another very popular variety in the series, strong doubling is evident on the date and LIBERTY. Virtually no doubling is visible on IN GOD WE TRUST.

Comments: Early die state specimens exhibit heavy die polish on the reverse just below the memorial.

	AU-50	MS-60	MS-63	MS-65
VARIETY	$100.00	$150.00	$225.00	$350
NORMAL	$0.01	$0.03	$0.09	$9

Note: Values for MS-60 and MS-63 coins are for RB (red and brown) specimens; values for MS-65 are for full red specimens.

1980-D

FS-01-1980D-000 (034.1)

VARIETY: Removed Listing
PUP: Date
URS-0 · I-0 · L-0

CONECA: N/L

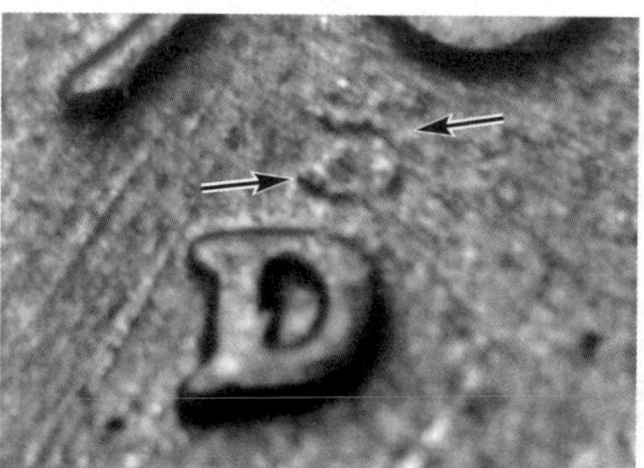

Description: This was previously listed as a 1980-D Over S cent, the old FS-034.1. The D Over S status has since been removed, and we feel very comfortable deleting this listing.

Comments: Should anyone offer this coin as a D Over S variety, be very suspicious of it and consider confirmation from a variety specialist.

	AU-50	MS-60	MS-63	MS-65
VARIETY	$0.01	$0.03	$0.09	$9
NORMAL	$0.01	$0.03	$0.09	$9

Note: Values for MS-60 and MS-63 coins are for RB (red and brown) specimens; values for MS-65 are for full red specimens.

1982, Copper Large Date — FS-01-1982-101 (034.5)

VARIETY: Doubled-Die Obverse
CONECA: 2-O-V
PUP: IN GOD WE TRUST
URS-10 · I-3 · L-3

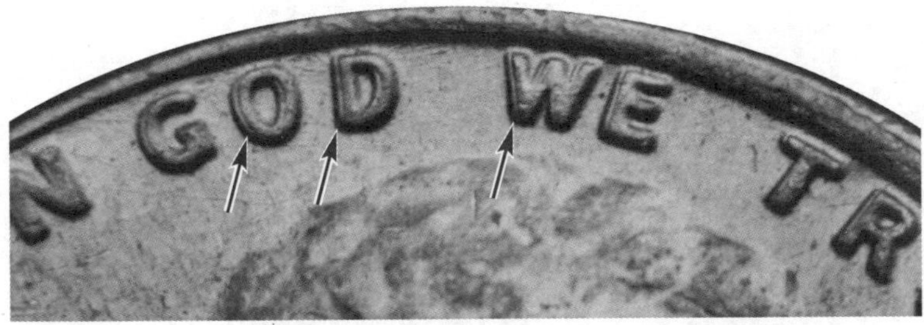

Description: Strong doubling is evident on IN GOD WE TRUST.

Comments: This is the only obverse doubled die for this date that is worth a significant premium.

	AU-50	MS-60	MS-63	MS-65
VARIETY	$15.00	$25.00	$50.00	$95
NORMAL	$0.01	$0.03	$0.09	$9

Note: Values for MS-60 and MS-63 coins are for RB (red and brown) specimens; values for MS-65 are for full red specimens.

1982, Zinc Small Date — FS-01-1982-1801

VARIETY: Doubled-Die Reverse
CONECA: 2-O-V
PUP: E PLURIBUS UNUM
URS-2 · I-4 · L-4

Description: Strong doubling is evident on UNITED STATES OF AMERICA, E PLURIBUS UNUM, and ONE CENT.

Comments: If ever there was a prime example a significant new variety can still be discovered, check this out. This variety was discovered in the summer of 2007, 25 years after production!

	AU-50	MS-60	MS-63	MS-65
VARIETY	$15.00	$25.00	$50.00	$95
NORMAL	$0.01	$0.03	$0.09	$9

Note: Values for MS-60 and MS-63 coins are for RB (red and brown) specimens; values for MS-65 are for full red specimens.

1983 — FS-01-1983-101 (035)

VARIETY: Doubled-Die Obverse
PUP: LIBERTY
URS-9 · I-3 · L-3

CONECA: 1-O-V

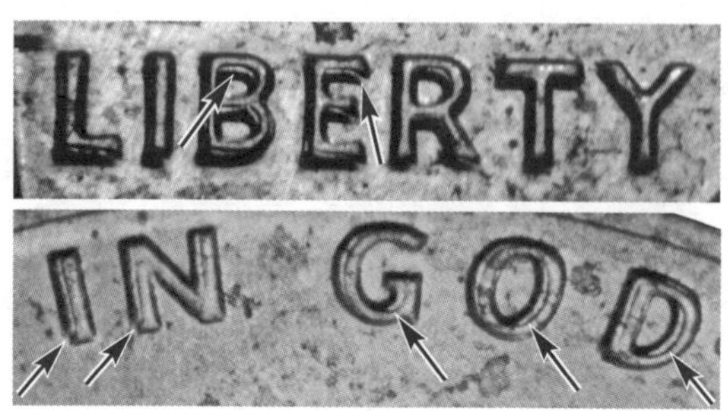

Description: Moderate doubling is evident on LIBERTY and IN GOD WE TRUST, and there is slight doubling on the date.

Comments: Relatively few collectors are aware of the obverse doubled dies for this date. Compare this listing with the next three.

	AU-50	MS-60	MS-63	MS-65
VARIETY	$10.00	$15.00	$25.00	$45
NORMAL	$0.01	$0.03	$0.09	$9

Note: Values for MS-60 and MS-63 coins are for RB (red and brown) specimens; values for MS-65 are for full red specimens.

1983 — FS-01-1983-102 (035.1)

VARIETY: Doubled-Die Obverse
PUP: LIBERTY
URS-9 · I-3 · L-3

CONECA: 2-O-V

Description: Moderate doubling is evident on the date, with slightly lesser doubling on IN GOD WE TRUST and LIBERTY.

Comments: Relatively few collectors are aware of the obverse doubled dies for this date.

	AU-50	MS-60	MS-63	MS-65
VARIETY	$10.00	$15.00	$25.00	$45
NORMAL	$0.01	$0.03	$0.09	$9

Note: Values for MS-60 and MS-63 coins are for RB (red and brown) specimens; values for MS-65 are for full red specimens.

1983

FS-01-1983-103 (035.2)

VARIETY: Doubled-Die Obverse
CONECA: 3-O-V
PUP: IN GOD WE TRUST
URS-9 · I-3 · L-3

Description: Moderate doubling is evident on IN GOD WE TRUST and LIBERTY.

Comments: Relatively few collectors are aware of the obverse doubled dies for this date.

	AU-50	MS-60	MS-63	MS-65
VARIETY	$10.00	$15.00	$25.00	$45
NORMAL	$0.01	$0.03	$0.09	$9

Note: Values for MS-60 and MS-63 coins are for RB (red and brown) specimens; values for MS-65 are for full red specimens.

1983

FS-01-1983-401 (035.3)

VARIETY: Obverse Die Clash
CONECA: N/L
PUP: Field above date
URS-6 · I-3 · L-3

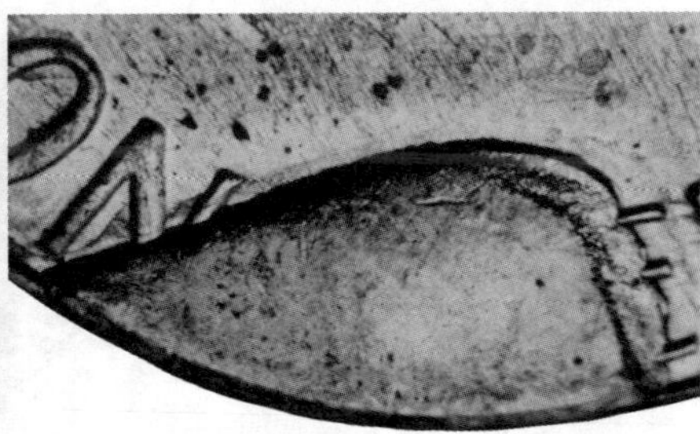

Description: Some weak impressions of letters in the word LIBERTY appear above the date.

Comments: The letters of LIBERTY above the date are not the result of a doubled die, but an unknown cause, possibly some type of die clash. The variety is also paired with a large reverse die break (cud) which may hold some key to the images on the obverse.

	AU-50	MS-60	MS-63	MS-65
VARIETY	$75.00	$100.00	$150.00	$250
NORMAL	$0.01	$0.03	$0.09	$9

Note: Values for MS-60 and MS-63 coins are for RB (red and brown) specimens; values for MS-65 are for full red specimens.

1983 — FS-01-1983-801 (036)

VARIETY: Doubled-Die Reverse
CONECA: 1-R-IV
PUP: ONE CENT
URS-14 · I-5 · L-5

Description: All reverse lettering is strongly doubled, including UNITED STATES OF AMERICA, E PLURIBUS UNUM, and ONE CENT. Also doubled are the designer's initials and portions of the memorial.

Comments: This is a well-known doubled-die reverse for the date. We suggest checking current price guides for constantly changing prices.

	AU-50	MS-60	MS-63	MS-65
VARIETY	$65.00	$80.00	$140.00	$360
NORMAL	$0.01	$0.03	$0.09	$9

Note: Values for MS-60 and MS-63 coins are for RB (red and brown) specimens; values for MS-65 are for full red specimens.

1984 — FS-01-1984-101 (037)

VARIETY: Doubled-Die Obverse
CONECA: 1-O-IV
PUP: Ear
URS-15 · I-5 · L-5

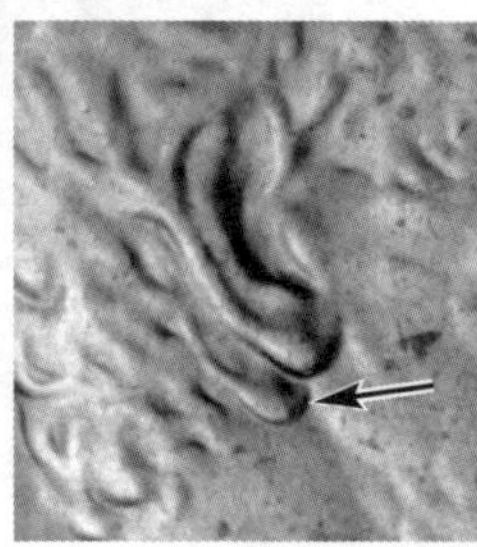
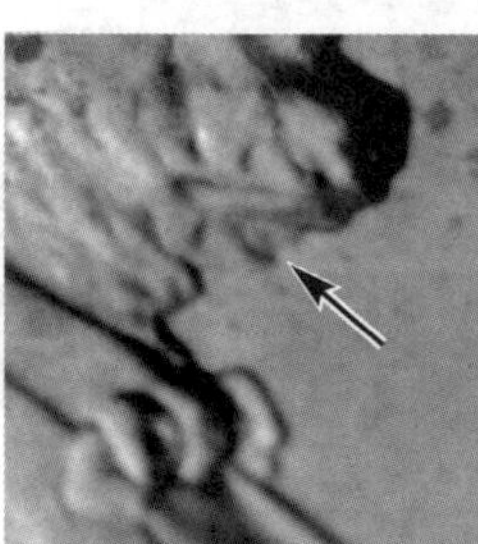

Description: Strong doubling is evident on the ear of Lincoln, with additional doubling on the beard and bowtie.

Comments: This variety is extremely popular among even regular collectors. It was discovered by Richard Allen in 1984.

	AU-50	MS-60	MS-63	MS-65
VARIETY	$85.00	$105.00	$135.00	$200
NORMAL	$0.01	$0.03	$0.09	$9

Note: Values for MS-60 and MS-63 coins are for RB (red and brown) specimens; values for MS-65 are for full red specimens.

1984 — FS-01-1984-102 (038)

VARIETY: Doubled-Die Obverse **CONECA: 2-O-II**
PUP: Date
URS-8 · I-3 · L-3

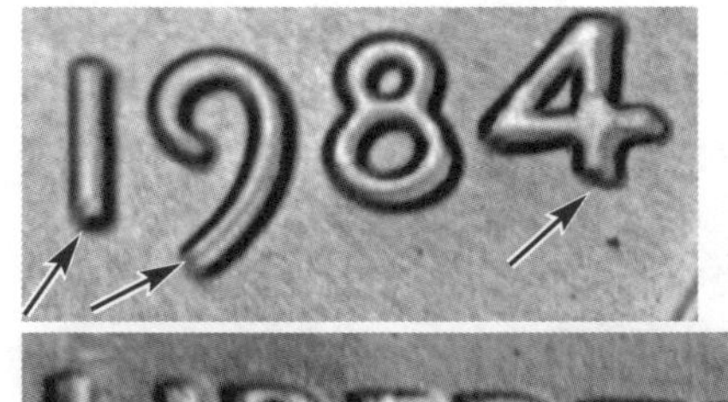

Description: Moderate doubling is evident on the date and LIBERTY.

Comments: Most of the reported examples of this coin are spotted. A true MS-65 specimen will be a quick sell.

	AU-50	MS-60	MS-63	MS-65
VARIETY	$35.00	$50.00	$75.00	$95
NORMAL	$0.01	$0.03	$0.09	$9

Note: Values for MS-60 and MS-63 coins are for RB (red and brown) specimens; values for MS-65 are for full red specimens.

1984-D — FS-01-1984D-101 (039)

VARIETY: Doubled-Die Obverse **CONECA: 1-O-II+VI**
PUP: Date
URS-8 · I-3 · L-3

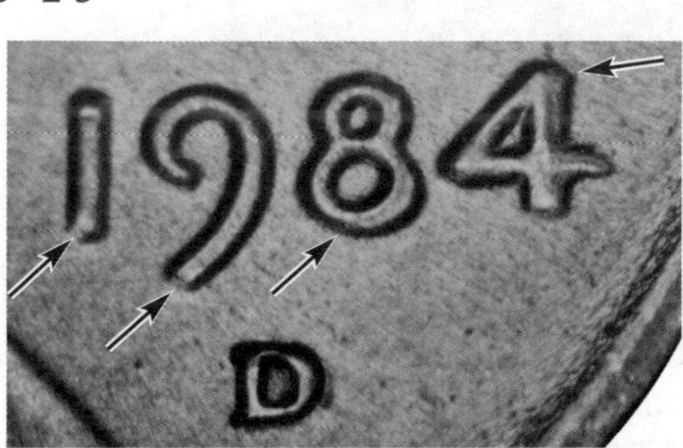

Description: Doubling is evident on the date and slightly on LIBERTY.

Comments: This variety is popular with Lincoln specialists and could be a neat find for you Westerners.

	AU-50	MS-60	MS-63	MS-65
VARIETY	$15.00	$25.00	$35.00	$45
NORMAL	$0.01	$0.03	$0.09	$9

Note: Values for MS-60 and MS-63 coins are for RB (red and brown) specimens; values for MS-65 are for full red specimens.

1990-(S) Proof FS-01-1990-101

VARIETY: No S Mintmark **CONECA: N/L**
PUP: Mintmark area
URS-6 · I-5 · L-5

Description: The S mintmark is missing.

Comments: These can still be picked, as evidenced by an eagle-eyed cherrypicker who found two sets at the 2008 FUN Convention and sold them shortly afterward for an $11,000 profit.

	PF-65	PF-66	PF-67
VARIETY	$4,500	$5,500	$6,250
NORMAL	$4	$7	$9

Note: Values listed for Proof Lincoln cents are for full red specimens. Red-and-brown and full brown specimens command less. Cameo and deep cameo specimens should command much greater prices.

1992-D FS-01-1992D-901

VARIETY: Proof Reverse **CONECA: N/L**
PUP: AMERICA
URS-4 · I-4 · L-4

Description: The normal business-strike reverse for the 1992 cents has the AM of AMERICA with a clear space between the letters. However, this 1992-D cent was struck with the Proof reverse for that year, which has the AM of AMERICA very close, almost touching.

Comments: The reverse hubs for 1992 were the opposite of those used in 1998, 1999, and 2000. See those listings later in this section.

	AU-50	MS-60	MS-63	MS-65
VARIETY	$25.00	$35.00	$50.00	$75
NORMAL	$0.01	$0.03	$0.09	$2

Note: Values for MS-60 and MS-63 coins are for RB (red and brown) specimens; values for MS-65 are for full red specimens.

1994 — FS-01-1994-801 (039.9)

VARIETY: Doubled-Die Reverse
CONECA: 1-R-IV
PUP: Last three columns of memorial
URS-3 · I-2 · L-2

Description: Doubling is evident as two extra columns within the three final columns.

Comments: This variety was first reported by James Mattaliano.

	AU-50	MS-60	MS-63	MS-65
VARIETY	$25.00	$35.00	$50.00	$75
NORMAL	$0.01	$0.03	$0.09	$2

Note: Values for MS-60 and MS-63 coins are for RB (red and brown) specimens; values for MS-65 are for full red specimens.

1995 — FS-01-1995-101 (040)

VARIETY: Doubled-Die Obverse
CONECA: 1-O-V
PUP: LIBERTY
URS-21 · I-4 · L-3

Description: Very strong doubling is evident on LIBERTY and IN GOD WE TRUST, with minor doubling on the date.

Comments: First reported by Felix Dausilio, this variety received rapid recognition when it appeared on the front page of *USA Today,* sending all of us on a nationwide treasure hunt.

	AU-50	MS-60	MS-63	MS-65
VARIETY	$25.00	$30.00	$35.00	$45
NORMAL	$0.01	$0.03	$0.09	$2

Note: Values for MS-60 and MS-63 coins are for RB (red and brown) specimens; values for MS-65 are for full red specimens.

1995-D — FS-01-1995D-103 (041)

VARIETY: Doubled-Die Obverse
CONECA: 3-O-V
PUP: LIBERTY
URS-7 · I-3 · L-3

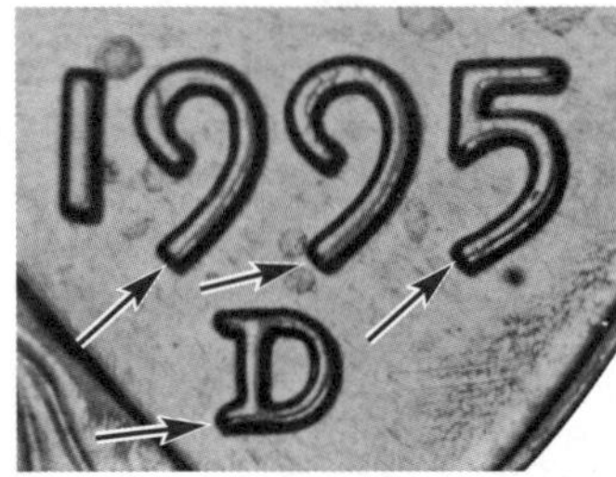

Description: Strong doubling is evident on IN GOD WE TRUST and to a lesser degree on the date, mintmark, and LIBERTY.

Comments: This variety is the direct result of the Philadelphia Mint specimen being reported. This is also interesting, as the Mint started to include the mintmarks on the master hubs during this time, hence the like doubling on the mintmark.

	AU-50	MS-60	MS-63	MS-65
VARIETY	$175.00	$250.00	$350.00	$500
NORMAL	$0.01	$0.03	$0.09	$2

Note: Values for MS-60 and MS-63 coins are for RB (red and brown) specimens; values for MS-65 are for full red specimens.

1997 — FS-01-1997-101 (043)

VARIETY: Doubled Ear
CONECA: 1-O-IV
PUP: Ear
URS-9 · I-3 · L-3

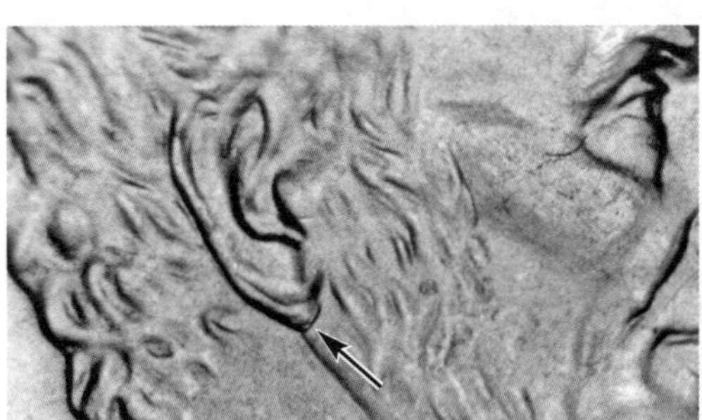

Description: Doubling on the ear gives the appearance of a second earlobe.

Comments: First reported by Larry Philbrick, this has become a controversial variety. It is listed by CONECA as a doubled die but we don't believe it is. However, this is a neat variety, whatever the cause.

	AU-50	MS-60	MS-63	MS-65
VARIETY	$175.00	$250.00	$350.00	$500
NORMAL	$0.01	$0.03	$0.09	$2

Note: Values for MS-60 and MS-63 coins are for RB (red and brown) specimens; values for MS-65 are for full red specimens.

1998
FS-01-1998-901

VARIETY: Proof Reverse   **CONECA: N/L**
PUP: AMERICA
URS-8 · I-4 · L-4

Description: The normal business-strike reverse for the 1998 cents has the AM of AMERICA very close, almost touching. This variety has the Proof (Type II) reverse, with the AM in AMERICA showing a clear space between the letters. The reverse with the AM almost touching is called the "close AM," or type I, reverse; the reverse with the AM apart is called the "wide AM," or type II, reverse.

Comments: These varieties have grown tremendously in popularity.

	AU-50	MS-60	MS-63	MS-65
VARIETY	$20.00	$25.00	$35.00	$50
NORMAL	$0.01	$0.03	$0.09	$2

Note: Values for MS-60 and MS-63 coins are for RB (red and brown) specimens; values for MS-65 are for full red specimens.

1999
FS-01-1999-901

VARIETY: Proof Reverse   **CONECA: N/L**
PUP: AMERICA
URS-4 · I-4 · L-4

Description: The normal business-strike reverse for the 1999 cents has the AM of AMERICA very close, almost touching. This variety has the Proof (Type II) reverse, with the AM in AMERICA showing a clear space between the letters. The reverse with the AM almost touching is called the "close AM," or type I, reverse; the reverse with the AM apart is called the "wide AM," or type II, reverse.

Comments: These varieties have grown tremendously in popularity.

	AU-50	MS-60	MS-63	MS-65
VARIETY	$150.00	$175.00	$250.00	$350
NORMAL	$0.01	$0.03	$0.09	$2

Note: Values for MS-60 and MS-63 coins are for RB (red and brown) specimens; values for MS-65 are for full red specimens.

1999-(S) Proof   FS-01-1999S-901

VARIETY: Business-Strike Reverse   **CONECA: N/L**
PUP: AMERICA
URS-7 · I-4 · L-4

Description: The normal Proof reverse for 1999 cents has the AM on AMERICA wide apart. This variety has the AM of AMERICA almost touching. The reverse with the AM almost touching is called the "close AM," or type I, reverse; the reverse with the AM apart is called the "wide AM," or type II, reverse.

Comments: These varieties have grown tremendously in popularity.

	PF-64	PF-65	PF-66	PF-67
VARIETY	$525	$650.00	$750	$850.00
NORMAL	$4	$4.75	$7	$9.50

2000   FS-01-2000-901

VARIETY: Proof Reverse   **CONECA: N/L**
PUP: AMERICA
URS-11 · I-4 · L-4

Description: The normal business strike reverse for the 2000 cents has the AM of AMERICA very close, almost touching. This variety has the Proof (Type II) reverse, with the AM in AMERICA showing a clear space between the letters. The reverse with the AM almost touching is called the "close AM," or type I, reverse; the reverse with the AM apart is called the "wide AM," or type II, reverse.

Comments: These varieties have grown tremendously in popularity.

	AU-50	MS-60	MS-63	MS-65
VARIETY	$20.00	$25.00	$35.00	$50
NORMAL	$0.01	$0.03	$0.09	$2

Note: Values for MS-60 and MS-63 coins are for RB (red and brown) specimens; values for MS-65 are for full red specimens.

2000-(S) Proof — FS-01-2000S-901

VARIETY: Business-Strike Reverse

CONECA: N/L

PUP: AMERICA

URS-7 · I-4 · L-4

Description: The normal Proof reverse for 2000 cents has the AM on AMERICA wide apart. This variety has the AM of AMERICA almost touching. The reverse with the AM almost touching is called the "close AM," or type I, reverse; the reverse with the AM apart is called the "wide AM," or type II, reverse.

Comments: These varieties have grown tremendously in popularity.

	PF-64	PF-65	PF-66	PF-67
VARIETY	$525	$650.00	$750	$850.00
NORMAL	$4	$4.75	$7	$9.50

THE CHERRYPICKERS' GUIDE **HELPFUL HINTS**

Don't get discouraged if you haven't found any significant varieties for a while—they're out there, and eventually you'll uncover some. Remember, knowledge is power, but it's only relevant when you use it!

Two-Cent Pieces, 1864–1873

The two-cent piece has increased in popularity among variety collectors since the first edition of the *Cherrypickers' Guide* was published. This section has grown slowly but steadily.

One recommended book for specialists and serious collectors is Frank Leone's *Longacre's Two-Cent Piece—An 1864 Attribution Guide.* Another is Kevin Flynn's *Getting Your Two Cent's Worth.*

1864, Small Motto — FS-02-1864-401 (000.5)

VARIETY: Small Motto
PUP: Motto
URS-11 · I-5 · L-5

Description: The motto for the earlier 1864 two-cent pieces was small compared to later issues.

Comments: One of the authors has fairly recently cherrypicked this variety. It can still be done!

	VF-20	EF-40	AU-50	MS-60	MS-63	MS-65
VARIETY, SMALL MOTTO	$385	$575	$660	$1,100	$1,600	$3,600
NORMAL, LARGE MOTTO	$25	$41	$72	$80	$125	$500

Note: Values for MS-60 and MS-63 coins are for brown specimens; values for MS-65 coins are for red and brown specimens. Full red specimens command far greater premiums.

1864, Large Motto — FS-02-1864-1101 (001)

VARIETY: Doubled-Die Obverse
LEONE: 64LG-06G
PUP: Motto
URS-7 · I-3 · L-3

Description: The doubling is most evident on the upper half of the coin, including IN GOD WE TRUST, the upper leaves, and the banner itself.

Comments: A small horizontal die gouge appears over the left side of the banner above IN. Later die states exhibit a cud (die break) at 8:00 on the obverse.

	VF-20	EF-40	AU-50	MS-60	MS-63	MS-65
VARIETY	$35	$65	$100	$135	$175	$595
NORMAL	$25	$41	$72	$80	$125	$500

Note: Values for MS-60 and MS-63 coins are for brown specimens; values for MS-65 coins are for red and brown specimens. Full red specimens command far greater premiums.

1864, Large Motto — FS-02-1864-1301 (001.5)

VARIETY: Repunched Date
LEONE: 64LG-100E

PUP: Date
URS-7 · I-3 · L-3

Description: The repunched date is evident as a tripled 1 and 8, with both secondary digits to the north of the primary numbers. There is no evident repunching easily visible on the 6, but the 4 is tripled, with both secondary digits very close to the primary.

Comments: This is one of the rarest repunched dates in the two-cent series and obviously very difficult to locate.

	VF-20	EF-40	AU-50	MS-60	MS-63	MS-65
VARIETY	$75	$100	$150	$225	$300	$650
NORMAL	$25	$41	$72	$80	$125	$500

Note: Values for MS-60 and MS-63 coins are for brown specimens; values for MS-65 coins are for red and brown specimens. Full red specimens command far greater premiums.

1864, Large Motto — FS-02-1864-1302 (001.7)

VARIETY: Repunched Date
LEONE: 64LG-24H

PUP: Date
URS-6 · I-3 · L-3

Description: The entire date was punched at least three times. Secondary digits are evident to the north of the 1 and 8, and to the southwest of the 6 and 4.

Comments: This is another nice and collectible repunched date in the two-cent series.

	VF-20	EF-40	AU-50	MS-60	MS-63	MS-65
VARIETY	$50	$85	$125	$175	$250	$650
NORMAL	$25	$41	$72	$80	$125	$500

Note: Values for MS-60 and MS-63 coins are for brown specimens; values for MS-65 coins are for red and brown specimens. Full red specimens commands far greater premiums.

1864, Large Motto — FS-02-1864-1901 (001.8)

VARIETY: Clashed Die
PUP: Reverse field
URS-4 · I-4 · L-4

LEONE: 64LG-16B

Description: Reminiscent of the mule clashed dies of 1857, this reverse die was clashed with an obverse die of an Indian Head cent. The profile of the Indian is evident to the right of the 2, the chin at the bottom on the TS in CENTS, and the neck running south from the left side of that same T.

Comments: This is a wild die clash, and very rare.

	VF-20	EF-40	AU-50	MS-60	MS-63	MS-65
VARIETY	$175	$250	$350	$450	$650	$950
NORMAL	$25	$41	$72	$80	$125	$500

Note: Values for MS-60 and MS-63 coins are for brown specimens; values for MS-65 coins are for red and brown specimens. Full red specimens commands far greater premiums.

1865, Plain 5 — FS-02-1865-101 (002)

VARIETY: Doubled-Die Obverse
PUP: TRUST
URS-9 · I-3 · L-3

LEONE: 65P-101R

Description: The doubling is most visible on the upper half of the obverse, particularly on the word TRUST, the berry stems and leaves, and the horizontal lines of the shield.

Comments: Interestingly, there is a die gouge above IN on the banner, similar to that on the 1864 doubled die (FS-1101).

	VF-20	EF-40	AU-50	MS-60	MS-63	MS-65
VARIETY	$50	$75	$125	$175	$250	$625
NORMAL	$25	$41	$72	$80	$125	$500

Note: Values for MS-60 and MS-63 coins are for brown specimens; values for MS-65 coins are for red and brown specimens. Full red specimens command far greater premiums.

1865, Plain 5   FS-02-1865-301 (002.3)

VARIETY: Repunched Date   **LEONE: 65P-501R**
PUP: Date
URS-6 · I-2 · L-2

Description: The base of a secondary 1 is evident between the center of the primary 1 and the 8. Portions of the other digits are also visible.

Comments: Many examples of this variety have a rotated reverse.

	VF-20	EF-40	AU-50	MS-60	MS-63	MS-65
VARIETY	$50	$75	$125	$175	$250	$625
NORMAL	$25	$41	$72	$80	$125	$500

Note: Values for MS-60 and MS-63 coins are for brown specimens; values for MS-65 coins are for red and brown specimens. Full red specimens command far greater premiums.

1865, Fancy 5   FS-02-1865-1301 (002.5)

VARIETY: Repunched Date   **LEONE: 65F-101R**
PUP: Date
URS-9 · I-3 · L-3

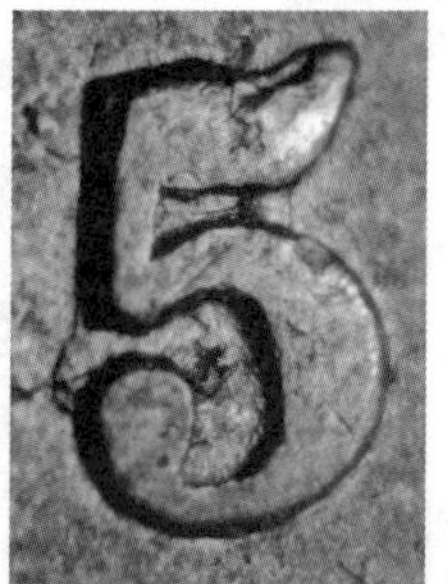

Description: A secondary 1 and 8 are evident to the northwest of the primary digits.

Comments: This variety was once believed to be an 1865/4 overdate. However, later research has proven that the image thought to be a 4 is actually an aberration to the date punch.

	VF-20	EF-40	AU-50	MS-60	MS-63	MS-65
VARIETY	$50	$75	$125	$175	$250	$625
NORMAL	$25	$41	$72	$80	$125	$500

Note: Values for MS-60 and MS-63 coins are for brown specimens; values for MS-65 coins are for red and brown specimens. Full red specimens command far greater premiums.

1865, Fancy 5 — FS-02-1865-1302 (002.7)

VARIETY: Repunched Date
PUP: Date
URS-9 · I-3 · L-3

LEONE: 65F-201R

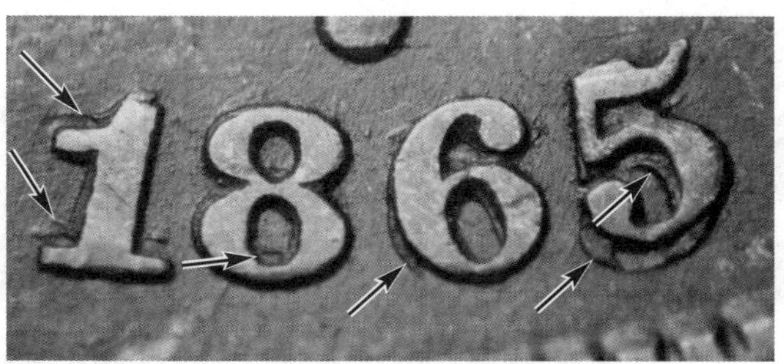

Description: A secondary 1 is evident slightly to the northwest of the primary 1, and a secondary 6 and 5 are evident to the southwest of the primary digits. Portions of a secondary 8 are evident within the lower loop of the primary 8.

Comments: A very similar variety exists, but the repunching is not quite as strong.

	VF-20	EF-40	AU-50	MS-60	MS-63	MS-65
VARIETY	$50	$75	$125	$175	$250	$625
NORMAL	$25	$41	$72	$80	$125	$500

Note: Values for MS-60 and MS-63 coins are for brown specimens; values for MS-65 coins are for red and brown specimens. Full red specimens command far greater premiums.

1865, Fancy 5 — FS-02-1865-1303 (002.8)

VARIETY: Repunched Date
PUP: Date
URS-9 · I-3 · L-3

 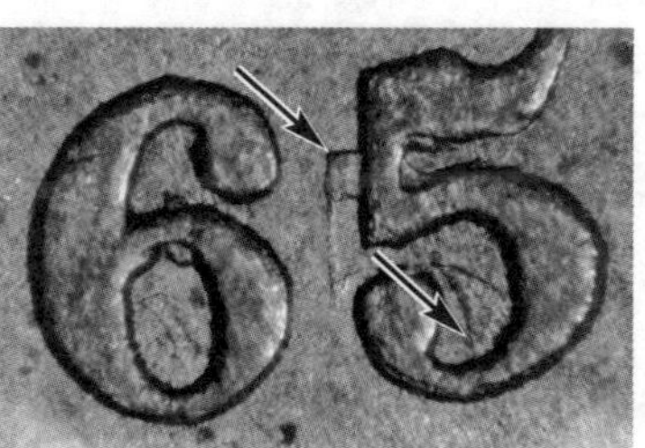

Description: This is one of the strongest repunched dates of the series, with a secondary 5 evident far to the southwest of the primary 5. A secondary 1 is visible slightly to the north of the primary 1.

Comments: A very similar variety exists, but the repunching is not quite as strong.

	VF-20	EF-40	AU-50	MS-60	MS-63	MS-65
VARIETY	$50	$75	$125	$175	$250	$625
NORMAL	$25	$41	$72	$80	$125	$500

Note: Values for MS-60 and MS-63 coins are for brown specimens; values for MS-65 coins are for red and brown specimens. Full red specimens command far greater premiums.

1865, Fancy 5 — FS-02-1865-1304 (002.9)

VARIETY: Misplaced Date
PUP: Denticles below date
URS-6 · I-3 · L-3

Description: The top of a digit, likely a 6, is evident in the denticles below and slightly to the right of the primary 8.

Comments: Strangely enough, there are relatively few MPDs known in this series. Certainly more exist.

	VF-20	EF-40	AU-50	MS-60	MS-63	MS-65
VARIETY	$35	$65	$110	$150	$200	$575
NORMAL	$25	$41	$72	$80	$125	$500

Note: Values for MS-60 and MS-63 coins are for brown specimens; values for MS-65 coins are for red and brown specimens. Full red specimens command far greater premiums.

1867 — FS-02-1867-101 (003)

VARIETY: Doubled-Die Obverse
PUP: IN GOD WE TRUST
URS-9 · I-4 · L-4

  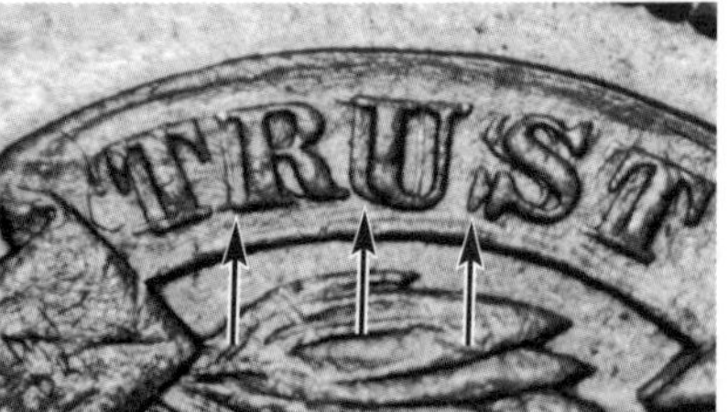

Description: This is by far the strongest doubled die known in the two-cent series. A secondary image is evident to the left of most of the primary devices.

Comments: This variety is somewhat common in low-end circulated grades, but is considered rare in Extremely Fine and About Uncirculated and very rare in Mint State.

	VF-20	EF-40	AU-50	MS-60	MS-63	MS-65
VARIETY	$75	$150	$225	$300	$450	$750
NORMAL	$44	$55	$90	$120	$170	$520

Note: Values for MS-60 and MS-63 coins are for brown specimens; values for MS-65 coins are for red and brown specimens. Full red specimens command far greater premiums.

1868 — FS-02-1868-301 (003.5)

VARIETY: Misplaced Date
PUP: Denticles below date
URS-8 · I-3 · L-3

Description: The top of a digit, most likely a 6, is evident protruding from the denticles below the primary 6.

Comments: This is another of the few known MPDs in the two-cent series.

	VF-20	EF-40	AU-50	MS-60	MS-63	MS-65
VARIETY	$75	$100	$150	$200	$295	$700
NORMAL	$46	$60	$100	$130	$190	$550

Note: Values for MS-60 and MS-63 coins are for brown specimens; values for MS-65 coins are for red and brown specimens. Full red specimens command far greater premiums.

1868 — FS-02-1868-302

VARIETY: Possible Overdate
PUP: 8 of date
URS-1 · I-3 · L-3

Description: There is a diagonal bar evident at the lower-right side of the upper loop and the upper left side of the lower loop of the last 8. This diagonal bar matches the relative position of a 7.

Comments: The authors would like to be able to examine and study additional high-grade examples of this variety.

	VF-20	EF-40	AU-50	MS-60	MS-63	MS-65
VARIETY	N/A	N/A	N/A	N/A	N/A	N/A
NORMAL	$46	$60	$100	$130	$190	$550

Note: It would be impossible to place any value on this variety at this time, given the lack of a definitive attribution.

1869 — FS-02-1869-101 (004.2)

VARIETY: Doubled-Die Obverse
PUP: IN GOD
URS-7 · I-3 · L-3

Description: A secondary image is evident below and slightly right of IN GOD in the motto. The doubling is also evident on the leaves.

Comments: This DDO is known on both circulation-strike and Proof coins. Actual sales include an MS-63 for $950, and a PF-63 for $1,500. This variety was discovered by Bob Grellman around 1991.

	VF-20	EF-40	AU-50	MS-60	MS-63	MS-65
VARIETY	$200	$300	$450	$600	$900	$1,750
NORMAL	$48	$72	$120	$160	$190	$585

Note: Values for MS-60 and MS-63 coins are for brown specimens; values for MS-65 coins are for red and brown specimens. Full red specimens command far greater premiums.

1869 — FS-02-1869-301 (003.9)

VARIETY: Repunched Date + Misplaced Date
PUP: Denticles below date
URS-6 · I-3 · L-3

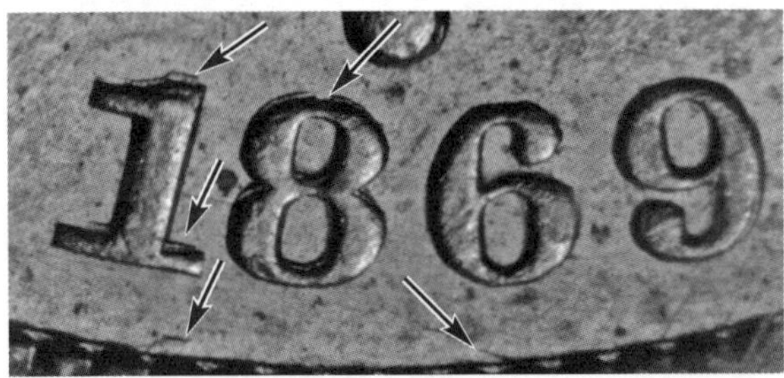

Description: The repunching is evident with a secondary 1 to the north of the primary 1. The top of a digit is protruding from the denticles below the 1.

Comments: There is a die scratch below the 6 of the date, once thought to possibly be portions of another digit.

	VF-20	EF-40	AU-50	MS-60	MS-63	MS-65
VARIETY	$75	$125	$195	$225	$350	$850
NORMAL	$48	$72	$120	$160	$190	$585

Note: Values for MS-60 and MS-63 coins are for brown specimens; values for MS-65 coins are for red and brown specimens. Full red specimens command far greater premiums.

1869 — FS-02-1869-302 (004)

Variety: Repunched Date
PUP: Date
URS-10 · I-3 · L-3

Description: A secondary 1 and 8 are evident to the north of the primary digits. There is also an image of a D to the left and slightly overlapping the G of GOD.

Comments: This variety was once considered to be an overdate, but further research has proven that wrong. Later die states exhibit a die crack through the bottom of the date.

	VF-20	EF-40	AU-50	MS-60	MS-63	MS-65
Variety	$75	$125	$195	$225	$350	$850
Normal	$48	$72	$120	$160	$190	$585

Note: Values for MS-60 and MS-63 coins are for brown specimens; values for MS-65 coins are for red and brown specimens. Full red specimens command far greater premiums.

1870 — FS-02-1870-101 (004.3)

Variety: Doubled-Die Obverse **Leone: 70B-101R**
PUP: TRUST
URS-17 · I-2 · L-2

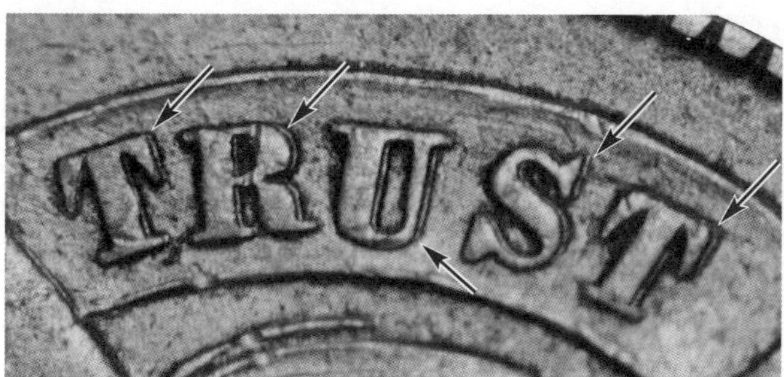

Description: Moderate doubling is evident on IN GOD WE TRUST, and there is slight doubling on the ribbon.

Comments: This variety was first reported in 1990.

	VF-20	EF-40	AU-50	MS-60	MS-63	MS-65
Variety	$125	$195	$250	$350	$450	$1,000
Normal	$80	$125	$180	$250	$310	$770

Note: Values for MS-60 and MS-63 coins are for brown specimens; values for MS-65 coins are for red and brown specimens. Full red specimens command far greater premiums.

1871 — FS-02-1871-101 (005)

VARIETY: Doubled-Die Obverse
LEONE: 71N-101R
PUP: IN GOD WE TRUST
URS-6 · I-3 · L-3

Description: Very strong doubling is evident on IN GOD WE TRUST, the ribbon, the leaves, the shield, and the arrows.

Comments: This same die was used to strike all Proof coins for the date. The Proof die is listed next. However, this doubled die on a circulation-strike coin is very rare and should command a hefty premium.

	VF-20	EF-40	AU-50	MS-60	MS-63	MS-65
VARIETY	$150	$250	$350	$450	$600	$1,100
NORMAL	$105	$145	$210	$275	$365	$670

Note: Values for MS-60 and MS-63 coins are for brown specimens; values for MS-65 coins are for red and brown specimens. Full red specimens command far greater premiums.

1871 Proof — FS-02-1871-102 (005)

VARIETY: Doubled-Die Obverse
LEONE: 71N-101R
PUP: IN GOD WE TRUST
URS-16 · I-3 · L-3

Description: Very strong doubling is evident on IN GOD WE TRUST, the ribbon, the leaves, the shield, and the arrows.

Comments: All 1871 Proof two-cent pieces exhibit this doubled die, therefore it commands no premium. This is the same die as used for the previous listing. Note that Proof coins usually have sharp, squared rims.

	PF-60Br	PF-63Br	PF-63RB	PF-63RD	PF-65BR	PF-65RB	PF-65RD
VARIETY	$275	$385	$410	$540	$715	$1,100	$2,500
NORMAL	$275	$385	$410	$540	$715	$1,100	$2,500

Note: Values are as indicated.

1872   FS-02-1872-101 (006)

VARIETY: Doubled-Die Obverse
PUP: TRUST
URS-7 · I-3 · L-3

LEONE: 72-101R

Description: The doubling is visible on the upper portion of the coin, with the spread growing stronger from left to right. It is most evident on TRUST.

Comments: As this is a very scarce date, remember the Fivaz axiom: "As the normal value of a coin increases, any premium one might expect for a variety on that coin will decrease." However, this doubled die is scarce in relation to the total 1872 population.

	VF-20	EF-40	AU-50	MS-60	MS-63	MS-65
VARIETY	$750	$950	$1,100	$1,600	$2,100	$4,250
NORMAL	$700	$880	$1,025	$1,510	$1,980	$4,070

Note: Values for MS-60 and MS-63 coins are for brown specimens; values for MS-65 coins are for red and brown specimens. Full red specimens command far greater premiums.

The Cherrypickers' Guide HELPFUL HINTS

Check the coins already in your collection. In many cases, collectors will find a variety they had no idea they had. In some cases, these unfound varieties can be quite valuable. This first happened to J.T. Stanton back in 1982, and it can happen to you!

Silver Three-Cent Pieces, "Trimes," 1851–1873

The three-cent sections are the least populated in the entire *Cherrypickers' Guide;* trimes were not included until the fourth edition, in 2000. We certainly hope there will be population growth in the near future.

Die clashes are widely known, more so for this series than any other. Die clashes are more likely on small coins than large ones, which made the tiny silver three-cent piece a prime target. A coin with clash marks will rarely bring a significant premium, if any at all.

1851   FS-3S-1851-301 (001)

VARIETY: Repunched Date   **BREEN-2902**
PUP: Date
URS-9 · I-2 · L-2

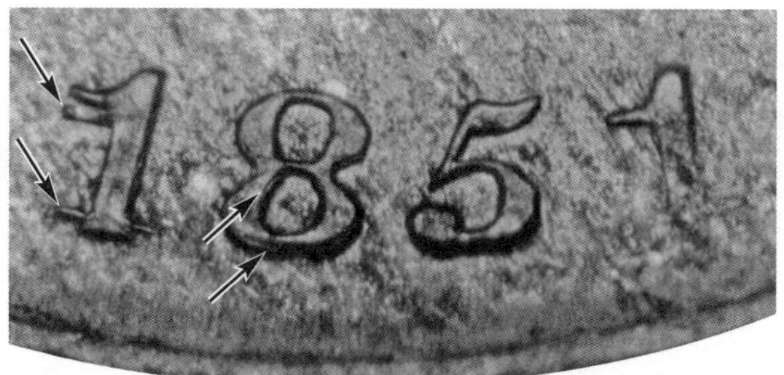

Description: For the first 1 and 8 only, secondary digits are evident to the south of the primary digits.

Comments: The secondary digits on this listing might not be visible on lower-grade specimens.

	VF-20	EF-40	AU-50	MS-60	MS-63	MS-65
VARIETY	$65	$75	$195	$240	$350	$1,000
NORMAL	$46	$57	$145	$165	$245	$920

1851   FS-3S-1851-302 (001.5)

VARIETY: Repunched Date   **BREEN: N/L**
PUP: Date
URS-7 · I-2 · L-2

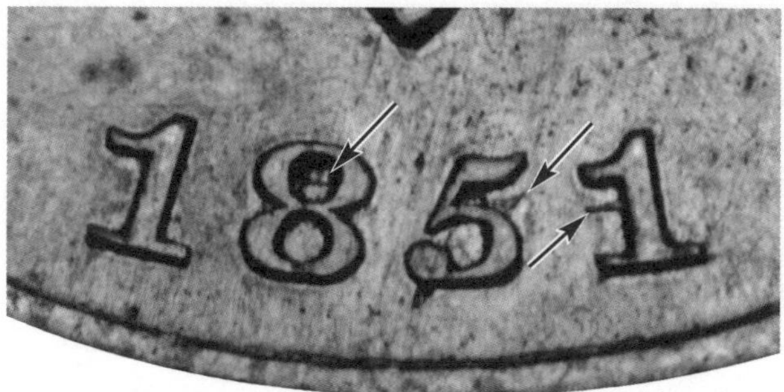

Description: Secondary digits are evident to the south of the primary digits on the 8, 5, and last 1.

Comments: This is a fairly strong RPD for this series.

	VF-20	EF-40	AU-50	MS-60	MS-63	MS-65
VARIETY	$75	$95	$225	$275	$375	$1,100
NORMAL	$46	$57	$145	$165	$245	$920

1852 — FS-3S-1852-301 (002)

VARIETY: Repunched Date
PUP: First 1 of date
URS-4 · I-4 · L-4

BREEN: N/L

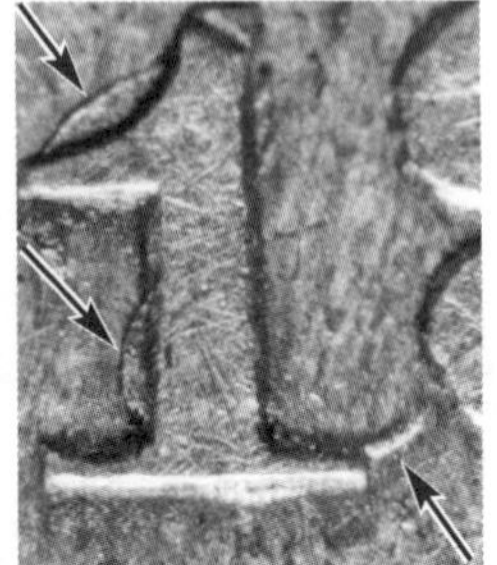

Description: An inverted 2 is evident underneath the primary 1. A secondary date punch was obviously punched into the die in an inverted orientation and then corrected after some effacing of the die.

Comments: Dan Brady discovered this variety in the mid-1990s.

	VF-20	EF-40	AU-50	MS-60	MS-63	MS-65
VARIETY	$600	$750	$900	$1,100	$1,350	$1,750
NORMAL	$46	$57	$145	$165	$245	$920

1852 — FS-3S-1852-302 (002.3)

VARIETY: Repunched Date
PUP: 5 and 2 of date
URS-4 · I-3 · L-3

BREEN: N/L

Description: Secondary digits are evident to the east of the primary digits on the 5 and 2.

Comments: To date very few examples of this RPD have been reported.

	VF-20	EF-40	AU-50	MS-60	MS-63	MS-65
VARIETY	$75	$95	$200	$300	$400	$1,050
NORMAL	$46	$57	$145	$165	$245	$920

1852 — FS-3S-1852-801 (002.5)

VARIETY: Doubled-Die Reverse
PUP: Reverse stars
URS-5 · I-3 · L-3

BREEN: N/L

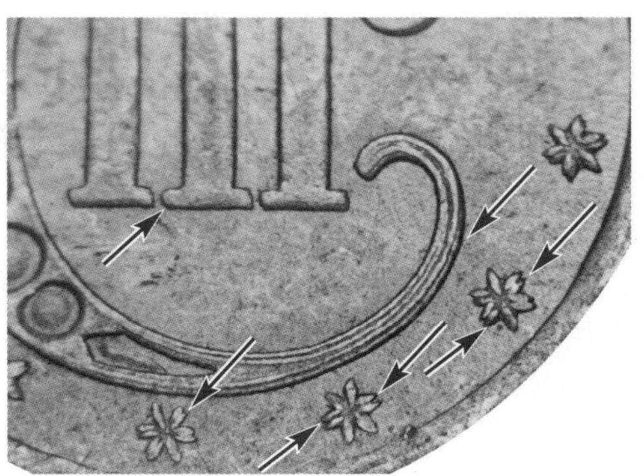

Description: Doubling is evident on the lower-right quadrant, especially the stars. Lesser doubling is also apparent on other reverse elements.

Comments: This is the only doubled die we have listed in the silver three-cent piece series.

	VF-20	EF-40	AU-50	MS-60	MS-63	MS-65
VARIETY	$75	$100	$225	$275	$400	$1,100
NORMAL	$46	$57	$145	$165	$245	$920

1853 — FS-3S-1853-301 (003)

VARIETY: Repunched Date
PUP: Date
URS-6 · I-2 · L-2

BREEN-2915

Description: Secondary digits are evident to the north of the primary 1 and 8.

Comments: This RPD can be detected on lower-grade specimens.

	VF-20	EF-40	AU-50	MS-60	MS-63	MS-65
VARIETY	$75	$95	$195	$250	$275	$1,000
NORMAL	$46	$57	$145	$165	$245	$920

1854 — FS-3S-1854-301 (004)

VARIETY: Repunched Date **BREEN-2917**
PUP: Date
URS-6 · I-3 · L-3

Description: Secondary digits are evident to the west of the primary digits on the 8 and 5.

Comments: This RPD is one of the most evident in the entire silver three-cent piece series.

	VF-20	EF-40	AU-50	MS-60	MS-63	MS-65
VARIETY	$95	$175	$300	$450	$750	$3,500
NORMAL	$46	$105	$200	$315	$600	$3,200

1862 — FS-3S-1862-301 (007)

VARIETY: Overdate **BREEN-2940**
PUP: Date
URS-10 · I-4 · L-4

 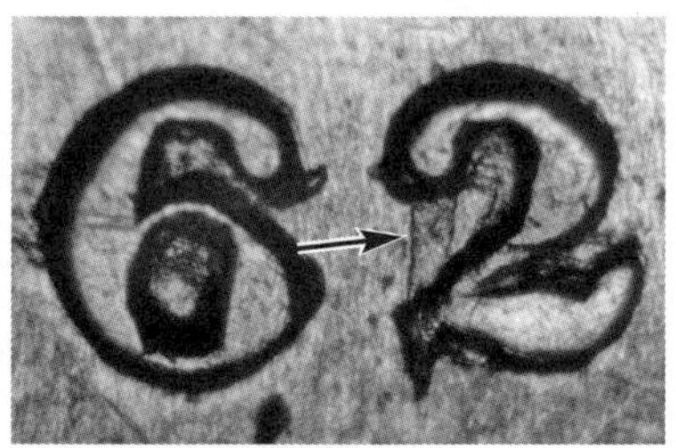

Description: There is a secondary 1 clearly visible beneath the 2 of the date.

Comments: This variety is well known and was originally discovered by John Cobb in 1963. The overdate is believed to be due more to economy (the Mint having used a good die another year) than to error. Circulated examples are about as common as the regular-dated coin.

	VF-20	EF-40	AU-50	MS-60	MS-63	MS-65
VARIETY	$60	$85	$175	$210	$365	$1,070
NORMAL	$60	$85	$175	$210	$250	$970

Nickel Three-Cent Pieces, 1865–1889

Any reference work of the magnitude of the *Cherrypickers' Guide* can be accomplished only with the help of outside sources—sources with detailed knowledge of the subject at hand. This section would not have been as complete or up-to-date without the selfless help and advice of Gary Rosner and Ed Fletcher. A big, hearty thanks to Ed and Gary for their contributions.

The nickel three-cent series is one of those few that have struggled for collectors over the years—at least when compared to most others. Yet the series is showing greater signs of popularity among collectors of "regular" coins and especially among those of us who enjoy the varieties.

As far as varieties go, the series contains many very nice repunched dates, misplaced dates, doubled-die obverses, doubled-die reverses, and even a nice overdate! Some of the misplaced dates are really dramatic, especially one with a 1 protruding from Miss Liberty's neck. Like many other series, some of the rarest varieties do not necessarily present the most eye appeal. Yet a couple of those varieties with super eye appeal are somewhat easy to find.

For those who have a greater interest in the varieties in the series, there are two fact-filled sources for more information. The first is a book by Kevin Flynn and Edward Fletcher entitled *The Authoritative Reference on Three Cent Nickels*. The book contains more than 150 pages filled with text and more than a hundred excellent photos.

The second excellent source is online—www.3centnickel.com. Gary Rosner has developed a terrific online source of information that can't be found anywhere else. Additionally, with the flexibility of Web-based information, the data is updated frequently, and new discoveries are published lightning-fast. You can be sure to read of new reference materials on Rosner's Web site. Pay him a visit and mention you heard of the site from the *Cherrypickers' Guide*.

1865 — FS-3N-1865-101 (003.5)

VARIETY: Doubled-Die Obverse — **FF: DDO-001**
PUP: AMERICA
URS-5 · I-3 · L-3

Description: Secondary letters are evident to the left of the primary letters on AMERICA. Slight doubling is also visible on the hair and some of the other letters.

Comments: Many specimens exhibit an unusual obverse die crack across the bust and curls to the rim at 4:30. This has proven to be a very elusive variety.

	VF-20	EF-40	AU-50	MS-60	MS-63	MS-65
VARIETY	$50	$75	$125	$175	$250	$750
NORMAL	$22	$36	$57	$95	$140	$620

1865 — FS-3N-1865-102

VARIETY: Doubled-Die Obverse — **FF: DDO-002**
PUP: UNITED STATES
URS-3 · I-3 · L-3

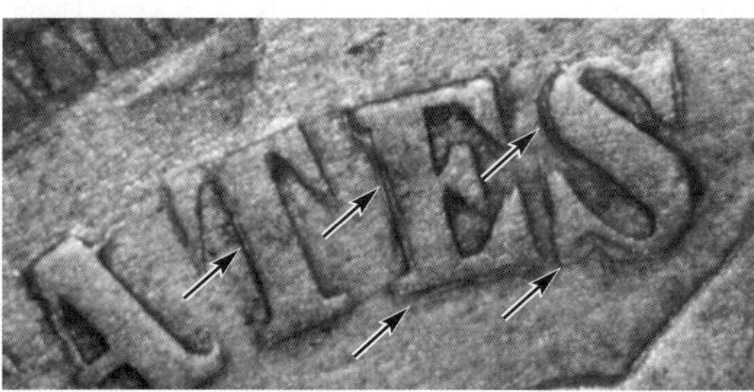

Description: Nice doubling is evident on UNITED STATES, LIBERTY, the nostril, the eyelid, and the front edge of the coronet.

Comments: There is a strong obverse cud at 2:00 and a triangular die gouge in the field below the denticles, above the T of UNITED (which is evident in the photo). This variety is easy to spot as soon as you see the retained cud on the rim.

	VF-20	EF-40	AU-50	MS-60	MS-63	MS-65
VARIETY	$50	$75	$125	$175	$250	$750
NORMAL	$22	$36	$57	$95	$140	$620

1865 — FS-3N-1865-301 (001)

VARIETY: Misplaced Date — **FF: MPD-001**
PUP: Denticles below date
URS-7 · I-3 · L-3

Description: The top flag of a 5 is evident protruding from the denticles below and between the 6 and 5 of the date.

Comments: This variety usually exhibits a slightly rotated reverse. It was discovered by Tom Miller.

	VF-20	EF-40	AU-50	MS-60	MS-63	MS-65
VARIETY	$35	$50	$75	$150	$225	$725
NORMAL	$22	$36	$57	$95	$140	$620

1865 — FS-3N-1865-302 (001.5)

VARIETY: Repunched Date — **FF: RPD-002**
PUP: Date
URS-5 · I-3 · L-3

Description: Secondary digits are evident to the west of the primary digits on all four numbers.

Comments: Numerous heavy die cracks were on the specimens examined by the authors, indicating the die may have been short-lived. There is a similar repunched date on a Proof die, which may in fact have been used for a few circulation strikes.

	VF-20	EF-40	AU-50	MS-60	MS-63	MS-65
VARIETY	$50	$75	$125	$175	$250	$750
NORMAL	$22	$36	$57	$95	$140	$620

1865 — FS-3N-1865-303 (002)

VARIETY: Misplaced Date **FF: MPD-002**
PUP: Denticles below date
URS-7 · I-2 · L-2

Description: The top of what is believed to be a secondary 5 is visible within the denticles below the 6.

Comments: There are other 1865 dies with similar misplaced dates. This variety has proven to be one of the most difficult of all nickel three-cent varieties to locate! It was first reported to us in early 1989.

	VF-20	EF-40	AU-50	MS-60	MS-63	MS-65
VARIETY	$50	$75	$125	$175	$250	$750
NORMAL	$22	$36	$57	$95	$140	$620

1865 — FS-3N-1865-304 (002.5, 003)

VARIETY: Repunched Date **FF: RPD-003**
PUP: Date
URS-7 · I-3 · L-3

Description: Secondary digits of all four numbers are evident to the south of the primary digits.

Comments: This variety was incorrectly listed twice in the fourth edition. FS-003 was a very early die state, and FS-002.5 was a very late die state, which explains how the mistake occurred. There are two known reverse dies paired with this obverse. Strong clash marks are evident on mid- and late-die-state coins; this likely explains the change of reverse dies. Specimens are also known with a retained cud on the reverse at 11:00.

	VF-20	EF-40	AU-50	MS-60	MS-63	MS-65
VARIETY	$50	$75	$125	$175	$250	$750
NORMAL	$22	$36	$57	$95	$140	$620

1865   FS-3N-1865-305

VARIETY: Repunched Date   **FF: RPD-006**
PUP: Date
URS-3 · I-3 · L-3

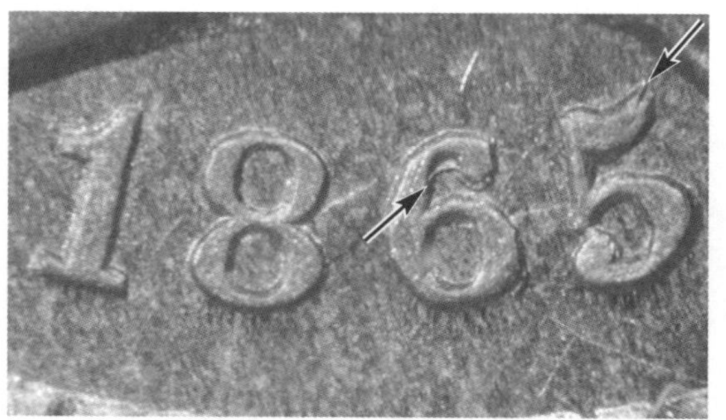

Description: Repunching is visible on the 6 to the south and the 5 to the north due to a date initially punched in a position rotated counterclockwise to the final date punch.

Comments: All known examples have a rotated reverse, approximately 190° clockwise.

	VF-20	EF-40	AU-50	MS-60	MS-63	MS-65
VARIETY	$50	$75	$125	$175	$250	$750
NORMAL	$22	$36	$57	$95	$140	$620

1866   FS-3N-1866-101 (004)

VARIETY: Doubled-Die Obverse   **FF: DDO-001**
PUP: AMERICA
URS-5 · I-3 · L-3

Description: Moderate doubling is evident on AMERICA and on portions of the hair.

Comments: The dies clashed midway through the obverse's life. Mid- and late-die-state coins exhibit the clash marks and die cracks as progression occurs. This variety has proven extremely scarce.

	VF-20	EF-40	AU-50	MS-60	MS-63	MS-65
VARIETY	$100	$150	$250	$350	$450	$900
NORMAL	$22	$36	$57	$95	$140	$620

1866 — FS-3N-1866-301

VARIETY: Repunched Date
PUP: Date
URS-3 · I-3 · L-3

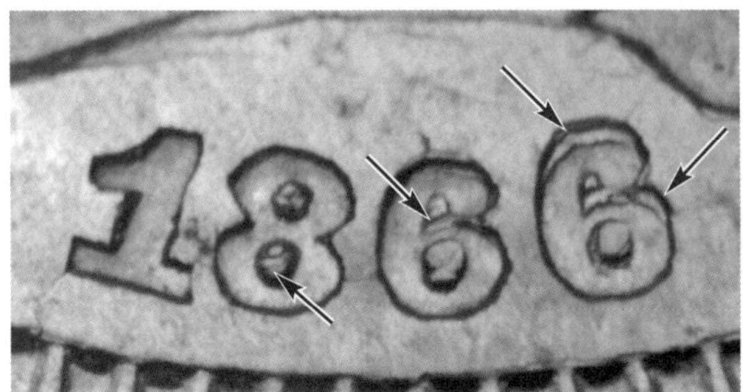

Description: Secondary digits are evident on the last three digits, strongest on the final 6. Slight repunching is visible on the 1.

Comments: This variety is a new listing and a fairly new discovery.

	VF-20	EF-40	AU-50	MS-60	MS-63	MS-65
VARIETY	$50	$75	$125	$175	$250	$750
NORMAL	$22	$36	$57	$95	$140	$620

1869 — FS-3N-1869-301 (004.3)

FF: RPD-002

VARIETY: Repunched Date
PUP: Date
URS-4 · I-3 · L-3

Description: A secondary 1 and 8 are evident to the north of the primary numbers.

Comments: This RPD is scarcer than the other RPDs for the date.

	VF-20	EF-40	AU-50	MS-60	MS-63	MS-65
VARIETY	$50	$75	$95	$150	$225	$850
NORMAL	$23	$36	$57	$105	$155	$700

1869 — FS-3N-1869-302 (004.5)

VARIETY: Repunched Date
PUP: Date
URS-9 · I-3 · L-3

FF: RPD-001

Description: Secondary digits are evident to the south of all four primary digits of the date.

Comments: Although stronger than the previous listing, and certainly holding more eye appeal, this variety has a slightly higher known population at this time. The obverse die is known paired with three reverse dies.

	VF-20	EF-40	AU-50	MS-60	MS-63	MS-65
VARIETY	$50	$75	$95	$150	$225	$850
NORMAL	$23	$36	$57	$105	$155	$700

1869 — FS-3N-1869-801 (004.7)

VARIETY: Doubled-Die Reverse
PUP: Ribbon
URS-9 · I-2 · L-2

FF: DDR-001

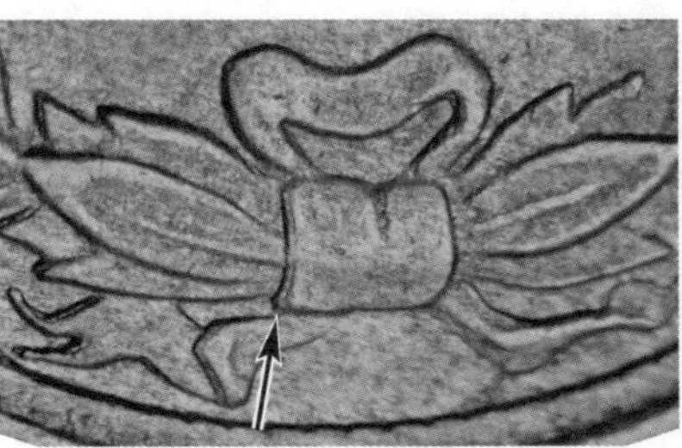
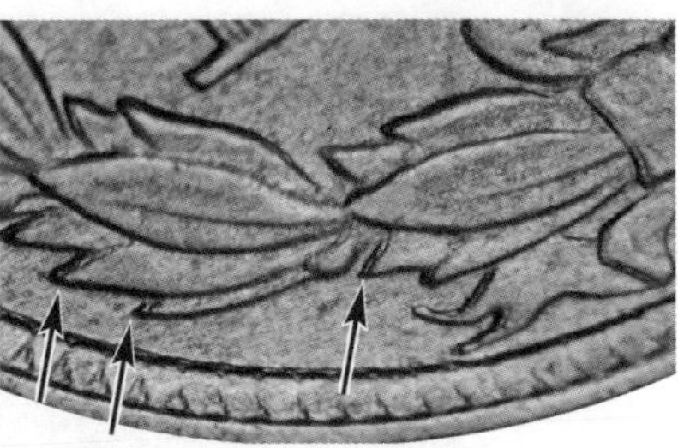

Description: The doubling is most evident in the lower-left quadrant of the reverse, especially on the ribbon bow.

Comments: This reverse die is known paired with two different obverse dies. This is not a very strong doubled die, but it is certainly worth the search.

	VF-20	EF-40	AU-50	MS-60	MS-63	MS-65
VARIETY	$45	$65	$95	$150	$200	$775
NORMAL	$23	$36	$57	$105	$155	$700

1870 — FS-3N-1870-101 (005)

VARIETY: Repunched Date + Doubled-Die Obverse   **FF: RPD-001, DDO-001**
PUP: Date
URS-6 · I-3 · L-3

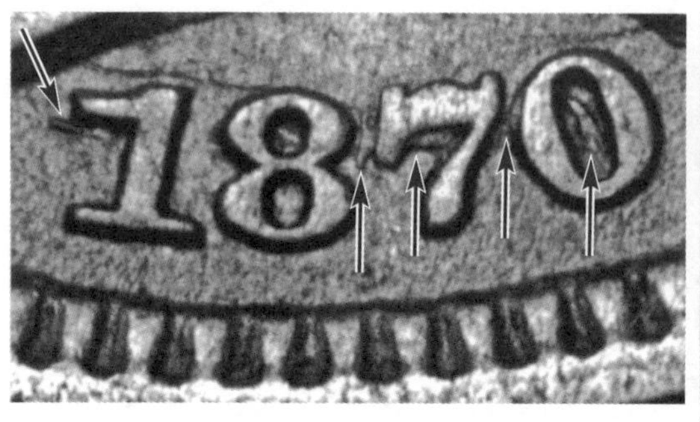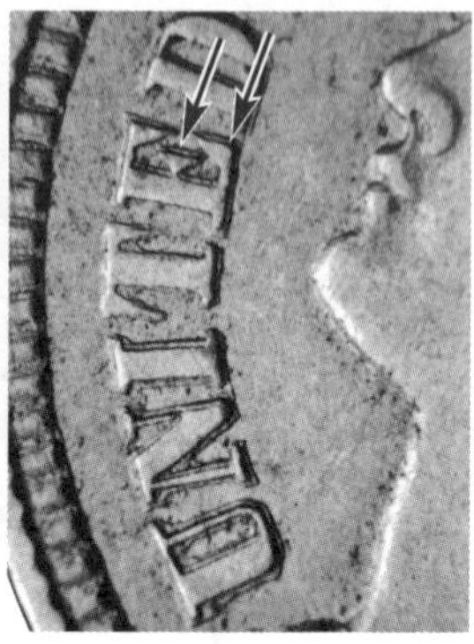

Description: Secondary digits are evident to the west of all four primary numbers.

Comments: This is also a minor doubled obverse die, with doubling most noticeable on the second E of STATES. However, the RPD is very strong and is the reason for the premium on this variety.

	VF-20	EF-40	AU-50	MS-60	MS-63	MS-65
VARIETY	$50	$75	$95	$150	$225	$850
NORMAL	$25	$36	$58	$120	$175	$700

1870 — FS-3N-1870-301 (005.5)

VARIETY: Misplaced Date   **FF: MPD-001**
PUP: Denticles below date
URS-4 · I-3 · L-3

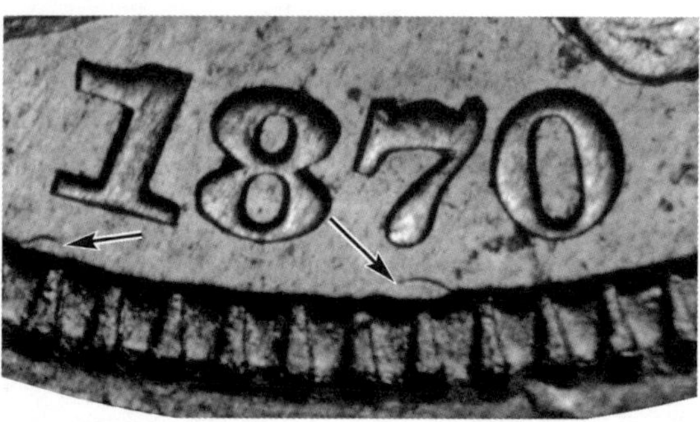

Description: The tops of two digits, supposedly a 1 and 0, are evident protruding from the denticles below the date.

Comments: A noted specialists feels that this is the third toughest variety in the series to locate.

	VF-20	EF-40	AU-50	MS-60	MS-63	MS-65
VARIETY	$65	$95	$125	$175	$300	$950
NORMAL	$25	$36	$58	$120	$175	$700

1870

FS-3N-1870-302 (005.6)

VARIETY: Misplaced Date + Doubled-Die Reverse
PUP: Denticles below date
URS-8 · I-3 · L-3

FF: MPD-002

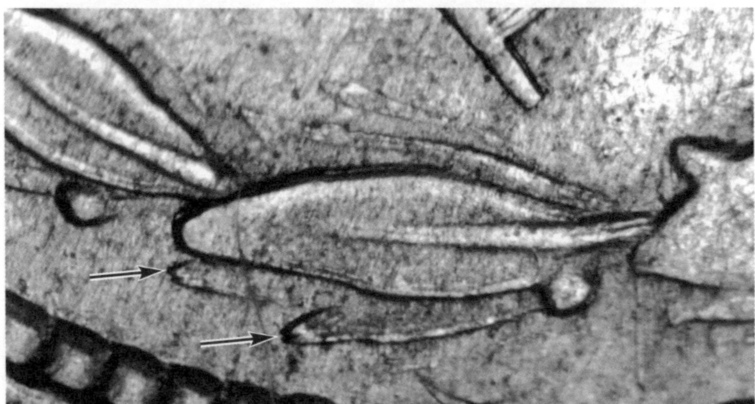

Description: Portions of several digits are evident in the denticles below the date. Minor doubling is evident on the reverse as split veins and leaf tips, mostly in the lower-left quadrant.

Comments: All the premium value in this variety comes from the misplaced date, not for the noted DDR. In fact, the MPD die was paired with at least two reverses, only one of which is the doubled die. This variety is much more common than the previous listings for the date.

	VF-20	EF-40	AU-50	MS-60	MS-63	MS-65
VARIETY	$45	$65	$95	$150	$225	$795
NORMAL	$25	$36	$58	$120	$175	$700

1871 — FS-3N-1871-101 (006)

VARIETY: Tripled-Die Obverse   **FF: TDO-001**
PUP: AMERICA
URS-7 · I-3 · L-3

Description: A tripled image is very evident on the letters of UNITED STATES OF AMERICA, with light doubling evident on LIBERTY.

Comments: The highly visible tripled die makes this variety very impressive, though not quite as impressive as FS-3N-1866-101. Additionally, the variety is relatively easy to locate in circulated grades, yet tough in Mint State.

	VF-20	EF-40	AU-50	MS-60	MS-63	MS-65
VARIETY	$45	$65	$95	$175	$225	$850
NORMAL	$27	$37	$60	$130	$185	$715

1873, Close 3 — FS-3N-1873-301

VARIETY: Repunched Date   **FF: RPD-001**
PUP: Date
URS-3 · I-3 · L-3

Description: A secondary 1 is evident to the south of the serif of the primary 1. A secondary 8 is also evident, inside the opening of the upper loop of the 8.

Comments: This is a new listing. The repunched serif of the 1 is very strong, making this almost a naked-eye variety—if you can find one. So far they have been very elusive.

	VF-20	EF-40	AU-50	MS-60	MS-63	MS-65
VARIETY	$45	$65	$100	$200	$300	$1,750
NORMAL	$29	$42	$65	$140	$200	$1,400

1875   FS-3N-1875-301 (006.5)

VARIETY: Misplaced Date   **FF: MPD-001**
PUP: Front of neck
URS-12 · I-3 · L-3

Description: The flag or base of a 1 is evident protruding from the front of Miss Liberty's neck.

Comments: This is likely the most readily available variety in the entire series. This being a very impressive MPD is the only reason it will command any premium.

	VF-20	EF-40	AU-50	MS-60	MS-63	MS-65
VARIETY	$40	$55	$95	$195	$225	$800
NORMAL	$30	$43	$80	$170	$200	$745

1881   FS-3N-1881-301 (006.8)

VARIETY: Repunched Date   **FF: RPD-005**
PUP: Date
URS-10 · I-2 · L-2

Description: This is an impressive RPD, a secondary 1 boldly evident between the final numerals of the date, 8 and 1. The top of an 8 is visible between the top of the two 8s, and the top of another 8 shows inside the upper loop of the second 8.

Comments: There are several obverse die chips and cracks in various progressions, suggesting Mint personnel stretched the die's life further than normal. This variety has proven to be relatively easy to locate.

	VF-20	EF-40	AU-50	MS-60	MS-63	MS-65
VARIETY	$35	$55	$85	$140	$200	$700
NORMAL	$22	$32	$50	$100	$150	$575

1887 — FS-3N-1887-301 (007)

VARIETY: Overdate
FF: OVD-001
PUP: Date
URS-5 · I-4 · L-4

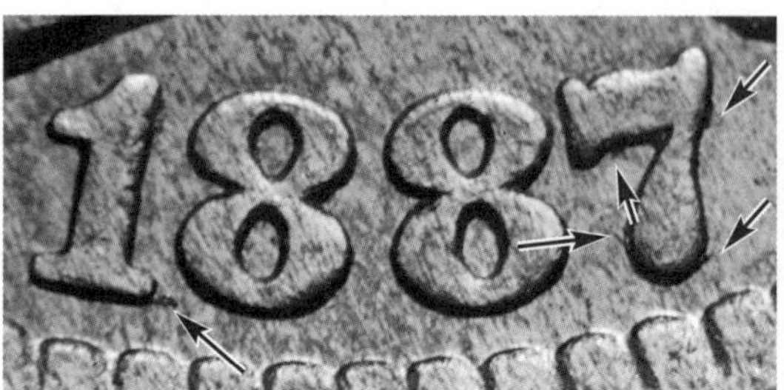 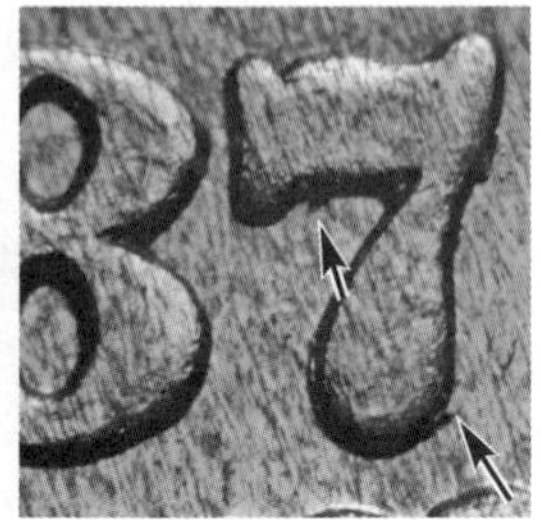

Description: The 1887 date was punched over a previously punched 1886 date. Faint remnants of the underlying 6 are evident on both lower sides of the 7. Secondary images are evident to the east of the primary 1 and both 8s.

Comments: Remember the Fivaz axiom: "As the value for a regular coin goes up, any premium one might expect for its variety will go down." This being an expensive "regular" coin, the percentage of premium for the variety is unimpressive.

	VF-20	EF-40	AU-50	MS-60	MS-63	MS-65
VARIETY	$425	$465	$500	$550	$600	$1,350
NORMAL	$380	$400	$435	$475	$550	$1,185

1887 Proof — FS-3N-1887-302

VARIETY: Overdate
FF: OVD-002
PUP: Date
URS-7 · I-2 · L-2

 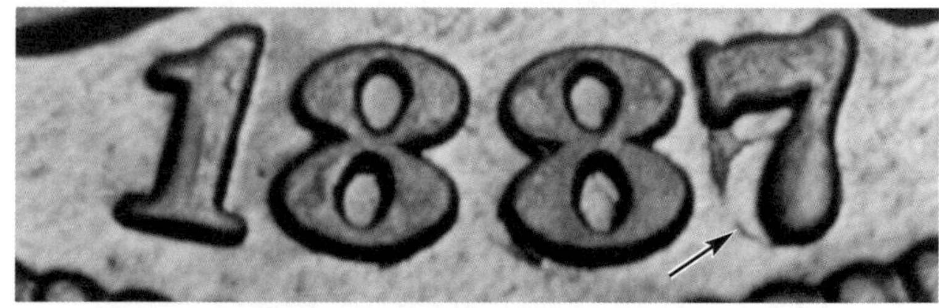

Description: This variety is similar to the previous listing, but on a Proof coin. The 1887 date was punched over a previously punched 1886 date. Strong remnants of the underlying 6 are visible on either side of the lower portion of the 7, with the 1 and both 8s clearly repunched.

Comments: According to all dealer price guides, the prices for PF-65 coins are the reverse of what one might expect. The non-overdate Proof coin is actually valued higher than the overdate Proof coin in PF-65. The Proof overdate is relatively common. Compare this listing with the preceding.

	PF-60	PF-63	PF-64	PF-65
VARIETY	$475	$550	$600	$910
NORMAL	$365	$400	$470	$975

1888

FS-3N-1888-301

VARIETY: Misplaced Date

PUP: Denticles below date

URS-3 · I-3 · L-3

FF: MPD-001

 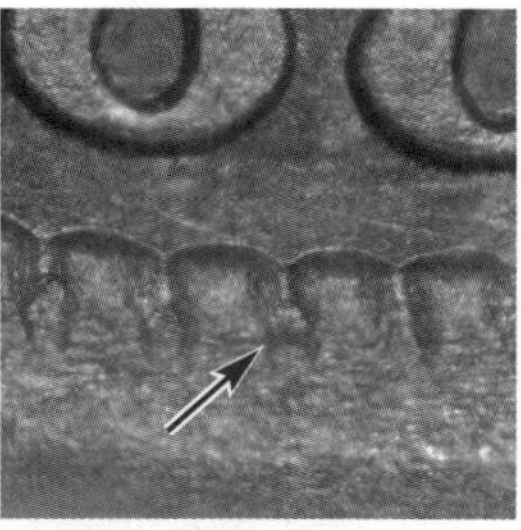

Description: The top of an 8 is evident protruding from the denticles below and between the first two 8s. Minor repunching of the last 8 is visible inside the upper loop.

Comments: This variety was discovered by Dick Osburn and reported by Gary Rosner. After the 1875 misplaced date, there are no reported misplaced dates in the series until this 1888. Then there is also a Proof 1889 with a misplaced date, which also has a repunched 1 to the south.

	VF-20	EF-40	AU-50	MS-60	MS-63	MS-65
VARIETY	$100	$125	$200	$350	$450	$750
NORMAL	$73	$90	$150	$275	$340	$645

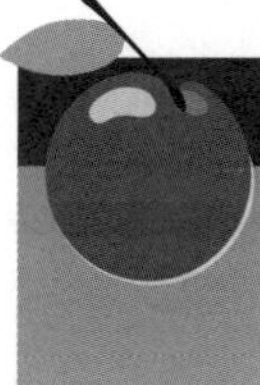

THE CHERRYPICKERS' GUIDE HELPFUL HINTS

Always check coins produced between 1941 and 1945. Many of the dramatic varieties from the 20th century were produced during WWII, when the U.S. government was trying to conserve metals, energy, and time. There are still significant discoveries to be made.

DAVE'S

The Collector's Friend®

SINCE 1983

When you're looking for rare varieties or regular issue key date buffalos, I am the guy to see.

I am proud to have handled some of the finest collections.

If you need help please call.

DAVE'S
DCW COLLECTION

P.O. BOX 500850
SAN DIEGO, CA 92150
FAX: 858-513-6557

VISA,
MASTERCARD

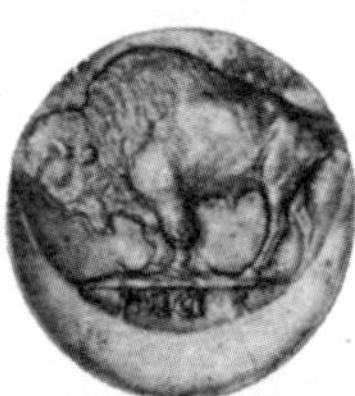

ANA L.M.
FUN, CONECA
HOBO SOCIETY
FLY-IN CLUB

www.thecollectorsfriend.com

800-346-6718

Shield Nickels, 1866–1883

Year for year, there are more varieties known in the Shield nickel series than in any other. In fact, with well over 100 listings, this is one of the largest sections in the *Cherrypickers' Guide.*

We have a theory as to why so many varieties are known in the Shield nickel series. The first circulating coin struck by the U.S. Mint in the very hard alloy of 75% copper and 25% nickel was the three-cent piece, which began production in 1865. The Shield design of the nickel five-cent piece, which is significantly larger, began production just a year later, in 1866.

The Mint was faced with a growing demand for minor coinage as commerce increased following the Civil War. Fractional silver coins (among others) had been hoarded. The nickel five-cent piece was a very useful denomination and demand for it quickly increased. The Mint was faced with production of a coin made of an alloy with which it had very little experience.

The dies used to make the new nickel five-cent coins deteriorated much faster than Mint personnel had anticipated, due in part to the hardness of the metal. Dies cracked, chipped, and broke faster than Mint personnel could make new ones. Quality control suffered. Dies were hubbed with different or misaligned hubs, creating dramatic doubled dies. Dates were punched with less care, resulting in hundreds of repunched dates, overdates, and misplaced dates. According to numismatic researcher R.W. Julian, many blanks were not properly annealed before striking, further adding to the stresses the dies received. Many dies continued to be used after slight damage, as new dies were in short supply. Die cracks were abundant, creating many varieties in themselves that are eagerly sought by collectors today.

There are literally hundreds upon hundreds of listed varieties in the Shield nickel series, and no doubt more will appear in future reference works.

We suggest you look not only at the date of these coins, but also at the annulet (circle) under the cross, to check for doubled dies. And be sure to examine the lettering on the obverse and reverse, and the stars on the reverse, for possible doubled dies.

An excellent reference for this series is the *Guide Book of Shield and Liberty Head Nickels,* by Q. David Bowers. Additionally, Ed Fletcher studies the series in detail, listing all known varieties in his wonderful book simply entitled *The Shield Five Cent Nickel.* His is by far the best book available for detailed study of the series. Howard Spindel, an avid collector and researcher, has developed an online club devoted to Shield nickels, at groups.yahoo.com/group/Shield_Nickels/. Spindel also has a great Web site devoted to the series, shieldnickels.net The information available on his Web site is invaluable.

SHIELD NICKEL MISSING LEAF VARIETIES

This section was contributed by Edward Fletcher.

When the master hub was produced for the Obverse Hub A, the outer leaf for the second right cluster was not engraved in the die. This missing leaf had to be hand engraved into each and every working die. This accounts for the many different shapes and sizes for the leaf in question. A handful of these dies passed through without the missing leaf being engraved into their surface. On these dies, the leaves on the right side of the shield are in clusters of 3/3/4/3 instead of the normal 3/4/4/3 clusters. They have been found on coins of 1866; 1867, Without Rays; 1868; and 1869, Wide Date. They are considered very rare.

Fewer than five of any Missing Leaf dies have been reported. Missing Leaf varieties that also have a repunched date or doubled-die obverse will command a higher premium.

Date	Number of dies known	With RPD	With DDO
1866	3	1	—
1867, With Rays	0	—	—
1867, Without Rays	7	—	—
1868	14	4	1
1869, Narrow Date	0	—	—
1869, Wide Date*	5	—	—

* Not all Missing Leaf varieties for the 1869, Wide Date, are found with the Reverse Hub IIb. One has also been found with Reverse Hub IIc.

Normal leaf cluster.

Missing leaf.

REVERSE HUBS OF THE SHIELD NICKEL

This section was contributed by Edward Fletcher.

Shield nickel reverse designs can be identified by the position of the stars in relation to the letters of UNITED STATES OF AMERICA. Use the outer point of the star for the identification. The star positions are as follows:

Reverse Hub I, With Rays

Below the left foot of the A in STATES
Below the right foot of E(S) in STATES
Below the left of the upright of the F in OF
Below AM in AMERICA
Below the left foot of the R in AMERICA

Reverse Hub I has rays engraved between the stars, radiating out from the center of the design. Reverse Hub I is found on all 1866 and some 1867 Shield nickels.

Reverse Hub IIa, Without Rays

Below the left foot of the A in STATES
Below the right foot of E(S) in STATES
Below the left of the upright of the F in OF
Below AM in AMERICA
Below the left foot of the R in AMERICA

Reverse Hub IIa is almost identical to Reverse Hub I, except the rays have been removed from the die. The star below the F has a broken point at 10:00. This hub is found on all 1867, Without Rays; some 1868; all 1869, Narrow Digit; and some 1869, Wide Digit nickels.

Reverse Hub IIb

Below the A in STATES
Below the left serif of the second S in STATES
To the center of the F in OF
Below the right edge of the foot of the M in AMERICA
Below the right of the upright of the R in AMERICA

Reverse Hub IIb is found with both solid and broken letters. It is found on some 1868 nickels.

Reverse Hub IIc

Below the left base of the A in STATES
Below the right foot of E(S) in STATES
Below the left of the upright of the F in OF
Below the M in AMERICA
Below the right side of the upright of the R in AMERICA

The first S in STATES is doubled slightly along the left side. The denticles are doubled, with the first set seen in the spaces between the final set. Reverse Hub IIc is found with both solid and broken letters. It is found on some 1869 and all 1870–1883 nickels. (Some 1868-dated nickels are said to exist with this reverse hub, but this has not been confirmed.)

Reverse Hub I

Reverse Hub IIa

Reverse Hub IIb

Reverse Hub IIc

Reverse Hub I

Reverse Hub IIa

Reverse Hub IIb

Reverse Hub IIc

OBVERSE AND REVERSE HUB MARRIAGES

This chart was contributed by Edward Fletcher.

Date	Obverse Hub	Reverse Hub
1866	A	I
1867, With Rays	A	I
1867, Without Rays	A	IIa
1868*	A	IIa
	A	IIb
	A	IIc
1869, Narrow Digit	A	IIa
1869, Wide Digit	A	IIa
	A	IIc
	B	IIa
	B	IIc
1870	A	IIa
	B	IIa
	B	IIc
1871	B	IIc
1872	B	IIc
	C	IIc
1873–1883	C	IIc

* Some 1868-dated nickels are said to exist with the Reverse Hub IIc, but this has not been confirmed.

1866   FS-05-1866-101 (001.7)

VARIETY: Doubled-Die Obverse   **FLETCHER-22**
PUP: Annulet
URS-3 · I-4 · L-4

Description: Strong doubling is evident on the classic area of this series, which is the annulet. A strong spread toward the southwest is evident on the annulet, the cross, the leaves, the scrolls, and the vertical lines in the shield.

Comments: Joseph Ambrulevich reportedly discovered this variety about 1988. This obverse die is paired with a very minor reverse doubled die.

	F-12	VF-20	EF-40	AU-50	MS-60	MS-63	MS-65
VARIETY	$75	$125	$175	$225	$300	$500	$2,500
NORMAL	$44	$63	$125	$175	$225	$400	$2,075

1866   FS-05-1866-102 (001.5)

VARIETY: Doubled-Die Obverse   **FLETCHER-21**
PUP: IN GOD WE TRUST
URS-3 · I-4 · L-4

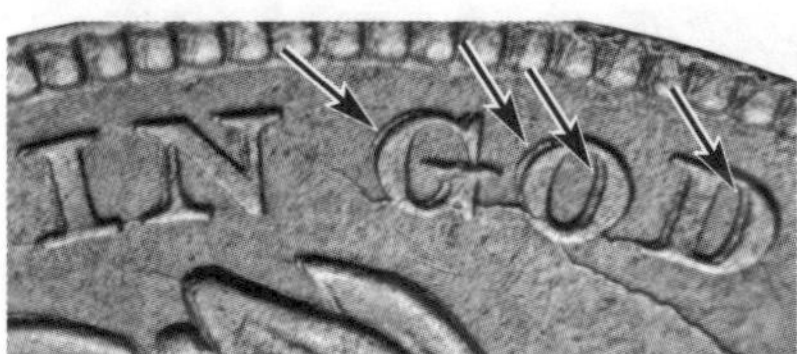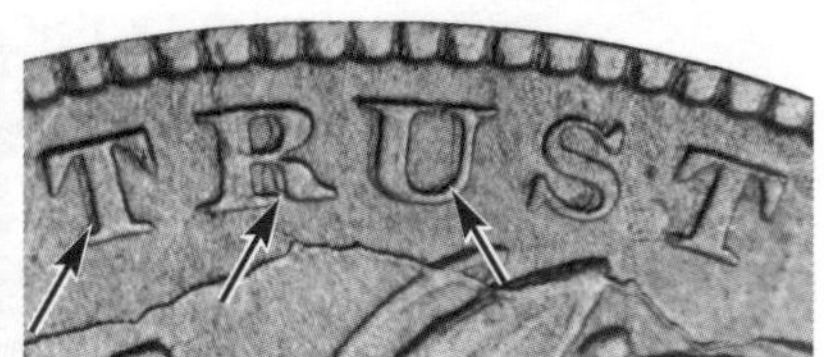

Description: Doubling is evident on all letters of IN GOD WE TRUST to the left of the primary image. There is also a repunched date to this variety. All four digits are repunched to the north.

Comments: This variety is unusual as it is one of very few Shield nickels that has a doubled obverse die with no doubling evident anywhere on the shield.

	F-12	VF-20	EF-40	AU-50	MS-60	MS-63	MS-65
VARIETY	$75	$125	$175	$225	$300	$500	$2,500
NORMAL	$44	$63	$125	$175	$225	$400	$2,075

1866 — FS-05-1866-301 (001)

VARIETY: Repunched Date
PUP: Date
URS-6 · I-4 · L-5

FLETCHER-08

Description: All four digits are repunched, with secondary images clearly visible east of the primary digits.

Comments: Varieties in low grades can easily be cherrypicked. There are at least four other similar, very strong repunched dates for this year.

	F-12	VF-20	EF-40	AU-50	MS-60	MS-63	MS-65
VARIETY	$75	$125	$175	$225	$300	$500	$2,500
NORMAL	$44	$63	$125	$175	$225	$400	$2,075

1866 — FS-05-1866-302 (001.1)

VARIETY: Repunched Date
PUP: Date
URS-4 · I-4 · L-5

FLETCHER-10

Description: All four digits are repunched, with secondary images clearly visible east of the primary digits.

Comments: Varieties in low grades can easily be picked. There are at least four other similar, very strong repunched dates for this year.

	F-12	VF-20	EF-40	AU-50	MS-60	MS-63	MS-65
VARIETY	$75	$125	$175	$225	$300	$500	$2,500
NORMAL	$44	$63	$125	$175	$225	$400	$2,075

1866 — FS-05-1866-303 (001.2)

VARIETY: Repunched Date
PUP: Date
URS-4 · I-4 · L-5

FLETCHER-20

Description: All four digits are repunched, with secondary images clearly visible east of the primary digits.

Comments: Varieties in low grades can easily be picked. There are at least four other similar, very strong repunched dates for this year.

	F-12	VF-20	EF-40	AU-50	MS-60	MS-63	MS-65
VARIETY	$75	$125	$175	$225	$300	$500	$2,500
NORMAL	$44	$63	$125	$175	$225	$400	$2,075

1866 — FS-05-1866-304 (001.3)

VARIETY: Repunched Date
PUP: Date
URS-4 · I-4 · L-4

FLETCHER-16

Description: All four digits are repunched, with secondary images clearly visible south of the primary digits.

Comments: Varieties in low grades can easily be picked. There are at least four other similar, very strong repunched dates for this year.

	F-12	VF-20	EF-40	AU-50	MS-60	MS-63	MS-65
VARIETY	$75	$125	$175	$225	$300	$500	$2,500
NORMAL	$44	$63	$125	$175	$225	$400	$2,075

1866 — FS-05-1866-305 (001.4)

VARIETY: Repunched Date
PUP: Date
URS-5 · I-3 · L-3

FLETCHER-13

Description: All four digits are repunched, with secondary images clearly visible north of the primary digits.

Comments: Varieties in low grades can easily be picked. There are at least four other similar, very strong repunched dates for this year.

	F-12	VF-20	EF-40	AU-50	MS-60	MS-63	MS-65
VARIETY	$75	$125	$175	$225	$300	$500	$2,500
NORMAL	$44	$63	$125	$175	$225	$400	$2,075

1866 — FS-05-1866-901

VARIETY: Clashed Reverse + Repunched Date
PUP: Reverse below 5, date
URS-6 · I-4 · L-4

FLETCHER-09A

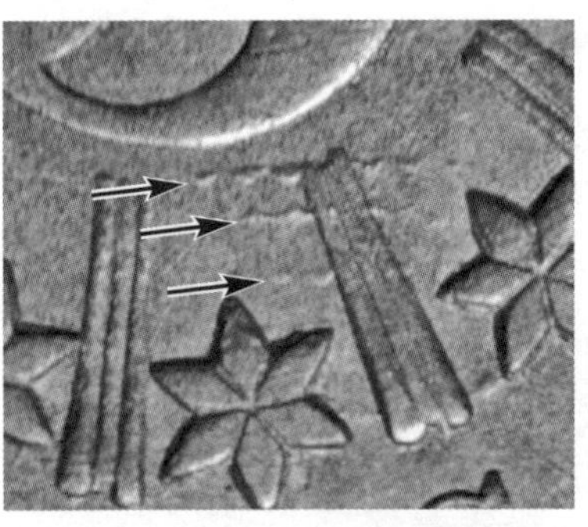 

Description: The reverse die was clashed with an unknown object, evident with three rows of images below and to the right of the 5. The date is also repunched, evident by the strong spread to the south on all four digits.

Comments: The value for this variety is primarily for the clashed die.

	F-12	VF-20	EF-40	AU-50	MS-60	MS-63	MS-65
VARIETY	$100	$150	$275	$350	$475	$750	$3,700
NORMAL	$47	$69	$160	$210	$325	$525	$3,175

1867, With Rays   FS-05-1867-301 (002.1)

VARIETY: Repunched Date   **FLETCHER-8**
PUP: Date
URS-4 · I-4 · L-4

Description: The primary date is punched over a larger date logotype, likely that of a dime or half dime. The top of a 1 is evident far to the west of the primary 1, and the top of a 7 is evident far to the east of the primary 7. Portions of the other secondary digits are visible within the primary digits.

Comments: To date, all six reported specimens of this variety have a reverse die rotated approximately 15° counterclockwise.

	F-12	VF-20	EF-40	AU-50	MS-60	MS-63	MS-65
VARIETY	$75	$125	$225	$300	$450	$750	$3,700
NORMAL	$47	$69	$160	$210	$325	$525	$3,175

1867, With Rays   FS-05-1867-302 (002.4)

VARIETY: Repunched Date + Doubled-Die Obverse   **FLETCHER-9**
PUP: Date, annulet
URS-4 · I-4 · L-4

Description: The repunched date is evident with a secondary 7 evident far to the east of the primary 7. Other digits of the secondary date are evident within the numbers of the primary date. The doubled die is evident with a doubled annulet, cross, leaves, and shield slightly to the southeast.

Comments: The value for this variety is primarily for the repunched date. However, this is the only doubled die listed by Fletcher for the 1867, With Rays type.

	F-12	VF-20	EF-40	AU-50	MS-60	MS-63	MS-65
VARIETY	$75	$125	$225	$300	$450	$750	$3,700
NORMAL	$47	$69	$160	$210	$325	$525	$3,175

1867, With Rays — FS-05-1867-303 (002.7)

VARIETY: Repunched Date
PUP: Date
URS-6 · I-3 · L-3

FLETCHER-2

Description: This repunched date exhibits a secondary 7 between the primary 6 and 7, and a secondary 6 between the primary 8 and 6.

Comments: Early and middle die states exhibit portions of a 1 to the left of the primary 1. This variety is known with a reverse rotated 155° counterclockwise.

	F-12	VF-20	EF-40	AU-50	MS-60	MS-63	MS-65
VARIETY	$75	$125	$225	$300	$450	$750	$3,700
NORMAL	$47	$69	$160	$210	$325	$525	$3,175

1867, With Rays — FS-05-1867-304 (002.6)

VARIETY: Misplaced Date (?)
PUP: Ball above date
URS-1 · I-4 · L-4

FLETCHER-01

Description: An image that appears to be the base of a misplaced 1 is evident protruding from the left side of the ball above the date.

Comments: To date, this still is a unique specimen. Hundreds of dedicated Shield nickel enthusiasts are looking for this variety.

	F-12	VF-20	EF-40	AU-50	MS-60	MS-63	MS-65
VARIETY	$75	$125	$225	$300	$450	$750	$3,700
NORMAL	$47	$69	$160	$210	$325	$525	$3,175

1867, With Rays — FS-05-1867-305 (002.75)

VARIETY: Misplaced Date
FLETCHER: N/L
PUP: Lower shield
URS-1 · I-4 · L-4

Description: The remnants of a 1 are evident errantly punched into the lower portion of the shield.

Comments: To date, this still is a unique specimen. Hundreds of dedicated Shield nickel enthusiasts are looking for this variety.

	F-12	VF-20	EF-40	AU-50	MS-60	MS-63	MS-65
VARIETY	$75	$125	$225	$300	$450	$750	$3,700
NORMAL	$47	$69	$160	$210	$325	$525	$3,175

1867, With Rays — FS-05-1867-901

VARIETY: Clashed Reverse
FLETCHER-11
PUP: Reverse at 12:00
URS-1 · I-4 · L-4

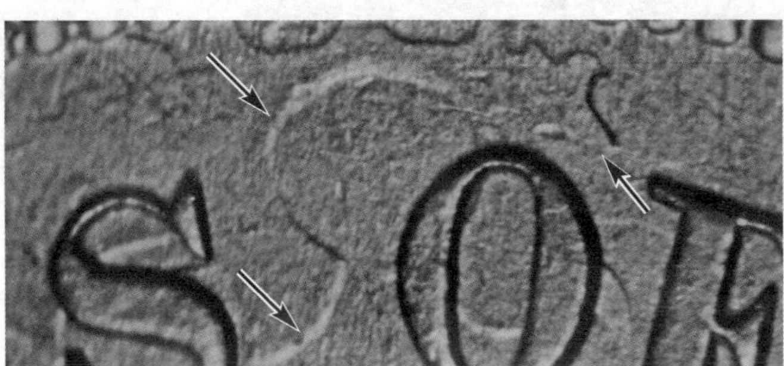

Description: The reverse die was clashed with an obverse die, evidenced by the image of the obverse ball at 12:00 on the reverse between the S of STATES and the O in OF.

Comments: Only one specimen has been reported.

	F-12	VF-20	EF-40	AU-50	MS-60	MS-63	MS-65
VARIETY	$100	$150	$275	$350	$475	$750	$3,700
NORMAL	$47	$69	$160	$210	$325	$525	$3,175

1867, No Rays — FS-05-1867-1101 (001.8)

VARIETY: Doubled-Die Obverse
FLETCHER-59
PUP: IN GOD WE TRUST
URS-2 · I-4 · L-4

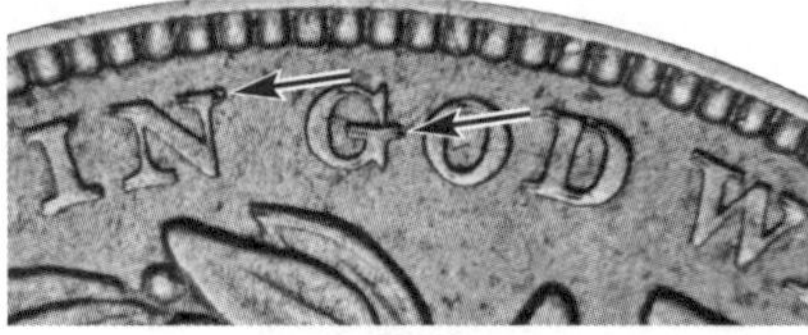

Description: Moderate doubling is evident on IN GOD WE TRUST, with the secondary image toward the center of the coin.

Comments: As of this writing, only a couple of specimens exist.

	F-12	VF-20	EF-40	AU-50	MS-60	MS-63	MS-65
VARIETY	$60	$75	$125	$195	$450	$250	$950
NORMAL	$25	$31	$52	$83	$120	$190	$745

1867, No Rays — FS-05-1867-1102 (002)

VARIETY: Doubled-Die Obverse + Repunched Date
FLETCHER-54
PUP: Annulet, date
URS-5 · I-4 · L-4

Description: Doubling is evident on the annulet, the cross, and the leaves; the horizontal lines are encroaching into the vertical lines. The date is strongly repunched, with secondary digits south of the primary digits on all four numbers.

Comments: This remains a highly sought-after variety.

	F-12	VF-20	EF-40	AU-50	MS-60	MS-63	MS-65
VARIETY	$85	$150	$250	$345	$500	$650	$1,200
NORMAL	$25	$31	$52	$83	$120	$190	$745

1867, No Rays — FS-05-1867-1301 (001.9)

Variety: Repunched Date

PUP: Date

URS-5 · I-4 · L-4

Fletcher-23

Description: All four digits of the date are repunched, with the secondary digits south of the primary date.

Comments: This is one of the more popular RPDs for this date.

	F-12	VF-20	EF-40	AU-50	MS-60	MS-63	MS-65
Variety	$95	$125	$195	$275	$300	$395	$950
Normal	$25	$31	$52	$83	$120	$190	$745

1867, No Rays — FS-05-1867-1302 (002.15)

Variety: Repunched Date

PUP: Date

URS-3 · I-3 · L-3

Fletcher-25

Description: All four digits of the date are repunched, with the secondary digits southeast of the primary date.

Comments: Late die states of this variety have a reverse cud.

	F-12	VF-20	EF-40	AU-50	MS-60	MS-63	MS-65
Variety	$95	$125	$195	$275	$300	$395	$950
Normal	$25	$31	$52	$83	$120	$190	$745

1867, No Rays   FS-05-1867-1303 (002.2)

VARIETY: Repunched Date   **FLETCHER-21**
PUP: Date
URS-4 · I-3 · L-3

Description: All four digits of the date are repunched, with the secondary digits to the southwest of the primary digits.

Comments: Ed Fletcher reports having examined three specimens, with all three having a die crack from the base of the 1 to the rim and a reverse rim cud at 4:30.

	F-12	VF-20	EF-40	AU-50	MS-60	MS-63	MS-65
VARIETY	$95	$125	$195	$275	$300	$395	$950
NORMAL	$25	$31	$52	$83	$120	$190	$745

1867, No Rays   FS-05-1867-1304 (002.25)

VARIETY: Repunched Date   **FLETCHER-20**
PUP: Date
URS-6 · I-3 · L-3

Description: This is a strong repunched date, with secondary digits evident to the west of the primary digits.

Comments: This variety is also rumored to have a 1 punched in the field above the primary 1, which we can't confirm at this time.

	F-12	VF-20	EF-40	AU-50	MS-60	MS-63	MS-65
VARIETY	$95	$125	$195	$275	$300	$395	$950
NORMAL	$25	$31	$52	$83	$120	$190	$745

1867, No Rays

FS-05-1867-1305 (002.3)

VARIETY: Repunched Date

FLETCHER-22

PUP: Date

URS-4 · I-3 · L-3

Description: A repunched date, with secondary digits (primarily the 6 and 7) evident far to the south of the primary digits.

Comments: This is another great RPD.

	F-12	VF-20	EF-40	AU-50	MS-60	MS-63	MS-65
VARIETY	$95	$125	$195	$275	$300	$395	$950
NORMAL	$25	$31	$52	$83	$120	$190	$745

1867, No Rays

FS-05-1867-1306 (002.35)

VARIETY: Repunched Date + Doubled-Die Obverse

FLETCHER-08.01

PUP: Date

URS-5 · I-3 · L-3

Description: The repunched date is evident with a secondary 1 and 8 to the north of the primary digits. The doubled die is evident on the annulet, cross, shield, and leaves, with the secondary image southeast of the primary images.

Comments: The value is primarily for the RPD.

	F-12	VF-20	EF-40	AU-50	MS-60	MS-63	MS-65
VARIETY	$95	$125	$195	$275	$300	$395	$950
NORMAL	$25	$31	$52	$83	$120	$190	$745

1867, No Rays — FS-05-1867-1307 (002.5)

VARIETY: Repunched Date
FLETCHER-38
PUP: Date
URS-3 · I-3 · L-3

Description: The date exhibits secondary digits south of the primary digits on the 6 and 7. (In the photo, the doubling on the 1 is the result of strike doubling.)

Comments: Notice the small die chip that connects the 8 to the ball.

	F-12	VF-20	EF-40	AU-50	MS-60	MS-63	MS-65
VARIETY	$95	$125	$195	$275	$300	$395	$950
NORMAL	$25	$31	$52	$83	$120	$190	$745

1867, No Rays — FS-05-1867-1308 (002.9)

VARIETY: Repunched Date
FLETCHER-46
PUP: Date
URS-3 · I-3 · L-3

Description: Secondary digits are evident south of the primary digits on the 6 and 7.

Comments: This is yet another very nice RPD for this date.

	F-12	VF-20	EF-40	AU-50	MS-60	MS-63	MS-65
VARIETY	$95	$125	$195	$275	$300	$395	$950
NORMAL	$25	$31	$52	$83	$120	$190	$745

1867, No Rays   FS-05-1867-1309 (002.45)

VARIETY: Misplaced Date   **FLETCHER-01.01**
PUP: Bottom of shield, date
URS-4 · I-3 · L-3

Description: The top of an apparent 8 is evident protruding within the "V" of the shield, just above the ball.

Comments: The line between the 8 and 6 is a die crack.

	F-12	VF-20	EF-40	AU-50	MS-60	MS-63	MS-65
VARIETY	$95	$125	$195	$275	$300	$395	$950
NORMAL	$25	$31	$52	$83	$120	$190	$745

1867, No Rays   FS-05-1867-1401

VARIETY: Obverse Clash   **FLETCHER-69**
PUP: Center of shield
URS-1 · I-4 · L-4

Description: An unusual, unexplained, and unidentified die clash is evident through the vertical lines of the shield, curving from upper right to lower left.

Comments: To the best of our knowledge, this is the only example reported to date.

	F-12	VF-20	EF-40	AU-50	MS-60	MS-63	MS-65
VARIETY	$95	$125	$195	$275	$300	$395	$950
NORMAL	$25	$31	$52	$83	$120	$190	$745

IDENTIFYING THE VARIETIES OF SHIELD NICKEL REVERSE DIES OF 1868

This section was contributed by Dennis Paulsen.

There are four known reverse hubs (types) used for the Shield nickel. These are identified in detail in Ed Fletcher's book, *The Shield Five Cent Series.* However, there are five varieties for just one of these hubs, the reverse of 1868. It is the varieties from this type that are most interesting. (The term *type* generally refers to an intentional change in the design, while the term *variety* generally refers to an accidental change.)

The reverse hubs (types) of the Shield nickel are as follows:

With Rays

Reverse Hub I (all 1866 and some 1867 coins)

Without Rays

Reverse Hub IIa ("Reverse of 1867," some 1867, 1868, and 1869 coins)

Reverse Hub IIb ("Reverse of 1868," only on a very small percentage of 1868)

Reverse Hub IIc (some 1869 and all 1870–1883 coins)

The five varieties, plus a transitional sub-variety, of the reverses of the 1868 Shield nickels are distinguished by a certain number of broken letters.

To identify the "Reverse of 1868" varieties, simply look at the star at 12:00. If the star points to the E of STATES, it is the more common "Reverse of 1867." If it points to the S, it is the "Reverse of 1868."

Reverse varieties of 1868 are as follows:

Variety 1—one broken letter (the C in CENTS); FS-05-1868-901 (002.94)

Variety 2—two broken letters (the C and the S in CENTS); FS-05-1868-902 (002.95)

Variety 3—three broken letters (the C and the S in CENTS; the first S in STATES); FS-05-1868-903 (002.96)

Variety 4—four broken letters (the C and the S in CENTS; the first S in STATES; the D in UNITED); FS-05-1868-904 (002.97)

Variety 5—no broken letters; FS-05-1868-905 (002.98)

Variety 5.5—a broken portion of the C in CENTS; FS-05-1868-906 (002.99)

Variety 1 (FS-05-1867-901)
Identified by the broken lower serif of the C in CENTS.

Variety 2 (FS-05-1867-902)
Identified by the broken C in CENTS (previously illustrated), and the broken lower loop of the S in CENTS.

Variety 3 (FS-05-1867-903)
Identified by the broken C and S in CENTS (previously illustrated), and a broken upper loop of the S in STATES.

Variety 4 (FS-05-1867-904)
Identified by the broken C and S in CENTS, the broken S in STATES (previously illustrated), and a broken upper curve in the D in UNITED.

Variety 5 (FS-05-1867-905)
No broken letters.

Variety 5.5 (FS-05-1867-906)

This is a transition between Variety 5 and Variety 1. The top portion of the lower serif of the C in CENTS is only partially broken, indicated by a weak up-stroke of the lower serif of the C. This C is sometimes found with slight vestiges of the broken portions (3:00 to 5:00 of the C). Bill Fivaz was the first to locate this transitional variety, and he refers to this as the "step-tail."

The rarest of the 1868 reverse varieties is FS-05-1868-905, "No Broken Letters." Examples are rarely encountered. They are the result of only one or two working reverse dies. FS-05-1868-901 and FS-05-1868-902, with one or two broken letters, are the most common, and represent almost 80 percent of all reverses of 1868.

Several years of study and examination of thousands of 1868 Shield nickels suggest that only about 10 percent of the 1868 Shield nickel population has the reverse type of 1868. Mint records indicate that 28,817,000 of the 1868 Shield nickel were struck. No one knows for sure the percentage minted with the reverse of 1868, but research indicates it to be 2,900,000. This chart shows estimates of value and rarity of the different varieties of the 1868 reverse. Rarity is estimated as that of FS-05-1868-906, and value similar to that of FS-05-1868-903.

	F-12	EF-40	AU-50	MS-60	Estimated Mintage	Percent of Total
FS-901	$20	$35	$75	$110	1,392,000	48%
FS-902	30	50	100	160	870,000	30%
FS-903	200	300	375	475	87,000	3%
FS-904	55	85	170	225	464,000	16%
FS-905	375	475	600	700	29,000	1%
FS-906	200	300	375	475	58,000	2%

Total Estimated Mintage: 2,900,000

1868

FS-05-1868-101 (003)

VARIETY: Doubled-Die Obverse

FLETCHER-42

PUP: Annulet

URS-10 · I-4 · L-4

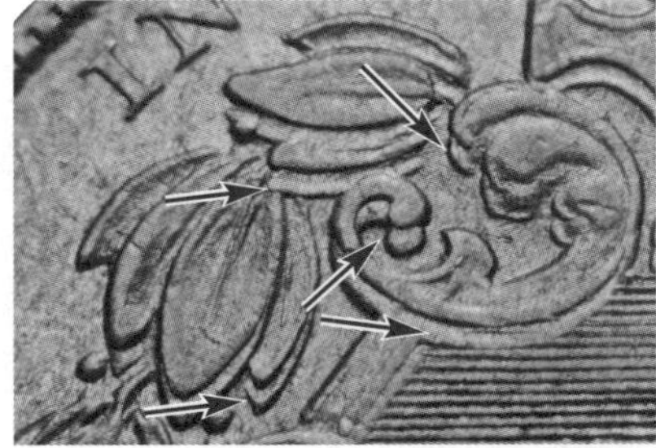 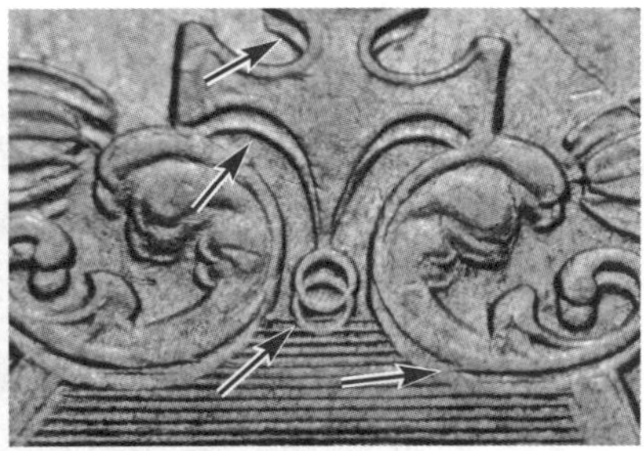

Description: Very strong doubling is evident on the upper portion of the design, including the annulet, the cross, the leaves, and the horizontal lines that "bleed" into the vertical lines.

Comments: This is the Reverse of 1867, hub IIa.

	F-12	VF-20	EF-40	AU-50	MS-60	MS-63	MS-65
VARIETY	$75	$125	$175	$250	$300	$450	$1,000
NORMAL	$25	$31	$52	$83	$120	$180	$780

THE CHERRYPICKERS' GUIDE **HELPFUL HINTS**

If you can't discern a variety with a 7x loupe, it probably isn't significant.

1868   FS-05-1868-102 (003.65)

VARIETY: Tripled-Die Obverse   **FLETCHER-111**
PUP: Annulet
URS-3 · I-4 · L-4

Description: Strong tripling is evident to the southwest and to the north on the annulet, cross, leaves, etc. A tripled die on the Shield nickel series is not typical.

Comments: This is the Reverse of 1868, hub IIb. This variety was first reported to us in January 2000 by Howard Spindel. Ken Hill reports having two specimens. This was first discovered by Terry Searcy.

	F-12	VF-20	EF-40	AU-50	MS-60	MS-63	MS-65
VARIETY	$75	$125	$175	$250	$300	$450	$1,000
NORMAL	$25	$31	$52	$83	$120	$180	$780

1868 — FS-05-1868-103 (003.8)

VARIETY: Doubled-Die Obverse — **FLETCHER-40**
PUP: Annulet
URS-3 · I-4 · L-4

Description: Strong doubling is evident on the upper portion of the design, including the annulet, the shield, the leaves, the berries, and the cross.

Comments: This is the Reverse of 1867, hub IIa.

	F-12	VF-20	EF-40	AU-50	MS-60	MS-63	MS-65
VARIETY	$75	$125	$175	$250	$300	$450	$1,000
NORMAL	$25	$31	$52	$83	$120	$180	$780

1868 — FS-05-1868-104 (003.9)

VARIETY: Doubled-Die Obverse — **FLETCHER-34**
PUP: Annulet
URS-10 · I-4 · L-4

Description: The doubling is evident slightly to the south of the primary image, most noticeably on the annulet, cross, and upper leaves.

Comments: This is the Reverse of 1867, hub IIa. The date on this variety is punched high and slanted slightly to the right, with the first 8 touching the ball.

	F-12	VF-20	EF-40	AU-50	MS-60	MS-63	MS-65
VARIETY	$75	$125	$175	$250	$300	$450	$1,000
NORMAL	$25	$31	$52	$83	$120	$180	$780

1868 — FS-05-1868-105 (003.95)

VARIETY: Doubled-Die Obverse & Reverse **FLETCHER-45**
PUP: IN GOD WE TRUST
URS-3 · I-4 · L-4

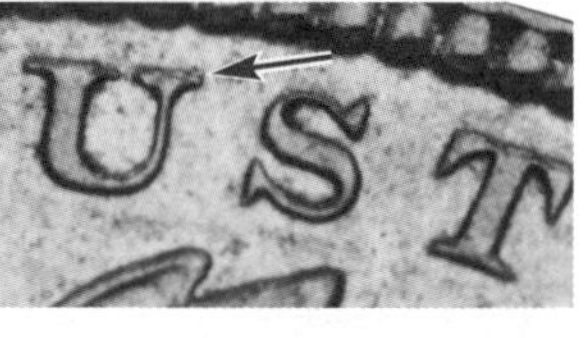

Description: On the obverse, moderate doubling is visible on IN GOD WE TRUST. On the reverse, slightly stronger doubling is visible on UNITED STATES OF AMERICA, CENTS, and some of the stars.

Comments: This is the Reverse of 1867, hub IIa. This variety continues to be very elusive and in high demand by Shield nickel variety collectors.

	F-12	VF-20	EF-40	AU-50	MS-60	MS-63	MS-65
VARIETY	$75	$125	$175	$250	$300	$450	$1,000
NORMAL	$25	$31	$52	$83	$120	$180	$780

1868 — FS-05-1868-106 (003.96)

VARIETY: Doubled-Die Obverse **FLETCHER-107.01**
PUP: Annulet
URS-3 · I-2 · L-2

Description: Moderate doubling is evident to the southwest on the cross, annulet, and leaves, and on the horizontal lines and lower border of the shield.

Comments: This is the Reverse of 1868, hub IIb. The date nearly touches the ball of the shield.

	F-12	VF-20	EF-40	AU-50	MS-60	MS-63	MS-65
VARIETY	$75	$125	$175	$250	$300	$450	$1,000
NORMAL	$25	$31	$52	$83	$120	$180	$780

1868

FS-05-1868-107 (003.97)

VARIETY: Doubled-Die Obverse + Repunched Date

FLETCHER-43

PUP: Date, annulet

URS-2 · I-3 · L-3

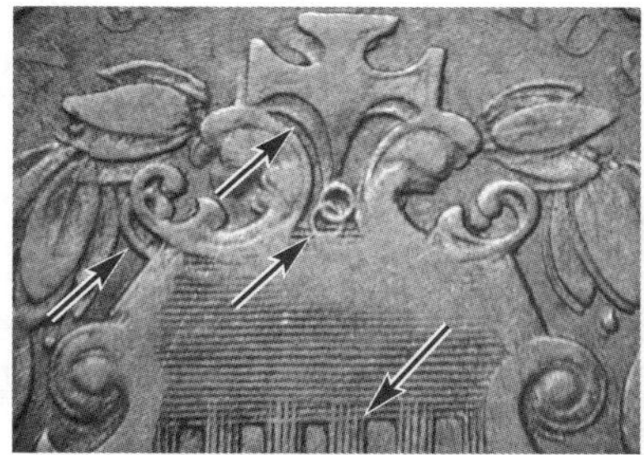 

Description: Very strong doubling is evident on the annulet, cross, and leaves, and on the horizontal lines and lower border of the shield. The 1 of the date is repunched north, and tilted slightly clockwise.

Comments: This is the Reverse of 1867, hub IIa. The date is very high, with the 8 touching the ball. There is a clear die crack running from the 6 through the top of the second 8 and on to the denticles. The "engraved" leaf is almost completely separated from the adjacent leaf.

	F-12	VF-20	EF-40	AU-50	MS-60	MS-63	MS-65
VARIETY	$75	$125	$175	$250	$300	$450	$1,000
NORMAL	$25	$31	$52	$83	$120	$180	$780

1868

FS-05-1868-109

VARIETY: Doubled-Die Obverse + Repunched Date

PUP: Annulet

URS-2 · I-4 · L-4

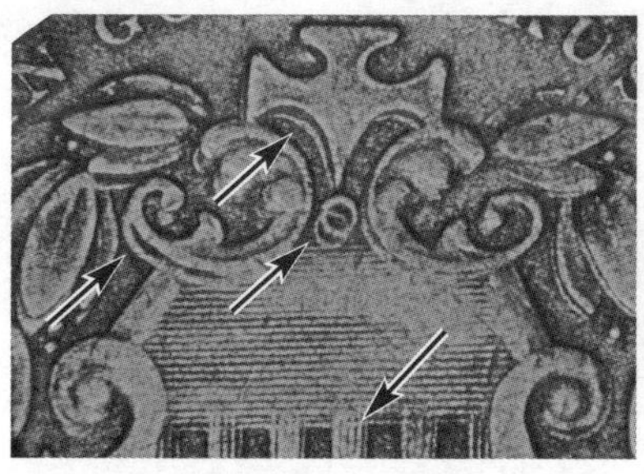 

Description: Doubling is evident by a strong secondary image to the southwest of the primary image, most noticeable on the annulet, cross, shield, and leaves. The RPD is visible by a secondary 1 closely north of the primary 1, evident mostly at the base.

Comments: This is the Reverse of 1868, hub IIb.

	F-12	VF-20	EF-40	AU-50	MS-60	MS-63	MS-65
VARIETY	$75	$125	$175	$250	$300	$450	$1,000
NORMAL	$25	$31	$52	$83	$120	$180	$780

1868 — FS-05-1868-110

VARIETY: Doubled-Die Obverse **FLETCHER-107**
PUP: Annulet
URS-2 · I-4 · L-4

Description: Doubling is evident by a strong secondary image to the southwest of the primary image on the annulet, cross, shield, and most leaves. The date nearly touches ball.

Comments: This is the Reverse of 1867, hub IIb.

	F-12	VF-20	EF-40	AU-50	MS-60	MS-63	MS-65
VARIETY	$75	$125	$175	$250	$300	$450	$1,000
NORMAL	$25	$31	$52	$83	$120	$180	$780

THE CHERRYPICKERS' GUIDE HELPFUL HINTS

Strike doubling can often be confused with the more valuable die doubling, such as a doubled die or repunched mintmark. To help ensure you know the difference, take time to read, read, and re-read appendix A.

1868   FS-05-1868-301 (003.2)

VARIETY: Repunched Date   **FLETCHER-19**
PUP: Date
URS-6 · I-3 · L-3

Description: This variety exhibits at least three date punches. Both secondary dates are evident starting north on the 1 and slanting downward from left to right. Secondary 6s and 8s (from the last 8) are evident south of the primary digits.

Comments: This is the Reverse of 1868, hub IIa.

	F-12	VF-20	EF-40	AU-50	MS-60	MS-63	MS-65
VARIETY	$75	$125	$175	$250	$300	$450	$1,000
NORMAL	$25	$31	$52	$83	$120	$180	$780

1868   FS-05-1868-302 (003.3)

VARIETY: Repunched Date   **FLETCHER-106.01**
PUP: Date
URS-6 · I-3 · L-3

Description: The initial date punch left the primary 86 touching the ball of the shield. The subsequent date punch aligned the 1s of both, but like the previous listing, the last 3 digits are south, with a progressively stronger spread going from left to right.

Comments: This is the Reverse of 1868, hub IIb. A die crack is evident on most specimens running from the rim west of the date, through the lower portion of the numbers, then downward to the rim southeast of the final 8.

	F-12	VF-20	EF-40	AU-50	MS-60	MS-63	MS-65
VARIETY	$75	$125	$175	$250	$300	$450	$1,000
NORMAL	$25	$31	$52	$83	$120	$180	$780

1868 — FS-05-1868-303 (003.35)

VARIETY: Repunched Date
PUP: Date
URS-4 · I-3 · L-3

FLETCHER-28.05

Description: This variety is extremely similar to the previous listing, except the 6 of the date does not touch the ball of the shield.

Comments: This is the Reverse of 1867, hub IIa. Aside from the repunched date being almost identical to the previous listing, there is a die crack that is eerily similar to the one on the previous listing. The primary difference to the die crack is that on this variety the crack leaves the second 8 farther to the right.

	F-12	VF-20	EF-40	AU-50	MS-60	MS-63	MS-65
VARIETY	$75	$125	$175	$250	$300	$450	$1,000
NORMAL	$25	$31	$52	$83	$120	$180	$780

1868 — FS-05-1868-304 (003.4)

VARIETY: Repunched Date
PUP: Date
URS-6 · I-3 · L-3

FLETCHER-25

Description: The secondary date was punched to the southeast of the primary date. All four digits are visible.

Comments: This is the Reverse of 1867, hub IIa. This variety was listed twice in the fourth edition of the *Cherrypickers' Guide* (003.75 as well as 003.4).

	F-12	VF-20	EF-40	AU-50	MS-60	MS-63	MS-65
VARIETY	$75	$125	$175	$250	$300	$450	$1,000
NORMAL	$25	$31	$52	$83	$120	$180	$780

1868

FS-05-1868-305 (003.45)

VARIETY: Repunched Date
PUP: Date
URS-3 · I-4 · L-4

FLETCHER: N/L

Description: Secondary digits are evident for all four digits, to the north of the primary digits. A secondary 1 is also evident to the east of the primary 1, actually closer to the first 8 than the 1.

Comments: This is a really neat RPD.

	F-12	VF-20	EF-40	AU-50	MS-60	MS-63	MS-65
VARIETY	$75	$125	$175	$250	$300	$450	$1,000
NORMAL	$25	$31	$52	$83	$120	$180	$780

1868

FS-05-1868-306 (003.5)

VARIETY: Repunched Date
PUP: Date
URS-4 · I-4 · L-4

FLETCHER-24

Description: There are at least four 8s evident for the last digit. The first 8 touches the ball and is the result of a broken date punch.

Comments: This is the Reverse of 1867, hub IIa.

	F-12	VF-20	EF-40	AU-50	MS-60	MS-63	MS-65
VARIETY	$75	$125	$175	$250	$300	$450	$1,000
NORMAL	$25	$31	$52	$83	$120	$180	$780

1868 — FS-05-1868-307 (003.7)

VARIETY: Repunched Date

PUP: Date

URS-7 · I-4 · L-4

FLETCHER-29.02

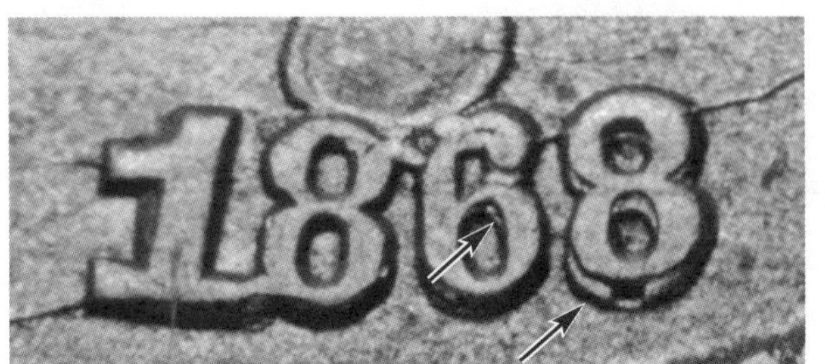

Description: A secondary 6 and secondary final 8 are evident south of the primary digits. The first 8 is touching the ball.

Comments: This is the Reverse of 1867, hub IIa. Early die states of this variety are missing the die cracks through the date but do exhibit some file marks on the obverse at 7:00.

	F-12	VF-20	EF-40	AU-50	MS-60	MS-63	MS-65
VARIETY	$75	$125	$175	$250	$300	$450	$1,000
NORMAL	$25	$31	$52	$83	$120	$180	$780

THE CHERRYPICKERS' GUIDE HELPFUL HINTS

Don't forget to inspect the denticles of a coin, especially those near and beneath the date, for variety characteristics. Dozens of significant varieties exhibit portions of numbers within or protruding from the denticles. Most of these are prized additions to a collection.

1868   FS-05-1868-309 (003.85)

VARIETY: Repunched Date   **FLETCHER: N/L**
PUP: Date
URS-3 · I-3 · L-3

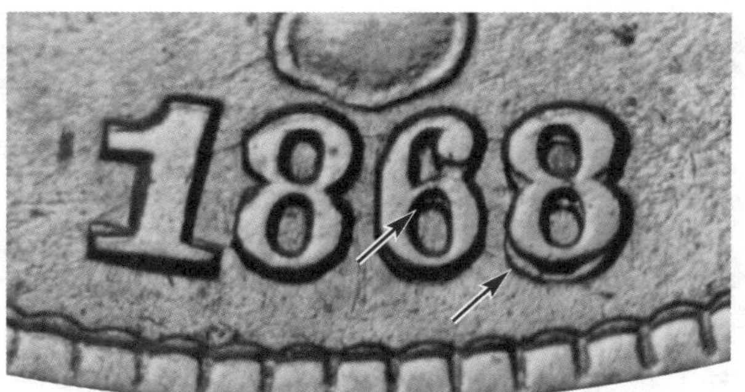

Description: Secondary digits are evident to the south of the primary digits on the 6 and the final 8.

	F-12	VF-20	EF-40	AU-50	MS-60	MS-63	MS-65
VARIETY	$75	$125	$175	$250	$300	$450	$1,000
NORMAL	$25	$31	$52	$83	$120	$180	$780

1868   FS-05-1868-310 (003.98)

VARIETY: Repunched Date   **FLETCHER-20**
PUP: Date
URS-3 · I-3 · L-3

Description: This is a very strong RPD, with secondary digits evident far to the south of the primary digits.

Comments: This is the Reverse of 1867, hub IIa.

	F-12	VF-20	EF-40	AU-50	MS-60	MS-63	MS-65
VARIETY	$75	$125	$175	$250	$300	$450	$1,000
NORMAL	$25	$31	$52	$83	$120	$180	$780

1868 — FS-05-1868-311 (003.985)

VARIETY: Repunched Date + Missing Leaf

PUP: Date

URS-4 · I-3 · L-3

FLETCHER-29.03

Description: Secondary digits are evident to the north of the 1 and first 8. This is also a Missing Leaf variety, of which there are several in the series.

Comments: This is the Reverse of 1867, hub IIa. The retained cud by the date area would likely indicate that very few coins ultimately were struck from this die.

	F-12	VF-20	EF-40	AU-50	MS-60	MS-63	MS-65
VARIETY	$75	$125	$175	$250	$300	$450	$1,000
NORMAL	$25	$31	$52	$83	$120	$180	$780

1868 — FS-05-1868-312 (003.1)

VARIETY: Misplaced Date

PUP: Ball above date

URS-4 · I-3 · L-3

FLETCHER-102

Description: A 1 is clearly evident protruding from the left side of the ball at the bottom of the shield.

Comments: This is the Reverse of 1868, hub IIb.

	F-12	VF-20	EF-40	AU-50	MS-60	MS-63	MS-65
VARIETY	$75	$125	$175	$250	$300	$450	$1,000
NORMAL	$25	$31	$52	$83	$120	$180	$780

1868

Variety: Misplaced Date
FLETCHER-02
PUP: Denticles below date
URS-1 · I-4 · L-4

Description: The top of a 6 or 8 is evident protruding from the denticles below the primary 6.

Comments: This is the Reverse of 1867, hub IIa. The discovery coin is still the only known specimen.

	F-12	VF-20	EF-40	AU-50	MS-60	MS-63	MS-65
Variety	$75	$125	$175	$250	$300	$450	$1,000
Normal	$25	$31	$52	$83	$120	$180	$780

The Cherrypickers' Guide HELPFUL HINTS

Don't get hung up on just the varieties listed in this book. There are many nice, yet-to-be-discovered "cherries" out there waiting for you to pick!

1868 — FS-05-1868-401 (003.99)

VARIETY: Missing Leaf + Scribe Mark   **FLETCHER-56**
PUP: Second right leaf cluster
URS-2 · I-4 · L-4

Description: The second right leaf cluster has three leaves, unlike the normal four leaves. This variety also exhibits a circular "scribe mark," for lack of a better term, circumventing the shield on the top and through the shield near the bottom.

Comments: This is the Reverse of 1867, hub IIa. All Missing Leaf varieties have only three leaves on the second cluster on the right.

	F-12	VF-20	EF-40	AU-50	MS-60	MS-63	MS-65
VARIETY	$75	$125	$175	$250	$300	$450	$1,000
NORMAL	$25	$31	$52	$83	$120	$180	$780

1869, Narrow Date — FS-05-1869-301 (005)

VARIETY: Narrow Date
PUP: Date
URS-8 · I-3 · L-3

FLETCHER-01

Description: The Normal Date 1869 Shield nickel variety is very scarce. Most dates for 1869 have short, fat digits. Previously referred to as the Tall Date, the name has been changed to Normal Date by Shield nickel specialists because the digits for other Shield nickels are this same relative size.

Comments: All known Normal Date varieties have the reverse of 1867, hub IIa. Those 1868 Normal Date varieties will have a three-digit Fivaz/Stanton number. All shorter-date Shield nickels will have a four-digit FS number.

	F-12	VF-20	EF-40	AU-50	MS-60	MS-63	MS-65
VARIETY	$75	$125	$175	$250	$300	$450	$1,000
NORMAL	$25	$31	$52	$83	$120	$180	$780

1869, Wide Date — FS-05-1869-1101 (004)

VARIETY: Doubled-Die Obverse
PUP: Motto, annulet
URS-6 · I-3 · L-3

FLETCHER-413

Description: Doubling is visible on IN GOD WE TRUST, rotated slightly counterclockwise. Doubling is also evident on the annulet, cross, leaves, and upper shield.

Comments: The date on this variety has the short, fat digits. This is the Reverse of 1867, hub IIc.

	F-12	VF-20	EF-40	AU-50	MS-60	MS-63	MS-65
VARIETY	$75	$125	$175	$250	$300	$450	$1,000
NORMAL	$25	$31	$52	$83	$120	$180	$780

1869, Wide Date — FS-05-1869-1102 (004.5)

VARIETY: Doubled-Die Obverse + Repunched Date — **FLETCHER-414**
PUP: Annulet, date
URS-3 · I-3 · L-3

 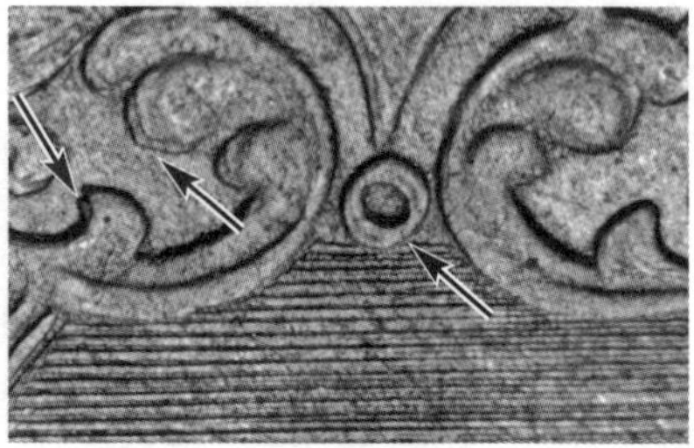

Description: Doubling is visible on IN GOD WE TRUST, the annulet, cross, leaves, and upper shield. The date is also repunched, with the secondary digits evident to the south of the primary digits.

Comments: Though this variety is very similar to the previous, compare the differences in the direction of the secondary annulet from the primary. The date on this variety has the short, fat digits. This is the Reverse of 1867, hub IIc.

	F-12	VF-20	EF-40	AU-50	MS-60	MS-63	MS-65
VARIETY	$75	$125	$175	$250	$300	$450	$1,000
NORMAL	$25	$31	$52	$83	$120	$180	$780

1869, Wide Date — FS-05-1869-1103 (005.67)

VARIETY: Doubled-Die Obverse + Repunched Date — **FLETCHER-411**
PUP: Annulet, date
URS-3 · I-3 · L-3

 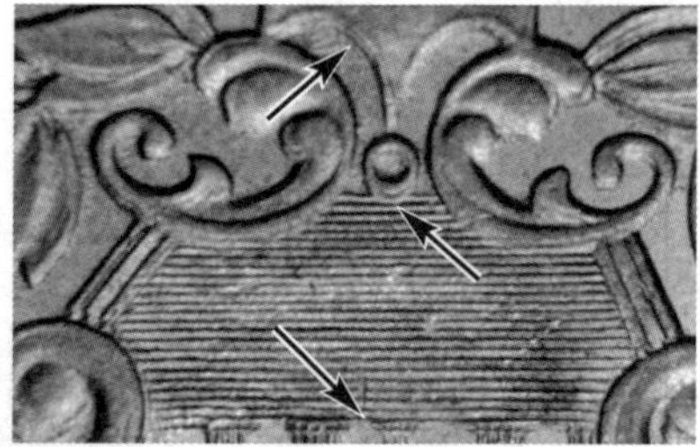

Description: Moderate doubling is evident to the south on the cross, annulet, leaves, and the horizontal lines and lower border of the shield. There is also doubling in the motto, rotated slightly counterclockwise. The date is also repunched, with a secondary 6 and 9 evident to the south of the primary digits, and a secondary 1 evident to the north of the primary digit.

Comments: The date on this variety has the short, fat digits. This is the Reverse of 1867, hub IIc.

	F-12	VF-20	EF-40	AU-50	MS-60	MS-63	MS-65
VARIETY	$75	$125	$175	$250	$300	$450	$1,000
NORMAL	$25	$31	$52	$83	$120	$180	$780

1869, Wide Date — FS-05-1869-1104

VARIETY: Doubled-Die Obverse + Repunched Date
FLETCHER: N/L
PUP: Motto, annulet, date
URS-1 · I-4 · L-4

Description: Doubling is evident on IN GOD WE TRUST, the annulet, shield, and leaves. The date shows evidence of repunching, with a close secondary image to the south of the primary image.

Comments: To the best of our knowledge, this is the only example reported to date.

	F-12	VF-20	EF-40	AU-50	MS-60	MS-63	MS-65
VARIETY	$75	$125	$225	$300	$450	$750	$3,700
NORMAL	$47	$69	$160	$210	$325	$525	$3,175

1869, WIDE Date — FS-05-1869-1301

VARIETY: Wide Date
FLETCHER: N/L
PUP: Date
URS-15 · I-1 · L-1

Description: This is the normal, common date punch for 1869.

Comments: The date on this variety has the short, fat digits. There is no significant value associated with the date style for this year.

	F-12	VF-20	EF-40	AU-50	MS-60	MS-63	MS-65
VARIETY	$25	$31	$52	$83	$120	$180	$780
NORMAL	$25	$31	$52	$83	$120	$180	$780

1869, Wide Date — FS-05-1869-1302 (005.3)

VARIETY: Repunched Date
PUP: Date
URS-4 · I-3 · L-3

FLETCHER-104

Description: Secondary digits are visible with a wide spread to the south of the primary digits. All four digits are repunched, though the 8 can be more difficult to view.

Comments: The date on this variety has the short, fat digits. This is the Reverse of 1867, hub IIa.

	F-12	VF-20	EF-40	AU-50	MS-60	MS-63	MS-65
VARIETY	$75	$125	$175	$250	$300	$450	$1,000
NORMAL	$25	$31	$52	$83	$120	$180	$780

1869, Wide Date — FS-05-1869-1303 (005.4)

VARIETY: Repunched Date
PUP: Date
URS-3 · I-3 · L-3

FLETCHER-202

Description: A secondary 1 and 8 are evident to the north of the primary digits. Notice that the secondary 8 is clearly touching the ball of the shield.

Comments: The date on this variety has the short, fat digits. This is the Reverse of 1867, hub IIc.

	F-12	VF-20	EF-40	AU-50	MS-60	MS-63	MS-65
VARIETY	$75	$125	$175	$250	$300	$450	$1,000
NORMAL	$25	$31	$52	$83	$120	$180	$780

1869, Wide Date — FS-05-1869-1304 (005.5)

VARIETY: Repunched Date
FLETCHER-408
PUP: Date
URS-4 · I-3 · L-3

Description: This date is actually triple-punched, with a set of secondary digits to the north and also to the east of the primary digits. The top of the northern secondary 86 is touching the ball of the shield.

Comments: The date on this variety has the short, fat digits. This is the Reverse of 1867, hub IIc.

	F-12	VF-20	EF-40	AU-50	MS-60	MS-63	MS-65
VARIETY	$75	$125	$175	$250	$300	$450	$1,000
NORMAL	$25	$31	$52	$83	$120	$180	$780

1869, Wide Date — FS-05-1869-1305 (005.6)

VARIETY: Repunched Date
FLETCHER-408
PUP: Date
URS-4 · I-3 · L-3

Description: Secondary digits are evident to the south of the primary digits. Early die states may show that certain digits are actually triple-punched.

Comments: The date on this variety has the short, fat digits. This is the Reverse of 1867, hub IIc.

	F-12	VF-20	EF-40	AU-50	MS-60	MS-63	MS-65
VARIETY	$75	$125	$175	$250	$300	$450	$1,000
NORMAL	$25	$31	$52	$83	$120	$180	$780

1869, Wide Date · FS-05-1869-1306 (005.68)

VARIETY: Repunched Date
PUP: Date
URS-4 · I-3 · L-3

FLETCHER-105

Description: Secondary digits are evident to the northeast of the primary digits. The secondary 8 and 6 are touching the ball of the shield.

Comments: The date on this variety has the short, fat digits. This is the Reverse of 1867, hub IIa.

	F-12	VF-20	EF-40	AU-50	MS-60	MS-63	MS-65
VARIETY	$75	$125	$175	$250	$300	$450	$1,000
NORMAL	$25	$31	$52	$83	$120	$180	$780

1869, Wide Date · FS-05-1869-1307 (005.2)

VARIETY: Misplaced Date
PUP: Ball of shield
URS-3 · I-3 · L-3

Description: A "spike" is evident protruding from the left side of the ball of the shield. We are not sure if this is a 1 or some other aberration.

Comments: The date on this variety has the short, fat digits. This is the Reverse of 1867, hub IIa.

	F-12	VF-20	EF-40	AU-50	MS-60	MS-63	MS-65
VARIETY	$75	$125	$175	$250	$300	$450	$1,000
NORMAL	$25	$31	$52	$83	$120	$180	$780

1870 — FS-05-1870-101 (005.7)

Variety: Doubled-Die Obverse + Repunched Date — **Fletcher-03**
PUP: Annulet, date
URS-5 · I-5 · L-5

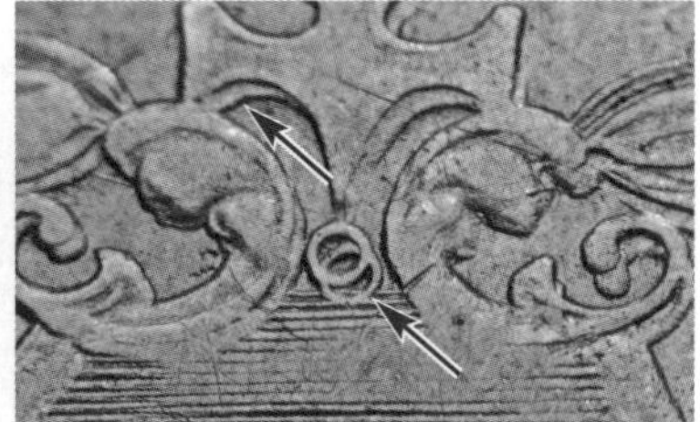

Description: This is an extremely strong doubled die, evident on the annulet, cross, upper shield, leaves, and berries. The date is also strongly repunched, with a secondary 7 and 0 evident to the south of the primary digits.

Comments: This is one of the Shield nickel varieties most actively sought by specialists.

	F-12	VF-20	EF-40	AU-50	MS-60	MS-63	MS-65
Variety	$100	$150	$200	$300	$400	$500	$2,200
Normal	$53	$68	$100	$145	$190	$265	$1,550

1870 — FS-05-1870-102 (005.74)

Variety: Doubled-Die Obverse — **Fletcher-12**
PUP: Annulet
URS-4 · I-4 · L-4

Description: Doubling is evident on the annulet, the cross, the upper shield, the leaves, the berries, and the horizontal lines running into the vertical lines.

Comments: This is another of the many popular Shield nickel doubled dies.

	F-12	VF-20	EF-40	AU-50	MS-60	MS-63	MS-65
Variety	$75	$125	$175	$250	$350	$450	$1,800
Normal	$53	$68	$100	$145	$190	$265	$1,550

1870 FS-05-1870-103 (005.75)

VARIETY: Doubled-Die Obverse + Repunched Date   **FLETCHER-03.01**
PUP: Annulet, date
URS-4 · I-4 · L-4

 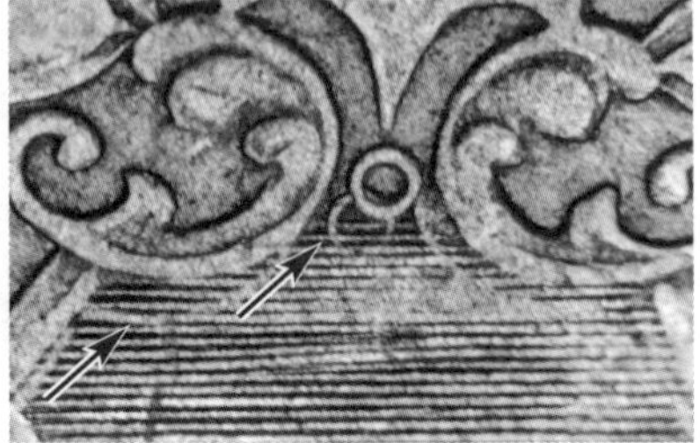

Description: This extremely strong doubled die is evident on the annulet, upper shield, leaves, and shows the horizontal lines running into the vertical lines. The repunched date is evident with the remains of a 0 far right of the primary 0.

Comments: This is likely one of the most eagerly sought varieties within the series. It is a super variety, with the wide spread on the doubled die and the tremendous spread on the repunched date. It was first reported to us by Brian Greer in July of 1995.

	F-12	VF-20	EF-40	AU-50	MS-60	MS-63	MS-65
VARIETY	$75	$125	$175	$250	$350	$450	$1,800
NORMAL	$53	$68	$100	$145	$190	$265	$1,550

1870 FS-05-1870-301 (005.77)

VARIETY: Repunched Date +   **FLETCHER-15**
    Clash with Indian Head Cent
PUP: Date, obverse
URS-3 · I-4 · L-4

Description: The date is quadruple-punched, with secondary 1s evident to the southwest, the south, and the southeast of the primary 1. Other digits are also doubled. The obverse exhibits weak clash marks of an Indian Head cent obverse.

Comments: This is a super variety with the clash of the Indian Head cent obverse and the strong repunched date.

	F-12	VF-20	EF-40	AU-50	MS-60	MS-63	MS-65
VARIETY	$75	$125	$195	$250	$350	$450	$2,250
NORMAL	$33	$43	$60	$86	$125	$280	$1,925

1870   FS-05-1870-302 (005.76)

VARIETY: Repunched Date + Misplaced Date   **FLETCHER-01**
PUP: Date
URS-4 · I-4 · L-4

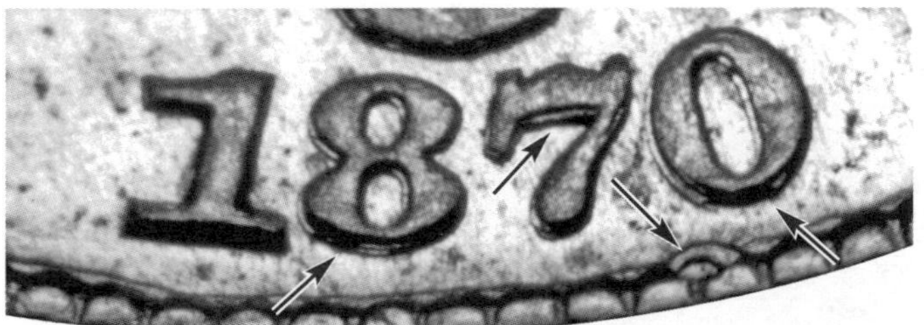

Description: The repunched date is evident with a close spread on the 8, 7, and 0 slightly to the south. The misplaced date is evident with the top of as many as three 0s protruding from the denticles.

Comments: The misplaced date is the primary feature of this variety.

	F-12	VF-20	EF-40	AU-50	MS-60	MS-63	MS-65
VARIETY	$75	$125	$195	$250	$350	$450	$2,250
NORMAL	$33	$43	$60	$86	$125	$280	$1,925

1870   FS-05-1870-801 (005.9)

VARIETY: Doubled-Die Reverse   **FLETCHER-14**
PUP: Reverse lettering
URS-5 · I-4 · L-4

Description: Doubling is evident on all reverse lettering, most stars, and the 5 in the center of the design. The doubling is very unusual, as the spread between the images is in different directions.

Comments: This doubled-die reverse is known paired with three different obverse dies.

	F-12	VF-20	EF-40	AU-50	MS-60	MS-63	MS-65
VARIETY	$75	$125	$195	$250	$350	$450	$2,250
NORMAL	$33	$43	$60	$86	$125	$280	$1,925

1871 — FS-05-1871-101 (006)

VARIETY: Doubled-Die Obverse   **FLETCHER: N/L**
PUP: Annulet
URS-5 · I-3 · L-3

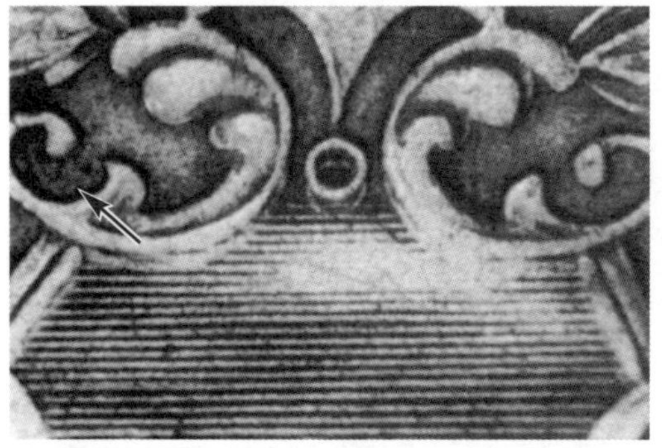

Description: Doubling is evident on the annulet, cross, leaves, and upper shield.

Comments: This is another typical Shield nickel doubled-die obverse.

	F-12	VF-20	EF-40	AU-50	MS-60	MS-63	MS-65
VARIETY	$195	$250	$350	$450	$525	$725	$2,250
NORMAL	$140	$210	$280	$360	$425	$625	$2,000

1871 — FS-05-1871-301 (006.5)

VARIETY: Repunched Date   **FLETCHER-02**
PUP: Date
URS-4 · I-3 · L-3

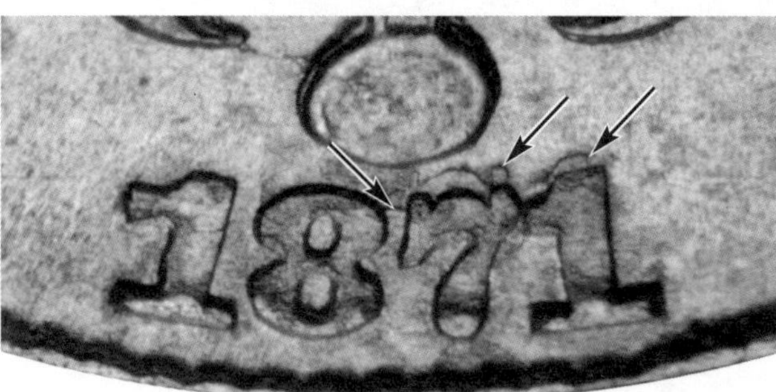

Description: All four digits are evidently repunched, with the secondary digits to the north of the primary digits. Later die states may show on only the 7 and the last 1.

Comments: There is a small, curved, raised line connecting the top of the 8 and the 7. This is likely a small die crack.

	F-12	VF-20	EF-40	AU-50	MS-60	MS-63	MS-65
VARIETY	$195	$250	$350	$450	$525	$725	$2,250
NORMAL	$140	$210	$280	$360	$425	$625	$2,000

1872 — FS-05-1872-101 (007)

VARIETY: Doubled-Die Obverse   **FLETCHER-121**
PUP: Annulet
URS-7 · I-3 · L-3

Description: Moderate doubling is evident on the annulet, cross, leaves, and shield, with the secondary image south-southeast of the primary image.

Comments: This date is well known with several doubled dies and repunched dates.

	F-12	VF-20	EF-40	AU-50	MS-60	MS-63	MS-65
VARIETY	$95	$125	$175	$225	$295	$350	$1,500
NORMAL	$85	$100	$140	$180	$225	$250	$1,250

1872 — FS-05-1872-102 (007.1)

VARIETY: Doubled-Die Obverse   **FLETCHER-123**
PUP: Annulet
URS-3 · I-4 · L-4

Description: Very strong doubling is evident on the annulet, upper shield, leaves, and the intersection of the horizontal and vertical lines.

Comments: This is a fabulous doubled die, as are many in the Shield nickel series.

	F-12	VF-20	EF-40	AU-50	MS-60	MS-63	MS-65
VARIETY	$125	$175	$275	$325	$395	$495	$1,750
NORMAL	$85	$100	$140	$180	$225	$250	$1,250

1872   FS-05-1872-103 (007.2)

VARIETY: Doubled-Die Obverse   **FLETCHER-124**
PUP: Annulet
URS-4 · I-4 · L-4

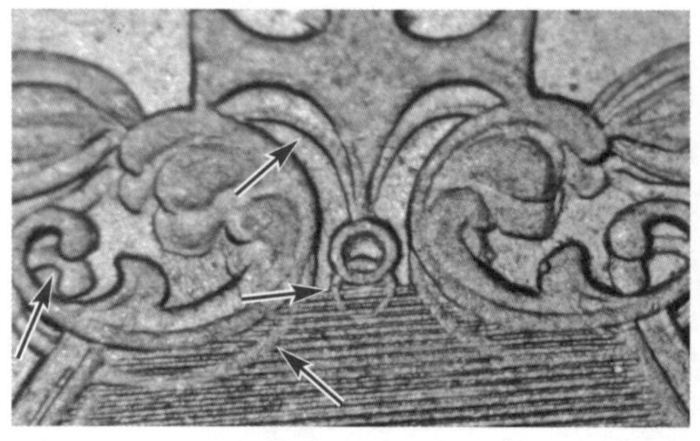 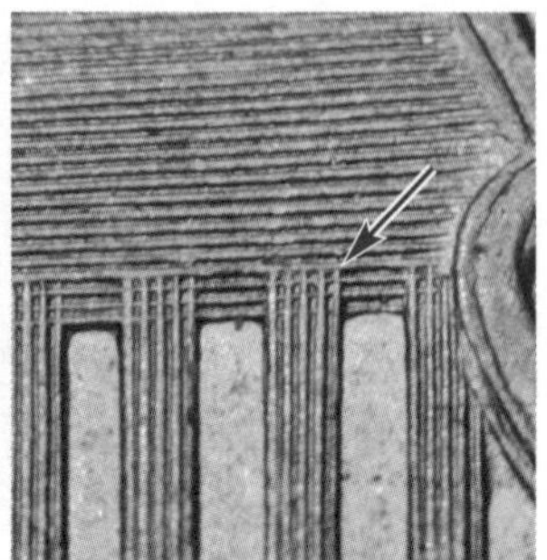

Description: Very strong doubling is evident on the annulet, upper shield, leaves, and the intersection of the horizontal and vertical lines.

Comments: Compare the photos of the doubling on the annulet for the differences in these varieties.

	F-12	VF-20	EF-40	AU-50	MS-60	MS-63	MS-65
VARIETY	$125	$175	$275	$325	$395	$495	$1,750
NORMAL	$85	$100	$140	$180	$225	$250	$1,250

1872   FS-05-1872-104 (007.3)

VARIETY: Doubled-Die Obverse   **FLETCHER-109**
PUP: Annulet
URS-4 · I-4 · L-4

Description: Very strong doubling is evident on the annulet, upper shield, leaves, berries, and the intersection of the horizontal and vertical lines.

Comments: Compare the photos of the doubling on the annulet for the differences in these varieties.

	F-12	VF-20	EF-40	AU-50	MS-60	MS-63	MS-65
VARIETY	$125	$175	$275	$325	$395	$495	$1,750
NORMAL	$85	$100	$140	$180	$225	$250	$1,250

1872

FS-05-1872-105 (007.4)

VARIETY: Tripled-Die Obverse
PUP: Annulet, upper shield
URS-4 · I-4 · L-4

FLETCHER-05

Description: Very strong tripling is evident on the annulet, with doubling evident on the upper shield and leaves.

Comments: This was the second tripled obverse die reported in the series, after the 1876. Others have since been reported.

	F-12	VF-20	EF-40	AU-50	MS-60	MS-63	MS-65
VARIETY	$125	$175	$275	$325	$395	$495	$1,750
NORMAL	$85	$100	$140	$180	$225	$250	$1,250

1872

FS-05-1872-106 (007.5)

VARIETY: Doubled-Die Obverse
PUP: Annulet
URS-3 · I-5 · L-5

FLETCHER-116

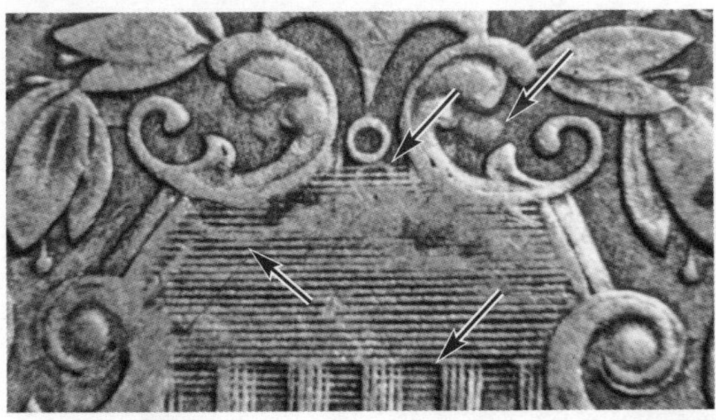

Description: Extremely strong doubling is evident on the annulet, with the top of the secondary annulet barely touching the bottom of the primary annulet. Strong doubling is also visible on the upper shield, leaves, berries, and the horizontal lines far south into the vertical lines.

Comments: This variety was first reported by Dave Brody.

	F-12	VF-20	EF-40	AU-50	MS-60	MS-63	MS-65
VARIETY	$125	$175	$275	$325	$395	$495	$1,750
NORMAL	$85	$100	$140	$180	$225	$250	$1,250

1872 — FS-05-1872-301 (007.6)

VARIETY: Repunched Date
PUP: Date
URS-4 · I-4 · L-4

FLETCHER-104

Description: The secondary digits are evident to the north of the primary digits. The separation increases from left to right.

	F-12	VF-20	EF-40	AU-50	MS-60	MS-63	MS-65
VARIETY	$125	$175	$275	$325	$395	$495	$1,750
NORMAL	$85	$100	$140	$180	$225	$250	$1,250

1872 — FS-05-1872-302 (007.65)

VARIETY: Repunched Date
PUP: Date
URS-4 · I-4 · L-4

Description: Several secondary 2s are evident beneath the 7. There are at least three 2s in the wrong position.

	F-12	VF-20	EF-40	AU-50	MS-60	MS-63	MS-65
VARIETY	$125	$175	$275	$325	$395	$495	$1,750
NORMAL	$85	$100	$140	$180	$225	$250	$1,250

1872 — FS-05-1872-303 (007.7)

VARIETY: Repunched Date
PUP: Date
URS-4 · I-4 · L-4

FLETCHER-103

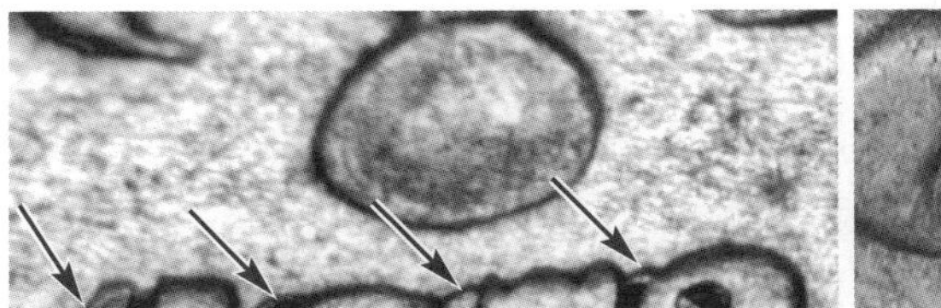 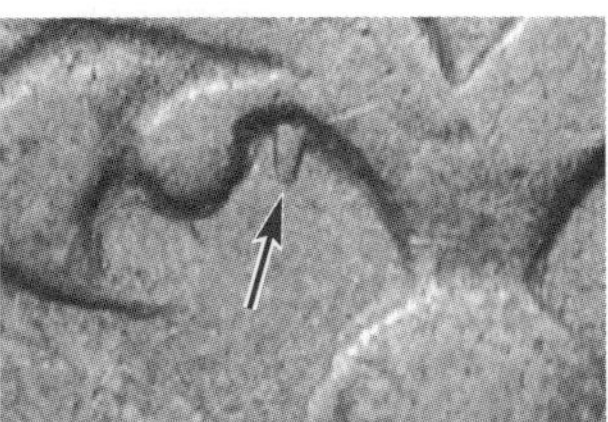

Description: All four secondary digits from the first date punch are evident to the west of the primary digits.

Comments: A "spike" protrudes from the bottom of the shield, just above the left side of the ball. This could be the flag of a misplaced 1, oriented horizontally, or could simply be a die chip.

	F-12	VF-20	EF-40	AU-50	MS-60	MS-63	MS-65
VARIETY	$125	$175	$275	$325	$395	$495	$1,750
NORMAL	$85	$100	$140	$180	$225	$250	$1,250

1872 — FS-05-1872-304 (007.76)

VARIETY: Repunched Date
PUP: Date
URS-5 · I-3 · L-3

FLETCHER-03.01

Description: Secondary digits are evident to the north of the primary 7 and 2.

	F-12	VF-20	EF-40	AU-50	MS-60	MS-63	MS-65
VARIETY	$100	$125	$175	$250	$350	$425	$1,500
NORMAL	$85	$100	$140	$180	$225	$250	$1,250

1872 — FS-05-1872-305 (007.77)

VARIETY: Repunched Date
PUP: Date
URS-4 · I-3 · L-3

FLETCHER-101.01

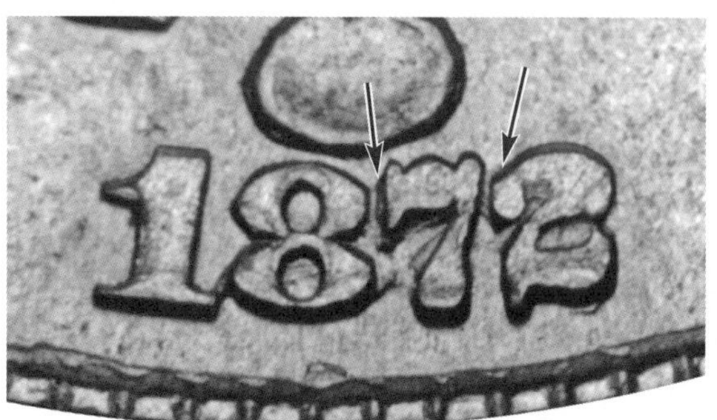

Description: Secondary digits are evident to the west of the primary 7 and 2. Also, the top of an apparent 1 is evident protruding from the denticles below the 8.

	F-12	VF-20	EF-40	AU-50	MS-60	MS-63	MS-65
VARIETY	$125	$175	$275	$325	$395	$495	$1,750
NORMAL	$85	$100	$140	$180	$225	$250	$1,250

1872 — FS-05-1872-306 (007.9)

VARIETY: Repunched Date
PUP: Date
URS-3 · I-3 · L-3

FLETCHER-02

Description: Portions of the secondary digits are evident to the north of the primary digits on the 1, 8, and 7.

Comments: Strike doubling is also evident on the digits of the date.

	F-12	VF-20	EF-40	AU-50	MS-60	MS-63	MS-65
VARIETY	$125	$175	$275	$325	$395	$495	$1,750
NORMAL	$85	$100	$140	$180	$225	$250	$1,250

1872

FS-05-1872-307 (007.75)

VARIETY: Misplaced Date

FLETCHER-101.02

PUP: Date

URS-3 · I-3 · L-3

Description: Portions of a misplace 2 are evident in the field immediately to the right of the ball.

	F-12	VF-20	EF-40	AU-50	MS-60	MS-63	MS-65
VARIETY	$125	$175	$275	$325	$395	$495	$1,750
NORMAL	$85	$100	$140	$180	$225	$250	$1,250

1872

FS-05-1872-308 (007.8)

VARIETY: Small Over Large Date

FLETCHER-102

PUP: Date

URS-4 · I-5 · L-5

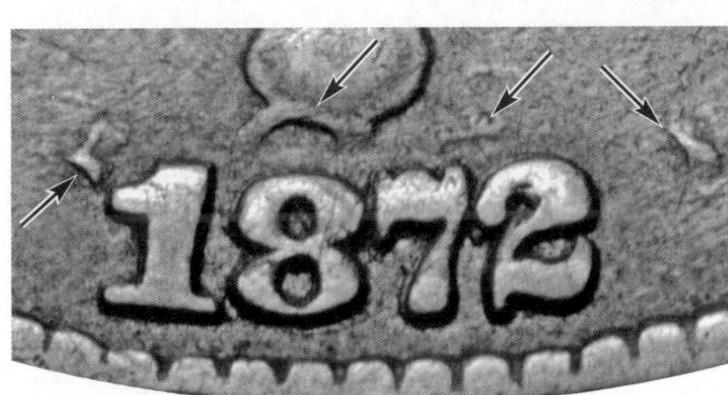

Description: A secondary, larger date punch was first placed into the die, then corrected with the normal date punch for the series. The flag of a 1 is evident northwest of the primary 1, the top of the secondary 8 is evident touching the ball, the top of the secondary 7 is evident northeast of the primary 7, and the upper right curve of a secondary 2 is evident far to the east of the primary 2.

Comments: It has been determined the secondary, larger date punch was that intended for a Liberty Seated dime. As of July 2008, there are six known examples, the finest graded Extremely Fine.

	F-12	VF-20	EF-40	AU-50	MS-60	MS-63	MS-65
VARIETY	$125	$175	$275	$325	$395	$495	$1,750
NORMAL	$85	$100	$140	$180	$225	$250	$1,250

1873, Close 3   FS-05-1873-101 (008, 008.85)

VARIETY: Doubled-Die Obverse   **FLETCHER-04**
PUP: Annulet
URS-5 · I-3 · L-3

Description: The secondary image is evident on the annulet, leaves, and cross. The horizontal lines barely encroach into the vertical lines.

Comments: This variety was listed twice in the fourth edition of the *Cherrypickers' Guide*, as FS-008 and FS-008.85.

	F-12	VF-20	EF-40	AU-50	MS-60	MS-63	MS-65
VARIETY	$75	$95	$125	$175	$250	$295	$2,400
NORMAL	$55	$70	$80	$135	$210	$235	$2,150

1873, Close 3 — FS-05-1873-102 (008.7)

VARIETY: Doubled-Die Obverse
FLETCHER-05
PUP: Annulet
URS-3 · I-5 · L-5

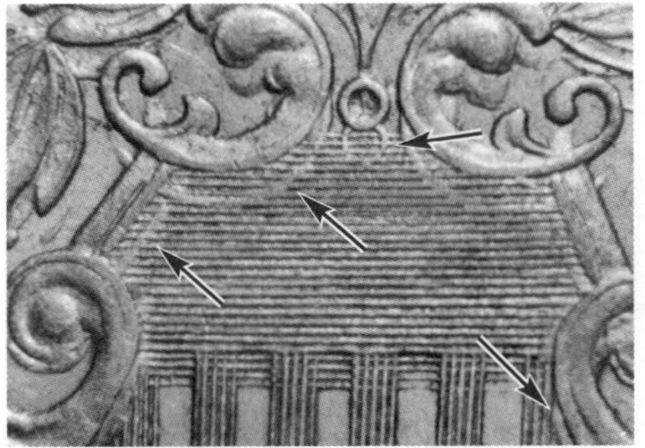

Description: This extremely strong doubled die is evident with the secondary annulet far to the south of the primary, barely touching. Doubling is also evident on the cross, leaves, shield, and berries.

Comments: This is one of the stronger doubled dies in the Shield nickel series and is on the want-list of virtually every collector.

	F-12	VF-20	EF-40	AU-50	MS-60	MS-63	MS-65
VARIETY	$125	$300	$450	$750	$950	$1,500	$3,500
NORMAL	$55	$70	$80	$135	$210	$235	$2,150

1873, Close 3 — FS-05-1873-103 (008.8)

VARIETY: Doubled-Die Obverse
FLETCHER-06
PUP: Annulet
URS-3 · I-5 · L-5

Description: Extremely strong doubling is evident, exhibiting the secondary annulet far to the south of the primary, not touching. Very strong doubling is also evident on the cross, leaves, shield, and berries. The horizontal lines protrude far into the vertical lines.

Comments: There is a die crack running northwest from a point just above the 3 through the left arrow toward the rim at 9:00.

	F-12	VF-20	EF-40	AU-50	MS-60	MS-63	MS-65
VARIETY	$125	$300	$450	$750	$950	$1,500	$3,500
NORMAL	$55	$70	$80	$135	$210	$235	$2,150

1873, Open 3 — FS-05-1873-1101 (008.3)

VARIETY: Doubled-Die Obverse
PUP: Annulet
URS-4 · I-4 · L-4

FLETCHER-113

Description: Very strong doubling is evident on the annulet, cross, leaves, and shield, with the spread to the west.

	F-12	VF-20	EF-40	AU-50	MS-60	MS-63	MS-65
VARIETY	$100	$125	$150	$225	$325	$425	$2,500
NORMAL	$55	$70	$80	$135	$210	$235	$2,150

1873, Open 3 — FS-05-1873-1102 (008.5)

VARIETY: Doubled-Die Obverse + Misplaced Date
PUP: Annulet, date
URS-5 · I-5 · L-5

FLETCHER-102

Description: The doubling is typical for the series, with a secondary annulet evident to the south of the primary. Doubling is also visible on the leaves, cross, and shield. Portions of several digits are evident protruding from the denticles below the date.

	F-12	VF-20	EF-40	AU-50	MS-60	MS-63	MS-65
VARIETY	$100	$125	$150	$225	$325	$425	$2,500
NORMAL	$55	$70	$80	$135	$210	$235	$2,150

1873, Open 3 — FS-05-1873-1301 (009)

VARIETY: Repunched Date (Large Over Small)   **FLETCHER-106**
PUP: Date
URS-3 · I-5 · L-5

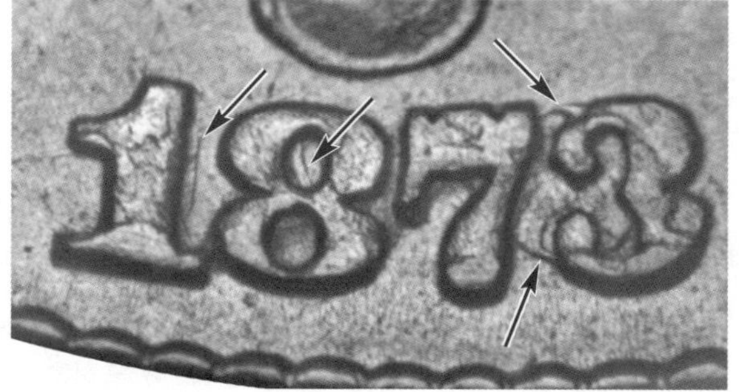

Description: The initial date punch was likely that intended for a three-cent piece or half dime. The primary date punch was normal for the date, creating a Large Date Over Small Date variety. The secondary 1 is evident between the primary 1 and 8, and a secondary 3 is evident between the primary 7 and 3.

Comments: This is a very rare variety, always sought by the many Shield nickel specialists.

	F-12	VF-20	EF-40	AU-50	MS-60	MS-63	MS-65
VARIETY	$500	$750	$1,000	$1,400	$1,750	$2,100	$3,500
NORMAL	$55	$70	$80	$135	$210	$235	$2,150

1873, Open 3 — FS-05-1873-1302 (009.3)

VARIETY: Repunched Date   **FLETCHER-103**
PUP: Date
URS-3 · I-3 · L-3

Description: The flag of a secondary 1 is evident high between the primary 1 and 8.

	F-12	VF-20	EF-40	AU-50	MS-60	MS-63	MS-65
VARIETY	$95	$125	$150	$200	$300	$400	$2,300
NORMAL	$55	$70	$80	$135	$210	$235	$2,150

1873, Open 3 — FS-05-1873-1303 (009.5)

VARIETY: Repunched Date

FLETCHER-110

PUP: Date

URS-4 · I-4 · L-4

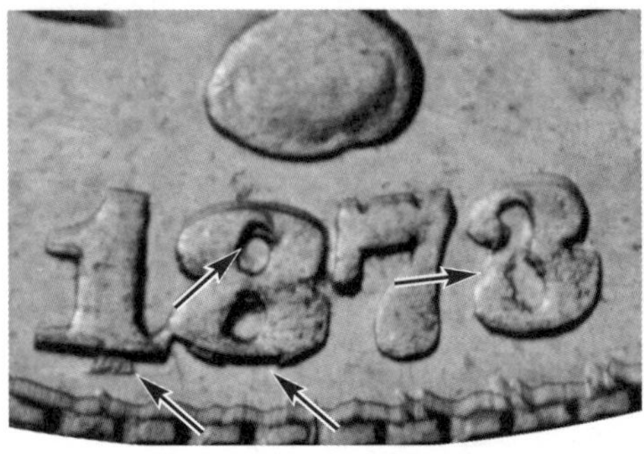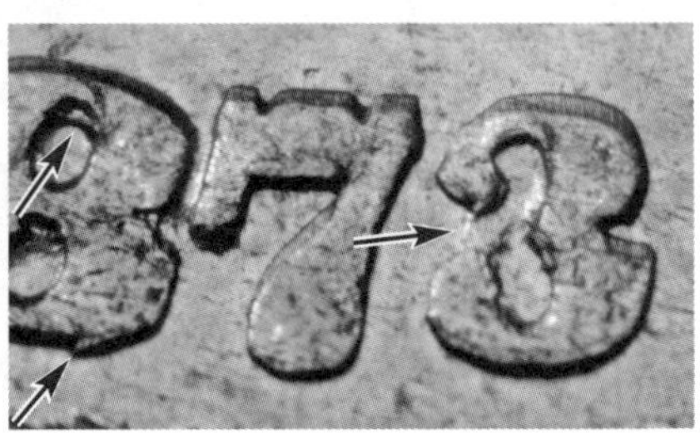

Description: A secondary 1 protrudes from the bottom of the primary 1, a secondary 8 barely protrudes from the bottom of the primary 8, and what appears to be a secondary 3 is evident inside the primary 3.

Comments: This is a very interesting repunched date. It may, in time, prove to be an 1873/2 overdate.

	F-12	VF-20	EF-40	AU-50	MS-60	MS-63	MS-65
VARIETY	$100	$175	$250	$350	$500	$750	$2,500
NORMAL	$55	$70	$80	$135	$210	$235	$2,150

1873, Open 3 — FS-05-1873-1304 (009.7)

VARIETY: Repunched Date

FLETCHER-108.01

PUP: Date

URS-1 · I-4 · L-4

Description: A secondary 7 is evident between the primary 73. A secondary 3 is evident far to the south but within the opening of the primary 3.

Comments: This is a very unusual repunched date.

	F-12	VF-20	EF-40	AU-50	MS-60	MS-63	MS-65
VARIETY	$95	$125	$150	$200	$300	$400	$2,300
NORMAL	$55	$70	$80	$135	$210	$235	$2,150

1874 — FS-05-1874-101 (010)

VARIETY: Doubled-Die Obverse
FLETCHER-05
PUP: Annulet
URS-6 · I-3 · L-3

Description: Typical Shield nickel doubling is evident on the annulet, cross, upper shield, and leaves. The horizontal lines barely creep into the vertical lines.

	F-12	VF-20	EF-40	AU-50	MS-60	MS-63	MS-65
VARIETY	$100	$125	$150	$200	$300	$350	$1,500
NORMAL	$75	$95	$120	$165	$245	$260	$1,350

1874 — FS-05-1874-102 (010.4)

VARIETY: Doubled-Die Obverse
FLETCHER-12
PUP: Annulet, motto
URS-2 · I-3 · L-3

Description: Typical Shield nickel doubling is evident on the annulet, cross, upper shield, and leaves. The horizontal lines barely creep into the vertical lines. Doubling is also evident on IN GOD WE TRUST.

Comments: This particular variety exhibits the strongest known doubling of the motto (IN GOD WE TRUST) of any Shield nickel doubled die.

	F-12	VF-20	EF-40	AU-50	MS-60	MS-63	MS-65
VARIETY	$150	$225	$350	$450	$500	$750	$1,750
NORMAL	$75	$95	$120	$165	$245	$260	$1,350

1874 — FS-05-1874-103 (010.5)

VARIETY: Doubled-Die Obverse
FLETCHER-08
PUP: Annulet
URS-3 · I-3 · L-3

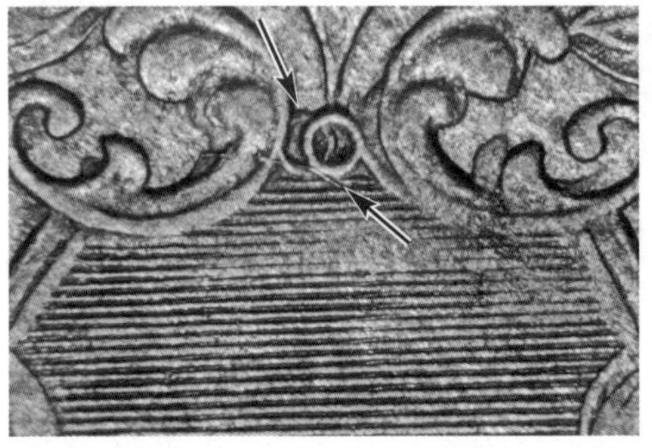

Description: Very strong doubling is evident to the west on the annulet, cross, upper shield, leaves, and berries.

Comments: This variety was discovered by J.T. Stanton in January of 1990. There is a die scratch on the lower portion of the annulet. It is unusual for the doubling to be to the west, as on this example.

	F-12	VF-20	EF-40	AU-50	MS-60	MS-63	MS-65
VARIETY	$150	$225	$350	$450	$500	$750	$1,750
NORMAL	$75	$95	$120	$165	$245	$260	$1,350

1874 — FS-05-1874-104 (010.6)

VARIETY: Doubled-Die Obverse
FLETCHER-09.01
PUP: Annulet
URS-5 · I-5 · L-5

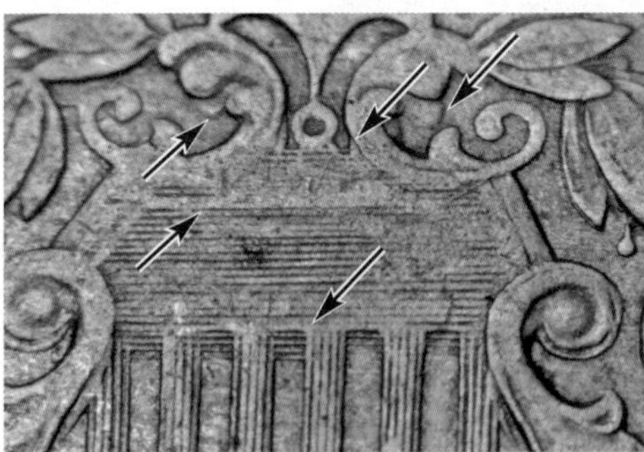

Description: This is a very strong doubled die, with the top of the secondary annulet barely touching the lower portion of the primary annulet. The doubling is also evident on the upper shield, cross, leaves, and berries. The horizontal lines protrude into the vertical lines.

	F-12	VF-20	EF-40	AU-50	MS-60	MS-63	MS-65
VARIETY	$150	$225	$350	$450	$500	$750	$1,750
NORMAL	$75	$95	$120	$165	$245	$260	$1,350

1874   FS-05-1874-301 (010.7)

VARIETY: Repunched Date
PUP: Date
URS-6 · I-3 · L-3

FLETCHER-02

Description: A secondary 1 and secondary 8 are evident to the north of the primary digits. The primary 8 touches the ball, with the secondary 8 "broken" around the ball.

Comments: The date is punched farther right than a normal position.

	F-12	VF-20	EF-40	AU-50	MS-60	MS-63	MS-65
VARIETY	$100	$125	$175	$250	$350	$450	$1,500
NORMAL	$75	$95	$120	$165	$245	$260	$1,350

1874   FS-05-1874-302 (010.8)

VARIETY: Repunched Date
PUP: Date
URS-2 · I-3 · L-3

FLETCHER-01

Description: The top serif or "flag" of a secondary 1 is evident protruding from the left side of the primary 1's upright.

Comments: The specimens we've seen exhibit very strong strike doubling on the date.

	F-12	VF-20	EF-40	AU-50	MS-60	MS-63	MS-65
VARIETY	$100	$125	$175	$250	$350	$450	$1,500
NORMAL	$75	$95	$120	$165	$245	$260	$1,350

1875 — FS-05-1875-101 (011)

VARIETY: Doubled-Die Obverse
PUP: Annulet
URS-4 · I-4 · L-4

FLETCHER-04

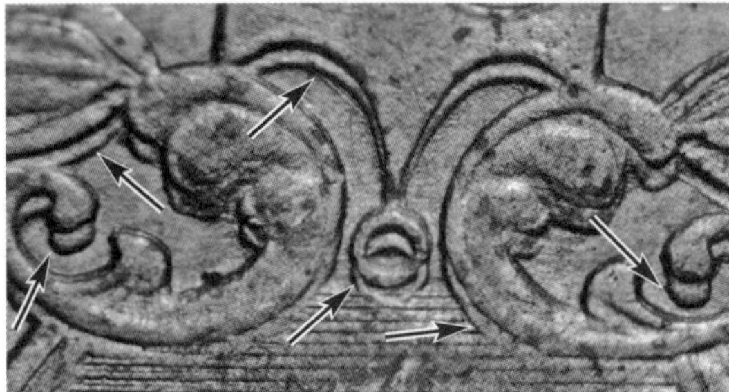 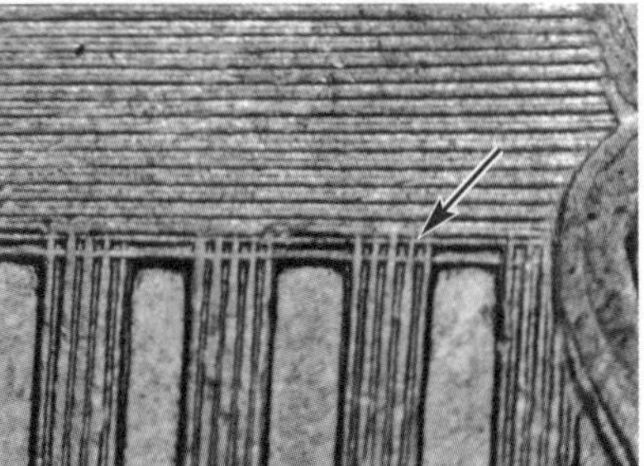

Description: Doubling is evident on the annulet, cross, leaves, berries, and upper shield. The horizontal lines protrude into the vertical lines.

	F-12	VF-20	EF-40	AU-50	MS-60	MS-63	MS-65
VARIETY	$135	$175	$225	$350	$450	$600	$2,000
NORMAL	$95	$125	$170	$225	$290	$320	$1,800

1875 — FS-05-1875-102 (011.3)

VARIETY: Doubled-Die Obverse
PUP: Annulet
URS-4 · I-4 · L-4

FLETCHER-05

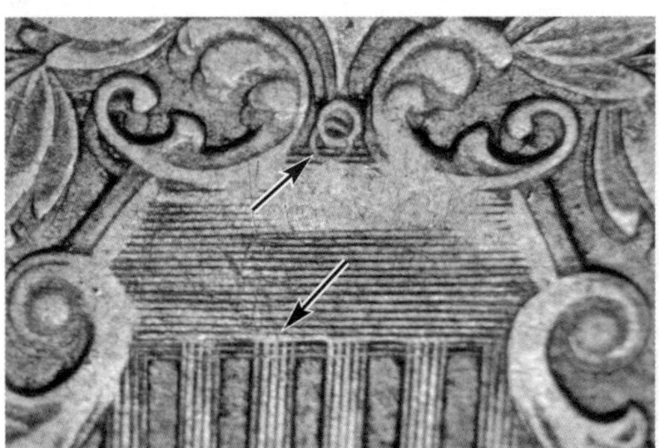

Description: Doubling is evident on the annulet, cross, upper shield, leaves, and berries. The horizontal lines protrude into the vertical lines.

Comments: This is a typical but very strong doubled die for the Shield nickel series.

	F-12	VF-20	EF-40	AU-50	MS-60	MS-63	MS-65
VARIETY	$150	$225	$300	$400	$550	$750	$2,400
NORMAL	$95	$125	$170	$225	$290	$320	$1,800

1875

FS-05-1875-103 (011.5)

VARIETY: Doubled-Die Obverse + Repunched Date

FLETCHER-03

PUP: Annulet, date

URS-3 · I-3 · L-3

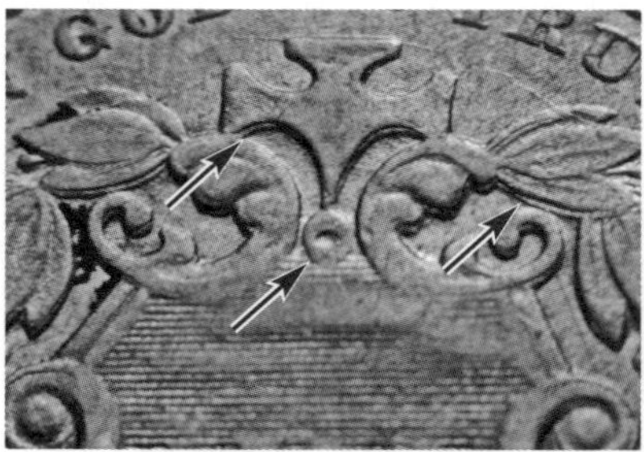 

Description: Moderate doubling is evident on the annulet, upper shield, cross, leaves, and berries. The horizontal lines protrude into the vertical lines. A secondary 7 and 5 are visible protruding from the tops of the primary digits.

	F-12	VF-20	EF-40	AU-50	MS-60	MS-63	MS-65
VARIETY	$150	$200	$250	$300	$450	$650	$2,000
NORMAL	$95	$125	$170	$225	$290	$320	$1,800

1876

FS-05-1876-101 (012)

VARIETY: Tripled-Die Obverse

FLETCHER-04

PUP: Annulet

URS-6 · I-5 · L-5

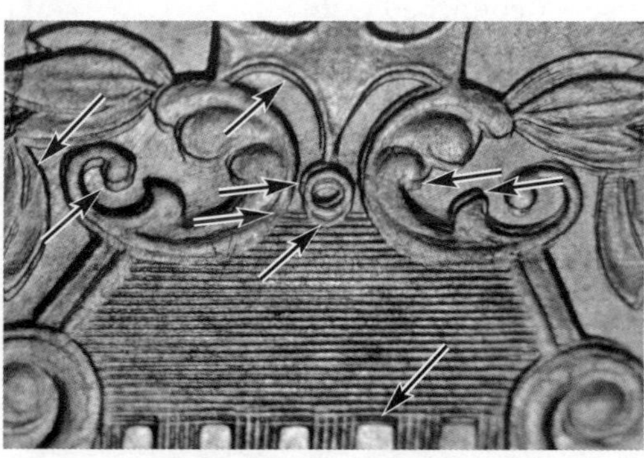

Description: This is a spectacular variety with the tripled image most evident on the annulet to the north and south. Doubling is evident on the upper shield, cross, leaves, and berries. The horizontal lines protrude into the vertical lines.

	F-12	VF-20	EF-40	AU-50	MS-60	MS-63	MS-65
VARIETY	$150	$200	$350	$450	$600	$750	$2,400
NORMAL	$90	$120	$150	$195	$260	$310	$1,725

1876 — FS-05-1876-102 (012.1)

VARIETY: Doubled-Die Obverse — **FLETCHER-05**
PUP: Annulet
URS-5 · I-3 · L-3

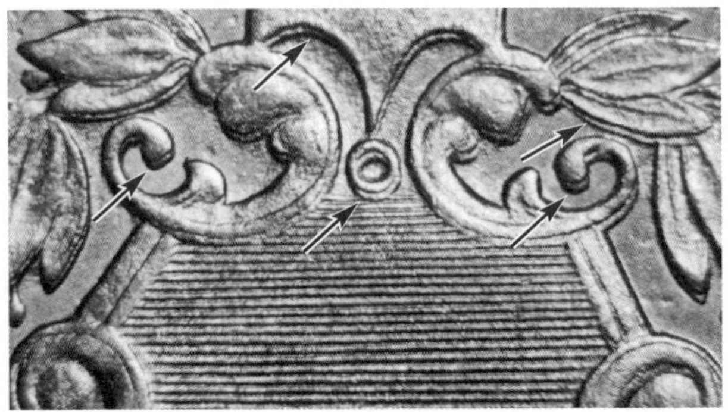

Description: Secondary images are evident on the annulet, cross, upper shield, leaves, and berries. The horizontal lines protrude into the vertical lines.

Comments: This is another typical doubled die for the series.

	F-12	VF-20	EF-40	AU-50	MS-60	MS-63	MS-65
VARIETY	$125	$175	$225	$300	$395	$500	$2,000
NORMAL	$90	$120	$150	$195	$260	$310	$1,725

1876 — FS-05-1876-103

VARIETY: Doubled-Die Obverse + Repunched Date — **FLETCHER-08**
PUP: Annulet, Date
URS-3 · I-3 · L-3

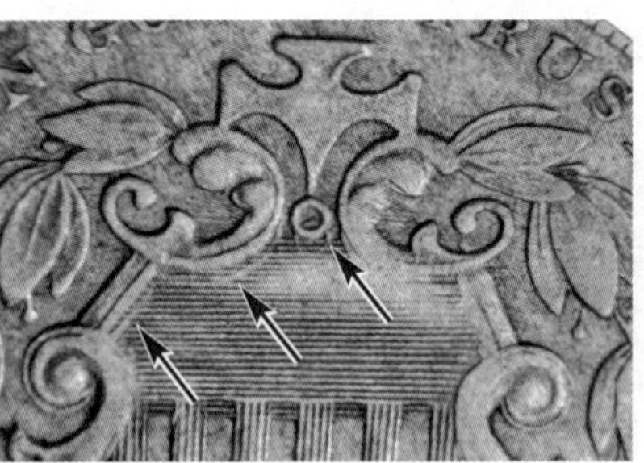 

Description: Moderate doubling is evident on the annulet, the lower right of the cross, the right leaf clusters, and very slightly on the right side of the shield. The RPD is evident by the base of a secondary 1 visible to the west of the primary 1's base.

Comments: To the best of our knowledge, there are only four specimens known.

	F-12	VF-20	EF-40	AU-50	MS-60	MS-63	MS-65
VARIETY	$125	$175	$225	$300	$395	$500	$2,000
NORMAL	$90	$120	$150	$195	$260	$310	$1,725

1882

FS-05-1882-101

VARIETY: Doubled-Die Obverse
PUP: Annulet
URS-1 · I-3 · L-3

FLETCHER-19

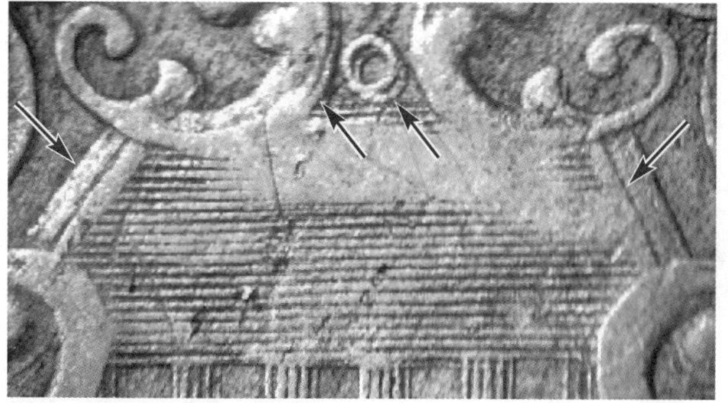

Description: Moderate doubling is evident on the annulet, the lower right of the cross, the right leaf clusters, and very slightly on the right side of the shield.

Comments: To the best of our knowledge, the discovery specimen is the only known example of this variety.

	F-12	VF-20	EF-40	AU-50	MS-60	MS-63	MS-65
VARIETY	$75	$100	$125	$200	$250	$350	$750
NORMAL	$25	$30	$50	$83	$118	$175	$580

1882

FS-05-1882-301 (012.5)

VARIETY: Repunched Date
PUP: Date
URS-4 · I-3 · L-3

FLETCHER-17.01

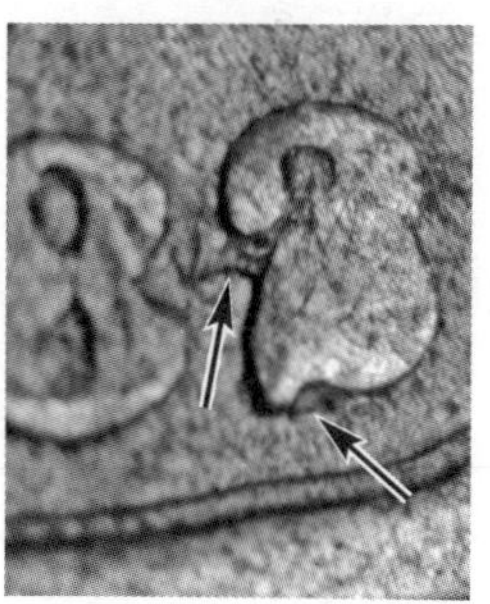

Description: The upper portion of a secondary 2 is evident low between the primary 82.

Comments: This repunched date (and other 1882 nickels with filled 2s) is often incorrectly identified as an 1883/2 overdate. Don't be confused!

	F-12	VF-20	EF-40	AU-50	MS-60	MS-63	MS-65
VARIETY	$75	$100	$125	$200	$250	$350	$750
NORMAL	$28	$35	$60	$110	$140	$195	$725

1882 — FS-05-1882-302

VARIETY: Repunched Date
PUP: Date
URS-3 · I-3 · L-3

FLETCHER-02

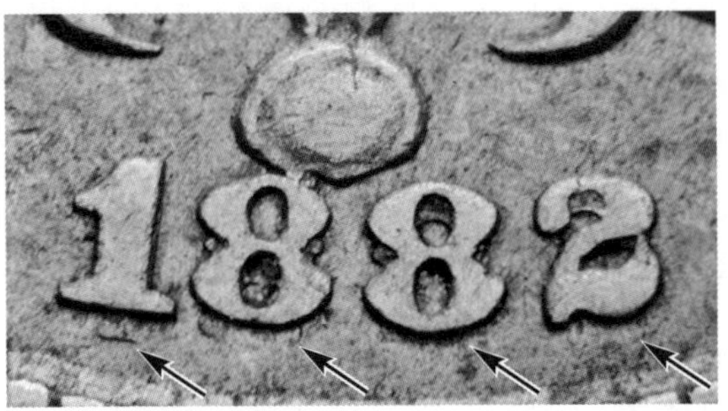

Description: This is a very strong repunched date, with secondary digits evident far to the south of the primary digits.

Comments: This is a relatively new discovery, located shortly after publication of the fourth edition of the *Cherrypickers' Guide*.

	F-12	VF-20	EF-40	AU-50	MS-60	MS-63	MS-65
VARIETY	$50	$75	$100	$150	$195	$350	$750
NORMAL	$25	$30	$50	$83	$118	$175	$580

1882 — FS-05-1882-999

VARIETY: Die Chip
PUP: Date
URS-50 · I-0 · L-0

FLETCHER: N/L

Description: The 2 of the date is filled, caused by a die chip. Various stages are known, and more than one die was affected.

Comments: This is a common die chip on a common coin and is not an 1883/2 overdate! We list this common variety solely to help collectors avoid purchasing it or a similar coin errantly attributed as an 1883/2 overdate. This coin is worth no more than a normal 1882 Shield nickel!

	F-12	VF-20	EF-40	AU-50	MS-60	MS-63	MS-65
VARIETY	$25	$30	$50	$83	$118	$175	$580
NORMAL	$25	$30	$50	$83	$118	$175	$580

1883 — FS-05-1883-301 (013)

VARIETY: Overdate
PUP: Date
URS-8 · I-5 · L-5

FLETCHER-08

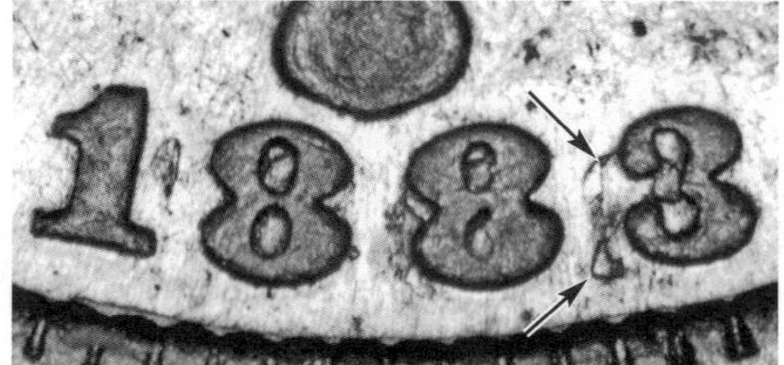

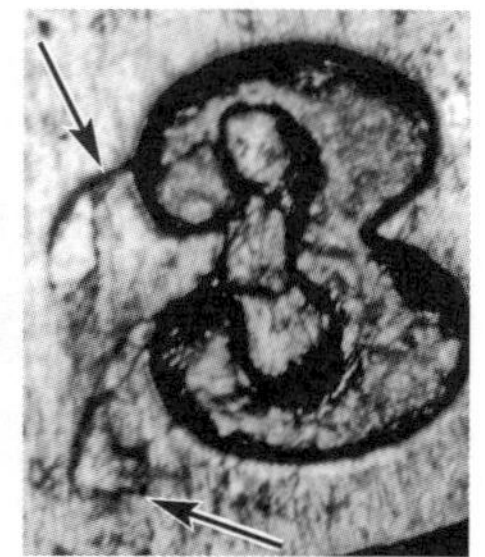

Description: The left half of an underlying 2 is evident between the last 8 and the 3. Secondary digits are also visible on the two 8s.

Comments: Compare this and the four other listed varieties. Additionally, read the text associated with FS-05-1882-999 on the previous page.

	F-12	VF-20	EF-40	AU-50	MS-60	MS-63	MS-65
VARIETY	$410	$650	$925	$1,400	$1,800	$2,000	$5,000+
NORMAL	$25	$30	$50	$83	$118	$175	$580

1883 — FS-05-1883-302 (013.1)

VARIETY: Overdate
PUP: Date
URS-4 · I-5 · L-5

FLETCHER-09

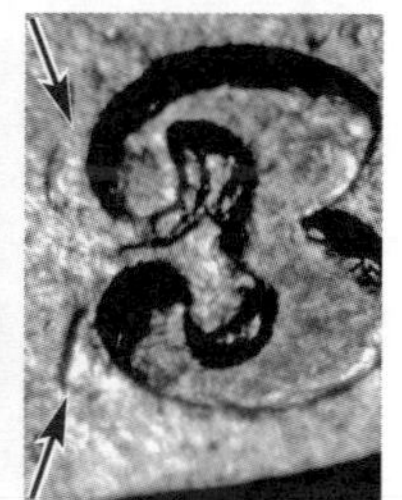

Description: The secondary 2 on this variety is evident to the west of the primary 3, but not as far left as on FS-301. The lower-left curve of the 2 is most evident. Secondary digits are also visible on the two 8s.

Comments: Compare this and the four other listed varieties. Additionally, read the text associated with FS-05-1882-999 on the previous page.

	F-12	VF-20	EF-40	AU-50	MS-60	MS-63	MS-65
VARIETY	$410	$650	$925	$1,400	$1,800	$2,000	$5,000+
NORMAL	$25	$30	$50	$83	$118	$175	$580

1883 — FS-05-1883-303 (013.2)

VARIETY: Overdate
PUP: Date
URS-11 · I-5 · L-5

FLETCHER-10

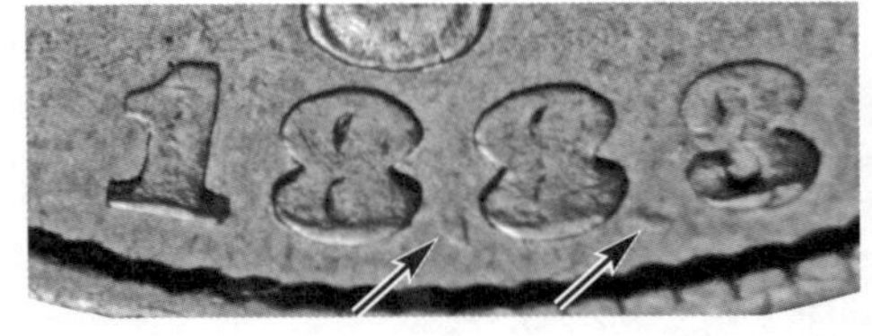

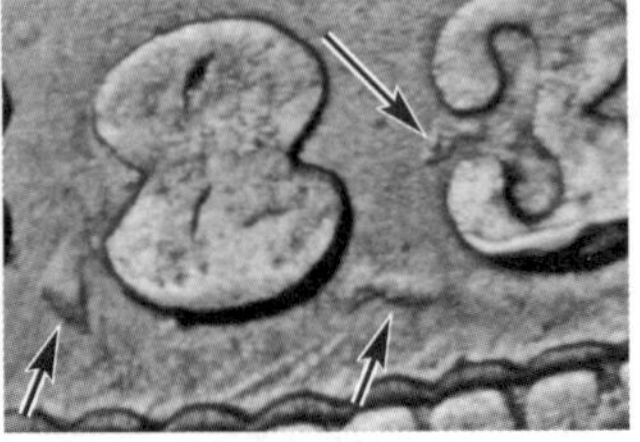

Description: The secondary 2 on this variety is evident far to the west of the primary 3; the lower-left portion of the 2 is most evident, almost touching the 8. The lower portion of a secondary 8 is also evident between the two primary 8s. Some specimens have a die crack running from the rim at 7:00 to the rim at 6:00, and touching the bottom of the 1 and the first 8. Still later die states show a full cud in this area.

Comments: This is likely the most common of the five known varieties. Some specialists feel this die may represent as much as 75 percent of all 1883/2 overdates. Compare this and the other four listed varieties. Additionally, read the text associated with FS-05-1882-999.

	F-12	VF-20	EF-40	AU-50	MS-60	MS-63	MS-65
VARIETY	$410	$650	$925	$1,400	$1,800	$2,000	$5,000+
NORMAL	$25	$30	$50	$83	$118	$175	$580

1883 — FS-05-1883-304 (013.3)

VARIETY: Overdate
PUP: Date
URS-3 · I-5 · L-5

FLETCHER-08.01

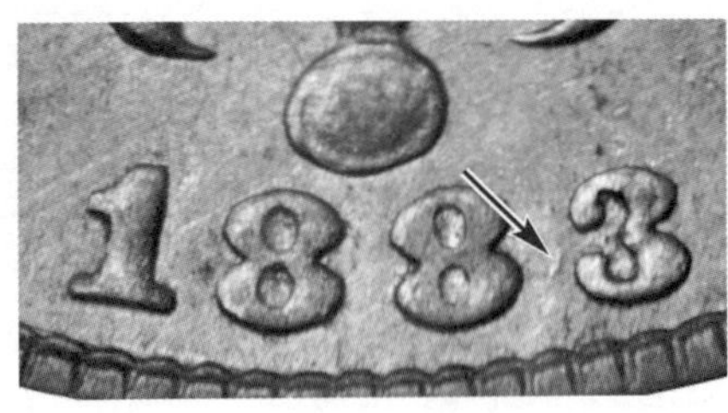

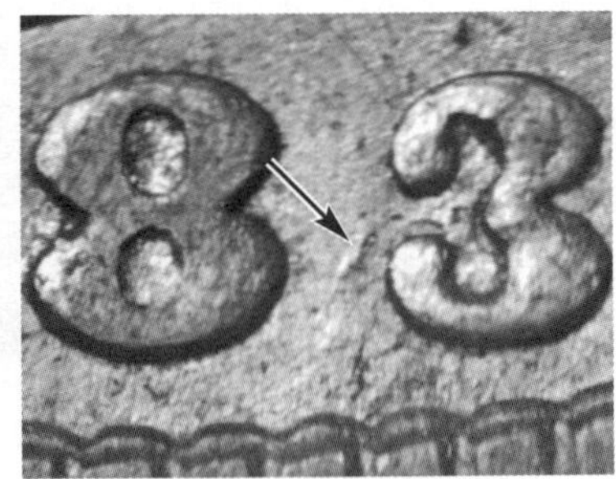

Description: The secondary 2 on this variety is weak but visible to the west of the primary 3. This is similar to the previous listing, but the 2 is not quite as far west. The lower-left curve of the 2 is most evident. Secondary digits are also visible on the two 8s.

Comments: Compare this and the four other listed varieties. Additionally, read the text associated with FS-05-1882-999.

	F-12	VF-20	EF-40	AU-50	MS-60	MS-63	MS-65
VARIETY	$410	$650	$925	$1,400	$1,800	$2,000	$5,000+
NORMAL	$25	$30	$50	$83	$118	$175	$580

1883   FS-05-1883-305

VARIETY: Overdate   **FLETCHER-07**
PUP: Date
URS-4 · I-5 · L-5

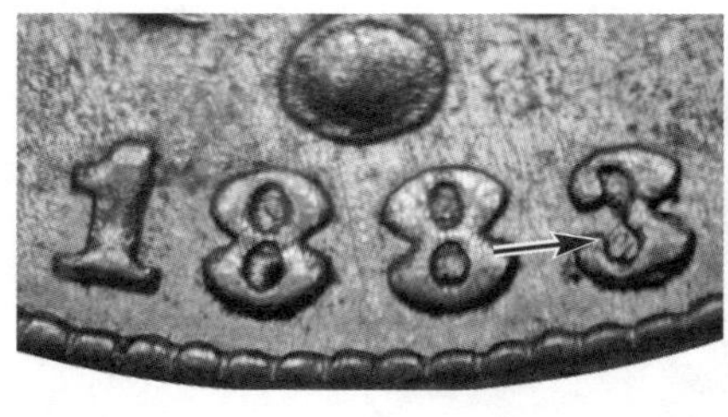
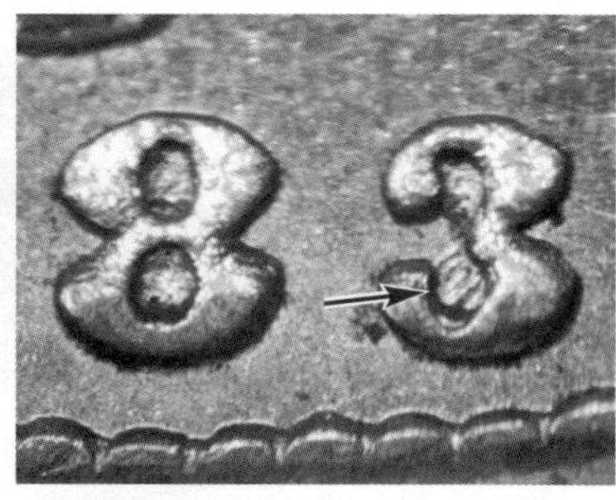

Description: The secondary 2 is centered under the 3. The left curve of the 2 is visible connecting the center point of the 3 with the tip of the lower serif. The lower-left corner of the 2 is visible protruding from the lower-left portion of the 3. This is the only one of the five known overdates where the 2 is not between the last 8 and the 3.

Comments: Compare this and the four other listed varieties. Additionally, read the text associated with FS-05-1882-999.

	F-12	VF-20	EF-40	AU-50	MS-60	MS-63	MS-65
VARIETY	$410	$650	$925	$1,400	$1,800	$2,000	$5,000+
NORMAL	$25	$30	$50	$83	$118	$175	$580

1883   FS-05-1883-311 (012.8)

VARIETY: Repunched Date   **FLETCHER-04**
PUP: Date
URS-4 · I-3 · L-3

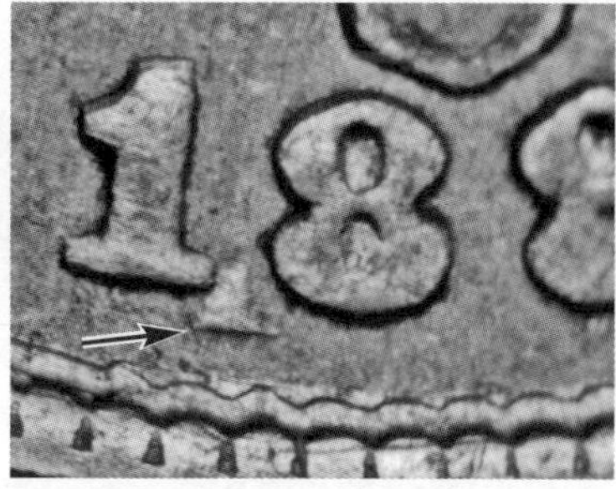

Description: The base of a secondary 1 is evident slightly below and between the 1 and the first 8.

	F-12	VF-20	EF-40	AU-50	MS-60	MS-63	MS-65
VARIETY	$50	$75	$100	$150	$195	$350	$750
NORMAL	$25	$30	$50	$83	$118	$175	$580

1883 — FS-05-1883-312 (012.9)

VARIETY: Repunched Date
PUP: Date
URS-6 · I-3 · L-3

FLETCHER-02

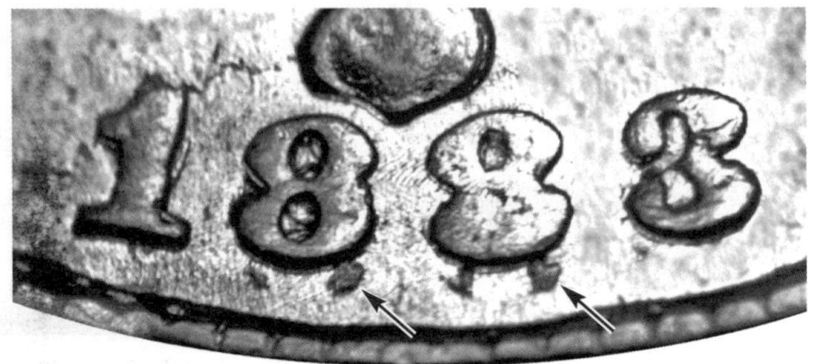

Description: Repunching is evident south of the primary date.

	F-12	VF-20	EF-40	AU-50	MS-60	MS-63	MS-65
VARIETY	$50	$75	$100	$150	$195	$350	$750
NORMAL	$25	$30	$50	$83	$118	$175	$580

A NOTE REGARDING THE OLD FS #5¢-003.55

This variety, illustrated and listed in the fourth edition of the *Cherrypickers' Guide,* is actually an Indian Head cent. It was listed as a Shield nickel by mistake. The old listing number has been deleted from the present text.

Liberty Head Nickels, 1883–1912

The first edition of the *Cherrypickers' Guide*, published in 1990, included a single variety of Liberty Head nickel—the 1887 doubled-die reverse.

Since then, the number of listed Liberty Head nickel die varieties has slowly grown. By the fourth edition, 10 were listed. The present edition includes a few more. Interest in the series has risen with the publication of references including the *Complete Guide to Shield and Liberty Head Nickels* (Peters and Mohon) and the *Guide Book of Shield and Liberty Head Nickels* (Bowers). No doubt, even more varieties will be listed in the next edition of the *Cherrypickers' Guide*.

1883, No Cents — FS-05-1883-1301 (013.7)

VARIETY: Repunched Date
PUP: Date
URS-4 · I-3 · L-3

BREEN: N/L

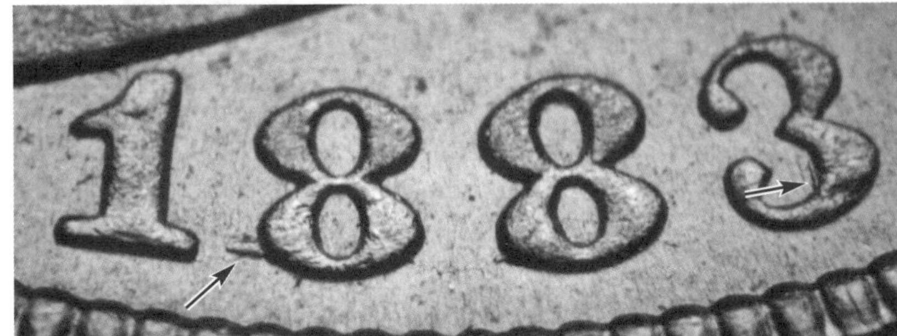

Description: The base of a secondary 1 is evident protruding from the lower-left side of the first 8.

Comments: This is a really interesting RPD, with the position one digit off to the right.

	VF-20	EF-40	AU-50	MS-60	MS-63	MS-65
VARIETY	$20	$35	$50	$75	$100	$275
NORMAL	$9	$10	$11	$22	$40	$230

1883, No Cents — FS-05-1883-1302

VARIETY: Repunched Date
PUP: Date
URS-3 · I-3 · L-3

BREEN: N/L

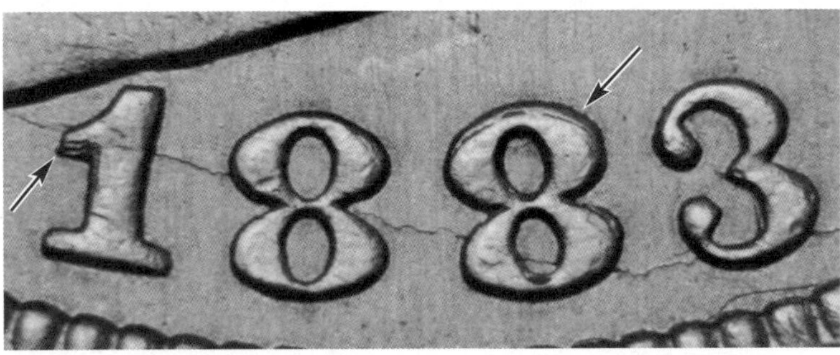

Description: The 1 of the date is actually triple-punched, with secondary digits evident barely to the south, under the flag of the primary 1. A secondary 8 is evident slightly north of the primary second 8.

Comments: It is very likely that more examples of this specimen will be located by observant collectors.

	VF-20	EF-40	AU-50	MS-60	MS-63	MS-65
VARIETY	$20	$35	$50	$75	$100	$275
NORMAL	$9	$10	$11	$22	$40	$230

1884 — FS-05-1884-301 (013.8)

VARIETY: Repunched Date
PUP: Date
URS-7 · I-3 · L-3

BREEN: N/L

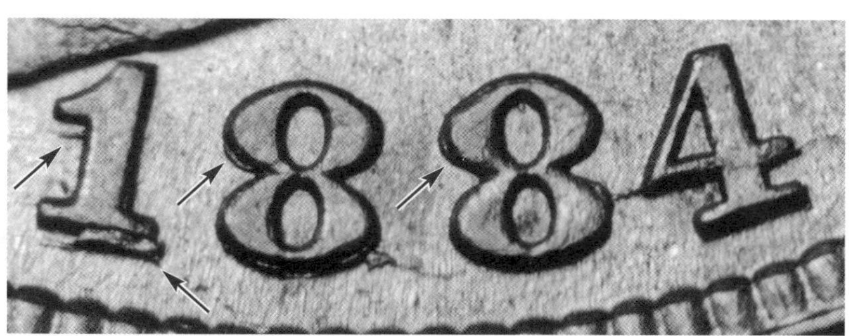

Description: All four digits exhibit secondary digits south, with the spread strongest on the 1 and weaker from left to right.

Comments: The secondary digits of the 8, 8, and 4 may not be visible on late-die-state specimens.

	VF-20	EF-40	AU-50	MS-60	MS-63	MS-65
VARIETY	$65	$100	$135	$200	$295	$1,550
NORMAL	$53	$80	$110	$165	$240	$1,450

1886 — FS-05-1886-301 (013.9)

VARIETY: Repunched Date
PUP: Date
URS-6 · I-3 · L-3

BREEN: N/L

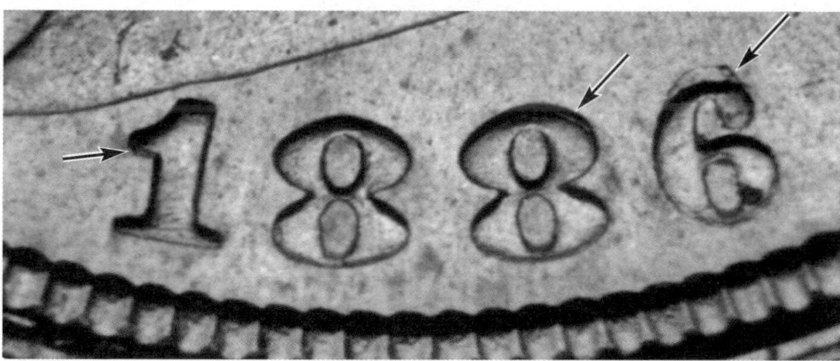

Description: There is a secondary 1 slightly to the south of the primary 1, and a strong secondary 6 to the north of the primary 6.

Comments: Occurring on what is itself a scarce coin, this Liberty Head nickel variety likely will have a very low total certified population, but a high percentage of total date population.

	VF-20	EF-40	AU-50	MS-60	MS-63	MS-65
VARIETY	$475	$650	$750	$1,000	$2,100	$7,200
NORMAL	$450	$620	$725	$950	$1,975	$7,000

1887 — FS-05-1887-801 (014)

VARIETY: Doubled-Die Reverse
PUP: STATES OF AMERICA
URS-6 · I-3 · L-3

BREEN: N/L

Description: Moderate doubling is evident on UNITED STATES OF AMERICA and E PLURIBUS UNUM.

Comments: This variety was first reported by Guy Araby, and very few specimens have been reported since.

	VF-20	EF-40	AU-50	MS-60	MS-63	MS-65
VARIETY	$75	$150	$200	$250	$350	$1,250
NORMAL	$39	$72	$105	$135	$185	$1,000

1888 — FS-05-1888-101

VARIETY: Doubled-Die Obverse
PUP: Ear
URS-2 · I-3 · L-3

BREEN: N/L

Description: Moderate doubling is evident in the form of a doubled earlobe.

Comments: Certainly more examples of this neat variety exist than have been reported.

	VF-20	EF-40	AU-50	MS-60	MS-63	MS-65
VARIETY	$125	$150	$195	$275	$375	$1,550
NORMAL	$93	$129	$171	$221	$300	$1,400

1889 FS-05-1889-301

VARIETY: Repunched Date
PUP: Date
URS-4 · I-3 · L-3

BREEN: N/L

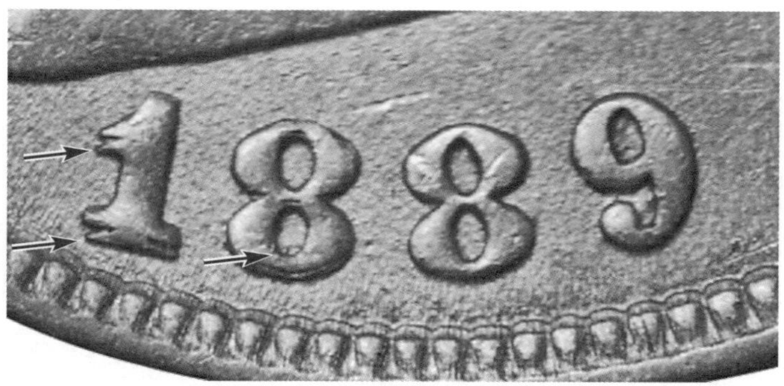

Description: There is a secondary 1 to the southeast of the primary 1, and the first 8 shows a secondary 8 to the southwest of the primary digit.

Comments: To date, only a couple examples of this very nice repunched date have been reported.

	VF-20	EF-40	AU-50	MS-60	MS-63	MS-65
VARIETY	$65	$100	$150	$175	$250	$750
NORMAL	$16	$29	$48	$75	$110	$580

1890 FS-05-1890-301 (014.3)

VARIETY: Repunched Date
PUP: Date
URS-4 · I-3 · L-3

BREEN: N/L

Description: Secondary digits are evident to the south of the primary digits on the 1, 8, and 9.

Comments: Though the first punch was fairly weak, the width of separation is fairly strong.

	VF-20	EF-40	AU-50	MS-60	MS-63	MS-65
VARIETY	$50	$75	$125	$195	$225	$1,500
NORMAL	$35	$60	$100	$155	$195	$1,400

1897 — FS-05-1897-301 (014.48)

VARIETY: Repunched Date
BREEN: N/L
PUP: Date
URS-3 · I-3 · L-3

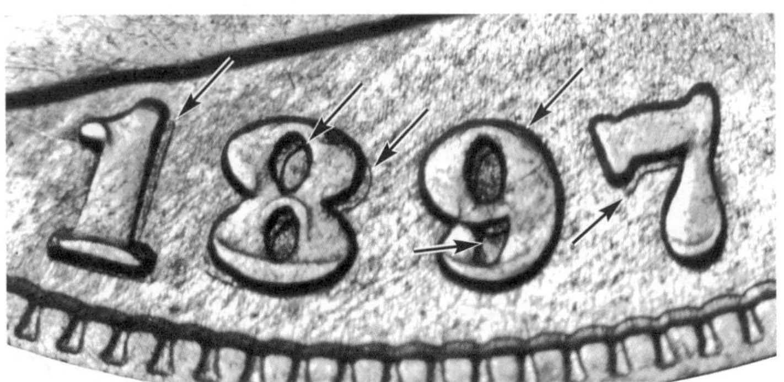

Description: All four digits of the date exhibit secondary digits to the east and south of the primary digits.

Comments: It is our belief that the Liberty Head nickel series is ripe for new finds.

	VF-20	EF-40	AU-50	MS-60	MS-63	MS-65
VARIETY	$35	$65	$100	$125	$195	$950
NORMAL	$25	$45	$65	$90	$150	$900

1898 — FS-05-1898-301 (014.49)

VARIETY: Repunched Date
BREEN: N/L
PUP: Date
URS-4 · I-2 · L-2

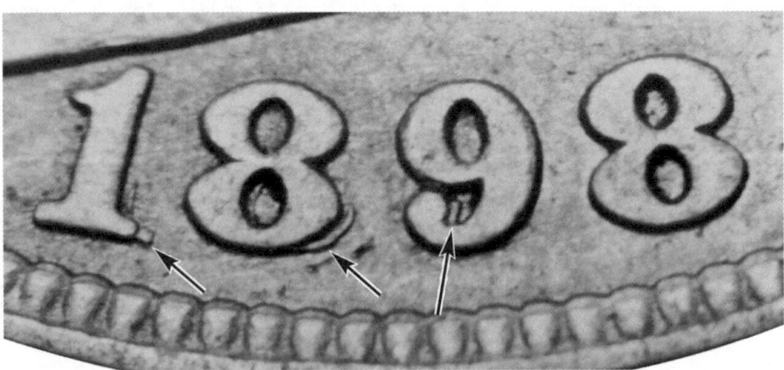

Description: Secondary digits are evident southeast on the 1, 8, and 9.

Comments: Compare this listing with the next.

	VF-20	EF-40	AU-50	MS-60	MS-63	MS-65
VARIETY	$35	$65	$95	$135	$175	$1,100
NORMAL	$20	$42	$65	$95	$145	$925

1898

FS-05-1898-302 (014.495)

VARIETY: Repunched Date
PUP: Date
URS-3 · I-2 · L-2

BREEN: N/L

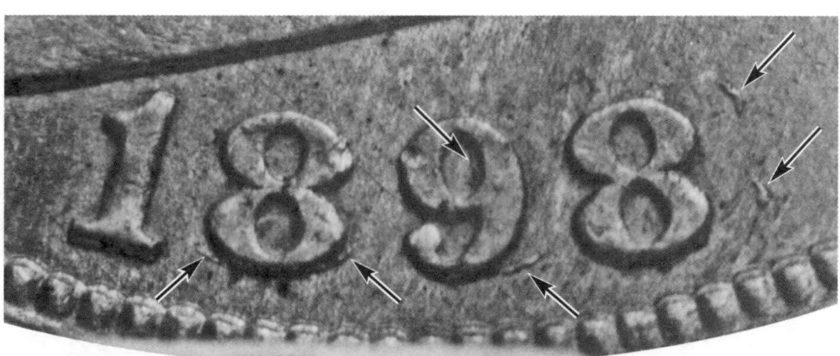

Description: This is actually a triple-punched date. A secondary digit is evident to the west of the lower curve of the first 8. There is a wide spread to the east on the last three primary digits.

Comments: An early-die-state specimen is a neat find!

	VF-20	EF-40	AU-50	MS-60	MS-63	MS-65
VARIETY	$45	$75	$100	$150	$200	$1,100
NORMAL	$20	$42	$65	$95	$145	$925

THE CHERRYPICKERS' GUIDE HELPFUL HINTS

Study and learn the Pick-Up-Points (PUPs) for each series so that you can focus your initial attention on these areas to find varieties. Don't forget the denticle area and the design above the date (especially on 19th century coinage such as the Liberty Seated series) for misplaced numbers, etc. They hide, so use a good loupe and good light.

1899   FS-05-1899-301 (014.5)

VARIETY: Repunched Date   **BREEN: N/L**
PUP: Date
URS-4 · I-3 · L-3

Early Die State

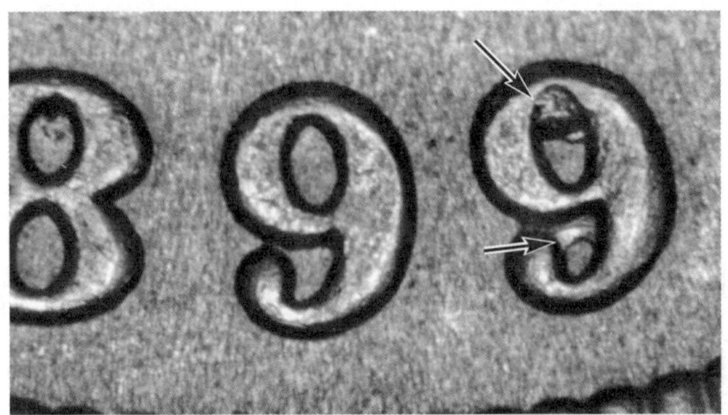

Late Die State

Description: The loop of a 9, or possibly (but unlikely) an 8, is evident within the lower loop of the second 9.

Comments: Some specialists believe this to be a 1899/8 overdate. However, we feel it is simply a repunched date, with the secondary 9 far to the south of the primary 9 at the last digit.

	VF-20	EF-40	AU-50	MS-60	MS-63	MS-65
VARIETY	$35	$75	$125	$175	$225	$750
NORMAL	$18	$30	$58	$85	$130	$600

1900

FS-05-1900-801 (014.7)

VARIETY: Doubled-Die Reverse
PUP: CENTS
URS-5 · I-3 · L-3

BREEN: N/L

Description: Doubling is evident on all reverse design elements, including the V, with a stronger spread on the lower quadrant of the reverse.

Comments: This variety is very popular among specialists.

	VF-20	EF-40	AU-50	MS-60	MS-63	MS-65
VARIETY	$65	$100	$150	$225	$300	$850
NORMAL	$18	$30	$58	$85	$130	$600

Buffalo Nickels, 1913–1938

The Buffalo nickel is one of the most widely collected series of American numismatics. It is very popular with all, in large part due to a great, all-American design concept.

New varieties in this section have been contributed by Marilyn and Leroy Van Allen, R.A. Medina, Rudy Gos, Norm Talbert, Ron Pope, and many others. The most significant variety is very likely the 1914/3 overdate, from both the Philadelphia and the San Francisco mints.

An excellent work on the subject is *Treasure Hunting Buffalo Nickels*, by John Wexler, Ron Pope, and Kevin Flynn. Another is David W. Lange's *Complete Guide to Buffalo Nickels*. Q. David Bowers's *Guide Book of Buffalo and Jefferson Nickels* is also recommended.

1913, Type I

FS-05-1913-901 (014.85)

VARIETY: 3-1/2-Legged Buffalo

CONECA: N/L

PUP: Front leg

URS-4 · I-4 · L-4

Description: The reverse die was heavily polished, possibly to remove clash marks. The result was a die with most of the bison's front leg missing, hence the nickname "3-1/2-Legged buffalo."

Comments: This variety was reportedly discovered by Joseph Ambrulevich about 1988.

	VF-20	EF-40	AU-50	MS-60	MS-63	MS-65
VARIETY	$200	$350	$450	$600	$750	$1,250
NORMAL	$15	$19	$23	$29	$50	$175

THE CHERRYPICKERS' GUIDE HELPFUL HINTS

Remember, if you can't see the characteristics of a coin clearly, you'll likely miss the important one. Don't take a chance. Always use a good, Hastings triplet magnifier (7x or 10x). The added expense will be more than offset by just one nice find. There are additional magnifying suggestions in appendix C.

1913, Type II   FS-05-1913-1101 (014.8)

VARIETY: Doubled-Die Obverse   **CONECA: 1-O-VI**
PUP: Date
URS-4 · I-4 · L-3

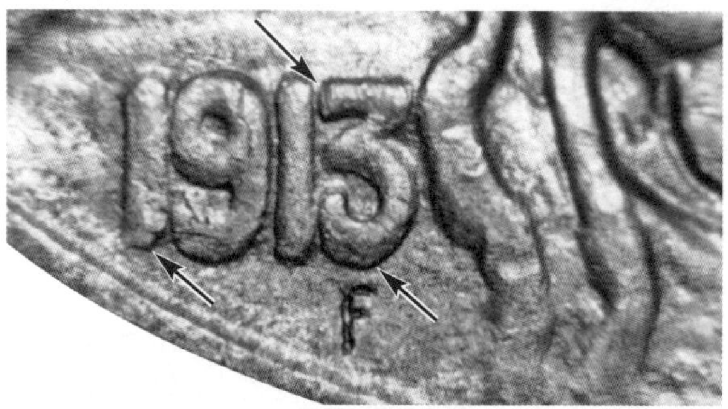

Description: Moderate doubling is evident on the date, with the secondary image visible south of the primary digits.

Comments: As a Class VI doubled die, doubling may not be evident on late stages, but would show extra-thick numerals.

	VF-20	EF-40	AU-50	MS-60	MS-63	MS-65
VARIETY	$35	$50	$75	$100	$150	$375
NORMAL	$13	$20	$24	$29	$55	$335

1913, Type II   FS-05-1913-1801 (014.86)

VARIETY: Doubled-Die Reverse   **CONECA: 1-R-II+VI**
PUP: FIVE CENTS
URS-5 · I-3 · L-3

Description: Doubling is evident to the south on the letters of FIVE CENTS.

Comments: The doubling on this variety is very similar to that on a variety from 1930 listed as FS-05-1930-801.

	VF-20	EF-40	AU-50	MS-60	MS-63	MS-65
VARIETY	$35	$50	$75	$100	$150	$375
NORMAL	$13	$20	$24	$29	$55	$335

1913-D, Type 1   FS-05-1913D-401 (014.861)

VARIETY: Two Feathers   **CONECA: N/L**
PUP: Feathers
URS-6 · I-3 · L-3

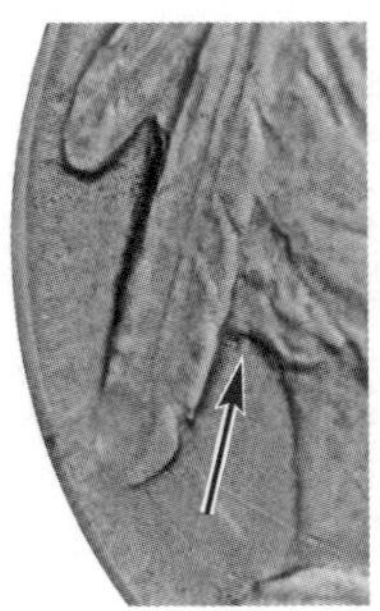 

Description: The obverse die was heavily polished, probably to remove clash marks. The result was a die with the innermost feather missing, hence the nickname "Two Feathers."

Comments: Recently more Two Feathers varieties have been found, creating a search for more while increasing interest in Buffalo nickels with abraded dies.

	VF-20	EF-40	AU-50	MS-60	MS-63
VARIETY	$75	–	–	–	–
NORMAL	$32	$42	$75	$80	$85

1914   FS-05-1914-101 (014.87)

VARIETY: Overdate   **CONECA: N/L**
PUP: Date
URS-7 · I-5 · L-4

Description: The overdate is seen as the straight top bar of the underlying 3 at the top of the 4 and the start of the 3's diagonal on the upper right outside of the 4. On some, a hint of the curve of the lower portion of the 3 shows just above the crossbar of the 4.

Comments: Since first being reported in January of 1997, many specimens have been found. Additionally, another overdate on the 1914-S has been confirmed (see FS-05-1914S-101) and a 1914-D is rumored. These facts lead many specialists to believe that this is the result of the date on a maser die being repunched, which could mean that many working dies would be affected. More study is being conducted. First reported by R.A. Medina with confirmation from Roger Alexander. There are several different overdate dies known for the Philadelphia Mint issue. The one illustrated here is the strongest.

	VF-20	EF-40	AU-50	MS-60	MS-63
VARIETY	$700	$800	$1,800	$3,500	$9,000
NORMAL	$25	$32	$45	$58	$90

1914-S — FS-05-1914S-101 (014.89)

VARIETY: Overdate
PUP: Date
URS-6 · I-5 · L-5

CONECA: N/L

Description: See the description for FS-05-1914-101, as both descriptions are the same.

Comments: See the comments for FS-05-1914-101.

	VF-20	EF-40	AU-50	MS-60	MS-63
VARIETY	$570	$675	$2,100	$4,000	$6,800
NORMAL	$65	$90	$160	$210	$475

1915 — FS-05-1915-101 (014.9)

VARIETY: Doubled-Die Obverse
PUP: Eye, nostril
URS-6 · I-4 · L-3

CONECA: 1-V-IV

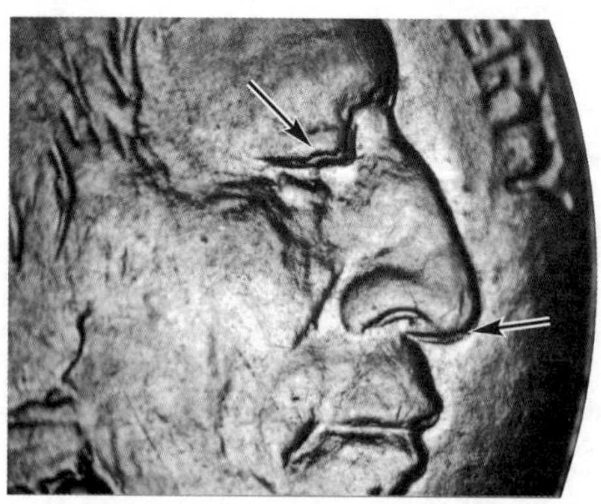

Description: The doubling is evident as a secondary image on the eyelid, nose, and nostril.

Comments: The doubling on this variety is very similar to that on FS-05-1930-101 (017).

	VF-20	EF-40	AU-50	MS-60	MS-63
VARIETY	$40	$80	$135	–	$150
NORMAL	$11	$24	$45	$60	$85

1915

FS-05-1915-401 (014.91)

VARIETY: Two Feathers

CONECA: N/L

PUP: Feathers

URS-8 · I-3 · L-3

 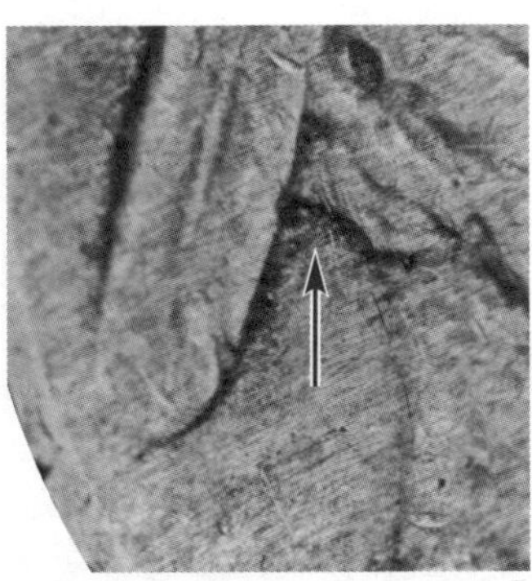

Description: The obverse die was heavily polished, probably to remove clash marks. The result was a die with the innermost feather missing, hence the nickname "Two Feathers."

Comments: Recently more Two Feathers varieties have been found, creating a search for more while increasing interest in Buffalo nickels with abraded dies.

	VF-20	EF-40	AU-50	MS-60	MS-63
VARIETY	$47	–	–	–	–
NORMAL	$11	$224	$45	$60	$85

1915-D

FS-05-1915D-501 (015)

VARIETY: Repunched Mintmark

CONECA: RPM-001

PUP: Mintmark

URS-4 · I-5 · L-3

Description: The second D is northeast of the primary image.

Comments: A very rare variety, especially in high grade.

	VF-20	EF-40	AU-50	MS-60	MS-63
VARIETY	–	$320	$500	$700	$1,400
NORMAL	$68	$120	$160	$275	$360

1915-S — FS-05-1915S-501 (015.5)

VARIETY: Repunched Mintmark
PUP: Mintmark
URS-1 · I-4 · L-3

CONECA: RPM-001

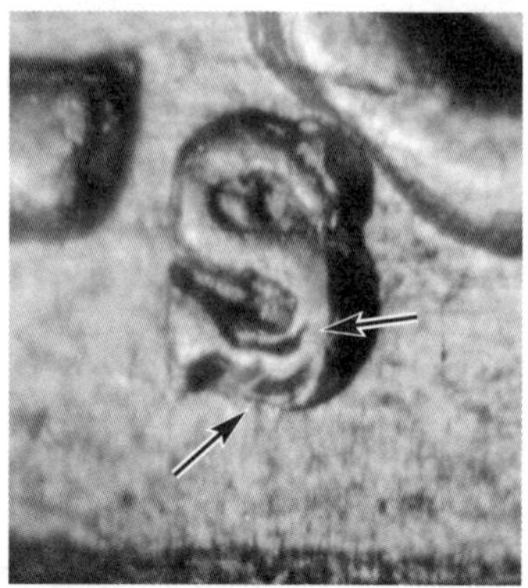

Description: Actually triple punched, with the secondary S's to the north and south of the primary image.

Comments: A very rare variety, especially in high grade.

	VF-20	EF-40	AU-50	MS-60	MS-63
VARIETY	$250	$485	$650	–	$1,300
NORMAL	$185	$420	$500	$630	$1,000

1915-S — FS-05-1915S-502 (015.6)

VARIETY: Repunched Mintmark
PUP: Mintmark
URS-1 · I-4 · L-3

CONECA: RPM-002

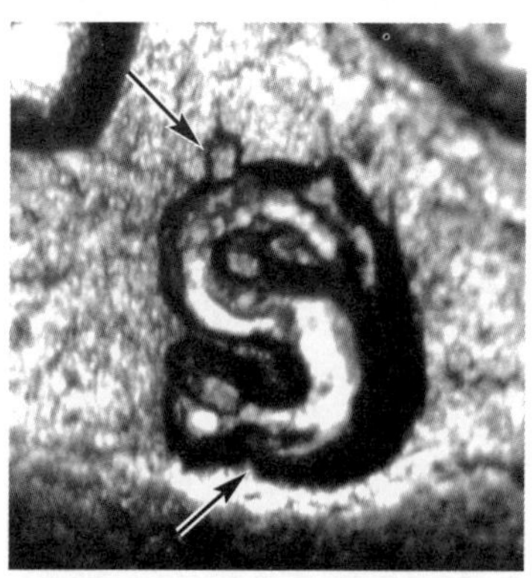

Description: Actually triple punched with the secondary S's to the northeast and south of the primary image.

Comments: Further study could prove four or more punchings!

	VF-20	EF-40	AU-50	MS-60	MS-63
VARIETY	$250	$485	$650	–	$1,300
NORMAL	$185	$420	$500	$630	$1,000

1916   FS-05-1916-101 (016)

VARIETY: Doubled-Die Obverse   **CONECA: 1-O-V**
PUP: Date
URS-9 · I-5 · L-5

Description: The date, chin, throat, feathers, and the tie on the braids are all doubled. The date is doubled to the southeast, with the top two-thirds of the 16 quite strong, and the lower two-thirds of the 19 virtually missing.

Comments: Although well known, this variety is quite rare. Beware of 1916 nickels with strike doubling on the date offered as this variety. Please read the appendix on other forms of doubling. The true doubled die must look like the coin shown here.

	VF-20	EF-40	AU-50	MS-60	MS-63
VARIETY	$11,500	$16,000	$35,000	$68,000	$175,000
NORMAL	$10	$13	$21	$48	$80

1916   FS-05-1916-401 (016.3)

VARIETY: Missing Designer's Initial   **CONECA: N/L**
PUP: Date area
URS-5 · I-3 · L-3

Description: The initial F, normally below the date, is obviously missing.

Comments: There are some dies with a partially missing or weak initial, but these do not command the premium of this variety with no trace showing.

	VF-20	EF-40	AU-50	MS-60	MS-63
VARIETY	–	$200	$280	–	$660
NORMAL	$10	$13	$21	$48	$80

1917   FS-05-1917-401 (016.411)

VARIETY: Two Feathers   **CONECA: N/L**
PUP: Feathers
URS-6 · I-3 · L-3

 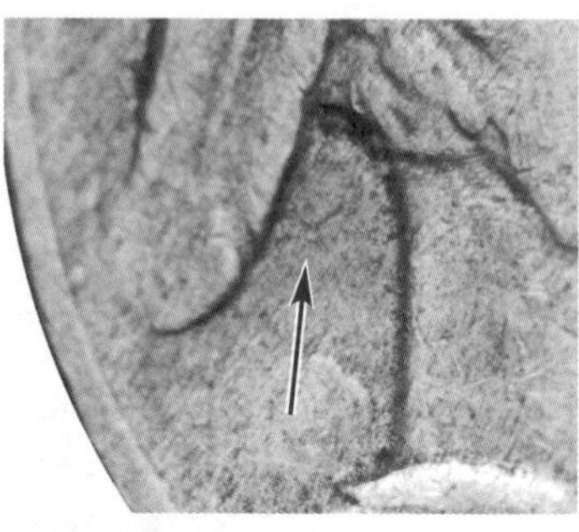

Description: The obverse die was heavily polished, probably to remove clash marks. The result was a die with the innermost feather missing, hence the nickname "Two Feathers."

	VF-20	EF-40	AU-50	MS-60	MS-63
VARIETY	–	–	$275	–	–
NORMAL	$9	$16	$32	$58	$145

1917   FS-05-1917-801 (016.4)

VARIETY: Doubled-Die Reverse   **CONECA: 1-R-III**
PUP: E PLURIBUS UNUM
URS-5 · I-4 · L-3

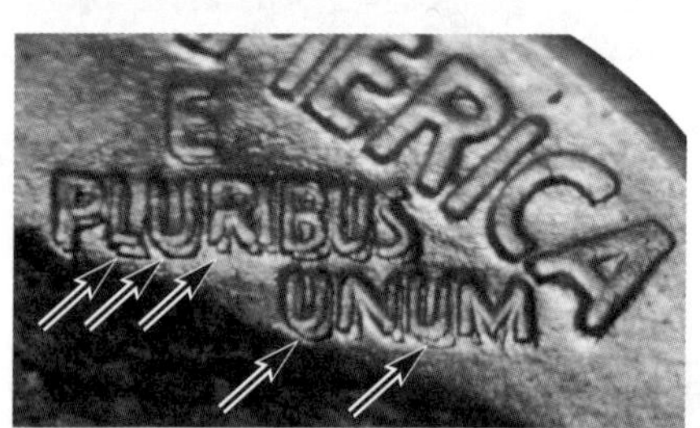

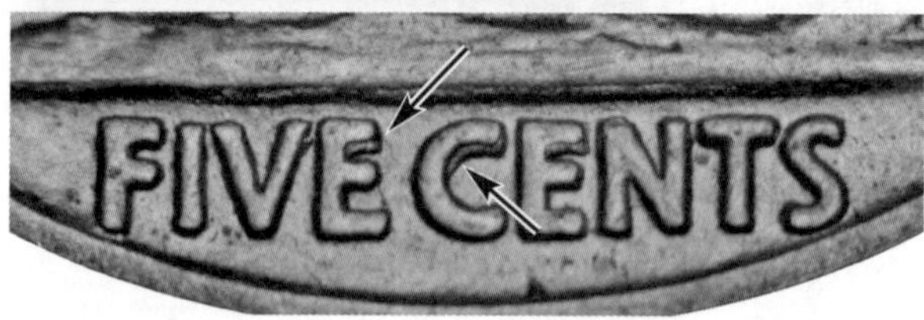

Description: Doubling is clearest on E PLURIBUS UNUM, the VE CE of FIVE CENTS, the lower ground, and the legs, horn, beard, and mane of the buffalo.

Comments: Another reverse doubled die variety has been discovered, but it is far less dramatic. (See FS-05-1917-802.)

	VF-20	EF-40	AU-50	MS-60	MS-63
VARIETY	–	$1,260	$1,750	–	–
NORMAL	$9	$16	$32	$58	$145

1917 — FS-05-1917-802 (016.41)

VARIETY: Doubled-Die Reverse

PUP: E PLURIBUS UNUM

URS-4 · I-3 · L-3

CONECA: 2-R-IV

Description: Doubling is clearest to the northeast on E PLURIBUS UNUM.

Comments: This is the weaker of the two reported 1917 DDRs. See FS-05-1917-801 for the other.

	VF-20	EF-40	AU-50	MS-60	MS-63
VARIETY	–	$120	$315	–	$600
NORMAL	$9	$16	$32	$58	$145

1917-D — FS-05-1917D-401 (016.43)

VARIETY: Two Feathers

PUP: Feathers

URS-6 · I-3 · L-3

CONECA: N/L

 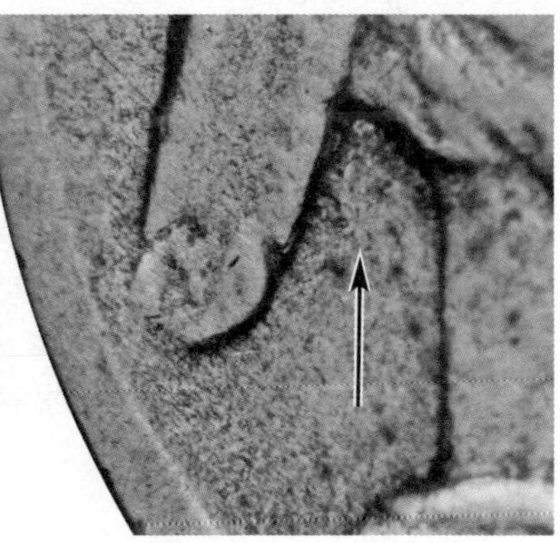

Description: The obverse die was heavily polished, probably to remove clash marks. The result was a die with the innermost feather missing, hence the nickname "Two Feathers."

	VF-20	EF-40	AU-50	MS-60	MS-63
VARIETY	$100	–	–	–	–
NORMAL	$85	$140	$250	$325	$820

1917-D · FS-05-1917D-901 (016.42)

VARIETY: 3-1/2-Legged Buffalo
PUP: Front leg of buffalo
URS-5 · I-4 · L-4

CONECA: N/L

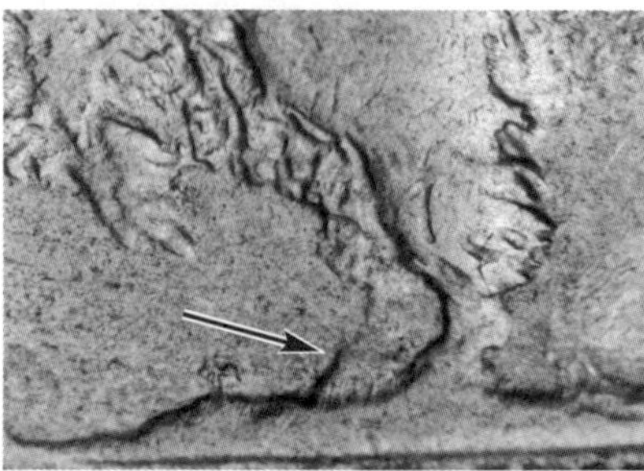

Description: The reverse die was heavily polished, probably to remove clash marks. The result was a die with portions of the buffalo's front leg missing, hence the nickname "3-1/2-Legged Buffalo."

Comments: This is the most recent discovery of a 3- or 3-1/2-Legged Buffalo, having been first reported in 1999 by Bob White. There is also a possibility that this is has a doubled-die obverse. The die state of the discovery piece makes it difficult to tell. We would love to see an earlier die state.

	VF-20	EF-40	AU-50	MS-60	MS-63
VARIETY	–	$260	$400	–	–
NORMAL	$85	$140	$250	$325	$820

1917-S · FS-05-1917S-401 (016.44)

VARIETY: Two Feathers
PUP: Feathers
URS-6 · I-3 · L-3

CONECA: N/L

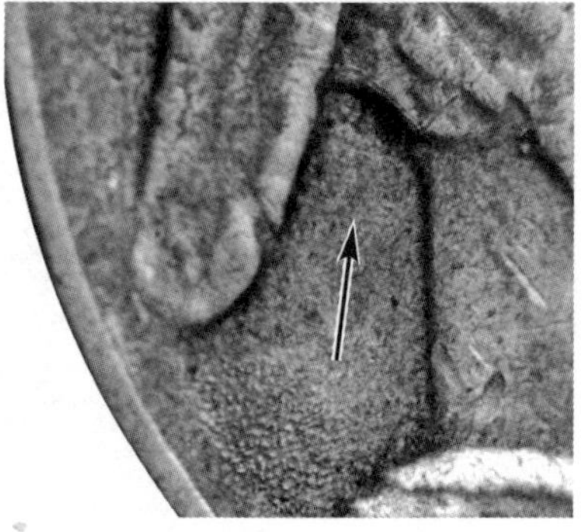

Description: The obverse die was heavily polished, probably to remove clash marks. The result was a die with the innermost feather missing, hence the nickname "Two Feathers."

	VF-20	EF-40	AU-50	MS-60	MS-63
VARIETY	$155	–	–	–	–
NORMAL	$105	$190	$340	$420	$1,400

1918

FS-05-1918-401 (016.46)

VARIETY: Two Feathers
PUP: Feathers
URS-6 · I-3 · L-3

CONECA: N/L

 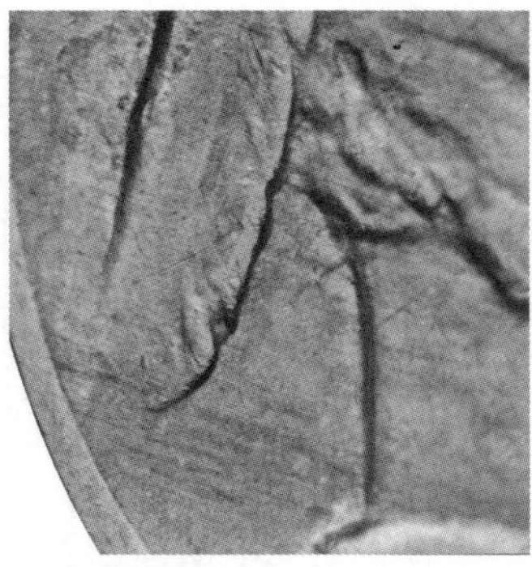

Description: The obverse die was heavily polished, probably to remove clash marks. The result was a die with the innermost feather missing, hence the nickname "Two Feathers."

	VF-20	EF-40	AU-50	MS-60	MS-63
VARIETY	$60	–	–	–	–
NORMAL	$16	$32	$48	$105	$350

1918

FS-05-1918-801 (016.45)

VARIETY: Doubled-Die Reverse
PUP: E PLURIBUS UNUM
URS-4 · I-3 · L-4

CONECA: 1-R-II

Description: Doubling is clearest to the north on E PLURIBUS UNUM.

Comments: We anticipate the interest in this relative newcomer will increase. Some specimens show a die crack on the reverse from the rim to the bison's rump, just below the tail.

	VF-20	EF-40	AU-50	MS-60	MS-63
VARIETY	$1,150	$1,400	$2,300	$3,500	$7,000
NORMAL	$16	$32	$48	$105	$350

1918-D   FS-05-1918D-101 (016.5)

VARIETY: Overdate   **CONECA: 1-O-III**
PUP: Date
URS-9 · I-5 · L-5

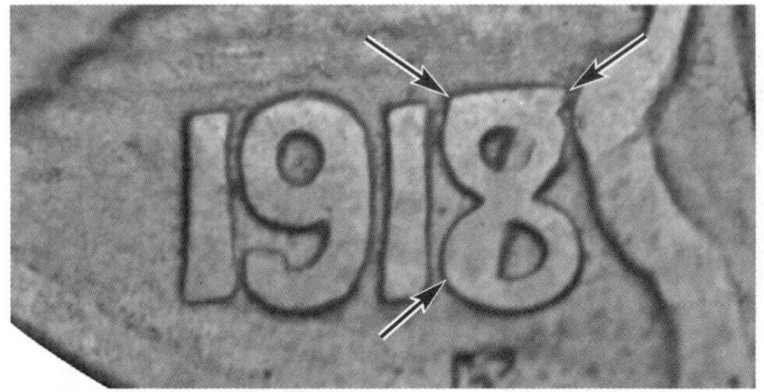

Description: A very rare overdate, with the top of the 8 extending halfway up into the horizontal bar of the 7. The two "ears" of the 7 show clearly, as well as the flat top surface of the 7. The diagonal of the 7 is straight, not curved, and appears on the right portion of the upper loop and the left half of the lower loop.

Comments: Look for the small die crack immediately above the tie on the braid, leading slightly downward to the Indian's jaw. The beginning of this die break can usually be seen even on lower grade coins.

	VF-20	EF-40	AU-50	MS-60	MS-63
VARIETY	$6,000	$10,000	$13,500	$35,000	$68,500
NORMAL	$135	$210	$340	$420	$1,300

1918-S   FS-05-1918S-401 (016.6)

VARIETY: Two Feathers   **CONECA: N/L**
PUP: Feathers
URS-6 · I-3 · L-3

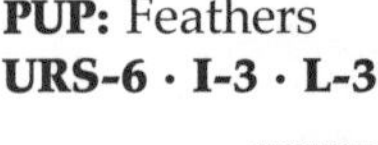

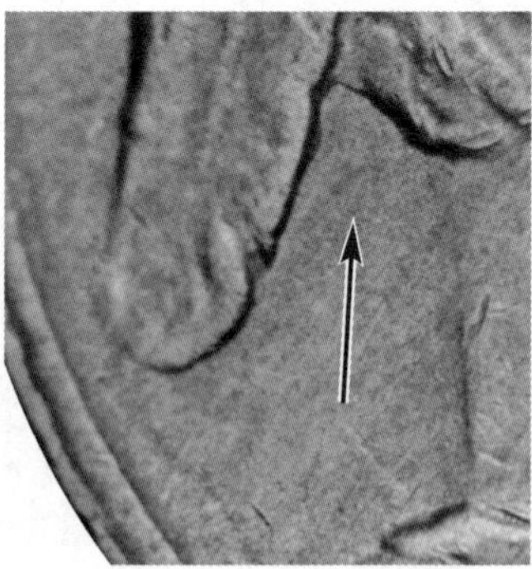

Description: The obverse die was heavily polished, probably to remove clash marks. The result was a die with the innermost feather missing, hence the nickname "Two Feathers."

	VF-20	EF-40	AU-50	MS-60	MS-63
VARIETY	$125	–	–	–	–
NORMAL	$105	$200	$325	$580	$3,400

1919 — FS-05-1919-401 (016.61)

VARIETY: Two Feathers + Missing Designer's Initial
PUP: Feathers
URS-6 · I-3 · L-3

CONECA: N/L

 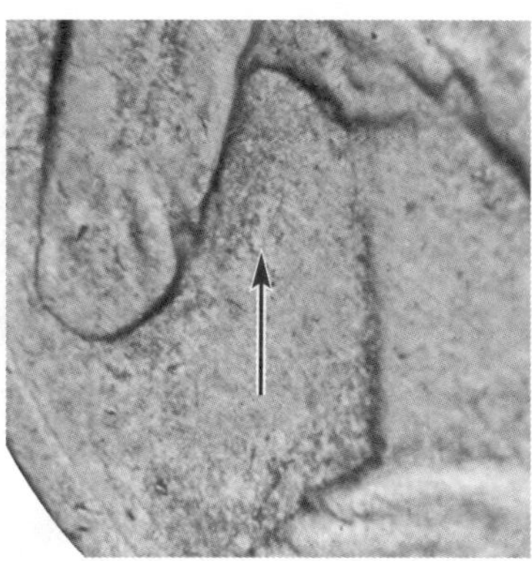

Description: The obverse die was heavily polished, probably to remove clash marks. The result was a die with the innermost feather missing, hence the nickname "Two Feathers." Also missing is the designer's initial.

	VF-20	EF-40	AU-50	MS-60	MS-63
VARIETY	$62	–	–	–	–
NORMAL	$8	$15	$32	$58	$135

1920-D — FS-05-1920D-501 (016.63)

VARIETY: Repunched Mintmark
PUP: Mintmark
URS-3 · I-3 · L-3

CONECA: RPM-001

Description: The secondary D is visible to the west of the primary D.

	VF-20	EF-40	AU-50	MS-60	MS-63
VARIETY	–	$340	$375	–	$2,100
NORMAL	$125	$290	$340	$550	$1,750

1920-S — FS-05-1920S-401 (016.631)

VARIETY: Two Feathers   **CONECA: N/L**
PUP: Feathers
URS-6 · I-3 · L-3

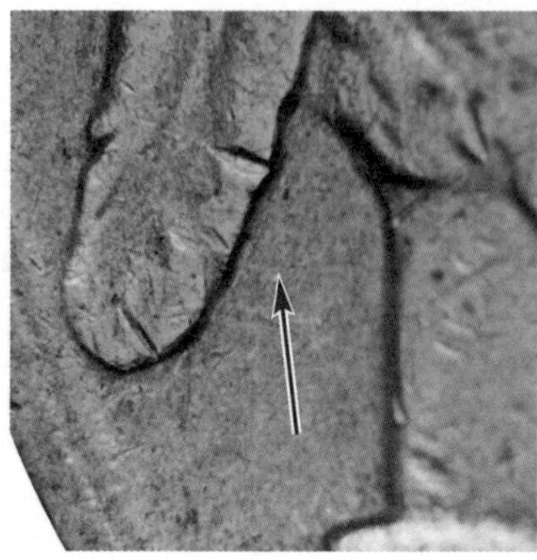

Description: The obverse die was heavily polished, probably to remove clash marks. The result was a die with the innermost feather missing, hence the nickname "Two Feathers."

	VF-20	EF-40	AU-50	MS-60	MS-63
VARIETY	$130	–	–	–	–
NORMAL	$95	$185	$325	$550	$2,300

1921 — FS-05-1921-401 (016.633)

VARIETY: Two Feathers   **CONECA: N/L**
PUP: Feathers
URS-6 · I-3 · L-3

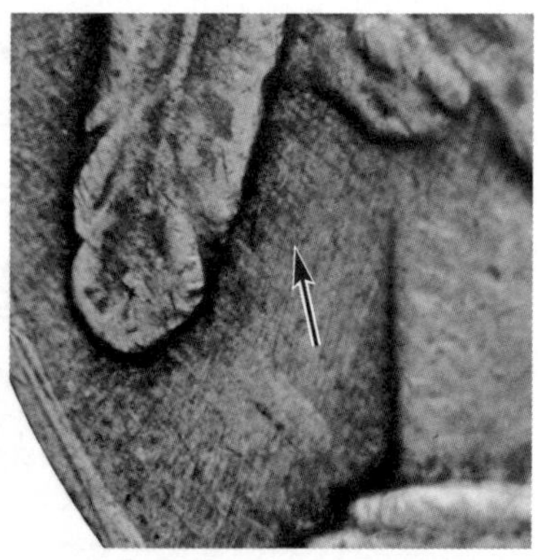

Description: The obverse die was heavily polished, probably to remove clash marks. The result was a die with the innermost feather missing, hence the nickname "Two Feathers."

	VF-20	EF-40	AU-50	MS-60	MS-63
VARIETY	$135	–	–	–	–
NORMAL	$26	$53	$80	$140	$340

1921-S
FS-05-1921S-401 (016.635)

VARIETY: Two Feathers
PUP: Feathers
URS-6 · I-3 · L-3

CONECA: N/L

Description: The obverse die was heavily polished, probably to remove clash marks. The result was a die with the innermost feather missing, hence the nickname "Two Feathers."

	VF-20	EF-40	AU-50	MS-60	MS-63
VARIETY	$670	–	–	–	–
NORMAL	$580	$1,000	$1,300	$1,700	$2,300

1925-D
FS-05-1925D-401 (016.638)

VARIETY: Two Feathers
PUP: Feathers
URS-6 · I-3 · L-3

CONECA: N/L

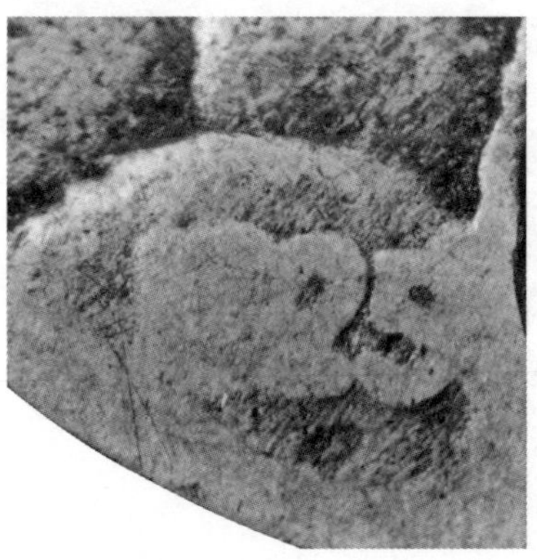 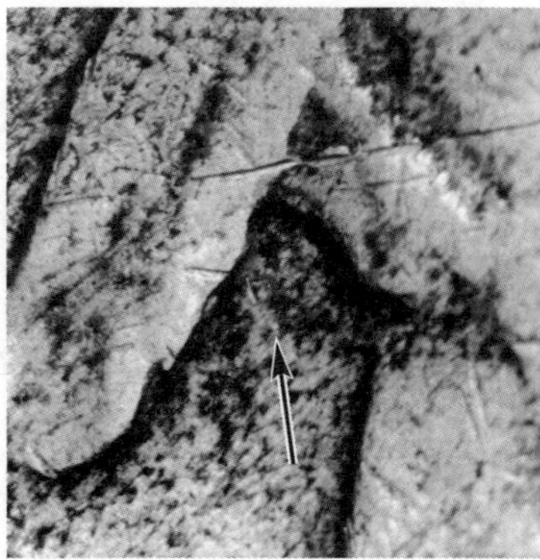

Description: The obverse die was heavily polished, probably to remove clash marks. The result was a die with the innermost feather missing, hence the nickname "Two Feathers."

	VF-20	EF-40	AU-50	MS-60	MS-63
VARIETY	–	$225	–	–	–
NORMAL	$95	$185	$265	$400	$800

1925-S — FS-05-1925S-401 (016.641)

VARIETY: Two Feathers
PUP: Feathers
URS-6 · I-3 · L-3

CONECA: N/L

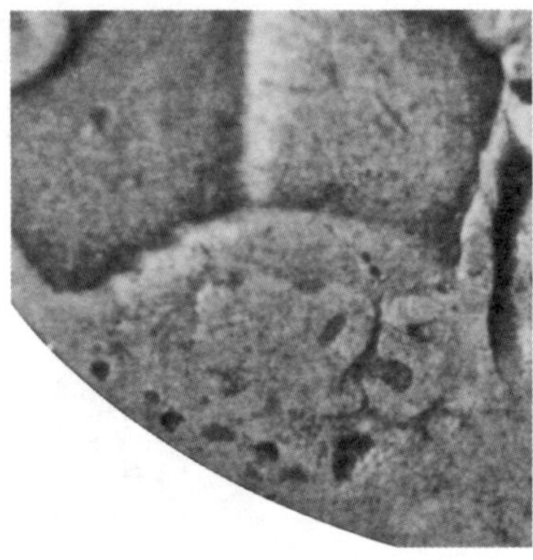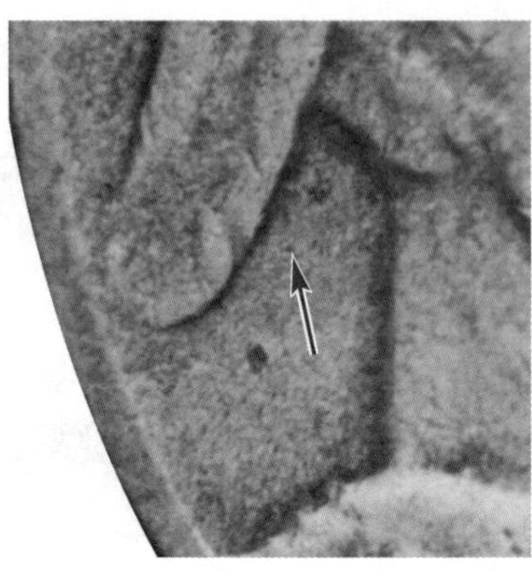

Description: The obverse die was heavily polished, probably to remove clash marks. The result was a die with the innermost feather missing, hence the nickname "Two Feathers."

	VF-20	EF-40	AU-50	MS-60	MS-63
VARIETY	$130	–	–	–	–
NORMAL	$95	$190	$265	$500	$2,500

1925-S — FS-05-1925S-501 (016.64)

VARIETY: Repunched Mintmark
PUP: Mintmark
URS-4 · I-3 · L-3

CONECA: RPM-001

Description: The secondary S is visible to the east of the primary S.

Comments: Known for a long time, this variety has received very little publicity.

	VF-20	EF-40	AU-50	MS-60	MS-63
VARIETY	–	$325	$5,000	–	–
NORMAL	$95	$190	$265	$500	$2,500

1927-D

FS-05-1927D-501 (016.7)

VARIETY: Repunched Mintmark
PUP: Mintmark
URS-3 · I-4 · L-4

CONECA: RPM-001

Description: There are remnants of two secondary mintmarks, one to the north and one to the south of the primary mintmark.

Comments: The prices listed are estimates, and will almost certainly change as more specimens surface and more transactions are recorded.

	VF-20	EF-40	AU-50	MS-60	MS-63
VARIETY	–	–	$340	$375	$475
NORMAL	$35	$90	$150	$175	$350

1927-D

FS-05-1927D-901 (016.65)

VARIETY: 3-1/2-Legged Buffalo
PUP: Front leg
URS-4 · I-4 · L-3

CONECA: N/L

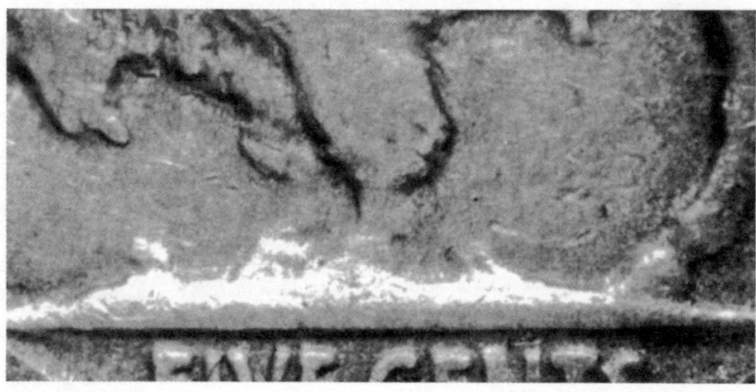

Description: The reverse die was heavily polished, possibly to remove clash marks. The result was a die with most of the bison's front leg missing, hence the nickname "3-1/2-Legged Buffalo."

Comments: First reported by Ron Pope.

	VF-20	EF-40	AU-50	MS-60	MS-63
VARIETY	–	$425	–	–	–
NORMAL	$35	$90	$150	$175	$350

1929-S — FS-05-1929S-101 (016.8)

VARIETY: Doubled-Die Obverse

CONECA: 1-O-IV

PUP: Date

URS-5 · I-3 · L-2

Description: The doubling is visible on the date, neck, and hair braid.

	VF-20	EF-40	AU-50	MS-60	MS-63
VARIETY	$45	$95	$165	$250	$400
NORMAL	$2	$13	$27	$58	$85

1930 — FS-05-1930-101 (017)

VARIETY: Doubled-Die Obverse

CONECA: 1-O-IV

PUP: Eyelid, nostril

URS-9 · I-3 · L-2

 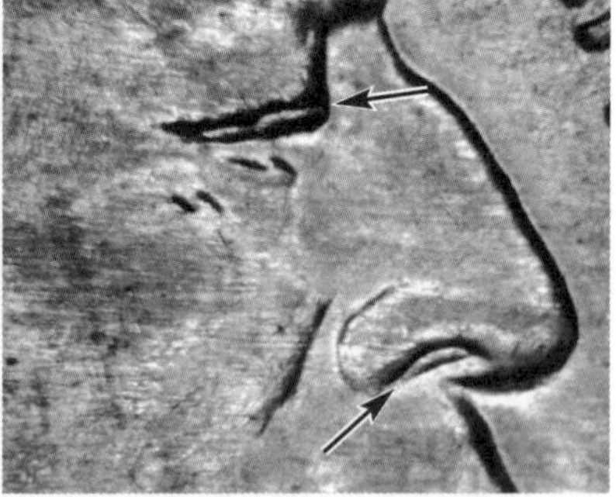

Description: There are at least six different varieties of doubled obverse dies for this date, the strongest pictured here. The doubling may be picked up on the upper eyelid, nostril, and upper lip. The date is also slightly doubled.

Comments: The doubling on one of the other varieties of this date is very similar to this one but not as strong. On a third, a strongly doubled brow on the Indian is the PUP.

	VF-20	EF-40	AU-50	MS-60	MS-63
VARIETY	–	$250	$325	$375	–
NORMAL	$4.50	$12	$21	$37	$80

1930   FS-05-1930-801 (017.5)

VARIETY: Doubled-Die Reverse—5-Legged Buffalo
CONECA: 1-R-IV
PUP: Left front leg
URS-5 · I-3 · L-3

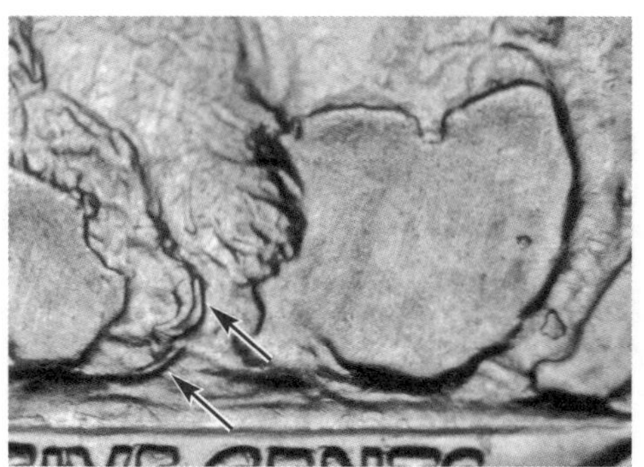

Description: Doubling is slight on E PLURIBUS UNUM, but most noticeable as an extra left front leg, hence the nickname "5-Legged Buffalo."

Comments: Discovered by Marilyn and Leroy Van Allen.

	VF-20	EF-40	AU-50	MS-60	MS-63
VARIETY	–	$275	–	–	$750
NORMAL	$4.50	$12	$21	$37	$80

1930   FS-05-1930-802 (017.3)

VARIETY: Doubled-Die Reverse
CONECA: 2-R-IV
PUP: E PLURIBUS UNUM
URS-4 · I-3 · L-2

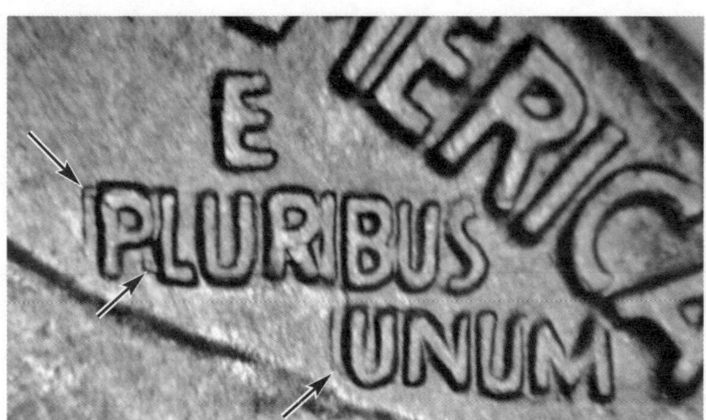

Description: Doubling is evident to the west on the PL of PLURIBUS and the first U of UNUM.

Comments: Though only portions are doubled, it is a very nice spread.

	VF-20	EF-40	AU-50	MS-60	MS-63
VARIETY	–	$360	–	–	–
NORMAL	$4.50	$12	$21	$37	$80

1930 — FS-05-1930-803 (017.4)

VARIETY: Doubled-Die Reverse
CONECA: 3-R-IV
PUP: E PLURIBUS UNUM and buffalo's appendage
URS-2 · I-2 · L-2

 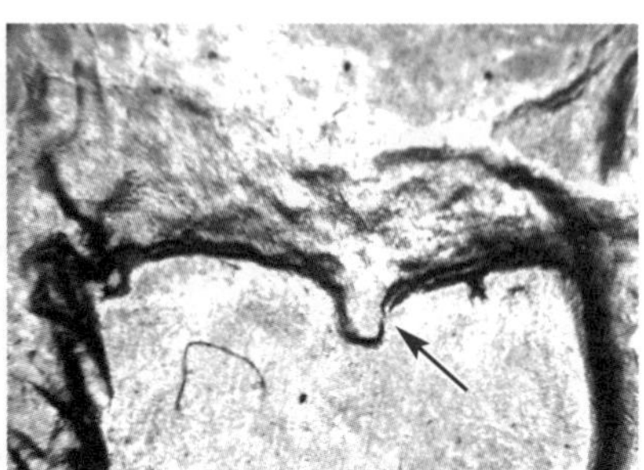

Description: Doubling is evident to the southeast on portions of E PLURIBUS UNUM and the bison's appendage.

Comments: The coin shown here is a rather late die state. We would like to see a much earlier die state.

	VF-20	EF-40	AU-50	MS-60	MS-63
VARIETY	–	$190	$290	–	–
NORMAL	$4.50	$12	$21	$37	$80

1930-S — FS-05-1930S-401 (017.711)

VARIETY: Two Feathers
CONECA: N/L
PUP: Feathers
URS-6 · I-3 · L-3

Description: The obverse die was heavily polished, probably to remove clash marks. The result was a die with the innermost feather missing, hence the nickname "Two Feathers."

Comments: At present, this is the latest date known with two feathers.

	VF-20	EF-40	AU-50	MS-60	MS-63
VARIETY	$37.00	–	–	–	–
NORMAL	$4.50	$15	$32	$58	$130

1930-S

FS-05-1930S-501 (017.71)

Variety: Repunched Mintmark
PUP: Mintmark
URS-4 · I-3 · L-3

CONECA: RPM-002

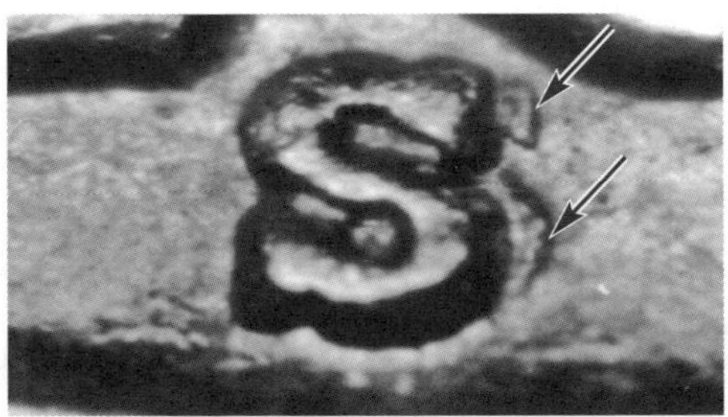

Description: The secondary mintmark is visible to the east of the primary mintmark.

Comments: This variety has been known for some time but seldom is seen.

	VF-20	EF-40	AU-50	MS-60	MS-63
Variety	–	$75	$110	–	–
Normal	$4.50	$15	$32	$58	$130

1935

FS-05-1935-801 (018)

Variety: Doubled-Die Reverse
PUP: FIVE CENTS
URS-10 · I-5 · L-5

CONECA: 1-R-V

Description: Strong doubled FIVE CENTS, E PLURIBUS UNUM, eye, horn, and mane on the buffalo.

Comments: This variety is extremely rare in any grade above Very Fine. About 10 are known in Mint State.

	VF-20	EF-40	AU-50	MS-60	MS-63
Variety	$170.00	$450.00	$1,700	$7,000	$15,500
Normal	$2.25	$3.50	$10	$24	$50

1935 — FS-05-1935-803 (018.1)

VARIETY: Doubled-Die Reverse
PUP: FIVE CENTS
URS-4 · I-3 · L-3

CONECA: 3-R-V

Description: Moderate doubling on FIVE CENTS, and to a lesser degree on UNITED and E PLURIBUS UNUM.

Comments: Though perhaps more rare than FS-05-1935-801, be careful not to confuse this with that listing, as the premiums are not nearly as high for this variety.

	VF-20	EF-40	AU-50	MS-60	MS-63
VARIETY	–	$100.00	$450	–	–
NORMAL	$2.25	$3.50	$10	$24	$50

1935-D — FS-05-1935D-502 (018.5)

VARIETY: Repunched Mintmark
PUP: Mintmark
URS-4 · I-4 · L-4

CONECA: RPM-002

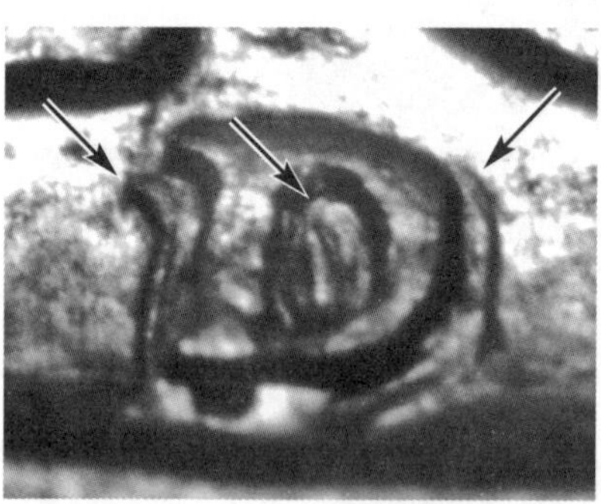

Description: This is, without a doubt, one of the nicer RPMs of this series. There are at least four mintmark punches, with two to the west and one to the east of the primary mintmark.

Comments: This coin was first reported to us by Denny Polly about 1987.

	VF-20	EF-40	AU-50	MS-60	MS-63
VARIETY	–	–	$150	$225	$275
NORMAL	$6.50	$16	$45	$80	$90

1935-S

FS-05-1935S-801 (018.6)

VARIETY: Doubled-Die Reverse
PUP: E PLURIBUS UNUM, FIVE CENTS
URS-3 · I-2 · L-2

CONECA: 1-R-IV

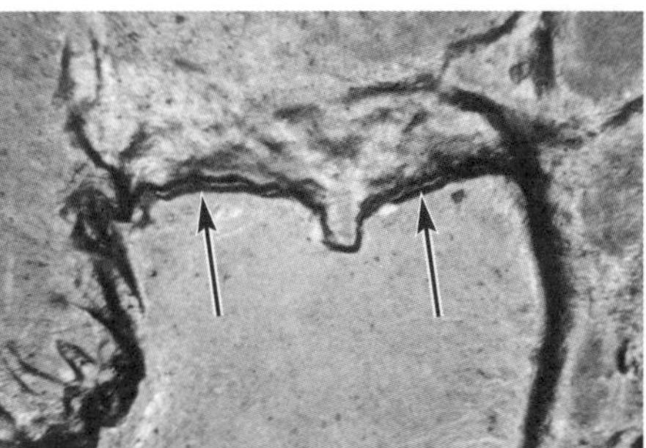

Description: Doubling is seen to the southeast on portions of E PLURIBUS UNUM and FIVE CENTS. It is also evident on the buffalo's belly.

Comments: More and more DDRs with similar doubling are being reported.

	VF-20	EF-40	AU-50	MS-60	MS-63
VARIETY	–	–	$90	–	–
NORMAL	$3	$4.50	$16	$58	$80

1936

FS-05-1936-101 (018.7)

VARIETY: Doubled-Die Obverse
PUP: Date, LIBERTY
URS-7 · I-3 · L-4

CONECA: 1-O-VI

Description: Doubling is seen as extreme thickness primarily on the date and LIBERTY.

Comments: This is the strongest known Class VI doubled-die obverse for the series.

	VF-20	EF-40	AU-50	MS-60	MS-63
VARIETY	–	–	$350	$500	$850
NORMAL	$2.25	$3.25	$10	$24	$50

1936 — FS-05-1936-801 (018.8)

VARIETY: Doubled-Die Reverse
PUP: UNITED STATES, CENTS
URS-5 · I-3 · L-3

CONECA: 1-R-II +VI (4)

Description: Doubling is seen as extreme thickness on all reverse lettering, with near separation on the dot between UNITED and STATES.

Comments: This is perhaps the strongest known Class VI Doubled-Die Reverse for the series and would make a great companion to the previous listing (FS-05-1936-101).

	VF-20	EF-40	AU-50	MS-60	MS-63
VARIETY	–	–	$175	$250	$375
NORMAL	$2.25	$3.25	$10	$24	$50

1936-D — FS-05-1936D-502 (019.5)

VARIETY: Repunched Mintmark
PUP: Mintmark
URS-12 · I-3 · L-4

CONECA: RPM-002

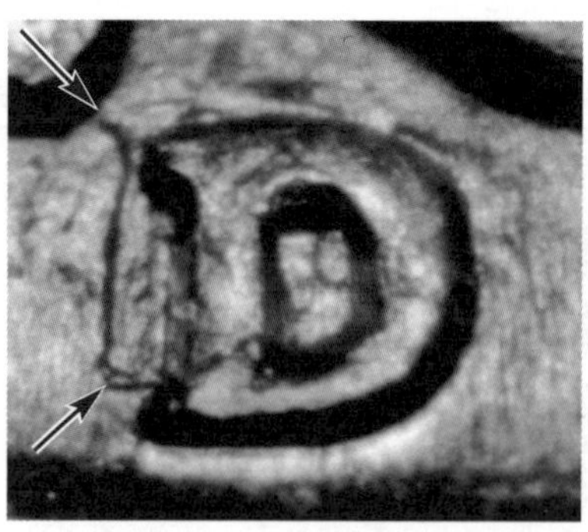

Description: The secondary mintmark is visible to the northwest of the primary mintmark.

Comments: A very popular RPM.

	VF-20	EF-40	AU-50	MS-60	MS-63
VARIETY	–	$17.00	$25	$60	$70
NORMAL	$2.25	$4.50	$13	$42	$50

1936-D   FS-05-1936S-511 (019.8)

VARIETY: Over Mintmark (D/D/S)
PUP: Mintmark
URS-4 · I-4 · L-4

CONECA: RPM-004

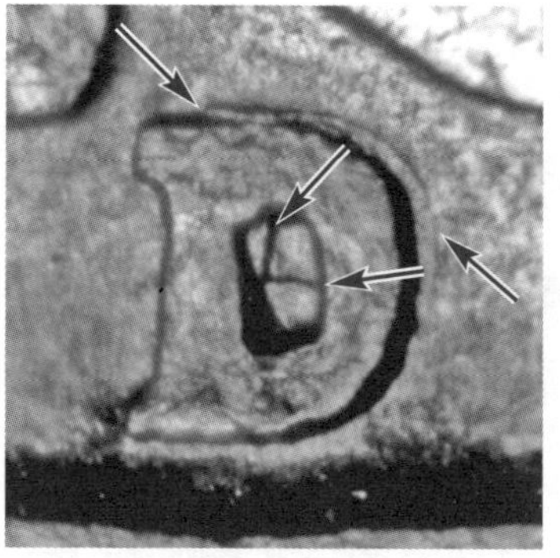

Description: An S mintmark was initially punched into the die, followed by two subsequent D mintmark punches.

Comments: This variety, first reported by Bill Fivaz, has received a fairly large amount of publicity, yet few have been found.

	VF-20	EF-40	AU-50	MS-60	MS-63
VARIETY	–	–	–	–	–
NORMAL	$2.25	$4.50	$13	$42	$50

1936-D   FS-05-1936D-901 (019)

VARIETY: 3-1/2-Legged Buffalo
PUP: Buffalo's right front leg
URS-7 · I-5 · L-5

CONECA: N/L

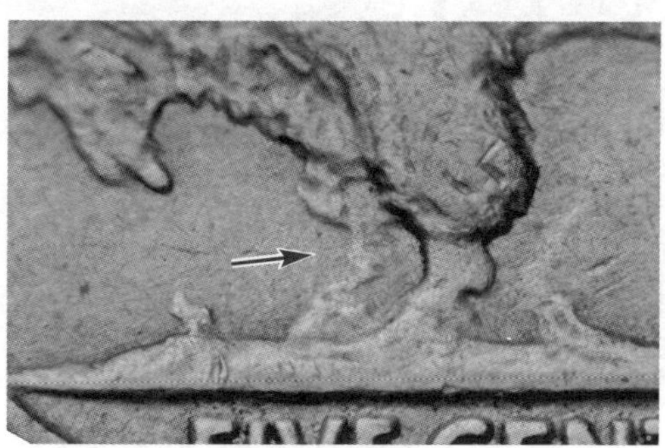

Description: The right front leg of the buffalo on this variety has been partially polished off the die—similar to the famous 1937-D 3-Legged variety, but not as severe. It is not from the same die as the 1937-D variety.

Comments: This is an extremely rare variety, with fewer than 40 known in any grade. This was incorrectly listed by Breen as 1936-P.

	VF-20	EF-40	AU-50	MS-60	MS-63
VARIETY	$5,500.00	$8,000.00	$10,000	$18,500	–
NORMAL	$2.25	$4.50	$13	$42	$50

1936-S
FS-05-1936S-501 (020)

VARIETY: Repunched Mintmark
PUP: Mintmark
URS-11 · I-4 · L-3

CONECA: RPM-001

Description: This is a very strong repunched mintmark, with the secondary S almost half a letter south of the primary S

Comments: Very scarce in grades above Extremely Fine, and rare in Mint State.

	VF-20	EF-40	AU-50	MS-60	MS-63
VARIETY	$50.00	$90	$170	$275	$340
NORMAL	$2.25	$4	$13	$42	$50

1937-D
FS-05-1937D-901 (020.2)

VARIETY: 3-Legged Buffalo
PUP: Buffalo's front leg
URS-14 · I-5 · L-5

CONECA: N/L

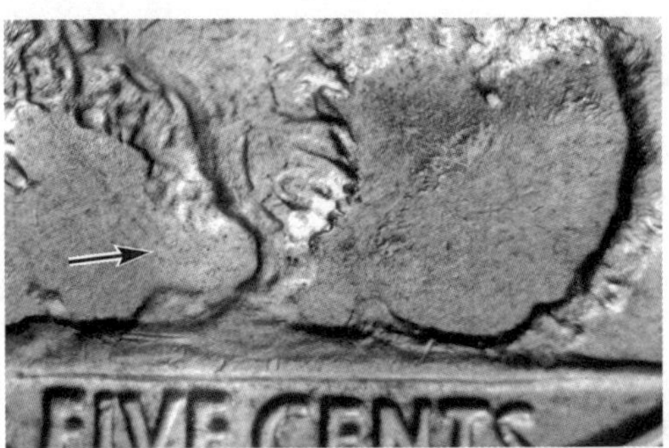

Description: This reverse die was heavily polished, possibly to remove clash marks. The result was a die with portions of the bison's right front leg missing, hence the nickname "3-Legged Buffalo."

Comments: There are many altered specimens passed as the genuine coin. Look for a line of raised dots from the middle of the bison's belly to the ground as one of the diagnostics on the genuine specimen.

	VF-20	EF-40	AU-50	MS-60	MS-63
VARIETY	$1,300.00	$1,400.00	$1,600	$3,000	$6,000
NORMAL	$3.25	$4.50	$11	$35	$42

1938-D

VARIETY: Over Mintmark (D/D/D/S)

CONECA: OMM-001

PUP: Mintmark

URS-13 · I-5 · L-4

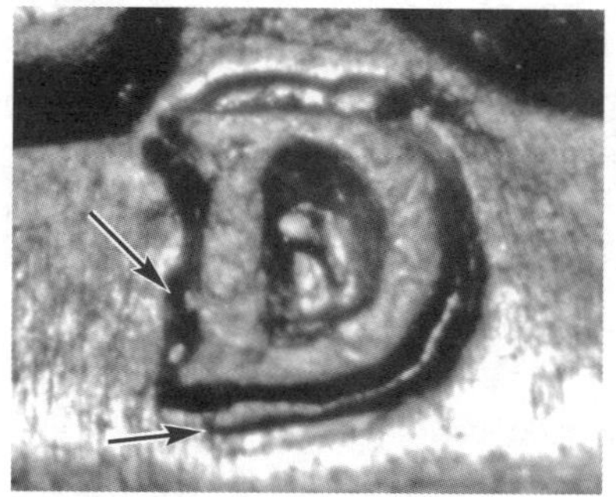

Description: An S mintmark was initially punched into the die, followed by three subsequent D mintmark punches. The alteration was deliberate, as the Mint was preparing the new Jefferson design dies, and it was cheaper to recycle dies marked for the San Francisco Mint but never shipped than to hub new dies and scrap the S-mint dies.

Comments: There are five different D Over S dies for this date. OMM-001, the variety illustrated here, is the variety listed in most major pricing guides. The other varieties command less of a premium.

	VF-20	EF-40	AU-50	MS-60	MS-63
VARIETY	$15	$21	$34	$58	$85
NORMAL	$5	$6	$9	$24	$40

THE CHERRYPICKERS' GUIDE HELPFUL HINTS

Keep in mind that as the numismatic value of a coin increases, the premiums attached to its varieties tend to decrease. A doubled die on a 1901-S Barber quarter would add no significant value to the coin because of the already high numismatic value, and very few dies were used to produce that date. Another so-called white elephant would be an RPM on a Mint State 1936-D Washington quarter.

Jefferson Nickels, 1938 to Date

The Jefferson nickel series is one of the most widely collected of all modern coin designs and most certainly as far as varieties are concerned. The popularity of collecting these varieties started full force with the beginning of PAK, the Full Steps Jefferson nickel club that originated in the 1970s.

Due in large part to PAK, most of the varieties listed in the *Cherrypickers' Guide* have been well known to specialists for several decades, yet still may be somewhat new to more novice collectors. In the earlier days of PAK, there was a list of the "10 Most Wanted" varieties within the series:

1. The 1939 Doubled-Die Reverse, FS-801
2. The 1942-D Over Horizontal D, FS-501
3. The 1943/2-P Overdate, FS-101
4. The 1943-P "Doubled Eye," FS-106
5. The 1945-P Doubled-Die Reverse, FS-801
6. The 1946-D Over Inverted D, FS-501
7. The 1949-D Over S, FS-501
8. The 1954-S Over D, FS-501
9. The 1955 Proof Tripled-Die Reverse, FS-801, and
10. The 1955-D Over S #1, FS-501.

These 10 are still popular today, though there have been many additions to collectors' "must have" lists.

An excellent reference for general information on the series is *A Guide Book of Buffalo and Jefferson Nickels* by Q. David Bowers. Included is a complete history of the series, price guidelines, grading information, variety information, and much more. A detailed date-by-date analysis defines strike characteristics, availability by grade, and many facts not available in any other reference. Add to this the accurate, interesting, and at times colorful writing by the best numismatic author of our time, and you will have the most interesting and informative book on the series.

As of this publication, there are several other books devoted to the varieties in the series which we can recommend to those interested in obtaining more information. *The Jefferson Nickel RPM Book—An Attribution Guide* by Dr. James Wiles describes and illustrates all known repunched and over mintmarks within the series. A second edition was produced in 2003 to include discoveries made after the initial publication. *The Best of the Jefferson Nickel Doubled Dies* by John A. Wexler and Brian A. Ribar describes and illustrates many of the doubled dies within the series. There is another important book by Bernard A. Nagengast entitled *The Jefferson Nickel Analyst*. This reference offers a date-by-date analysis of the series, and also describes and rates rarity of Full Steps nickels.

1938 — FS-05-1938-1101 (021)

VARIETY: Doubled-Die Obverse
CONECA: 2-O-II
PUP: Date
URS-10 · I-3 · L-2

Description: A moderate spread is evident on the motto, star, and date. The secondary image is rotated slightly counterclockwise.

Comments: Once a very popular Jefferson nickel variety, this doubled die can still be cherrypicked with some searching.

	EF-40	AU-50	MS-60	MS-63	MS-65
VARIETY	$10	$15	$20	$25	$35
NORMAL	<$1	$2	$3	$5	$20

1938 — FS-05-1938-1105 (021.5)

VARIETY: Quadrupled-Die Obverse
CONECA: 5-O-II
PUP: Date, LIBERTY
URS-10 · I-3 · L-2

Description: This is a moderate quadrupled die, with secondary images evident toward the center of the coin on LIBERTY, IN GOD WE TRUST, the date, and the star.

Comments: Early-die-state specimens especially are quite attractive, with the four images very clear on all the lettering and the date.

	EF-40	AU-50	MS-60	MS-63	MS-65
VARIETY	$10	$15	$20	$25	$35
NORMAL	<$1	$2	$3	$5	$20

1939 — FS-05-1939-801 (022)

VARIETY: Doubled-Die Reverse
CONECA: 1-R-IV
PUP: MONTICELLO, CENTS
URS-10 · I-5 · L-5

Description: Very strong doubling is evident to the east of the primary letters, most noticeably on MONTICELLO, and FIVE CENTS. Lesser doubling is also visible on UNITED STATES OF AMERICA and the right side of the building.

Comments: Early-die-state specimens especially are quite attractive.

	EF-40	AU-50	MS-60	MS-63	MS-65
VARIETY	$50	$95	$125	$195	$450
NORMAL	<$1	$2	$3	$5	$20

1939 — FS-05-1939-802 (022.5)

VARIETY: Quadrupled-Die Reverse
CONECA: 1-R-IV
PUP: MONTICELLO, CENTS
URS-10 · I-4 · L-3

Description: Strong multiple images are evident on all reverse lettering with a close spread. The final O of MONTICELLO is almost egg-shaped.

Comments: This variety is still fairly scarce to rare in Mint State.

	EF-40	AU-50	MS-60	MS-63	MS-65
VARIETY	$15	$25	$50	$95	$150
NORMAL	<$1	$2	$3	$5	$20

1939 Proof   FS-05-1939-901 (023)

VARIETY: Reverse of 1940   **CONECA: N/L**
PUP: Steps of Monticello
URS-9 · I-4 · L-4

Description: The vast majority of the 1939 Proof Jefferson mintage was produced with the reverse of 1938, which had "wavy," ill-defined steps on Monticello. However, a very few of the Proof coins were produced using the new, enhanced design of 1940, with sharp, well-defined steps. The photo here is of the steps of 1940.

Comments: Circulation-strike coins produced in 1939 from all three mints are known with both reverse designs, but the Proof coins from 1939 are rare with the "type II" steps of 1940.

	PF-63	PF-65	PF-67
VARIETY	$70	$220	$3,000
NORMAL	$48	$110	$400

1940 Proof   FS-05-1940-901 (024)

VARIETY: Reverse of 1938   **CONECA: N/L**
PUP: Steps of Monticello
URS-8 · I-5 · L-5

Description: The vast majority of the 1940 Proof Jefferson mintage was produced with the reverse of 1940, which had sharp, well-defined steps. However, a very few of the Proof coins were produced using the older hub, with ill-defined steps of 1938. The photo here is of the reverse of 1938.

Comments: This is an extremely rare variety. There are no known business strikes with the reverse of 1938.

	PF-63	PF-65	PF-67
VARIETY	$85	$315	$1,900
NORMAL	$35	$94	$360

1941-D — FS-05-1941D-501 (024.3)

VARIETY: Repunched Mintmark
PUP: Mintmark
URS-5 · I-2 · L-2

CONECA: RPM-003

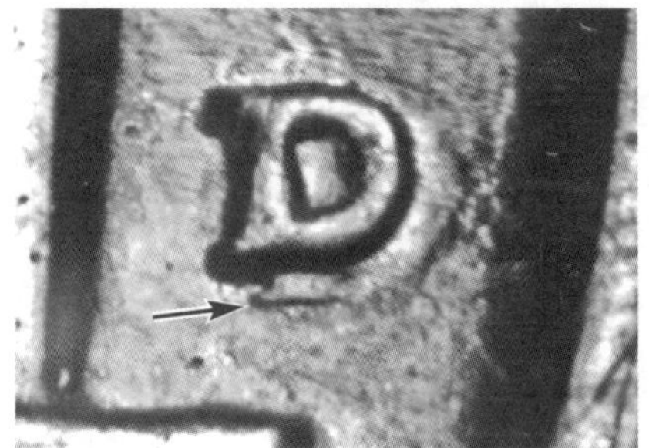

Description: A secondary D is evident to the southeast of the primary D.

Comments: This variety is included primarily to remind novices that RPMs are known and available in this series for almost any dated coin bearing a mintmark through the 1950s, and with many dates later.

	AU-50	MS-63	MS-65
VARIETY	$25	$50	$95
NORMAL	$1	$5	$10

Values: Please note that relatively minor varieties such as this are very difficult to sell in grades below About Uncirculated.

1941-S — FS-05-1941S-501 (024.5)

VARIETY: Large S Mintmark
PUP: Mintmark
URS-5 · I-4 · L-4

CONECA: N/L

Large Mintmark

Small Mintmark

Description: Two mintmark styles were used on 1941-S nickels; the large S (shown on the left) is far rarer than the normal or "small" S (shown on the right).

Comments: This variety is extremely difficult to locate in any grade.

	AU-50	MS-63	MS-65
VARIETY	$25	$75	$125
NORMAL	$1	$5	$20

1941-S — FS-05-1941S-502

VARIETY: Repunched Mintmark
CONECA: RPM-002
PUP: Mintmark
URS-5 · I-3 · L-3

Description: A secondary S is evident to the south of the primary S. This is the large S variety.

Comments: Most of the value for this RPM is for the Large S–style mintmark.

	AU-50	MS-63	MS-65
VARIETY	$25	$50	$95
NORMAL	$1	$5	$20

1941-S — FS-05-1941S-503 (024.6)

VARIETY: Inverted Mintmark
CONECA: N/L
PUP: Mintmark
URS-3 · I-3 · L-3

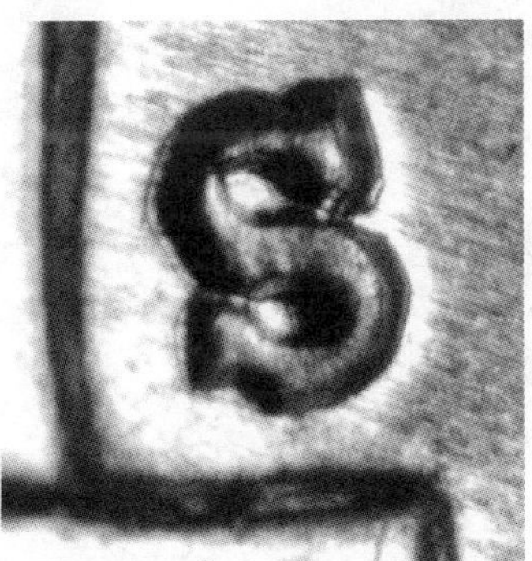

Description: The normal or small S mintmark on this particular die was placed in an inverted orientation.

Comments: Inverted S mintmarks are a relatively new area of interest with respect to varieties. This is one of the earlier reported such varieties.

	AU-50	MS-63	MS-65
VARIETY	$25	$50	$95
NORMAL	$1	$5	$10

1942 — FS-05-1942-101 (025)

VARIETY: Doubled-Die Obverse
PUP: Nose, date, GOD
URS-7 · I-3 · L-3

CONECA: 2-O-IV

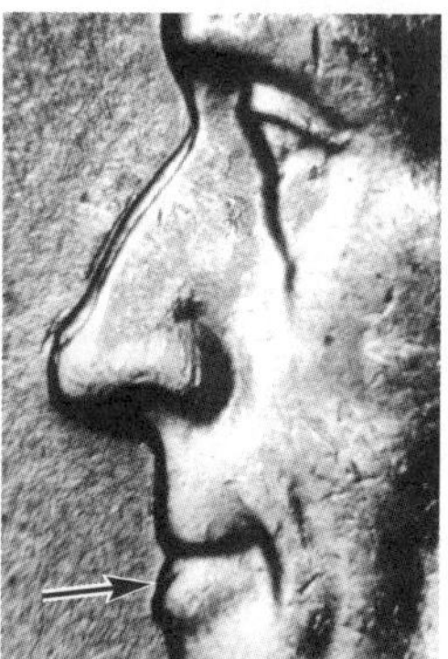

Description: Strong doubling is evident on Jefferson's profile, especially the nose, and on the date, motto, and LIBERTY.

Comments: This is a much underrated variety and extremely difficult to locate.

	EF-40	AU-50	MS-60	MS-63	MS-65
VARIETY	$25	$35	$60	$100	$300
NORMAL	<$1	<$1	$2	$7	$24

1942 — FS-05-1942-102 (026)

VARIETY: Doubled-Die Obverse
PUP: Eye, nose
URS-9 · I-3 · L-3

CONECA: 3-O-IV

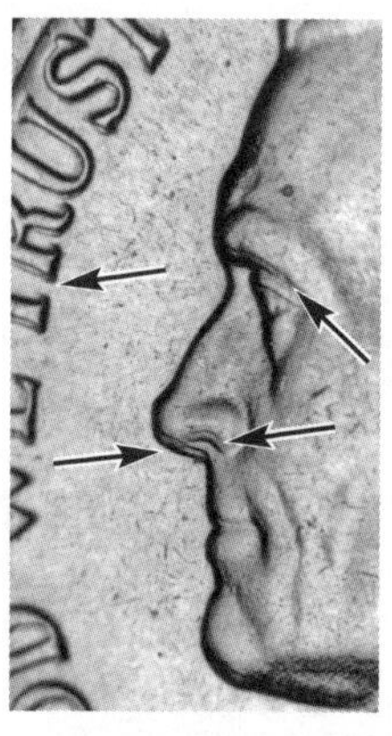

Description: Strong doubling is evident on the eyebrow, lower nose, lips, jaw, and all the obverse lettering.

Comments: This and the previous listings are quite rare, yet not well known.

	EF-40	AU-50	MS-60	MS-63	MS-65
VARIETY	$25	$35	$60	$100	$300
NORMAL	<$1	<$1	$2	$7	$24

1942-D

FS-05-1942D-501 (027)

VARIETY: D Over Horizontal D
PUP: Mintmark
URS-11 · I-5 · L-5

CONECA: RPM-001

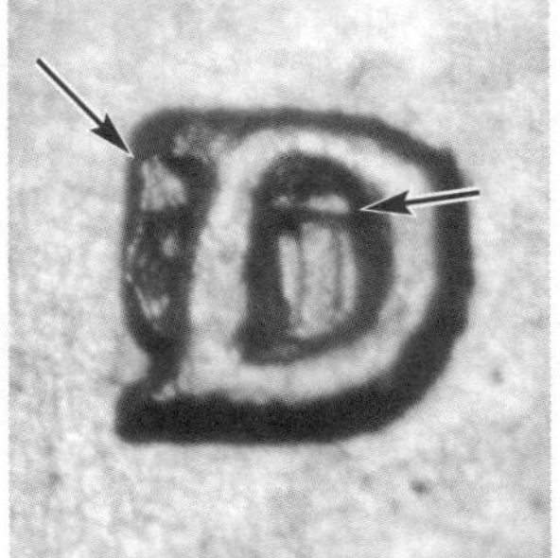

Description: The initial D mintmark was punched into the die horizontally, then corrected, creating the D Over Horizontal D variety.

Comments: This is the rarest of the major Jefferson nickel varieties in Mint State, yet can still be picked on rare occasions.

	EF-40	AU-50	MS-60	MS-63	MS-65
VARIETY	$75	$100	$350	$500	$1,000
NORMAL	$2	$4	$15	$20	$27

1943-P

FS-05-1943P-101 (028)

VARIETY: Doubled-Die Obverse + Overdate
PUP: Date
URS-13 · I-5 · L-5

CONECA: 3-O-II+III+V

Description: This popular variety was created when the die was first hubbed with a 1942-dated hub, then subsequently hubbed with a 1943-dated hub. The diagonal of the 2 is visible within the lower opening of the 3. Doubling is also visible on LIBERTY and IN GOD WE TRUST. Most of the high-grade specimens available are late die states with heavy metal flow lines toward the rim and somewhat "mushy" numbers and letters. The reverse is also a tripled die.

Comments: There is at least one 1943-P five-cent piece that has a faint, short die gouge extending upward from the lower ball of the 3; this is often mistaken for the overdate. The true overdate must look like the variety pictured here. This variety is very difficult to sell below About Uncirculated. Discovered by Del Romines.

	EF-40	AU-50	MS-60	MS-63	MS-65
VARIETY	$100.00	$175.00	$240.00	$275.00	$650
NORMAL	$1.50	$2.75	$5.50	$8.50	$16

1943-P · FS-05-1943P-106 (029)

VARIETY: Doubled-Die Obverse   **CONECA: 6-O-I**
PUP: Eye
URS-9 · I-5 · L-5

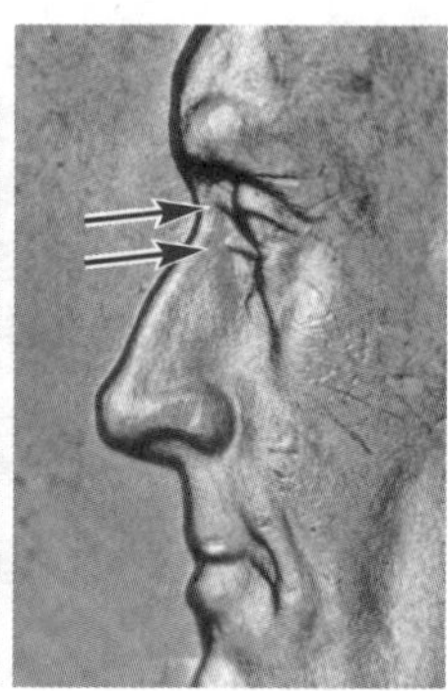

Description: The doubling is visible on the date, LIBERTY, the motto, and (most noticeably) the eye. There is a secondary eye below the primary eye, hence the nickname "Doubled Eye" variety.

Comments: This is one of the Jefferson nickel original "Top 10" varieties. It is becoming more and more difficult to locate.

	EF-40	AU-50	MS-60	MS-63	MS-65
VARIETY	$55.00	$80.00	$105.00	$175.00	$400
NORMAL	$1.50	$2.75	$5.50	$8.50	$16

1945-P · FS-05-1945P-801 (030)

VARIETY: Doubled-Die Reverse   **CONECA: 1-R-II**
PUP: Last O of MONTICELLO
URS-11 · I-5 · L-4

Description: The reverse is strongly doubled, with the spread increasing from left to right.

Comments: There are at least two other collectible DDRs for this date.

	EF-40	AU-50	MS-60	MS-63	MS-65
VARIETY	$35.00	$55.00	$80.00	$150.00	$340
NORMAL	$1.50	$2.75	$5.50	$8.50	$19

1945-P FS-05-1945P-803 (030.3)

VARIETY: Doubled-Die Reverse
PUP: UNUM, AMERICA
URS-10 · I-3 · L-3

CONECA: 3-R-II+VI

Description: Doubling is evident on all reverse lettering, especially E PLURIBUS UNUM, UNITED STATES OF AMERICA, FIVE CENTS, and LLO of MONTICELLO.

Comments: This variety is not as dramatic as the preceding or following listings, but it is still a nice doubled die.

	EF-40	AU-50	MS-60	MS-63	MS-65
VARIETY	–	–	$135.00	$300.00	–
NORMAL	$1.50	$2.75	$5.50	$8.50	$19

1945-P FS-05-1945P-804 (030.5)

VARIETY: Tripled-Die Reverse
PUP: AMERICA, mintmark
URS-10 · I-3 · L-3

CONECA: 4-R-VI-3, RPM-001

Description: The tripling is evident on the final O of MONTICELLO, CENTS, UNITED STATES OF AMERICA, and on portions of E PLURIBUS UNUM. The mintmark is punched at least three times.

Comments: Aside from the tripled die, this is one of the nicer RPMs of 1945.

	EF-40	AU-50	MS-60	MS-63	MS-65
VARIETY	–	$80.00	$175.00	$300.00	–
NORMAL	$1.50	$2.75	$5.50	$8.50	$19

1946-D — FS-05-1946D-501 (031)

VARIETY: Repunched Mintmark
CONECA: RPM-002
PUP: Mintmark
URS-8 · I-5 · L-5

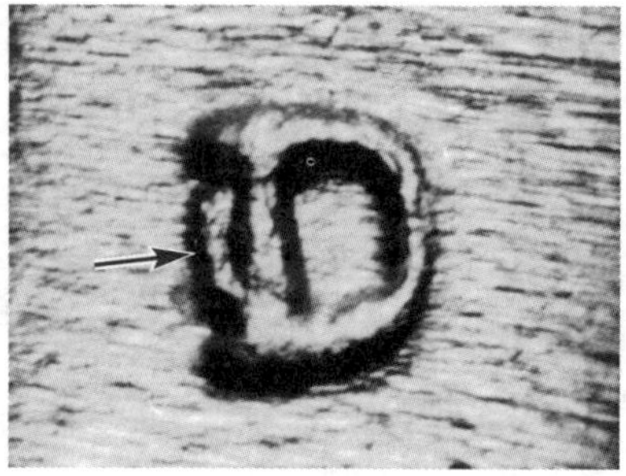

Description: The initial mintmark punch was inverted, with the subsequent punch in the correct position.

Comments: This is considered the second rarest of the original Jefferson "Top 10" in Mint State, second only to the 1942-D Over Horizontal D.

	EF-40	AU-50	MS-60	MS-63	MS-65
VARIETY	–	–	–	$700.00	$1,000.00
NORMAL	$0.45	$0.50	$1.25	$2.25	$6.50

1946-S — FS-05-1946S-101 (031.5)

VARIETY: Doubled-Die Obverse
CONECA: 1-O-V
PUP: LIBERTY, date
URS-5 · I-4 · L-4

Description: The doubling is evident as a counterclockwise spread primarily on LIBERTY, the star, and the date.

Comments: John Wexler first reported this variety in 1979.

	EF-40	AU-50	MS-60	MS-63	MS-65
VARIETY	–	$150.00	$350.00	$700.00	$950.00
NORMAL	$0.50	$0.55	$1.25	$1.75	$3.75

1949-D

FS-05-1949D-501 (032)

VARIETY: Over Mintmark (D/S)

CONECA: OMM-001

PUP: Mintmark

URS-9 · I-5 · L-5

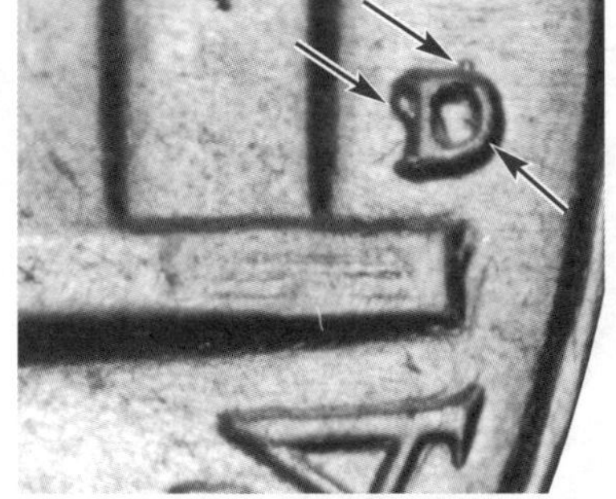
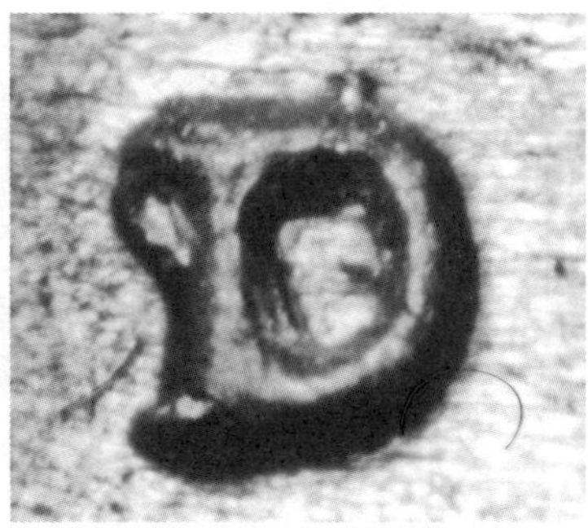

Description: The die initially received an S mintmark punch and later received a D mintmark on top of that. The top serif of the S is visible to the north of the D, with the upper left loop of the S visible to the west of the D.

Comments: This variety is quite rare in Mint State and highly sought after. Some may still be found in circulated grades. Some specimens have been located in original Mint sets.

	MS-60	MS-63	MS-65
VARIETY	$160.00	$210.00	$425
NORMAL	$1.75	$2.25	$6

1951 Proof

FS-05-1951-101 (032.5)

VARIETY: Doubled-Die Obverse

CONECA: 1-O-V

PUP: Eye, chin, TRUST

URS-6 · I-3 · L-3

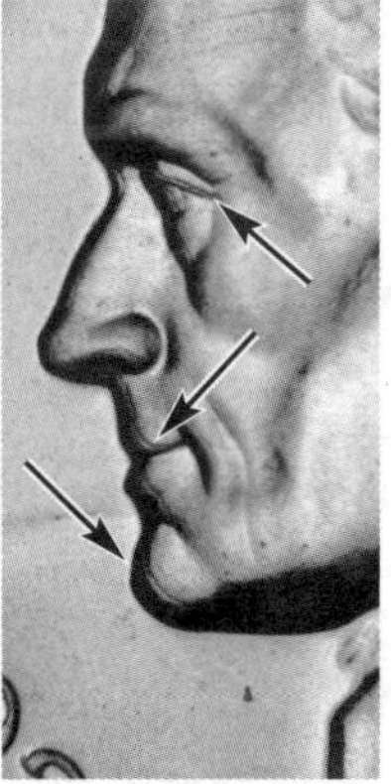

Description: The doubling is evident on the entire profile, including the chin, lips, nose, and eye. Some letters also show doubling, especially TRUST.

	PF-63	PF-64	PF-65
VARIETY	$200	–	$350
NORMAL	–	–	$65

1953 Proof FS-05-1953-101 (032.7)

VARIETY: Doubled-Die Obverse
CONECA: 1-O-II
PUP: IN GOD WE TRUST
URS-6 · I-3 · L-3

Description: The doubling is evident on all the letters of IN GOD WE TRUST.

	PF-63	PF-64	PF-65
VARIETY	$125	–	$300
NORMAL	–	–	$40

1954-D FS-05-1954D-501 (032.9)

VARIETY: Over Mintmark (?)
CONECA: RPM-003
PUP: Mintmark
URS-8 · I-4 · L-2

Description: The die possibly received an S mintmark and later was punched with a D mintmark.

	MS-60	MS-63	MS-65
VARIETY	–	$1,000.00	$1,200.00
NORMAL	$0.65	$1.25	$1.75

1954-S   FS-05-1954S-501 (033)

VARIETY: Over Mintmark   **CONECA: OMM-001**
PUP: Mintmark
URS-10 · I-5 · L-5

Description: The die initially received a D mintmark and later was punched with an S mintmark.

Comments: Finding an early-die-state specimen that is well struck is quite difficult, and such a coin would command a high premium. The overall strength of the strike is the important factor in the value of this OMM.

	MS-60	MS-63	MS-65
VARIETY	$28	$42.00	$85.00
NORMAL	$2	$2.25	$3.25

1954-S   FS-05-1954S-502 (033.1)

VARIETY: Repunched Mintmark   **CONECA: RPM-001**
PUP: Mintmark
URS-10 · I-2 · L-2

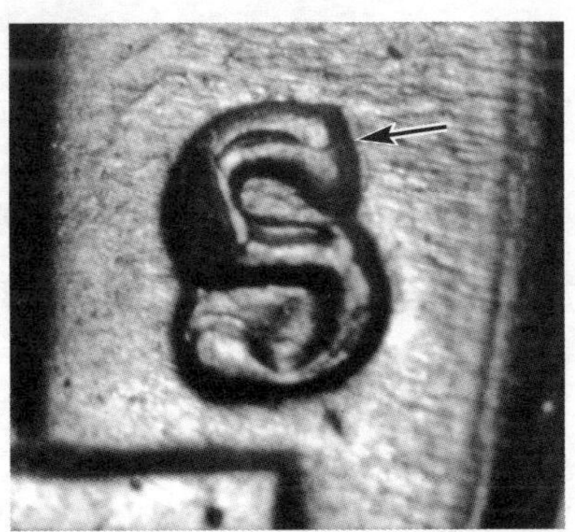

Description: The secondary S is visible to the north of the primary S.

Comments: This is one of the more popular Jefferson nickel RPMs.

	MS-60	MS-63	MS-65
VARIETY	–	$100.00	–
NORMAL	$2	$2.25	$3.25

1955 Proof   FS-05-1955-801 (035)

VARIETY: Tripled-Die Reverse   **CONECA: 1-R-II-C (3)**
PUP: MONTICELLO
URS-11 · I-4 · L-3

Description: The reverse die is tripled, which is most evident on the last O of MONTICELLO, and the lower portions of the letters in UNITED STATES OF AMERICA.

Comments: There are at least three doubled reverse dies for this date, but they do not command the premium for this variety. This variety was discovered by Frank Capper in 1978.

	PF-63	PF-64	PF-65
VARIETY	$175	–	–
NORMAL	$12	–	$16

1955-D   FS-05-1955D-501 (034)

VARIETY: Over Mintmark   **CONECA: OMM-001**
PUP: Mintmark
URS-13 · I-4 · L-4

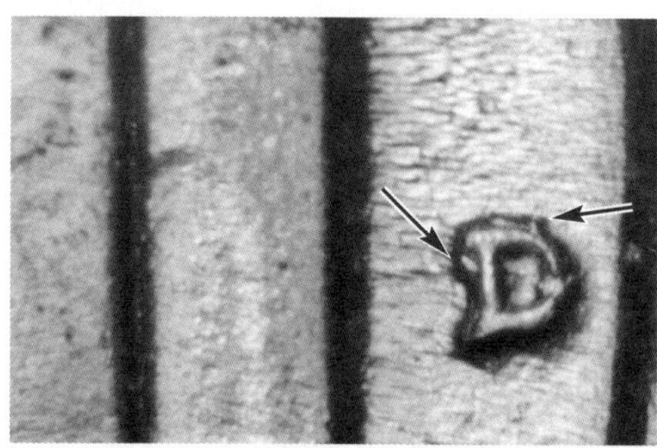

Description: A D mintmark was punched over an S mintmark. The top curve of the S is visible slightly to the north of the D. This probably occurred as production ceased in San Francisco and remaining usable reverse dies were repunched in Philadelphia.

Comments: There are some 10 different D Over S varieties for 1955, but the strongest (OMM-001), shown here, is the most sought after. Others bring less than the prices listed.

	MS-60	MS-63	MS-65
VARIETY	$38.00	$60.00	$95.00
NORMAL	$0.55	$0.80	$1.15

1956 Proof FS-05-1956-102 (035.4)

VARIETY: Doubled-Die Obverse **CONECA: 2-O-II+VI**
PUP: IN GOD WE TRUST
URS-6 · I-3 · L-2

Description: The doubling is evident on all the letters of IN GOD WE TRUST.

Comments: There are many different doubled dies, both obverse and reverse, on Proof Jefferson nickels. Many are outstanding multiple hubbings.

	PF-63	PF-64	PF-65
VARIETY	$95.00	–	–
NORMAL	$3.25	–	$3.75

1956 FS-05-1956-801 (035.2)

VARIETY: Quadrupled-Die Reverse **CONECA: 18-R-II**
PUP: E PLURIBUS UNUM, AMERICA
URS-6 · I-3 · L-2

Description: The reverse die is at least quadrupled, which is most evident on the last O of MONTICELLO, and the lower portions of the letters of UNITED STATES OF AMERICA and E PLURIBUS UNUM.

Comments: First reported to us by Frank Baumann.

	MS-60	MS-63	MS-65
VARIETY	–	$475.00	–
NORMAL	$0.55	$0.80	$1.10

1956 — FS-05-1956-802 (035.6)

VARIETY: Tripled-Die Reverse
PUP: AMERICA, UNUM
URS-6 · I-3 · L-2

CONECA: 24-R-II-C (3)

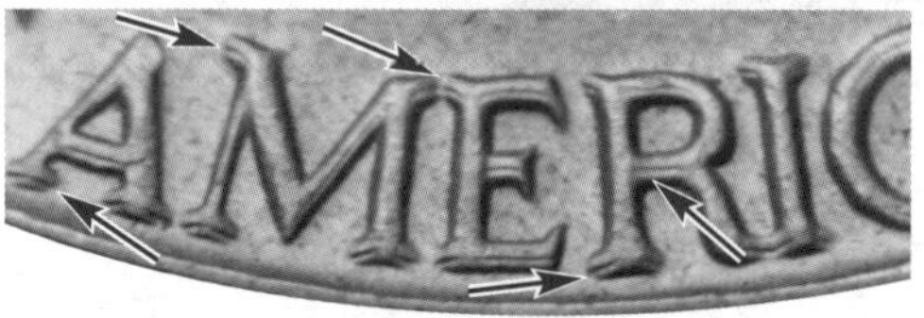

Description: The reverse die is tripled; this is most evident on the letters of UNITED STATES OF AMERICA and E PLURIBUS UNUM.

Comments: There are many very nice doubled-die reverses known for the late 1950s to the early 1960s business-strike Jefferson nickels.

	MS-60	MS-63	MS-65
VARIETY	–	$160.00	–
NORMAL	$0.55	$0.80	$1.10

1957 Proof — FS-05-1957-101 (035.8)

VARIETY: Quadrupled-Die Obverse
PUP: LIBERTY, date, star
URS-7 · I-3 · L-2

CONECA: N/L

Description: The quadrupling is most evident on all the letters of LIBERTY, the date, and the star.

Comments: There are many different doubled dies, both obverse and reverse, on Proof Jefferson nickels. Many are outstanding multiple hubbings.

	PF-63	PF-64	PF-65
VARIETY	$100.00	–	–
NORMAL	$3.25	–	$3.75

1960 Proof — FS-05-1960-801 (036)

VARIETY: Quadrupled-Die Reverse
CONECA: 1-R-II-C (4)
PUP: AMERICA, O in MONTICELLO
URS-9 · I-3 · L-2

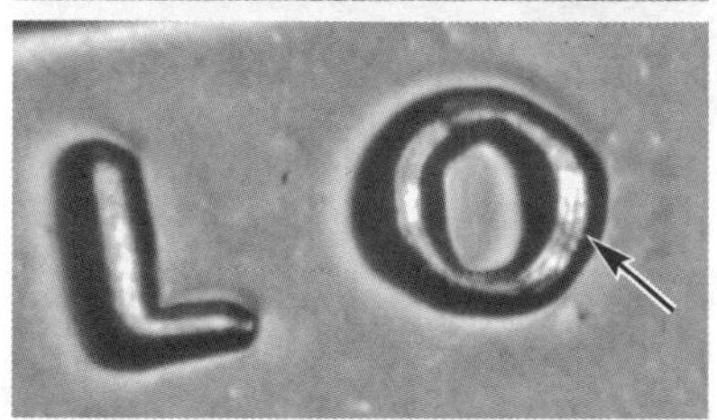

Description: The reverse die is quadrupled, most evident on MONTICELLO and most of the lettering around the rim, especially on UNUM and AMERICA.

Comments: There are also several doubled reverse dies for this date.

	PF-63	PF-64	PF-65
VARIETY	$85.00	–	–
NORMAL	$1.75	–	$2.25

1961 Proof — FS-05-1961-801 (037)

VARIETY: Tripled-Die Reverse
CONECA: 13-R-II-C (3)
PUP: UNUM, OF AMERICA
URS-7 · I-2 · L-2

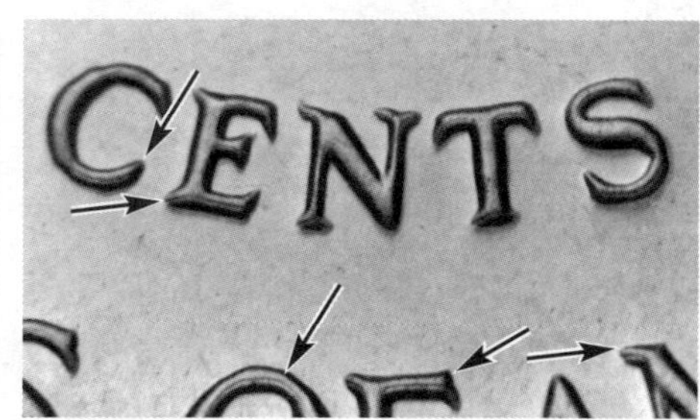

Description: The reverse die is tripled, most evident on UNUM, OF AMERICA, and CENTS.

Comments: There are many different doubled dies, both obverse and reverse, on Proof Jefferson nickels. Many are outstanding multiple hubbings.

	PF-63	PF-64	PF-65
VARIETY	$65.00	–	–
NORMAL	$1.50	–	$1.85

1963 — FS-05-1963-801 (037.3)

VARIETY: Tripled-Die Reverse
CONECA: 80-R-II
PUP: E PLURIBUS UNUM
URS-6 · I-2 · L-2

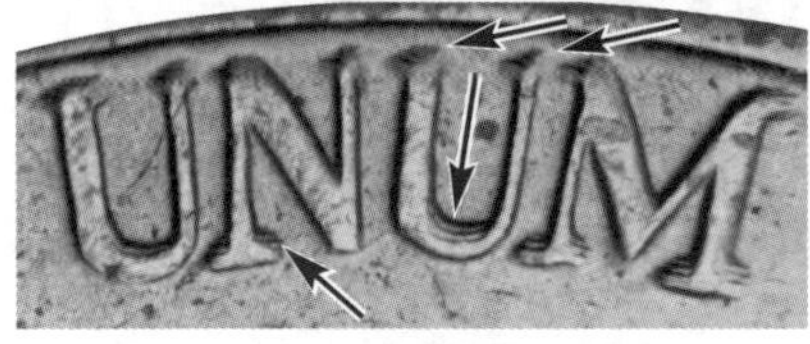

Description: The reverse die is tripled and most evident on E PLURIBUS UNUM, with doubling to a lesser extent on most reverse lettering.

Comments: There are many doubled-die reverses for the early 1960s business-strike Jefferson nickels. This is one of the nicer ones.

	MS-60	MS-63	MS-65
VARIETY	–	$125.00	–
NORMAL	$0.30	$0.55	$1.10

1964-D — FS-05-1964D-501 (037.5)

VARIETY: Repunched Mintmark
CONECA: RPM-005
PUP: Mintmark
URS-9 · I-2 · L-3

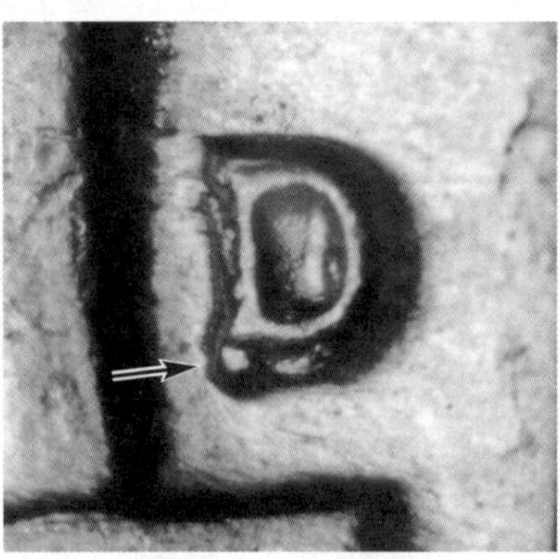

Description: The secondary D is visible to the south of the primary D.

Comments: If you like Jefferson nickel RPMs, we strongly recommend James Wiles's *Jefferson Nickel RPM Book.*

	MS-60	MS-63	MS-65
VARIETY	–	$105.00	–
NORMAL	$0.30	$0.55	$1.10

1968-S Proof

FS-05-1968S-501 (038)

VARIETY: Repunched Mintmark
PUP: Mintmark
URS-5 · I-3 · L-3

CONECA: RPM-002

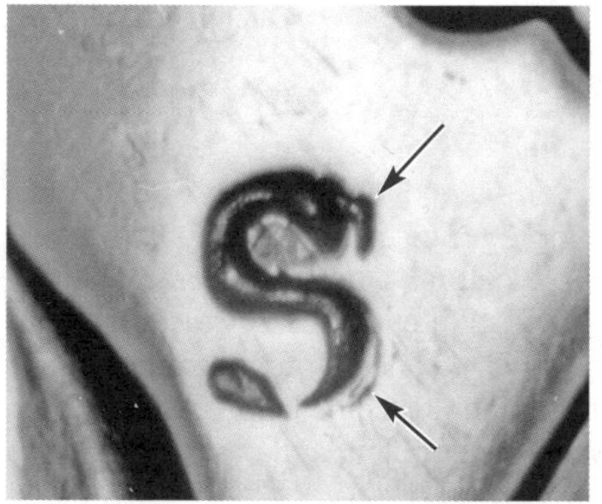

Description: The secondary S is visible to the southeast of the primary S.

Comments: This is one of only a few nice RPMs found on Proof coinage.

	PF-63	PF-64	PF-65
VARIETY	$125.00	–	–
NORMAL	$0.85	–	$1.10

THE CHERRYPICKERS' GUIDE HELPFUL HINTS

The varieties listed in this book are only the tip of the iceberg. Even more are yet to be discovered. Always examine closely any coin you obtain. You may soon discover that one great variety wanted by every collector in the hobby! And let us know when you do.

Doubled Dies vs. Other Forms of Doubling

The difference between die doubling (doubled dies, repunched dates, and repunched mintmarks, among others) and the more confusing forms of doubling can be very challenging to explain, and even more difficult for a novice to comprehend. Additionally, there are times when determining the difference can be frustrating even for a very experienced collector. This section will help you learn the differences. But reading alone will not do it all; you must examine numerous coins before you can expect to have a solid grasp of the differences between die doubling and other forms of doubling.

DIE DOUBLING: THOSE ABNORMALITIES WE LOVE TO COLLECT!

Die doubling is the type of doubling that exhibits a doubled image on the die itself, even before the coin is struck. Die doubling includes doubled dies, repunched dates, repunched mintmarks, overdates, over mintmarks, and repunched letters. It almost always exhibits splits in the serifs of the letters and/or numerals, with rounded, secondary images.

On this Jefferson nickel, the distinctive splits in the serifs are evident, and the secondary images are "rounded" and can easily be detected.

The photograph shown here of a true 1969-S doubled-die Lincoln cent exhibits the typical rounded secondary images. Notice also the "crease" between the images.

Many 19th-century coins have letters and numerals that are flat on their top surfaces as compared to the rounded appearance of most 20th-century letters and numerals. Therefore, the key to identifying true die doubling on 19th-century coins is the distinctive splits in the serifs.

There is one class of doubled die that would not exhibit the normal characteristics mentioned for die doubling. Known as Class VI doubled dies, these exhibit extra thickness

The splits in the serifs on this 1887 Indian Head cent doubled-die obverse are typical of what one would expect for most 19th-century coins with true die doubling.

on some letters and numbers. Most widely known on Lincoln cents, the doubling sometimes exhibits letters that are slightly misshapen, such as the lower bar of an E being curved. This curved shape often is convex. Although some specialists may disagree, Class VI doubled dies *generally* command very small premiums—except in rare cases.

Notice the extra thickness of the letters in LIBERTY. This is typical of a Class VI doubled die, shown here on a Lincoln cent.

STRIKE DOUBLING

Strike doubling is the type of doubling most often confused with, and very often misidentified as, a doubled die or repunched mintmark. Not only do novices confuse this type of doubling with doubled dies, but specialists disagree as to what the correct terminology should be.

Strike doubling is the term we prefer and what we feel most accurately describes the cause. Strike doubling occurs during the striking process. If one of the dies is loose as they come together to strike the coin, the loose die will twist slightly immediately as the hammer die starts to retract. This twisting die will actually cause some of the metal on the relief areas of the coin to shear. Remember that the relief area on the coin is

This LIBERTY on a Lincoln cent exhibits typical strike doubling. Notice the flat, shelf-like appearance of the secondary image.

the recessed area on the die. This shear will almost always be flat and shelf-like, and will appear as if the metal has actually been moved.

Some might argue that the striking of the coin ends when the hammer die reaches the very end of its stroke. By this argument, this should not be called *strike doubling*, but rather *mechanical* or *machine doubling*. In our opinion, this is like trying to split a hair. Additionally, we feel that *machine* or *mechanical* doubling can be even more confusing, as neither term indicates in which part of the minting process this happens. Either of those terms could refer to the coin counters at the end of the process! We feel *strike doubling* is best suited to indicate the point of the minting process in which this doubling occurs.

Furthermore, numismatists agree there are three basic areas of the minting process: planchet, die, and striking. This doubling occurs during the striking process, and not in the die-making or planchet-making process. (We don't refer to incomplete planchets as a machine problem, although a machine causes them.)

During our tours of the mints in Philadelphia and Denver, the personnel in both facilities confirmed the cause of strike doubling. Additionally, they stated that when they do encounter this doubling they tighten the dies into their holding collars and the doubling ceases.

Whether you refer to this as *strike doubling, machine doubling, mechanical doubling,* or *ejection doubling,* your primary focus should be to understand the differences and educate others.

As a rule, strike doubling exhibits a flat, shelf-like secondary image, not like the rounded secondary images of true die doubling. Usually this secondary image is low to the field. There are no splits in the serifs. On most Uncirculated and Proof coins, strike doubling gives the appearance that the metal has been "moved," much like that on hobo nickels or love tokens, and has a very shiny appearance.

On this 1937 Buffalo nickel, the secondary images exhibit the flat, shelf-like doubling typical of strike doubling. The secondary image is low, close to the field.

Strike doubling can affect all lettering on one or both sides, or could be detected on only one letter or a small portion of a device. Proof coins often exhibit strike doubling due to the excessive force employed in their manufacture. Strike doubling can also be evident on a coin with a true doubled die or true repunched mintmark.

There are several dates (and runs of dates) in several series that are well known for strike doubling. Examples include Mercury dimes from 1936 through 1942 and Lincoln cents from 1968 through 1972.

Compare this 1969-S Lincoln cent doubled die with the strike-doubling specimen to the right.

In this 1969-S cent, strike doubling is evident on the date and mintmark. Whenever the date and mintmark both are doubled, odds are that the doubling is strike doubling.

Although it can be difficult for a novice to understand, strike doubling might affect only the mintmark on a coin, creating what some may interpret as a repunched mintmark. In fact, this is fairly common, especially on Franklin halves and Washington quarters. This is often because strike doubling first affects the deepest part of the die (the highest part of the coin), which in many cases is the deeply punched mintmark.

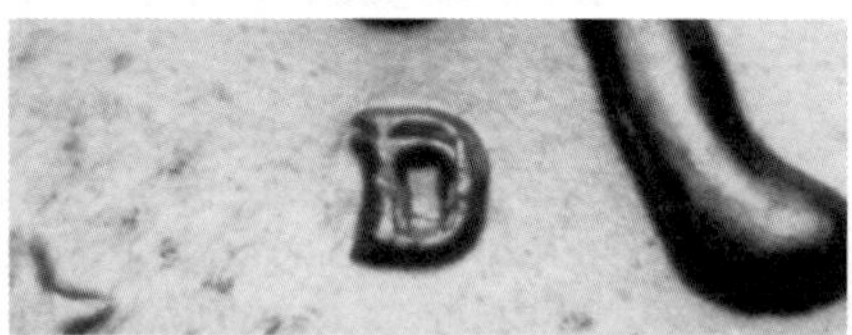

This is a genuine repunched mintmark on a Kennedy half dollar. Compare the doubling here with the next, which was caused by strike doubling.

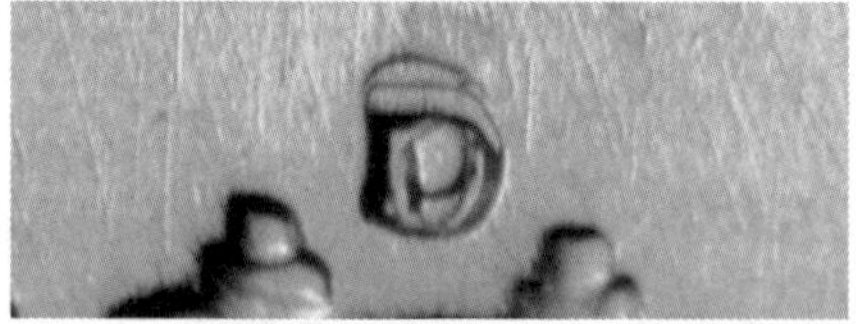

This mintmark on a Franklin half dollar is the result of strike doubling. Notice the flat, shelf-like doubling, which is the primary characteristic of strike doubling.

OTHER FORMS OF DOUBLING

In addition to strike doubling, there are other forms of doubling that are often mistaken for die doubling. Among these are doubling caused by die fatigue or die polish, and doubling that is typical on coins designed by James B. Longacre, possibly intentionally.

324

Die Fatigue

Die fatigue is very often confused with a doubled die. In general, as a die deteriorates, the letters and/or numbers develop wear, causing a secondary image on both sides of the letters or numbers (as though their edges have crumbled). This is due to stress in the metal of the die. This doubling will often, but not always, occur in combination with an "orange-peel" effect on the fields of the coin, created by the stress in the metal on the dies.

Die fatigue is very evident and extreme in this Jefferson nickel. Notice the secondary images on both sides of the letters, and the "orange-peel" effect on the field.

Here is another example of die fatigue. Notice the edges of the I and T appearing to merge into the field. Also, the letters have less definition than one would expect.

Die fatigue is very common on Washington quarters from the 1980s and 1990s, Jefferson nickels from 1955 to date, and Roosevelt dimes from 1965 to date. Die fatigue is a prime example of what can happen when the Mint tries to get maximum production out of every single die.

Die Polish

Excessive polishing of the dies can also cause a doubled image on the struck coin. As dies are being polished, excessive force is sometimes used in certain areas. When this occurs, the result of the polishing can be the appearance of a doubled image due to "spreading" the edges of the letters or numbers.

Excessive die polishing is the cause of the doubled image on the 3 of the date.

"Longacre" Doubling

This term was coined by J.T. Stanton as an easy way to describe the doubling that is typical on many coins designed by James Barton Longacre. These include Indian Head cents, nickel three-cent pieces, Shield nickels, and many gold issues. We're certain many readers have seen this doubling before; almost all of the letters are doubled, with the secondary

In this Indian Head cent, the doubling that is typical on many of Longacre's designs is evident. Notice that the secondary image is visible on both sides of the letters.

image appearing on both sides of the letters. Some specialists believe this is from the shoulder of the punch penetrating the die, causing the secondary step. Others feel it was an intentional design on Longacre's part, to help the metal flow into the tight crevices of the die. Although this doubling is evident on many of the coins that Longacre designed, it is not seen on all of his coins. This would likely remove the theory that the secondary or "stepped" image was planned to help with metal flow.

Longacre doubling does not add premium to a coin's value.

SUMMARY

We hope this long, but educational, article will help our readers learn the difference between die doubling and other forms of doubling. However, the best learning tool is experience. In that light, we suggest that you look—and look carefully—at as many coins as possible, especially in the date ranges mentioned. Look especially carefully at Proof quarters from 1968 and 1969 for strike doubling, Indian Head cents from the 1860s, 1870s, and 1880s for "Longacre" doubling, nickels from the 1980s for die fatigue, and Franklin half dollars for strike doubling on the mintmark. Don't pass up the opportunity to buy a good example of one of these for your reference, if it's not too expensive.

DIE-DOUBLING I.Q. TEST

The 10 photographs here exhibit some examples of die doubling, strike doubling, and even some other forms of doubling. Take a few minutes to see for yourself whether you can accurately identify the various forms of doubling.

Note: Most variety collectors feel coins exhibiting other forms of doubling should not command a premium. However, some collectors believe they are collectable and actively seek them. We feel there is absolutely nothing wrong with this and encourage those who decide to take this course. The question is and should be, "Are you having *fun* in your collecting pursuits?"

Test photo 1

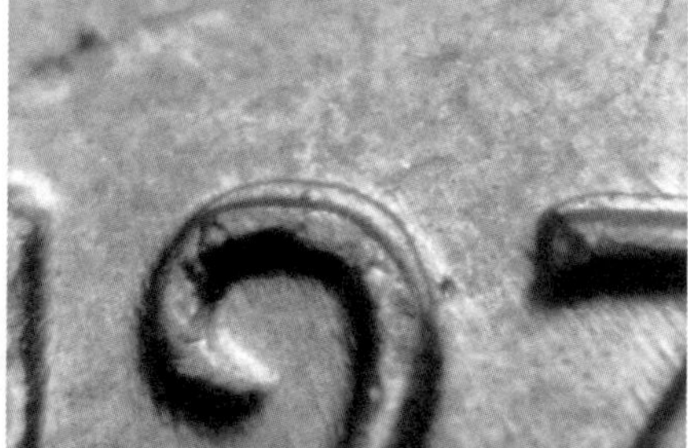

Test photo 2

Test photo 3

Test photo 4

Test photo 5

Test photo 6

Test photo 7

Test photo 8

Test photo 9

Test photo 10

Answers to the test photographs:
1. strike doubling; 2. strike doubling; 3. doubled die; 4. strike doubling; 5. doubled die; 6. die fatigue; 7. strike doubling; 8. repunched mintmark; 9. doubled die; 10. strike doubling.

In test photo 10, notice that the date and the mintmark both exhibit similar doubling. This should be a red flag. There are very few examples on which a doubled die and a repunched mintmark both are evident on the same side of the same coin. Keep in mind that until very recently, the mintmark was punched into the die after the die was made. Therefore, if the die is doubled, the mintmark is not necessarily doubled.

Appendix B
The Minting Process

WHY STUDY THE MINTING PROCESS?

In the study of Mint errors and varieties—and the study of the "regular" segment of numismatics, as well—a basic knowledge of the minting process is vital. If one does not understand how an error or variety occurred, he or she will not be able to determine whether it is genuine. The description that follows is an abbreviated one, but the basics remain the same.

There are four basic processes that take place at the U.S. Mint, and it is during second through fourth processes that all errors and varieties occur. First is the design process, in which the coin is designed and a model is engraved. Next is the die-making process, whereby the design is transferred to a "die steel" to strike the coin. The third process is the making of planchets—coin blanks that are created and specially prepared for striking. The last process is the striking of these planchets to make them into coins. The last three processes—die making, planchet production, and striking—are where errors occur. Some have described this trio of areas as "P-D-S" (planchets, dies, and striking); the resemblance of these initials to the P, D, and S mintmarks of the three primary minting facilities (Philadelphia, Denver, and San Francisco) makes it easy to remember remembering these areas of production.

Error vs. Variety

Occasionally there is disagreement as to whether a certain aberrant coin is an error or a variety. Generally speaking, most specialists consider an error a one-time occurrence that is not repeated in exactly the same way, and a variety an occurrence that *is* repeated in exactly the same way. An off-center strike, therefore, would be considered an error. True, some off-center strikes look quite similar, but generally speaking, each one will be different. However, a doubled die will repeat exactly with each strike, and is thus considered a variety.

THE DESIGN PROCESS

Sculptors and engravers are employed by the Mint to design coins and medals and to sculpt and engrave other designs into workable subjects for coining. These highly trained specialists take a design from a drawing, painting, or other two-dimensional object and transform it onto a plaster model, approximately 15 inches in diameter, that will ultimately be transferred to a coin or medal. The design on the model is always in raised above the surrounding area (i.e., it is "positive" or "in relief"), just as it will appear on the finished coin. This plaster sculpture, after slight changes and improvements, is coated with epoxy resins to act as a preservative and a hardener. The epoxy-coated plaster sculpture is called a *galvano* and is forwarded to the die-making area of the Mint.

THE DIE-MAKING PROCESS

Since the galvano is usually many times larger than the intended coin, its design must be reduced. To accomplish this, the galvano is placed onto a Janvier transfer-reducing machine. This machine traces the design on the galvano and, using the principle of the fulcrum, transfers the design onto the end of a piece of steel bar the actual size of the coin to be produced. This is called the *reducing* stage of die production, and this finished piece of steel is called the *master hub.* When the master hub has been produced, it is heated to extreme temperatures, then quenched (cooled) quickly in a vat of oil. This heating-and-cooling process, called *tempering,* hardens the steel even further.

The large galvano is reduced on a Janvier transfer reducing machine to create a master hub (a "positive") that is the actual size of the coin.

The master hub has the design in the same relief design as on the galvano and as it will appear on the finished coin. It is placed into a hydraulic hubbing press, opposite a piece of die steel that is about four inches long. When each is seated into the press, hydraulic force brings the two together, transferring the image from the master hub onto the end of the die steel. When complete, this is called the *master die,* with the design pressed (incused) into its surface.

This operation, known as *hubbing,* used to take several impressions to bring the design to the depth specifications. After each hubbing, the die would be annealed to make the steel even more hardened. If the die were to receive the image deep enough in the first hubbing, stress on the die steel would result and very likely create cracks, or at least would weaken the die. Strength and durability are stringent requirements. This process is now done by the "single-squeeze method," using one high-pressure compression.

After the master die is produced, it is placed into the hubbing press to create the working hub in the same manner. Several working hubs are produced. These working hubs then produce working dies in the manner described before. The working dies are then placed into the coining presses to strike coins and medals.

Traditionally, all dies were made in the Philadelphia Mint. Until 1987 the dies were produced without mintmarks, which were added by hand with punches before the dies were shipped to the branch-mint facilities for completion. However, beginning in 1987 the mintmark was added to the master die, and in 1990 it was added to the original plaster sculpture. Subsequently, the mintmark is transferred to the master hub and on down the die-production chain. Beginning in 1996, the Denver Mint started producing dies for its own and the San Francisco Mint's production facilities.

Remember that the plaster sculpture, the galvano, the master hub, and the working hub all have the image of the coin in relief, or positive, just as the finished coin will appear. Master dies and working dies have the image coin incuse, or negative—a mirror image of the finished coin.

PLANCHET MAKING

Cent and nickel planchets are primarily made outside the Mint, as is the sheet metal for the other denominations. However, the process is much the same as when the Mint produced their own planchets and metal. Raw metal, after being melted, is rolled into long sheets until it is the proper thickness for the intended coin. These long sheets are then coiled for storage, shipping, and eventual use. The sheets are uncoiled and fed into a blanking press—which is nothing more than a series of punches that cut blanks out of the metal coils—either at the outside facility or at the Mint. Notice the word "blank" instead of "planchet": Technically speaking, a *blank* is a disc of metal that has not been prepared for striking, whereas a *planchet* is a blank that has been prepared for striking.

Once the blanks are produced, they pass through what is known as a *riddler,* which passes the blanks over a three-tiered, vibrating screen, with holes in the first tier slightly larger than the intended blanks. The blanks that are of proper diameter drop through, and blanks that are too large are retained on the upper tier and carried to a scrap bin. The second-tier screen has holes slightly smaller than a proper-sized blank. Blanks that are too small pass through these holes to the third tier, from which they are carried

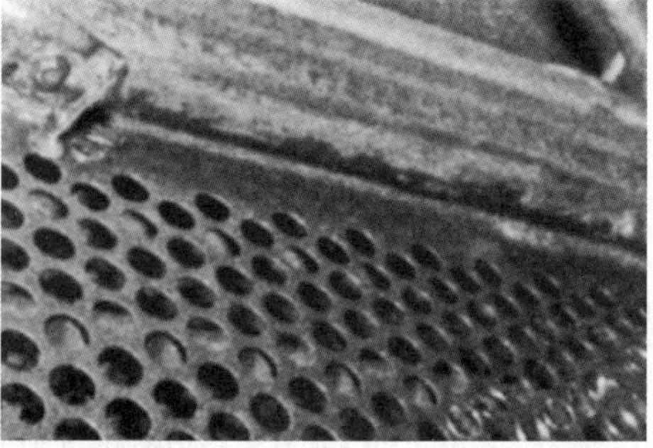

Once the blanks are produced, they pass through what is known as a riddler, which removes imperfectly-sized blanks.

away to the scrap bin. The blanks that remain on the second tier are presumed to be of accurate size, and are forwarded to the next process.

At this point, the blanks must be annealed and cleaned. The annealing process softens the blanks to improve striking and reduce wear on the dies. After annealing, they are passed through a wash for cleaning, then through a dryer to remove any soap or water (which might cause spots).

The blanks are then ready for the *upset mill.* This is a machine with two primary components: (1) a stationary die with V-shaped grooves, and (2) a rotating die in the center, also with V-shaped grooves. Blanks are fed into one end of the upset mill, fitting into the grooves. As the center die rotates, the blanks pass between the outer, stationary die and the inner, rotating die. As the blanks go through the mill, the spacing between the two dies is gradually reduced, forcing the metal on the edge of the blank to be raised above the flat surfaces. When the disc of metal exits the upset mill, generally with raised metal all around the edge, it is considered a planchet.

The reason for putting raised edges on planchets before striking is that it greatly helps in coin production: it helps force the metal, during striking, toward the center of the coin and then into the crevices of the die; it also helps the coins stack neatly as they are struck.

A blank remains a blank until it has been through the upsetting mill and received a raised edge, at which time it becomes a planchet. Blanks are frequently (and erroneously) referred to as "Type 1 planchets," but because they do not have raised edges, they should not be called planchets of any kind. There are no Type 1 or Type 2 planchets; the disc of metal is either a blank or a planchet, period.

The planchets are then fed into a furnace. This furnace is much like a long dryer with the planchets being fed in one end and tumbled as they travel through the furnace. Planchets are heated in the furnace to make them softer, which helps with striking. When the planchets exit the furnace, they are washed in a chemical bath and slowly tumbled dry. By the end of this process, most planchets made of nickel will have a yellowish tint.

STRIKING

The striking process begins with the planchets' being brought to the coining presses via overhead conveyors with small bins. These conveyors deposit the planchets into a hopper above the coining presses. From that point the planchets are fed by gravity through feeder tubes and down into the *coining chamber* (the area of the coining press where striking takes place).

The planchets drop from the feeder tubes into *feeder fingers,* each of which has a slot in the end to push out the struck coin and a hole a couple of inches back that holds the next planchet to be deposited into the chamber. These fingers slide back and forth over a smooth steel surface.

The coining chamber consists primarily of the anvil (lower) die, hammer (upper) die, collar, and feeder fingers. The *anvil die,* which usually strikes the reverse of the coin, moves only when coins are being ejected and planchets received. The *hammer die,* which usually strikes the obverse, comes down and strikes the planchet. The *collar* is a metal ring that retains the planchet during the strike, preventing the metal from expanding outside the desired diameter. The collar also serves as a third die, creating the reeding or lettering on coins intended to have reeded or lettered edges.

When the planchet is deposited on the anvil die and within the collar by the feeder finger, the finger retracts and the hammer die comes down and strikes the planchet. As the hammer die retracts, the anvil die (riding on a cam) rises; the feeder finger pushes the struck coin out of the chamber, continues forward, and deposits another planchet onto the anvil die. The feeder finger retracts and the striking process begins again. The finished coins pass through an additional riddler to catch further errors; this has greatly reduced the number of error coins escaping the Mint.

COUNTING AND BAGGING

Once the coins are ejected from the coining press, they fall down a chute and are carried to the counting room on conveyors. In the counting room, the coins are counted, packaged, and weighed. Some coins are bagged in the well-known Mint-sewn bags, while others (usually cents) are placed in large totes containing 1,500 pounds of coins within a heavy plastic liner. The bagged coins are then shipped to the various Federal Reserve banks.

Appendix C
What Are the Best Magnifiers?

"What level of magnification should I use when searching for varieties?" "Which magnifier is the best to use?" "Do I need a microscope?" These are three of the more common questions ever broached concerning this subject. All too often a collector will believe *more* magnification is better—when in fact less is usually best. With coin collecting in general and variety collecting in particular, the strength of the magnification is not as important as the *quality*.

Virtually every variety of any significance can be detected with a 7x glass, if it's of good quality. (A good 7x magnifier is also the recommended loupe for the most accurate coin grading.) A lesser-quality magnifier will only distort the image, making proper identification even more difficult. On the other hand, a good-quality glass with too much magnification is almost always overkill, as it can cause you to overlook key identification points.

An H.E. Harris magnifier (or *loupe,* pronounced "loop") is a common sight at coin shows. You will see dealers and collectors slip them out of their pocket to examine interesting coins. (Some wear them on a chain or string around their neck, for constant easy access.) These magnifiers fold into their chrome cases to protect the lens, which is usually 4x to 8x or greater strength.

Most serious collectors and almost all dealers use a Hastings triplet magnifier; usually a 7x or 10x power is preferred. "Hastings" is not a brand but a method of manufacture. The Hastings triplet has a three-glass (or plastic) optic, which ensures clarity throughout the entire lens and produces virtually no distortion.

Some manufacturers use 10x or 17x designations. However, without good-quality optics, the 10x or 17x means nothing. We've seen some magnifiers marked as 17x, compared to which a 10x Hastings triplet provides more detail, better clarity, and a wider field of view. And remember, if you can't see a variety with a 7x glass, it's likely not worth searching for.

A good 7x Bausch & Lomb Hastings triplet will normally run about $45. However, with some searching on the Internet, you can find a good 7x Hastings triplet for less than $25.

Stereoscopes (microscopes) are handy, fun, and very educational, but these are not absolutely necessary for the study of varieties. Should you have the desire to add one to your array of collecting tools, a good stereoscope can be obtained for as little as $250 (though most will run around $500 or more). Be sure to get a stereoscope—one that has two eyepieces. This will allow the very best in clarity and use. A stereoscope is great for taking photographs, and for studying the minute differences evident on every coin.

Check with your local supplier or favorite online dealers. See what they recommend. We strongly advise spending a little more for a good-quality product. You'll reap the rewards soon afterward.

Appendix D

Popular Varieties From Proof and Mint Sets

This list, of Proof sets and Mint sets that contain significant varieties, should be useful for all collectors. Beginning with those modern Mint sets from 1947, and Proof sets from 1950, there are many years of one or the other that are absent of a significant variety. Not all of the known varieties are significant. Should you encounter a significant variety that is not listed, please contact the publisher so the list can be updated.

Again, this list is just to be used as a guide. Those Proof listings in **bold type** are considered the most desirable.

Mint Sets

1949	5¢	D/S–over mintmark (although known, most have already been removed)
1954, Small Date	25¢	doubled-die reverse
1960, Small Date	5¢	(P)–doubled-die obverse (found in sets labeled as Small Date)
1960, Small Date	10¢	(P)–doubled-die obverse (found in sets labeled as Small Date)
1960, Small Date	25¢	(P)–doubled-die obverse (found in sets labeled as Small Date)
1961	50¢	D/D–repunched mintmark
1963	10¢	(P)-doubled-die obverse
1963	25¢	(P)–doubled-die obverse (P)–doubled-die reverse
1963	50¢	(P)–doubled-die obverse (P)–doubled-die reverse
1968	10¢	(P)–doubled-die obverse
1968	25¢	D–doubled-die reverse
1969	5¢	D/D–repunched mintmark
1969	10¢	D/D–repunched mintmark
1969	25¢	D/D–repunched mintmark
1969	50¢	D–doubled-die reverse
1970	1¢	D/D–repunched mintmark D–doubled-die obverse
1970	10¢	D–doubled-die reverse
1970	25¢	D–doubled-die reverse
1970, Small Date	50¢	D–doubled-die reverse
1971	5¢	D/D–repunched mintmark
1971	10¢	D/D–repunched mintmark D–doubled-die reverse
1971	50¢	D–doubled-die obverse D–doubled-die reverse
1972	1¢	(P)–doubled-die obverse
1972	5¢	D–doubled-die reverse
1972	50¢	D–doubled-die reverse
1973	50¢	(P)–doubled-die obverse D–doubled-die obverse
1974	50¢	D–doubled-die obverse
		D–doubled-die reverse
1981	5¢	D–doubled-die reverse
1984	50¢	D/D–repunched mintmark
1987	5¢	D/D–repunched mintmark
1987	10¢	D/D–repunched mintmark
1989	5¢	D–doubled-die reverse
1989	10¢	P–doubled-die reverse
1989	50¢	D/D–repunched mintmark
1991	5¢	D–doubled-die obverse

Proof Sets

Year	Denom.	Variety
1950	10¢	doubled-die reverse
1950	50¢	doubled-die obverse
1951	1¢	doubled-die obverse
1951	**5¢**	**doubled-die obverse**
1952	**25¢**	**"Superbird"**
1953	1¢	doubled-die obverse
1953	**5¢**	**doubled-die obverse**
1953	25¢	doubled-die obverse recut tail feathers
1954	1¢	doubled-die obverse
1954	10¢	doubled-die obverse
1954	50¢	doubled-die obverse
1955	1¢	doubled-die obverse doubled-die reverse
1955	**5¢**	**tripled-die reverse**
1956	1¢	doubled-die reverse
1956	10¢	doubled-die obverse
1956	50¢	doubled-die obverse doubled-die reverse
1957	**5¢**	**quadrupled-die obverse**
1957	50¢	doubled-die reverse
1959	25¢	doubled-die obverse
1960, Small Date	**1¢**	**doubled-die obverse** (Large/Small) **doubled-die obverse** (Small/Large)
1960	5¢	doubled-die reverse
1960	10¢	doubled-die obverse
1960	**10¢**	**doubled-die reverse**
1960	**25¢**	**doubled-die reverse**
1960	50¢	doubled-die obverse
1961	5¢	doubled-die reverse
1961	25¢	doubled-die obverse
1961	**50¢**	**doubled-die reverse**
1962	25¢	doubled-die obverse
1962	50¢	doubled-die obverse
1963	**10¢**	**doubled-die reverse**
1963	25¢	doubled-die reverse
1964	10¢	doubled-die obverse
1964	50¢	doubled-die obverse
1968-S	1¢	doubled-die obverse
1968-S	5¢	repunched mintmark
1968-S	10¢	doubled-die obverse
1968-S	**10¢**	**doubled-die reverse** **doubled-die obverse**
1968-S	**10¢**	**No S**
1968-S	25¢	repunched mintmark
1968-S	**25¢**	**doubled-die reverse**
1968-S	**50¢**	**doubled-die obverse**
1969-S	25¢	doubled-die obverse
1969-S	**25¢**	**repunched mintmark**
1970-S	**10¢**	**No S**
1970-S	50¢	doubled-die obverse
1971-S	1¢	doubled-die obverse
1971-S	**5¢**	**No S**
1971-S	50¢	doubled-die obverse
1975-S	10¢	doubled-die reverse
1975-S	**10¢**	**No S**
1979-S	1¢	Type II mintmark
1979-S	5¢	Type II mintmark
1979-S	10¢	Type II mintmark
1979-S	25¢	Type II mintmark
1979-S	50¢	Type II mintmark
1979-S	$1	Type II mintmark
1981-S	1¢	Type II mintmark
1981-S	5¢	Type II mintmark
1981-S	10¢	Type II mintmark
1981-S	25¢	Type II mintmark
1981-S	50¢	Type II mintmark
1981-S	$1	Type II mintmark
1982-S	25¢	doubled-die obverse
1983-S	**10¢**	**No S**
1990-S	**1¢**	**No S**
1990-S	25¢	doubled-die obverse
1995-S	25¢	doubled-die obverse

When Cherrypickin', Use Courtesy and Respect!

Many years ago, a dealer friend of ours indicated he would never let anyone, other than a few people, cherrypick his stock (fortunately, we were among that select group). He had legitimate complaints regarding most of those who try to cherrypick varieties. His experiences are not unlike those of many dealers. Too often, collectors who are most interested in cherrypickin' varieties disregard the dealer's other (and potentially more profitable) customers. Many cherrypickers will take up space and time, and then walk away without a single purchase. Is that right? Is that fair to the dealer?

Before we get directly into the *courtesy* aspect of this article, we would like to remind you that there is nothing wrong with cherrypickin'. We use our knowledge just as another dealer or collector would use their knowledge to buy the best deal. A dealer trying to buy an 1892-S Barber quarter in Fine condition for a client will usually cherrypick to get the best possible value. Dealers with excellent grading skills can cherrypick undergraded coins, making a nice profit in a later sale. That has been occurring for decades in our hobby.

When the term *cherrypick* is used today, most hobbyists automatically think of those who search for varieties among a stock of normal coins. Those of us involved with varieties have studied long and hard for our knowledge. However, to make the most of this knowledge, we must use some common sense, and we must *always* respect a dealer's main objective—to earn a living. Dealers are at shows and in the coin business to make money to support their families. This is their livelihood, and we must always respect their time and space. If you don't feel you can afford them this courtesy, don't consider cherrypickin' for varieties. Those of us who do respect a dealer's time and space do not want a few inconsiderate people to ruin the pickings for the rest of us.

There are a few "courtesy" pointers that we'd like you to keep in mind. Remember that you are very likely a small customer for the typical dealer. They can almost certainly make more money from another customer in a tenth of the time they might spend with you. Remember that *you need the dealers* for cherrypickin'—they could make their living without cherrypickers!

If you're at a show and you've spotted a dealer whose stock you would like to search, and that dealer is busy, simply go to another dealer for a while. If you are seated at a dealer's table looking over their stock, and they start to get busy, let them know in a respectful way that you realize you're taking up their space and time, and that you will come back when they aren't as busy. We promise the dealer will remember your courtesy and respect, and you're more likely to be welcomed back when time permits.

We've often had dealers ask what we're looking for. We generally tell them that we're looking for various varieties, and that will usually suffice. Don't lie. Never lie!

But you don't have to tell everything. If the dealer persists, you might tell them about a few of the more scarce varieties, and explain that there is a market for those varieties. Remember most dealers couldn't care less about the popular varieties that aren't listed in the Red Book. They will usually say "fine," and you can continue looking.

However, the best-case scenario is that you can teach this dealer something about varieties. As you become better acquainted, the dealer might start to look for some of the varieties, and save them for you. Sure, you'll likely pay a little more for them than the price of the normal coin, but far less than the actual value of the variety. In short, you'll have added a pair of eyes to *your* cherrypickin'. You'll get a new supply for varieties and at prices that will enable you to realize a very nice profit. We've even had dealers tell us to name the price, and we've had dealers ask for only the value of the normal coin.

Here's a tip that we think is extremely important. If you're at a dealer's table, and if for some reason you need to reach into your pocket or lap, plainly open your hands above the table, turn them over and rub them together, then do what you need to do. You don't need to say anything, and don't make a big deal of it, but make sure it's obvious. Why? The dealer will know for sure that you are not "palming" a coin. Do this with dealers you know well, and with dealers you don't know. Make it a habit. The main point here is to *never* give any dealer any opportunity to even think you are doing something wrong. We've seen people who hold a want list or magnifier in their lap, then take the coin below the table's surface, out of view of the dealer. That is very wrong, whether cherrypickin' or not, and will often discourage a dealer from welcoming you back. Always think of how you would want a customer to act if you were the dealer, and *always be respectful*—even if the dealer may seem rude.

Here are some other important points: Never let a dealer feel cheated when you buy a coin, or you'll never be welcomed back. Never brag about what you've purchased from a dealer if there is any way possible it could get back to the dealer. Always be polite and courteous—and being friendly doesn't hurt, either. Try to put yourself in their shoes once in a while. Usually, a dealer's main objective is to sell coins they have and know best for a profit. Many dealers specialize in certain areas, and leave other coins to others. We cherrypickers are the ones who know varieties best, and so they will usually leave this area for us.

One last tip: Suppose you find a super variety for the price of a regular coin, and for some reason you don't want the dealer to key in on that one coin. You might buy a few other coins at the same time to draw less attention to the coin you really want. Who cares about the added expense? You'll make a bundle on that nice cherry! And if the extra coins are ones with firm markets, such as an MS-63 Morgan dollar or a Proof set, you'll be able to turn around and sell them quickly.

Above all, *always use courtesy and respect* in all your dealings, be honest, and always act in a professional manner. You'll make some friends along the way, and we guarantee you'll come out ahead in the long run!

Appendix F
1979-S and 1981-S Proof-Mintmark Varieties

The Type I and Type II mintmark varieties for the 1979-S and 1981-S Proof sets are very well known, yet many people become confused when trying to differentiate them. This appendix illustrates the four mintmark styles for each denomination.

Compare these descriptions to the photos, and you'll be able to identify the correct types:

- The *1979-S Type I* mintmark has a squared, filled S, very indistinct.
- The *1979-S Type II* mintmark is clear and well formed.
- The *1981-S Type I* is a worn version of the 1979-S Type II.
- The *1981-S Type II,* although somewhat similar to the Type I, is distinguishable by the flattened top surface of the S. Some specialists argue that the S must be clear in both loops. Most agree that the S can show some slight filling, but the mintmark punch must show that flattened top surface. This is usually the most difficult type to comprehend. But the key is really very simple—that flatness on the top surface.

Cents

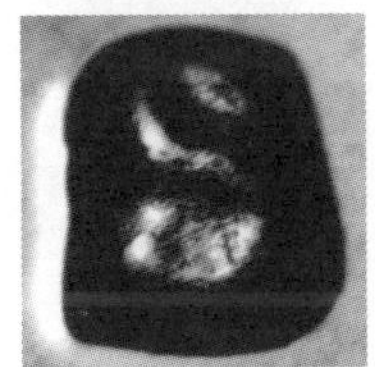 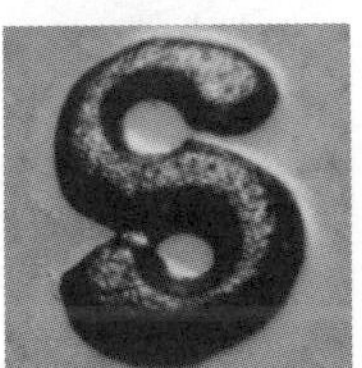  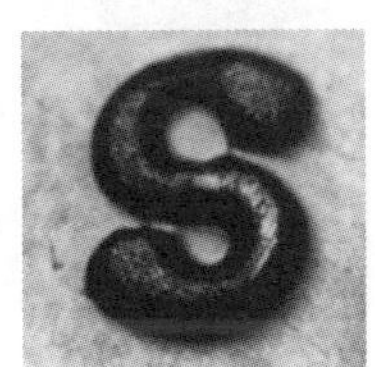

1979-S Type I　　**1979-S Type II**　　**1981-S Type I**　　**1981-S Type II**

Nickels

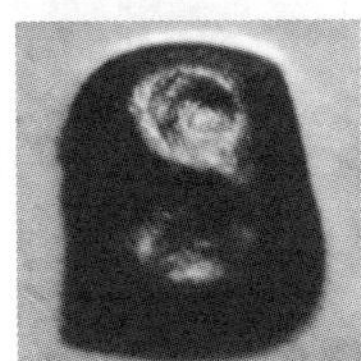 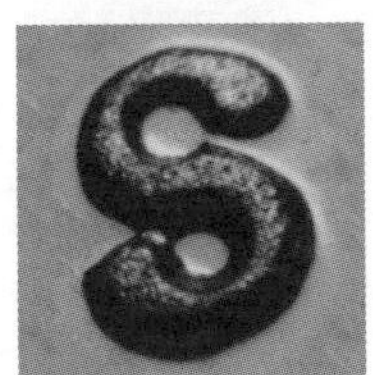 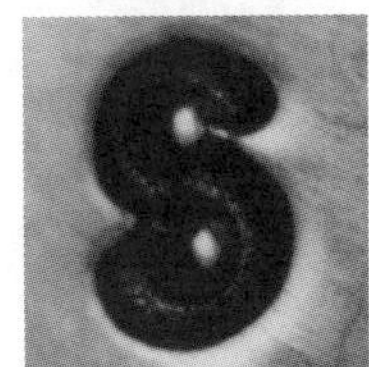 

1979-S Type I　　**1979-S Type II**　　**1981-S Type I**　　**1981-S Type II**

Dimes

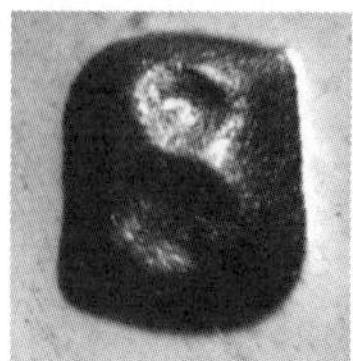

1979-S Type I

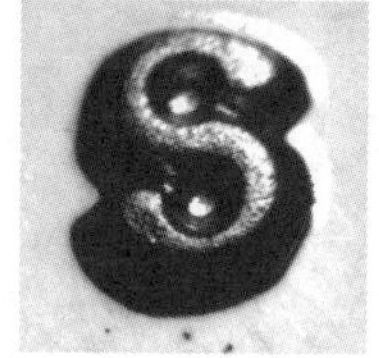

1979-S Type II

1981-S Type I

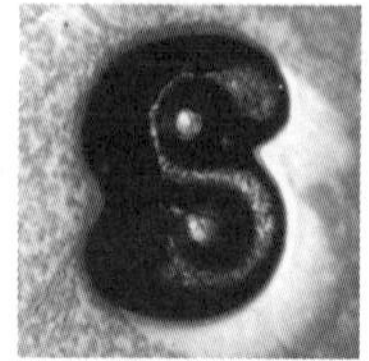

1981-S Type II

Quarter Dollars

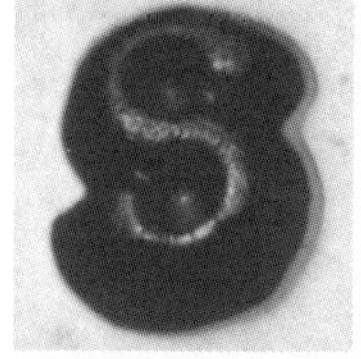

1979-S Type I

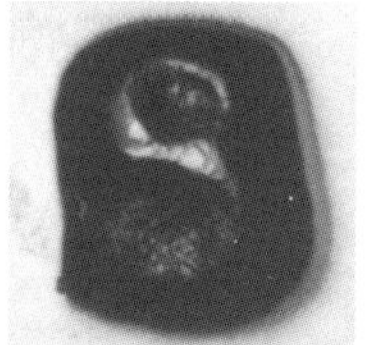

1979-S Type II

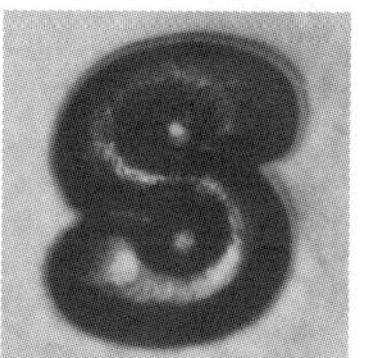

1981-S Type I

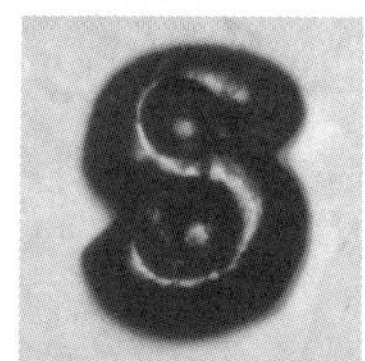

1981-S Type II

Half Dollars

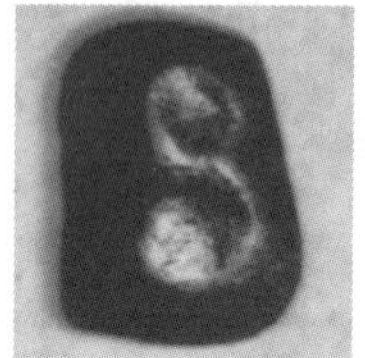

1979-S Type I

1979-S Type II

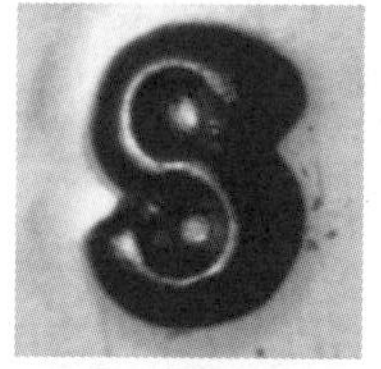

1981-S Type I

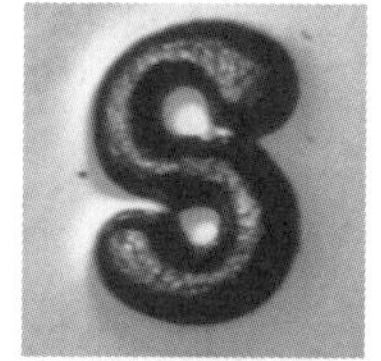

1981-S Type II

Dollars

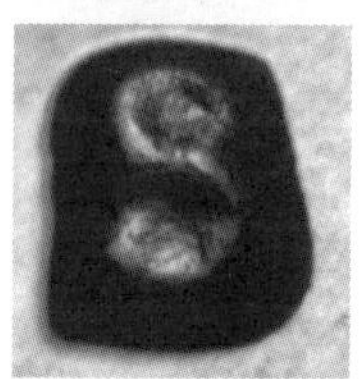

1979-S Type I

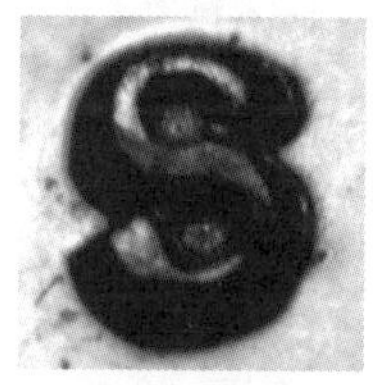

1979-S Type II

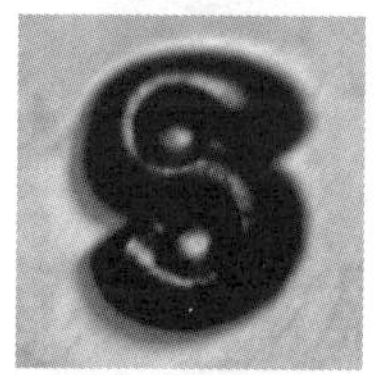

1981-S Type I

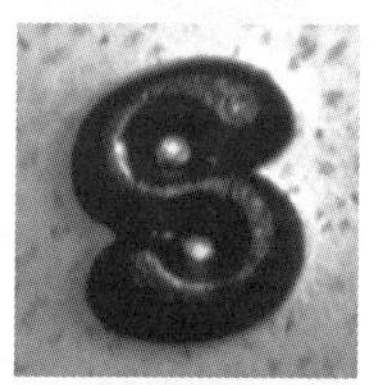

1981-S Type II

Appendix G
Recommended Reading

The axiom "Buy the book before the coin" applies even more strongly to the error/variety collector than to the regular segment of the hobby. The following is a list of recommended readings. It can by no means stay complete—new books become available regularly—but it gives you an excellent foundation for building your knowledge. Most of these books are available online, or through any coin dealer. The abbreviation OOP indicates the book is out of print.

GENERAL

The following books cover not only errors and varieties, but regular coins as well. These books should be included in any numismatist's library:

A Guide Book of United States Coins, by R.S. Yeoman, edited by Kenneth Bressett. Popularly known as the "Red Book," this is the book with which any numismatic library should begin.

Walter Breen's Complete Encyclopedia of U.S. and Colonial Coins. This is undoubtedly the best book anyone interested in die varieties can add to their library. It's not cheap, but much of the information it contains cannot be found anywhere else.

SERIES TOPICS

The following books highlight a specific series or subject. Each is a tremendous asset for anyone seriously interested in its topic.

A Guide Book of Flying Eagle and Indian Head Cents, by Richard Snow.

Flying Eagle and Indian Cent Die Varieties, by Larry R. Steve and Kevin Flynn. (OOP)

Flying Eagle, Indian Cent, Two Cent & Three Cent Doubled Dies, by Kevin Flynn. (OOP)

The Complete Guide to Lincoln Cents, by David Lange.

A Guide Book of Lincoln Cents, by Q. David Bowers.

The Lincoln Cent Doubled Die, by John Wexler. (OOP)

The RPM Book—Second Edition: Lincoln Cents, by James Wiles.

The Complete Price Guide and Cross Reference to Lincoln Cent Mint Mark Varieties, by Brian Allen and John A. Wexler. (OOP)

The Authoritative Reference on Lincoln Cents, by John Wexler and Kevin Flynn. (OOP)

Looking Through Lincoln Cents, by Charles Daughtrey.

The Authoritative Reference of Three Cent Nickels, by Kevin Flynn.

A Guide Book of Shield and Liberty Head Nickels, by Q. David Bowers.

The Shield Five Cent Series, by Ed Fletcher. (OOP)

The Complete Guide to Shield and Liberty Nickels, by Gloria Peters and Cynthia Mohon. (OOP)

Treasure Hunting Liberty Head Nickels, by Kevin Flynn and Bill Van Note. (OOP)

The Complete Guide to Buffalo Nickels, second edition, by David W. Lange.

Treasure Hunting Buffalo Nickels, by John Wexler, Ron Pope, and Kevin Flynn. (OOP)

A Guide Book of Buffalo and Jefferson Nickels, by Q. David Bowers.

The Best of the Jefferson Nickel Doubled Dies, by John Wexler and Brian Ribar.

The Jefferson Nickel RPM Book, by James Wiles.

The Complete Guide to Liberty Seated Half Dimes, by Al Blythe. (OOP)

The Complete Guide to Liberty Seated Dimes, by Brian Greer. (OOP)

The Complete Guide to Barber Dimes, by David Lawrence. (OOP)

The Authoritative Reference on Barber Dimes, by Kevin Flynn.

The Complete Guide to Mercury Dimes, second edition, by David W. Lange.

Treasure Hunting Mercury Dimes, by Kevin Flynn. (OOP)

The Authoritative Reference on Roosevelt Dimes, by John Wexler and Kevin Flynn.

The Comprehensive Encyclopedia of United States Liberty Seated Quarters, by Larry Briggs. (OOP)

The Complete Guide to Barber Quarters, by David Lawrence. (OOP)

The Authoritative Reference on Barber Quarters, by Kevin Flynn.

A Guide Book of Washington and State Quarters, by Q. David Bowers.

The Washington Quarter Dollar Book—Volume One, 1932–1941, by James Wiles.

The Washington Quarter Dollar Book—Volume Two, 1942–1944, by James Wiles.

The Washington Quarter Dollar Book—Volume Three, 1945–1949, by James Wiles.

The Best of the Washington Quarter Doubled Dies, by John Wexler and Kevin Flynn. (OOP)

The Ultimate Guide to Attributing Bust Half Dollars, by Glenn R. Peterson.

Early Half Dollar Varieties, by Al C. Overton.

The Complete Guide to Liberty Seated Half Dollars, by Randy Wiley and Bill Bugert. (OOP)

The Complete Guide to Barber Halves, by David Lawrence. (OOP)

Treasure Hunting Walking Liberty Half Dollars, by Kevin Flynn and Brian Raines.

The Complete Guide to Walking Liberty Half Dollars, by Bruce Fox. (OOP)

Treasure Hunting Franklin and Kennedy Half Dollar Doubled Dies, by Kevin Flynn and John Wexler.

The Kennedy Half Dollar, by James Wiles.

Commemorative Coins of the United States—A Complete Encyclopedia, by Q. David Bowers. (OOP)

A Guide Book of United States Commemorative Coins, by Q. David Bowers.

A Guide Book of Morgan Silver Dollars, by Q. David Bowers.

Comprehensive Catalog and Encyclopedia of Morgan and Peace Dollars, fourth edition, by Leroy C. Van Allen and George Mallis.

Top 100 Morgan Dollar Die Varieties: The VAM Keys, by Michael Fey and Jeff Oxman.

A Guide Book of Peace Dollars, by Roger W. Burdette.

The Authoritative Reference on Eisenhower Dollars, by John Wexler, Bill Crawford, and Kevin Flynn.

The RPM Book, by John Wexler and Tom Miller. (OOP)

The Error Coin Encyclopedia, by Arnold Margolis.

The Encyclopedia of Doubled Dies, volumes 1 and 2, by John Wexler.

Periodicals

These magazines regularly feature varieties and errors.

ERRORSCOPE. The bi-monthly magazine of CONECA (Combined Organizations of Numismatic Error Collectors of America), the national error/variety club. Membership information is available from online at www.conecaonline.org

Error Trends Coin Magazine. This highly educational monthly magazine is devoted to the error/variety hobby, weighted toward errors. Subscription information is available from Arnold Margolis, P.O. Box 158, Oceanside, New York, 11572-0158.

Appendix H
Coin Clubs

Joining a coin club is an important part of your hobby fulfillment. Membership brings many advantages, most important of which are camaraderie and the accumulation of knowledge. We all need both.

Even if you can't travel to meeting locations and shows, most clubs produce newsletters that are highly educational and encourage members to contribute articles. This is one of the best ways to learn about a specific numismatic subject. With every article you write, you'll travel new avenues of research and add to your numismatic knowledge. It never fails.

Many specialized coin clubs have been born in the virtual environment of the Internet. These clubs often are interactive, offering all members a great opportunity to ask questions of specialists, share knowledge, and meet others with similar interests.

This appendix lists numismatic organizations dedicated to subjects that should interest most of our readers. The information noted, including membership fees and addresses, is as accurate as possible at the time of publication. A visit to a group's Web site can provide the latest information.

NATIONWIDE CLUBS AND GROUPS

The American Numismatic Association. This is the largest coin-collecting group in the world. The monthly magazine, *The Numismatist,* contains articles submitted by members on a wide array of topics. Additionally, the ANA's library is second to none and is available to all members. Other great benefits are also included as a part of your membership.

American Numismatic
  Association
818 N. Cascade Ave.
Colorado Springs, CO 80903-3279
Phone: 719-632-2646
Fax: 719-634-4085
Email: ana@money.org
Web site: www.money.org

CONECA (Combined Organizations of Numismatic Error Collectors of America). CONECA is a worldwide organization that specializes in the study of errors and varieties. Its bimonthly newsletter, *Errorscope,* is filled with educational topics. Additionally, CONECA's Web site has a huge listing with descriptions of several thousand repunched mintmarks and doubled dies. And access to that is free to all!

CONECA
c/o Mr. Robert Neff, Membership
321 Kingslake Drive
Debary, FL 32713
Web site: www.conecaonline.org

NCADD (National Collectors Association of Die Doubling). NCADD is a group devoted to collecting coins with die doubling, repunched mintmarks, over mintmarks, doubled dies, overdates, etc. *The Hub,* NCADD's bi-monthly newsletter, is loaded with features and general educational articles.

NCADD
c/o Brian Ribar
2053 Edith Place
Merrick, NY 11566-3306
Web site: www.geocities.com/
ResearchTriangle/Facility/4968/
NCADD.html

ONLINE CLUBS AND GROUPS

Variety Coins. This is a great online group with a very active discussion board. Most variety specialists belong and are active on the boards. Ask a question, get several answers, each of which will prove useful. Membership is free.

Web site: groups.msn.com/
VarietyCoins /

Coin Varieties. Much like the above, this is a discussion group for those with an interest in coin varieties. Many variety specialists and enthusiasts hold membership (free) and are active in the discussions.

Web site: groups.yahoo.com/
group/coinvarieties

Error World. This online group specializes in coin errors and varieties. Most consider Error World one of the first online groups for this segment of the hobby. Like the majority of others, membership is free.

Web site: www.surok.addr.com/
index.html

Shield Nickels. Another excellent online group for enthusiasts of Shield nickels. Like many of the others, the discussion groups are filled with excellent information. There is no better discussion group available for the variety enthusiast. And best of all, you can join free!

Web site: groups.yahoo.com/
group/Shield_Nickels

SPECIALIZED CLUBS AND GROUPS

John Reich Collectors Society. "The purpose of the John Reich Collectors Society is to encourage the study of numismatics, particularly United States gold and silver coins minted before the introduction of the Liberty Seated design, and to provide technical and educational information concerning such coins." JRCS has a great newsletter and conducts meetings at various times throughout the year.

John Reich Collectors Society
P.O. Box 135
Harrison, OH 45030-0135
Email: jrcs19@adelphia.net
Web site: www.jrcs.org

Liberty Seated Collectors Club. LSCC is one of the strongest groups dedicated to any coin design or series. LSCC members receive the quarterly *Gobrecht Journal*, which is filled with some of the most educational numismatic articles available anywhere.

LSCC
Leonard Augsburger, Secretary-Treasurer
Email: leonard_augsburger@hotmail.com
Web site: www.lsccweb.org

Appendix I
Tips on Mailing Coins

Sooner or later, most of us will send coins through the mail. They might be worth a dollar or two, or several thousand. Whatever their value, you'll want to protect and insure those coins in the best way possible and ensure they arrive at their destination safely and in good condition. The following information will guide you as you choose the best way to package and mail your coins.

PACKAGING AND MAILING

Envelopes

Many valuable coins are lost in the mail as a result of improper packaging. In most such cases, the packages are flimsy, too small, or improperly addressed; or they display no return address, or use materials too thin to withstand the stress of our mail system. A package that is smaller than normal can easily fall off a conveyor, and might not be spotted for several days. Always assume that your package will encounter harsh handling, slip off conveyors, get caught in machinery, fall off a truck, or worse (always expect the worst). Yes, your package *should* be handled perfectly, and in most cases it *is* handled perfectly. However, even with the most exacting machinery and qualified staff, packages still have a chance of getting damaged or lost.

Are you willing to risk that your irreplaceable coins will be handled perfectly on their journey through our mail system? The United States Postal Service does a great job at a very reasonable price. But even they will tell you that perfection is unknown—with them, and with any other business.

If you're sending just a few coins, they can be secured in a corrugated cardboard self-sealing enclosure, such as a Safe-T-Mailer. You can even place the coins carefully between two pieces of heavy cardboard and tape it securely closed. Tape is far preferable over staples, as staple scratches can ruin a coin. The continued use of staples sooner or later will result in damage. The Safe-T-Mailer (or similar brand) package can be placed in a regular business-size envelope (the heavier the paper, the better) for safe mailing. If the coins are too heavy or bulky for an envelope, use a box (provided the coins are well protected). You should make sure your coins do not rattle or even move in the box. There should be no noise or shifting coming from the package. Not only are coins *lost* because of improper packaging and protection, but even more are *damaged*.

If you mail coins frequently, consider purchasing 28-lb., #11 brown kraft policy envelopes. These open and close on the end, rather than along the length, which offers better security—they are easier to seal, and are less likely to come open during transit. If by chance they do come open, the opening is smaller, decreasing the chance of the contents falling out. Additionally, 28# brown kraft envelopes are heavier than normal business envelopes, for better security. Their slightly larger size enables you to include as many as two corrugated mailers, plus additional papers. Also, this size will easily handle several 4" x 6" photographs, with no folding and without infringing on the margins of the envelope.

Number-11 kraft policy envelopes can be purchased from almost any local printer or most stationery stores—physical or online. Do not settle for a number-11 "regular" envelope, which has the normal v-flap on the long side. You want the sealing flap on the short end, which makes it a "policy" envelope.

Consider having your envelopes pre-printed with your name and address, and the words PHOTOS—PLEASE DO NOT BEND about two thirds of the way down on the left side. Those five simple words further disguise the contents—just another small step in providing as much security as possible while the package travels through the system. You should never write the word COINS or indicate the contents of the package in any way, as advertising such valuable items might jeopardize their delivery. Don't worry about the PHOTOS statement on the outside; there is nothing wrong with using these for other purposes.

The envelopes will cost about $60 to $75 per 500 without printing, or about $110 to $135 with printing. Although these are more expensive than regular number-10 envelopes, consider that the cost per piece is only about 15¢—not much, considering the total package cost including postage and insurance. Your 15¢ is negligible when you consider the added security.

Boxes

When you use a box to package and mail coins, make sure it's sturdy enough to withstand a rough trip. It's a good idea to protect the coins using bubble pack, packing peanuts, wadded-up paper, or similar fill. Use a box somewhat larger than needed, adding fill as necessary. Coins should be positioned at least a half inch from any side of the box. A large box and fill will reduce the chance of damage to the coins when the box is opened. We've often received very small boxes, sealed so securely we had no idea where the seams were, forcing us to cut the carton with a box cutter. When we do that, there is always a chance of the knife blade contacting a coin, damaging it. Obviously, when cutting we keep the blade of the cutter near an edge—but we have known people to place coins in contact with the edge of a box.

Consider how the recipient might try to open the package. Tape the box securely with heavy-duty tape prior to wrapping with an outer wrap. We've found that a kraft-paper grocery bag does a very adequate job for wrapping, and you should use brown kraft tape (the kind you moisten) on the outside. The proper tape is also available in white and with reinforced threads. The reinforced tape adds yet another level of security. We have even drawn a dotted line on the outside, with a notation of "Cut here to open," which indicates for the recipient the best place to cut the box safely. Remember to use only a tape that will clearly retain and not smear the ink from the rubber stamps of the Post Office. Never use cellophane tape, or any tape with a shiny surface! This tape will often tear, or cause ink to smear when it is fresh (and at times even when dry), and it can often be removed without evidence of such removal. The ability of the tape to resist undetected removal is critical, as the postal stamp is a vital part of security when using Registered Mail (or any mail for that matter). When the Post Office receives a Registered Mail package, the clerk is charged with affixing their cancellation stamp along each and every seam or tape edge. The purpose of this is so that anyone can easily determine if the package has been opened, or if tape has been added or removed. This is the basis for the requirement of the specified tapes. Many post offices have a brown tape available for use in sealing packages, but those we have seen do not meet the standards for Registered Mail. Plastic tape and duct tape are also not acceptable for Registered Mail.

You can usually find the proper tape at your local stationery store, at superstores, and even online. Don't skimp on the tape—it's inexpensive and using too much is better than too little. Even if your local Post Office accepts a tape that will allow the rubber stamp to smear, don't use it. These are your coins, or you are otherwise responsible for them. These guidelines are for security. If you insure your coins or send a package via Registered Mail, don't take a chance with inferior or inappropriate tape or packaging. If the coins are important enough to use Registered Mail, then they are important enough to use proper supplies.

The Return Address

The advantage of having envelopes printed with your return address reduces the chances of a thief placing their own return address in that position, especially if the return address is printed with large type. If a bogus return-address label is placed on your package and the package cannot be delivered, it will be returned to that bogus address. Place your Registered Mail label very close to the top of the addressee line. Thieves have been known to place an addressee label over the mailing address on the package so the merchandise will be delivered to a location where the culprits can obtain it. Placing that Registered Mail label very close to the addressee block makes it more difficult to place a bogus address label over the address you intended.

Address all packages carefully. Make sure your return address is properly displayed, and as large as feasible on the package. It's a very good habit to include the addressee and sender information inside the package. We have actually had packages returned after being destroyed in transit, because we had an invoice in the package with a name and address on it, which enabled the USPS to return the package and its contents.

The above instructions and recommendations apply to both Insured and Registered/Insured letters and packages. The best option now available to reduce odds of an address being changed is to use the USPS online mailing system. This system saves time and money. After you enter the package data, you print a label that contains your return address, the recipient's name and address, Registration or Insured numbers, and the postage! And when you use the online shipping for Priority Mail and other services, Delivery Confirmation is free. You can also have the USPS send an email to the recipient acknowledging the package is coming (this includes any tracking information).

Signing up for this Web service is free and simple. The USPS bills your credit card for the postage. You need only enter your address once. (From that time forward, the system will have your name and address for label data.) Next you enter the recipient's name and address; you can save this to your own personal address file on the USPS Web site. If you mail to that person again, their information is readily available, and you don't have to enter it again.

SHIPPING SERVICES
Insured / First Class Mail

While the maximum coverage on Insured Mail is now $5,000, compare the costs of Registered Mail with Insured / First Class. Consider that Registered Mail is many times more secure than simple Insured / First Class Mail. To give you an idea, banks and the Bureau of Engraving and Printing use Registered Mail to transport extremely large sums of currency. That is due to the security the USPS places on Registered Mail. Visit their Web site at usps.com for the most current shipping and insurance rates.

Insured / First Class parcels are signed for by the recipient (or his/her agent) upon delivery, and the Post Office retains the signature slip. When mailing, you retain a portion of the insured form for your records, with an adhesive portion of the label affixed to the package. This small label on the package includes the insurance item number of the package, and the Postal Service can obtain any information they might need from that number. You will complete the reverse of the primary insurance form yourself for your own records.

A risk involved with Insured Mail: there is no paper trail other than the shipping documents and the receiving documents. If the package is accidentally delivered to the wrong address, there will be no record of the person who received the package, other than a signature, and a person cannot be tracked solely by a signature. Identification is rarely required for Insured / First-Class Mail, and in some instances insured mail is left in a mailbox (or P.O. box) without the requirement of a signature.

You can file a claim on lost Insured Mail packages after a prescribed period subsequent to mailing (usually 30 days), and recover the total insured amount if the parcel is not located. However, you must jump through a lot of hoops to get the insured amount, including the submission of actual receipts. As a rule, the USPS will only reimburse the cost of the item(s) and not the owner's stated value. Be advised that this process takes time—often up to three months, and it's been known to take over six months to recover a loss!

The Most Secure Way of Mailing Merchandise

Registered Mail is by far the safest way to send merchandise, coins, currency, or even large sums of cash through the postal system, although in some cases it is more expensive than Insured / First Class. For shipping coins that are expensive, or difficult or impossible to replace, Registered Mail is worth its cost. The importance of sending your packages by Registered Mail cannot be overemphasized. Certified Mail never offers any insurance if a package is lost. Coins should never be sent via Certified Mail. Never!

With Registered Mail, each postal employee who handles the package along the delivery path must sign for it. This is maximum accountability. If a Registered Mail package is lost the last employee who signed for the package is responsible—with no exception. USPS employees realize this accountability.

In most post offices, only one or two employees have access to Registered Mail. Registered Mail awaiting claim is stored in a locked cabinet. Employees are required to obtain positive ID before delivery. With regular mail, if an employee knows the recipient, he might release the package after simply obtaining a signature, without requiring ID. The requirements for release of a Registered Mail package are so stringent that employees cannot release a Registered Mail package even to the addressee's spouse, unless the addressee has signed an authorization form.

Registered Mail packages are only insured if insurance has been purchased at the time of mailing. With Registered Mail, there is a fee for postage, a fee for the Registered Mail service, and if insurance is desired, the cost of that insurance. A package can be mailed via Registered Mail without insurance, but the minimum insurance is only a few cents more. Consult your local Post Office or usps.com for fees, including insurance and maximum coverage.

The major difference between Insured / First Class and Registered Mail is that Registered Mail is recorded, accounted for, and signed for by every postal employee who takes charge of the package along the way until the recipient acknowledges possession. Any lost article can be traced to the point where the receipt signature ceased.

As with Insured Mail, the recipient signs a slip upon receipt and the Post Office retains the form. The receipt the sender keeps is much more complete than that for Insured Mail, as it lists full addresses of both the sender and the recipient, the Registry number of the parcel, the total cost breakdown including the amount it is registered for, and (as on an Insured / First Class receipt) the round Post Office date stamp. You can use a book specially designed to track these packages, with a place for all the necessary information. The two key advantages of this book are that the sender's name and address is entered only once for as many as eight packages, and the sender can maintain a copy of the page in their Firm Mailing Book (USPS Form 3877). Some postal centers will allow the sender to use only two or three entries, but some will require all eight entries to be completed. Talk to your local postal service representative.

Be Wary of Certified Mail!

Never send coins or anything of value by Certified Mail—never! Certified Mail offers no monetary protection whatsoever, and if your package is lost you cannot recover any part of the value. It is strictly a method to ensure a certain letter or parcel is delivered—nothing more. There is not even assurance the package is received by the actual addressee. Anyone can receive the package. With Certified Mail you have no recourse if the package is lost, and the Post Office declines responsibility. If a Certified Mail package is lost, it will be up to you to prove the addressee was the actual recipient, which is next to impossible, and then up to your civil resources to obtain the lost value.

Return Receipt

For a small additional fee, you may include a Return Receipt Request on the letter or package that you are mailing. When this card is returned to you, it will be a confirmation that your package was received. The person who accepted it at the other end must sign and date the card, which verifies delivery. However, this can only be secured at the time your package is presented for mailing.

USPS.com

The U.S. Postal Service has produced something they can be proud of: the usps.com Web site is excellent! There are hundreds of pages of informative, searchable data that will help you determine what best suits your shipping needs. Plus (and this is the best part), you can obtain postage and official forms online. Forms that are not available on the site can be ordered online, along with boxes, envelopes, and supplies—all delivered to your door.

This information should help you understand the mailing options that are best for you. If all else fails, call your local Postal Service office and speak to a customer service representative. They are there to help you.

Appendix J
Fivaz-Stanton Numbers Cross-Reference Chart

The Fivaz-Stanton numbering system changed in the fourth edition of the *Cherry-pickers' Guide*. The earlier numbering system was very confined, limiting the number of new listings that could be added. The newer system is rational and infinite. For details, consult the "How to Use This Book" section.

This chart cross-references the current FS numbers assigned to all previous listings. The first column indicates the *new* FS number, with other columns showing the old FS number (if there was a listing), the date and mint of the coin, and a brief description. (Abbreviations listed in the date/mint column include L for Longacre's initial; LL for Large Letters; br for bronze; and NC for No Cents.) Due to space limitations, the description is very short and should not be used in an attempt to identify a variety.

These new numbers can easily be used in an abbreviated format, by using only the final three or four digits in the full number. A variety is always described with the denomination and date, so duplicating that number in a description is not really necessary. The final digits will describe the variety's FS number when the denomination and date are identified.

New FS#	Old FS#	Date/Mint	Brief Description
Half Cents			
HC-1804-301	001	1804	Cohen 2
HC-1804-302	002	1804	Cohen 4
HC-1805-301	003	1805	Cohen 2
HC-1806-301	004	1806	Cohen 3
HC-1808-301	005	1808	Cohen 1
HC-1809-301	006	1809 L	Cohen 1
Large Cents			
LC-1843-301	001	1843	Newcomb 17
LC-1846-301	002	1846	Newcomb 23
LC-1846-302	002.5	1846	Newcomb 25
LC-1847-301	003	1847	Newcomb 36
LC-1847-302	004	1847	Newcomb 43
LC-1849-301	005	1849	Newcomb 25
LC-1850-301	005.5	1850	Newcomb 24
LC-1851-301	006	1851	Newcomb 42
LC-1851-302	006.5	1851	Newcomb 44
LC-1856-301	007	1856	Newcomb 22
Flying Eagle Cents			
01-1857-101	002	1857	DDO 2-0-I; UNITED STATES OF AMERICA, beak, eye, tail
01-1857-102	002.3	1857	DDO 3-0-I; UNITED STATES OF AMERICA, beak, eye, tail; not as strong as 101
01-1857-103	002.7	1857	DDO 6-0-I and RPD; doubling on UNITED STATES OF AMERICA, beak, and eye

New FS#	Old FS#	Date/Mint	Brief Description
01-1857-104	002.8	1857	DDO 5-0-II; doubling evident on UNITED STATES OF AMERICA, beak, and wing
01-1857-105	002	1857	DDO; doubling evident on UNITED STATES OF AMERICA, beak, eye, and tail
01-1857-301	001.5	1857	RPD very strong south on all four digits
01-1857-401	001	1857	Obv of '56; rectangular opening of 0, long center serifs of F
01-1857-402	003	1857	Obverse clashed with Liberty Seated half dollar obverse
01-1857-403	004	1857	Obverse clashed with Liberty Head $20 gold obverse
01-1857-901	005	1857	Reverse clashed with Liberty Seated quarter reverse
01-1858-101	005.5	1858LL	Snow 2, DDO
01-1858-301	006	1858LL	Snow 1, Overdate 8/7 Die 1
01-1858-302	006.1	1858LL	Snow 7, Overdate 8/7 Die 2
Indian Head Cents			
01-1859-301	006.3	1859	Snow 1, RPD
01-1859-302	006.2	1859	Snow 2, RPD
01-1859-303	006.35	1859	Snow 3, RPD
01-1860-401	006.4	1860	Transitional design; Pointed Bust of 1860
01-1861-301	006.45	1861	Snow 1, RPD
01-1862-301		1862	Snow 2, MPD
01-1862-801		1862	Snow 5, DDR
01-1863-301		1863	Snow 2, RPD

New FS#	Old FS#	Date/Mint	Brief Description
01-1863-302		1863	MPD
01-1863-801	006.46	1863	Snow 10, DDR
01-1864-401		1864	Snow 5, Polished Die
01-1864-1101	006.47	1864 br	Snow 4, DDO, RPD
01-1864-1301	006.48	1864 br	Snow 2, RPD
01-1864-2301	006.7	1864 L	Snow 1, RPD
01-1864-2302	006.71	1864 L	Snow 3, RPD
01-1864-2303	006.72	1864 L	Snow 4, RPD
01-1864-2304	006.5, 006.55	1864 L	Snow 5, RPD
01-1864-2305		1864 L	Snow 2, RPD
01-1864-2306	006.73	1864 L	Snow 10, RPD
01-1865-301	007.4	1865	Snow 1, Plain 5–RPD
01-1865-302	007.45	1865	Plain 5–RPD
01-1865-303	007.5	1865	Snow 3, Plain 5–RPD
01-1865-304	007.56	1865	Snow 2, Plain 5–MPD
01-1865-1301	007.3	1865	Snow 1, Fancy 5–RPD
01-1865-1302	007.55	1865	Snow 4, Fancy 5–RPD
01-1865-1401	007.2	1865	Snow 14, Fancy 5–Obverse Die Gouge
01-1865-1801	007	1865	Snow 2, Fancy 5–DDR
01-1866-101	007.6	1866	Snow 1, DDO, Multiple MPD
01-1866-301	007.7	1866	Snow 2, RPD
01-1866-302	007.9	1866	Snow 3, RPD
01-1866-303	007.8	1866	Snow 9, RPD
01-1867-301	008	1867	Snow 1, RPD
01-1867-302	008.1	1867	Snow 4, RPD
01-1868-101	008.2	1868	Snow 1, DDO
01-1868-102	008.26	1868	Snow 4, DDO, RPD
01-1868-103	008.25	1868	Snow 5, DDO. RPD, MPD
01-1868-301	008.23	1868	Snow 8, MPD
01-1869-301	008.3	1869	Snow 3, RPD (formerly believed to be 1869/8)
01-1869-302	008.5	1869	Snow 1, RPD
01-1870-101	008.6	1870	Snow 1, 2, 13, 22, 28, DDO
01-1870-102	008.82	1870	Snow 5, DDO, RPD, MPD
01-1870-301	008.81	1870	Snow 4, RPD
01-1870-302	008.8	1870	Snow 8, MPD, DDR
01-1870-801	008.7	1870	Snow 2, 3, 14, DDR
01-1870-901		1870	Shallow N reverse
01-1871-901		1871	Shallow N reverse
01-1872-301	008.9	1872	Snow 1, RPD
01-1872-901		1872	Shallow N reverse
01-1873-101	009	1873	Snow 1, Close 3 DDO
01-1873-102	009.1	1873	Snow 2, Close 3 DDO
01-1873-1301	009.3	1873	Snow 1, Open 3 RPD
01-1874-101	009.33	1874	Snow 1, DDO
01-1875-301		1875	Snow 1, RPD
01-1875-302		1875	Snow 2, RPD
01-1875-303		1875	Snow 3, RPD
01-1875-801		1875	Snow 16, Die Alteration
01-1878-301	009.4	1878	Snow 2, MPD
01-1880-101	009.41	1880	Snow 1, DDO, MAD Reverse
01-1882-401	009.43	1882	Snow 6, MPD
01-1883-401	009.45	1883	Snow 8, MPD
01-1883-402		1883	Snow 7, MPD
01-1883-403		1883	Snow 1, MPD
01-1883-801	009.46	1883	Snow 6, DDR
01-1884-401	009.48	1884	Snow 1, MPD
01-1887-101	009.5	1887	Snow 1, DDO
01-1888-301	010	1888/7	Snow 1, Overdate
	010.5	1888	No variety–delisted
01-1888-302	010.7	1888/7	Snow 2, RPD
01-1888-303	010.73	1888	MPD; base of 1 in ribbon
01-1888-304	010.74	1888	MPD; 8 in hair curl
01-1888-305	010.75	1888	MPD; two 8's in hair curl
01-1889-301	010.8	1889	Snow 3, RPD
01-1889-801	010.81	1889	Snow 1, DDR
01-1889-802		1889	Snow 11, DDR
01-1890-101	010.85	1890	Snow 1, TDO
01-1890-401	010.82	1890	Snow 3, MPD
01-1890-402	010.84	1890	Snow 6, MPD
01-1891-101	010.88	1891	Snow 1, DDO
01-1891-301	010.87	1891	Snow 3, RPD
01-1892-301	010.89	1892	Snow 8, RPD
01-1892-302	010.9	1892	Snow 1, RPD, DDR
01-1892-401	010.91	1892	Heavy die scratches
01-1893-301	010.95	1893	Snow 2, RPD
01-1894-301	011	1894	Snow 1, RPD
01-1894-402	011.2	1894	Snow 2, MPD
01-1895-301	011.3	1895	Snow 1, RPD
01-1895-302	011.31	1895	Snow 9, RPD
01-1896-301	011.4	1896	Snow 1, RPD
01-1897-401	011.5	1897	Snow 1, MPD
01-1897-402	011.6	1897	Snow 8, RPD
01-1898-401	011.65	1898	MPD; 8 in denticles
01-1898-402	011.66	1898	Snow 5, MPD
01-1899-301	011.7	1899	Snow 1, RPD
01-1899-302	011.75	1899	Snow 13, RPD
01-1899-303		1899	Snow 9, RPD
01-1900-301	011.751	1900	Snow 1, RPD
01-1900-302		1900	Snow 3, RPD
01-1901-301		1901	Snow 19, RPD
01-1902-401		1902	Snow 4, Die gouge
01-1903-301	011.76	1903	Snow 10, MPD
01-1903-302	011.765	1903	Snow 6, MPD
01-1903-303		1903	Snow 7, RPD
01-1903-304		1903	Snow 3, RPD
01-1904-301		1904	Snow 10, RPD
01-1905-301		1905	Snow 1, RPD
01-1906-301		1906	Snow 7, RPD
01-1906-302		1906	Snow 14, MPD, RPD
01-1906-303		1906	Snow 20, RPD
01-1907-301		1907	Snow 1, RPD
01-1907-302		1907	Snow 2, RPD
01-1907-303		1907	Snow 27, RPD
01-1908-201		1908	Snow 1, RPM
01-1908-301	011.77	1908	Snow 4, MPD
01-1908-302	011.79	1908	Snow 9, MPD
01-1909-101	011.9	1909	Snow 1, Doubled L

Lincoln Cents

New FS#	Old FS#	Date/Mint	Brief Description
01-1909-1101	012	1909 V.D.B.	DDO, 1-O-IV
01-1909-1102	012.1	1909 V.D.B.	DDO, 2-O-VI
01-1909S-1501	012.2	1909-S	S/S RPM
01-1909S-1502	012.3	1909-S	S/S, Horizontal S, RPM

New FS#	Old FS#	Date/Mint	Brief Description
01-1910S-501		1910-S	RPM
01-1910S-502	012.7	1910-S	S/S, RPM
01-1911D-501	012.8	1911-D	D/D, RPM
01-1911D-502	012.81	1911-D	D/D, RPM
01-1911D-503	012.82	1911-D	D/D, RPM
01-1911D-504	012.83	1911-D	D/D, RPM
01-1911S-501	012.85	1911-S	S/S, RPM
01-1917-101	013	1917	DDO, 1-0-V
01-1922-401	013.2	1922	"No D" Variety; Die Pair #2 only
01-1925S-101	013.3	1925-S	DDO, 1-0-VI
01-1925S-501	013.31	1925-S	S/S RPM
01-1927-101	013.5	1927	DDO, 1-0-I
01-1927D-501	013.51	1927-D	D/D, RPM
01-1928S-501	013.6	1928-S	Large S mintmark variety
01-1929S-501	013.65	1929-S	S/S, RPM
01-1930D-501		1930-D	RPM
01-1930D-502	013.7	1930-D	D/D, RPM
01-1930S-501	013.73	1930-S	S/S, RPM
01-1934-101	013.79	1934	DDO
01-1934D-503	013.81	1934-D	D/D/D/D, RPM
01-1934D-504	013.8	1934-D	D/D, RPM
01-1935-101	013.9	1935	DDO, 1-0-V
01-1936-101	014	1936	DDO, 1-0-IV
01-1936-102	015	1936	DDO, 2-0-V
01-1936-103	016	1936	DDO, 3-0-V
01-1938D-501	016.4	1938-D	D/D, RPM
01-1938S-501	016.51	1938-S	S/S, RPM
01-1938S-502	016.5	1938-S	S/S/S, RPM
01-1939-101	017	1939	DDO, 1-0-I
01-1941-101	018	1941	DDO, 1-0-I
01-1941-102	018.1	1941	DDO, 2-0-I
01-1941-103	018.3	1941	DDO, 5-0-IV
01-1942-102	018.7	1942	DDO, 4-0-V
01-1942-103	018.9	1942	DDO, 6-0-IV
01-1942D-502	018.91	1942-D	D/D, RPM
01-1942D-504	018.92	1942-D	D/D, RPM
01-1942S-101	018.94	1942-S	DDO, 1-0-IV and S/S RPM
01-1942S-512	018.93	1942-S	S/S/S, RPM; very strong north and west
01-1943-101	018.97	1943	DDO, 1-0-VI; very strong class VI
01-1943D-501	019	1943-D	D/D, RPM; very strong D/D southwest
01-1943D-513	019.1	1943-D	D/D, RPM
01-1943S-101	019.5	1943-S	DDO, 1-0-IV
01-1944D-502	021.1	1944-D	D/D, RPM
01-1944D-507	021.11	1944-D	D/D, RPM
01-1944D-511	020	1944-D	D/S, OMM; very wide north
01-1944D-512	021	1944-D	D/S, OMM; centered under D
01-1946S-511	021.2	1944-S	S/D, OMM; D well centered under S
01-1947-101	021.3	1947	DDO, 1-0-I
01-1947S-504	021.31	1947-S	S/S, RPM
01-1949D-501	021.33	1949-D	D/D/D, RPM
01-1950S-504	021.34	1950-S	S/S, RPM
01-1951-101	021.35	1951 PF	DDO, 1-0-II
01-1951D-101	021.4	1951-D	DDO, 1-0-V
01-1951D-511	021.5	1951-D	D/S, OMM; S well centered under D
01-1951D-512	021.52	1951-D	D/S, OMM; S slightly south of being centered under D
01-1951D-521	021.51	1951-D	Misplaced D mintmark in date
01-1952D-511	021.6	1952-D	D/S, OMM; very likely over S mintmark
01-1953-101	021.7	1953 PF	DDO, 1-0-II
01-1953D-501	021.73	1953-D	D/D, RPM
01-1954D-501	021.76	1954-D	D/D/D, RPM; very strong north and south of primary D
01-1955-101	021.8	1955	DDO, 1-0-I
01-1955-102	021.9	1955	2-0-II+V
01-1955D-101	021.93	1955-D	DDO, 1-0-IV+VII
01-1955D-503	021.94	1955-D	D/D/D, RPM; secondary D centered and wide east
01-1955D-504	021.95	1955-D	D/Horizontal D (presently unique)
01-1955S-501	021.97	1955-S	S/S/S, RPM; both secondary stepped northwest
01-1956D-501	022.1	1956-D	D/D, RPM
01-1956D-508	022	1956-D	D/D, RPM; separated south
01-1958-101	022.15	1958	DDO, 1-0-I
01-1959-101	022.2	1959	DDO, 1-0-II
01-1959-104	022.3	1959	DDO, 4-0-II
01-1959D-501	022.5	1959-D	D/D/D, RPM
01-1960-101	025	1960 PF	DDO, Large/Small Date 1-0-III
01-1960-102	024	1960 PF	DDO, Small/Large Date 2-0-III
01-1960-103	023	1960 PF	TDO, Large/Small Date 3-0-III
01-1960D-101	025.5	1960-D	DDO, Small/Large Date, RPM
01-1961D-501		1961-D	RPM, D/Horizontal D
01-1963D-101	025.8	1963-D	DDO
01-1964-801	026	1964	DDR, 1-R-I
01-1964-802	027	1964	DDR, 58-R-II
01-1964-803		1964	DDR
01-1966-101		1966	DDO
01-1968D-501	027.3	1968-D	RPM
01-1968D-801	027.4	1968-D	DDR, 1-R-V
01-1968S-101	027.5	1968-S PF	DDO
01-1969D-901		1969-D	Missing Designer's Initials
01-1969S-101	028	1969-S	DDO, 1-0-I
01-1970S-101	029	1970-S	DDO, 1-0-I
01-1970S-102	030	1970-S PF	DDO, 3-0-III, Large/Small Date
01-1970S-103	030.1	1970-S	DDO, 5-0-VII
01-1970S-107	030.4	1970-S PF	DDO, 7-0-I
01-1970S-113	030.6	1970-S PF	DDO, 13-0-I
01-1970S-1401		1970-S	Small Date; circulation strike
01-1970S-1402	030.2	1970-S PF	Small Date; Proof
01-1971-101	031	1971	DDO, 1-0-II
01-1971-102	030.7	1971	DDO
01-1971S-101	032	1971-S PF	DDO, 1-0-II
01-1971S-102	033	1971-S PF	DDO, 2-0-II+V
01-1971S-103	033.1	1971-S PF	DDO, 4-0-V
01-1972-101	033.3	1972	DDO, 1-0-I
01-1972-102	033.52	1972	DDO, 2-0-I
01-1972-103	033.53	1972	DDO, 3-0-I
01-1972-104	033.54	1972	DDO, 4-0-I
01-1972-105	033.55	1972	DDO, 5-0-I
01-1972-106	033.56	1972	DDO, 6-0-I

New FS#	Old FS#	Date/Mint	Brief Description
01-1972-107	033.57	1972	DDO, 7-O-I
01-1972-108	033.58	1972	DDO, 8-O-I
01-1972-109	033.59	1972	DDO, 9-O-VII
01-1972S-101	033.7	1972-S PF	DDO, 1-O-I 3
	034.1	1980-D	removed listing
01-1980-101	034	1980	DDO, 1-O-V
01-1982-101	034.5	1982	CLD, DDO, 2-O-V
01-1982-1801		1982	ZSD, DDR
01-1983-101	035	1983	DDO, 1-O-V
01-1983-102	035.1	1983	DDO, 2-O-V
01-1983-103	035.2	1983	DDO, 3-O-V
01-1983-401	035.3	1983	Obverse die clash
01-1983-801	036	1983	DDR, 1-R-IV
01-1984-101	037	1984	DDO, 1-O-IV
01-1984-102	038	1984	DDO, 2-O-II
01-1984D-101	039	1984-D	DDO, 1-O-II+VI
01-1990-101		1990-(S) PF	No mintmark
01-1992D-901		1992-D PF	Type 1 reverse; touching AM of AMERICA
01-1994-801	039.9	1994	DDR, 1-R-IV
01-1995-101	040	1995	DDO, 1-O-V
01-1995D-103	041	1995-D	DDO, 3-O-V
01-1997-101	043	1997	DDO (?); Doubled Ear
01-1998-901		1998	Type 2 reverse; wide AM of AMERICA
01-1999-901		1999	Type 2 reverse; wide AM of AMERICA
01-1999S-901		1999-S PF	Type 1 reverse; close AM of AMERICA
01-2000-901		2000	Type 2 reverse; wide AM of AMERICA
01-2000S-901		2000-S PF	Type 1 reverse; close AM of AMERICA

Two-Cent Pieces

New FS#	Old FS#	Date/Mint	Brief Description
02-1864-401	000.5	1864	Small Motto
02-1864-1101	001	1864	DDO, 1-O-II (Leone-64Lg-06G)
02-1864-1301	001.5	1864	RPD (Leone 64Lg-100E)
02-1864-1302	001.7	1864	RPD (Leone 64-Lg-24H)
02-1864-1901	001.8	1864	Reverse die clashed with obverse of Indian Head cent
02-1865-101	002	1865	Plain 5; DDO 2-O-III (Leone 65P-1o1r)
02-1865-301	002.3	1865	Plain 5; RPD (Leone 65P-5o1r)
02-1865-1301	002.5	1865	Fancy 5; RPD (Leone 65F-1o1r)
02-1865-1302	002.7	1865	Fancy 5; RPD (Leone 65F-2o1r)
02-1865-1303	002.8	1865	Fancy 5; RPD
02-1865-1304	002.9	1865	Fancy 5; MPD (6 or 8 in digits below primary 8)
02-1867-101	003	1867	DDO, 1-O-V
02-1868-301	003.5	1868	MPD (6 in digits below primary 6)
02-1868-302		1868	Possible overdate
02-1869-101	004.2	1869	DDO
02-1869-301	003.9	1869	RPD and MPD (6 in digits below primary 6)
02-1869-302	004	1869	RPD
02-1870-101	004.3	1870	DDO

New FS#	Old FS#	Date/Mint	Brief Description
02-1871-101	005	1871	DDO; circulation strike
02-1871-102		1871 PF	DDO; common
02-1872-101	006	1872	DDO

Three-Cent Silver Pieces

New FS#	Old FS#	Date/Mint	Brief Description
3S-1851-301	001	1851	RPD
3S-1851-302	001.5	1851	RPD
3S-1852-301	002	1852	1852/inverted date
3S-1852-302	002.3	1852	RPD
3S-1852-801	002.5	1852	Doubled-Die Reverse
3S-1853-301	003	1853	RPD
3S-1854-301	004	1854	RPD–wide west
3S-1862-301	007	1862	2/1 overdate

Nickel Three-Cent Piece

New FS#	Old FS#	Date/Mint	Brief Description
3N-1865-101	003.5	1865	DDO
3N-1865-102		1865	DDO
3N-1865-301	001	1865	MPD; flag of 5 in denticles
3N-1865-302	001.5	1865	RPD; wide west
3N-1865-303	002	1865	MPD; flag of 5 deep in denticles
3N-1865-304	002.5, 003	1865	RPD; strong south (blunt tip 5)
3N-1865-305		1865	RPD
3N-1866-101	004	1866	DDO
3N-1866-301		1866	RPD
3N-1869-301	004.3	1869	RPD
3N-1869-302	004.5	1869	RPD
3N-1869-801	004.7	1869	DDR
3N-1870-101	005	1870	DDO, RPD
3N-1870-301	005.5	1870	MPD
3N-1870-302	005.6	1870	MPD, DDR
3N-1871-101	006	1871	TDO, 1-O-I
3N-1871-301		1871	RPD
3N-1875-301	006.5	1875	MPD; 1 in neck; very common (~1 in 3)
3N-1881-301	006.8	1881	RPD
3N-1887-301	007	1887	Overdate 7/6; circulation-strike version only
3N-1887-302	007	1887 PF	Overdate 7/6; Proof version
3N-1888-301		1888	MPD

Shield Nickels

New FS#	Old FS#	Date/Mint	Brief Description
05-1866-101	001.7	1866	DDO, F-22
05-1866-102	001.5	1866	DDO, F-21
05-1866-301	001	1866	RPD, F-08
05-1866-302	001.1	1866	RPD, F-10
05-1866-303	001.2	1866	RPD, F-20
05-1866-304	001.3	1866	RPD, F-16
05-1866-305	001.4	1866	RPD, F-13
05-1866-901		1866	Clashed reverse, RPD, F-09a
05-1867-301	002.1	1867	With Rays; RPD, F-8; likely a small/large date
05-1867-302	002.4	1867	With Rays; RPD, F-9
05-1867-303	002.7	1867	With Rays; RPD, F-2
05-1867-304	002.6	1867	With Rays; MPD, F-01
05-1867-305	002.75	1867	With Rays; 1 punched in shield
05-1867-901		1867	With Rays; rev die clashed with obv; date showing very strong; *super!*
05-1867-1101	001.8	1867	No Rays; DDO, 3-O-III F-59
05-1867-1102	002	1867	NR; DDO, 1-O-IV and RPD

New FS#	Old FS#	Date/Mint	Brief Description
05-1867-1301	001.9	1867	No Rays; RPD, F-23
05-1867-1302	002.15	1867	No Rays; RPD, F-25
05-1867-1303	002.2	1867	No Rays; RPD, F-21
05-1867-1304	002.25	1867	No Rays; RPD, F-20
05-1867-1305	002.3	1867	No Rays; RPD, F-22
05-1867-1306	002.35	1867	No Rays; RPD, DDO, F-08.01
05-1867-1307	002.5	1867	No Rays; RPD, F-38
05-1867-1308	002.9	1867	No Rays; RPD, F-46
05-1867-1309	002.45	1867	No Rays; MPD, F-01.01
05-1867-1401		1867	Obverse die clash, F-69
05-1868-101	003	1868	DDO, 1-0-IV
05-1868-102	003.65	1868	TDO, 10-0-III+IV; Reverse of '68
05-1868-103	003.8	1868	DDO, 6-0-III
05-1868-104	003.9	1868	DDO, 9-0-IV
05-1868-105	003.95	1868	DDO, DDR
05-1868-106	003.96	1868	DDO, 3-0-IV; Reverse of '68
05-1868-107	003.97	1868	DDO, 11-0-IV and RPD
05-1868-109		1868	DDO, RPD
05-1868-110		1868	DDO
05-1868-301	003.2	1868	RPD, F-19
05-1868-302	003.3	1868	RPD; Reverse of '68
05-1868-303	003.35	1868	RPD, south, F-28.05
05-1868-304	003.4	1868	RPD, east, F-25
05-1868-305	003.45	1868	RPD, multiple
05-1868-306	003.5	1868	RPD, date touching ball, F-24
05-1868-307	003.7	1868	RPD
	003.75	1868	duplicate, removed listing
05-1868-309	003.85	1868	RPD
05-1868-310	003.98	1868	RPD, F-20
05-1868-311	003.985	1868	RPD and missing leaf
05-1868-312	003.1	1868	MPD; 1 in ball of shield; Reverse of '68
	003.55	1868	removed listing; photo was an Indian Head cent
05-1868-313	003.6	1868	MPD; 6 or 8 in denticles; F-2
05-1868-401	003.99	1868	Missing leaf and circular scribe mark
05-1868-901	002.94	1868	Variety 1 has a fully broken C of CENTS
05-1868-902	002.95	1868	Variety 2 has a broken C and S of CENTS
05-1868-903	002.96	1868	Variety 3 has a broken C and S of CENTS, plus the S of STATES
05-1868-904	002.97	1868	Variety 4 is same as #903 plus a broken D of UNITED
05-1868-905	002.98	1868	Variety 5 has no broken letters; earliest die state
05-1868-906	002.99	1868	Variety 5.5 has a partially broken C of CENTS
05-1869-301	005	1869	Narrow Date
05-1869-1101	004	1869	Wide Date, DDO 1-0-III
05-1869-1102	004.5	1869	Wide Date, DDO 2-0-V and RPD (tripled)
05-1869-1103	005.67	1869	Wide Date, DDO 3-0-IV+V and RPD
05-1869-1104		1869	Wide Date, DDO and RPD
05-1869-1301		1869	Normal or "wide" date as opposed to the narrow date FS-301
05-1869-1302	005.3	1869	Wide Date, RPD, F-104
05-1869-1303	005.4	1869	Wide Date, RPD, F-202
05-1869-1304	005.5	1869	Wide Date, RPD, F-408
05-1869-1305	005.6	1869	Wide Date, RPD, F-408
05-1869-1306	005.68	1869	Wide Date, RPD, F-105
05-1869-1307	005.2	1869	Wide Date, MPD; 1 in ball above date
05-1870-101	005.7	1870	DDO, 1-0-III and RPD, F-03
05-1870-102	005.74	1870	DDO, F-12
05-1870-103	005.75	1870	DDO and RPD, very wide east
05-1870-301	005.77	1870	RPD, wide southwest, and die clash
05-1870-302	005.76	1870	MPD with 0 in denticles southwest of primary 0
05-1870-801	005.9	1870	DDR 2-R-III rev of '70 over rev of '67
05-1871-101	006	1871	DDO
05-1871-301	006.5	1871	RPD, F-02
05-1872-101	007	1872	DDO, F-121
05-1872-102	007.1	1872	DDO, F-123
05-1872-103	007.2	1872	DDO, 1-0-III, F-124
05-1872-104	007.3	1872	DDO, 4-0-III, F-109
05-1872-105	007.4	1872	TDO, F-05
05-1872-106	007.5	1872	DDO, F-116
05-1872-301	007.6	1872	RPD, F-104; moderate north
05-1872-302	007.65	1872	RPD; very strong with 7 south 3x
05-1872-303	007.7	1872	RPD, F-103
05-1872-304	007.76	1872	RPD, 72 repunched north
05-1872-305	007.77	1872	RPD, MPD
05-1872-306	007.9	1872	RPD, F-02
05-1872-307	007.75	1872	MPD; 2 north right of ball
05-1872-308	007.8	1872	Small over large date
05-1873-101	008, 008.85	1873	Close 3; DDO, 2-0-IV, F-04
05-1873-102	008.7	1873	Close 3; DDO, 3-0-IV, F-05
05-1873-103	008.8	1873	Close 3; DDO, F-06
05-1873-1101	008.3	1873	Open 3; DDO, F-113
05-1873-1102	008.5	1873	Open 3; DDO, MPD, F-102
05-1873-1301	009	1873	Open 3; RPD, Large Date over Small Date
05-1873-1302	009.3	1873	Open 3; RPD, F-103
05-1873-1303	009.5	1873	Ooen 3; RPD, F-110
05-1873-1304	009.7	1873	Open 3; RPD
05-1874-101	010	1874	DDO, F-05
05-1874-102	010.4	1874	DDO, F-12; very strong on shield and motto
05-1874-103	010.5	1874	DDO, 4-0-V, F-08
05-1874-104	010.6	1874	DDO; very strong south; full annulet separation
05-1874-301	010.7	1874	RPD, F-02
05-1874-302	010.8	1874	RPD, F-01
05-1875-101	011	1875	DDO, 1-0-III, F-04
05-1875-102	011.3	1875	DDO, 2-0-V, F-05
05-1875-103	011.5	1875	DDO, RPD, F-03
05-1876-101	012	1876	TDO, 1-0-II+III, F-04
05-1876-102	012.1	1876	DDO, 2-0-III
05-1876-103		1876	DDO, RPD, F-08
05-1882-101		1882	DDO, F-19
05-1882-301	012.5	1882	RPD

New FS#	Old FS#	Date/Mint	Brief Description
05-1882-302		1882	RPD, F-02
05-1882-999		1882	Die chip
05-1883-301	013	1883	Overdate Die #1, F-08
05-1883-302	013.1	1883	Overdate Die #2, F-09
05-1883-303	013.2	1883	Overdate Die #3, F-10
05-1883-304	013.3	1883	Overdate Die #4, F-08.01
05-1883-305		1883	Overdate Die #5, F-07
05-1883-311	012.8	1883	RPD, F-04
05-1883-312	012.9	1883	RPD, F-02

Liberty Head Nickels

New FS#	Old FS#	Date/Mint	Brief Description
05-1883-1301	013.7	1883	No cents; RPD; base of 1 low and left from first 8
05-1883-1302		1883	No cents; RPD; base of 1 low and left from first 8
05-1884-301	013.8	1884	RPD
05-1886-301	013.9	1886	RPD
05-1887-801	014	1887	DDR, 1-R-III
05-1888-101		1888	DDO; most evident on Liberty's ear
05-1889-301		1889	RPD
05-1890-301	014.3	1890	RPD
05-1897-301	014.48	1897	RPD
05-1898-301	014.49	1898	RPD
05-1898-302	014.495	1898	RPD; very strong east of primary date
05-1899-301	014.5	1899	RPD; some believe to be a 9/8
05-1900-801	014.7	1900	DDR; moderate on all reverse elements

Buffalo Nickels

New FS#	Old FS#	Date/Mint	Brief Description
05-1913-901	014.85	1913	Type 1; 3-1/2 leg reverse
05-1913-1101	014.8	1913	Type II; DDO, 1-O-VI (listed in *CPG* 4-1 as Type I)
05-1913-1801	014.86	1913	Type II; DDR, 1-R-II+VI
05-1913D-401	014.861	1913-D	Two Feather Variety
05-1914-101	014.87	1914	DDO; Overdate 4/3
05-1914S-101	014.89	1914-S	DDO; Overdate 4/3
05-1915-101	014.9	1915	DDO, 1-O-IV
05-1915-401	014.91	1915	Two Feather Variety
05-1915D-501	015	1915-D	RPM, D/D north
05-1915S-501	015.5	1915-S	RPM
05-1915S-502	015.6	1915-S	RPM
05-1916-101	016	1916	DDO, 1916/1916
05-1916-401	016.3	1916	No F; missing designer's initial
05-1917-401	016.411	1917	Two Feather Variety
05-1917-801	016.4	1917	DDR, 1-R-III
05-1917-802	016.41	1917	DDR, 2-R-IV
05-1917D-401	016.43	1917-D	Two Feather Variety
05-1917D-901	016.42	1917-D	3-1/2 leg reverse
05-1917S-401	016.44	1917-S	Two Feather Variety
05-1918-401	016.46	1918	Two Feather Variety
05-1918-801	016.45	1918	DDR, 1-R-II
05-1918D-101	016.5	1918-D	Overdate
05-1918S-401	016.6	1918-S	Two Feather Variety
05-1919-401	016.61	1919	Two Feather Variety, Missing initial
05-1920D-501	016.63	1920-D	RPM
05-1920S-401	016.631	1920-S	Two Feather Variety

New FS#	Old FS#	Date/Mint	Brief Description
05-1921-401	016.633	1921	Two Feather Variety
05-1921S-401	016.635	1921-S	Two Feather Variety
05-1925D-401	016.638	1925-D	Two Feather Variety
05-1925S-401	016.641	1925-S	Two Feather Variety
05-1925S-501	016.64	1925-S	RPM
05-1927D-501	016.7	1927-D	RPM
05-1927D-901	016.65	1927-D	3-1/2 leg reverse
05-1927S-101	016.75	1927-D	DDO
05-1929-101	016.8	1929	DDO
05-1930-101	017	1930	DDO, 1-O-IV
05-1930-801	017.5	1930	DDR, 1-R-IV
05-1930-802	017.3	1930	DDR, 2-R-IV
05-1930-803	017.4	1930	DDR, 3-R-IV
05-1930S-401	017.711	1930-S	Two Feather Variety
05-1930S-501	017.71	1930-S	S/S, RPM
05-1935-801	018	1935	DDR, 1-R-V
05-1935-803	018.1	1935	DDR, 3-R-V
05-1935D-502	018.5	1935-D	D/D/D/D, RPM
05-1935S-801	018.6	1935-S	DDR, 1-R-IV
05-1936-101	018.7	1936	DDO, 1-O-VI
05-1936-801	018.8	1936	DDR, 1-R-II+VI (4)
05-1936D-502	019.5	1936-D	D/D/D, RPM
05-1936D-511	019.8	1936-D	D/D/S, OMM; actually D/D/D/S
05-1936D-901	019	1936-D	3-1/2 leg reverse
05-1936S-501	020	1936-S	S/S south; RPM
05-1937D-901	020.2	1937-D	3-legged variety
05-1938D-511	020.5	1938-D/S	D/D/D/S, OMM

Jefferson Nickels

New FS#	Old FS#	Date/Mint	Brief Description
05-1938-1101	021	1938	DDO, 1-O-III
05-1938-1105	021.5	1938	DDO, 5-O-II-(4)
05-1939-801	022	1939	DDR, 1-R-IV
05-1939-802	022.5	1939	DDR, 2-R-II+VI
05-1939-901	023	1939 PF	Reverse of 1940; Type II Steps
05-1940-901	024	1940 PF	Reverse of 1938; Type I Steps
05-1941D-501	024.3	1941-D	RPM; D/D southeast
05-1941S-501	024.5	1941-S	Large S mintmark
05-1941S-502		1941-S	Large S; RPM, S/S overlapping
05-1941S-503	024.6	1941-S	Inverted mintmark
05-1942-101	025	1942	DDO, 2-O-IV
05-1942-102	026	1942	DDO, 3-O-IV
05-1942D-501	027	1942-D	RPM, D/Horizontal D
05-1943P-101	028	1943-P	DDO, 1943/2-P
05-1943P-106	029	1943-P	DDO, 6-O-I; Doubled Eye variety
05-1945P-801	030	1945-P	DDR, 1-R-III
05-1945P-803	030.3	1945-P	DDR, 3-R-II+VI
05-1945P-804	030.5	1945-P	DDR, 4-R-II-(6), RPM
05-1946D-501	031	1946-D	D/Inverted D, RPM
05-1946S-101	031.5	1946-S	DDO, 1-O-V
05-1949D-501	032	1949-D	D/S, OMM
05-1951-101	032.5	1951 PF	DDO, 1-O-V
05-1953-101	032.7	1953 PF	DDO, 1-O-I
05-1954D-501	032.9	1954-D	RPM; some believe this to be an OMM, D/S
05-1954S-501	033	1954-S	OMM, D/S
05-1954S-502	033.1	1954-S	S/S, RPM

New FS#	Old FS#	Date/Mint	Brief Description
05-1955D-501		1955-D	OMM
05-1955-801	035	1955 PF	DDR, 1-R-II-(3)
05-1956-102	035.4	1956 PF	DDO
05-1956-801	035.2	1956	QDR, 18-R-II-(4)
05-1956-802	035.6	1956	TDR
05-1957-101	035.8	1957 PF	QDO
05-1960-801	036	1960 PF	DDR, 1-R-II
05-1961-801	037	1961 PF	DDR, 13-R-II
05-1963-801	037.3	1963	TDR
05-1964D-501	037.5	1964-D	RPM
05-1968S-501	038	1968-S PF	S/S east; RPM

Bust Half Dimes

New FS#	Old FS#	Date/Mint	Brief Description
H10-1829-301	000.1	1829	1829/8; 8 on top surface of 9
H10-1834-301	000.3	1834	3 Over Inverted 3 in date

Liberty Seated Half Dimes

New FS#	Old FS#	Date/Mint	Brief Description
H10-1838-901		1838	Rusted die reverse; rusting evident at about K-3 and K-4
H10-1840o-901	000.5	1840-O	Transitional reverse; Large Letter reverse with open buds
H10-1842o-301		1842-O	Repunched Date; evident on 8 and 2
H10-1843-301	000.6	1843	RPD; 1 and 8 evident south of primary, 4 visible light south
H10-1844-301	000.63	1844	RPD; 1, 8, and 4 south of primary, also 1 north of primary
H10-1845-301	000.65	1845	RPD; 84 protruding south from base of rock
H10-1845-302	000.66	1845	RPD; all 4 digits doubled WNW of the primary date
H10-1848-301	001	1848	Large Date
H10-1848-302	001.3	1848	Overdate; 1848/7/6
H10-1849-301	001.5	1849	Overdate; 1849/8
	001.55	1849	Overdate; 1849/6 (?)
H10-1853-301	001.8	1853	MPD; date protruding from rock; Blythe says 1853/2
H10-1856-301	001.9	1856	MPD; 8 in rock above primary 8
H10-1858-301	002	1858	RPD; Breen 3090
H10-1858-302	003	1858	RPD; date over inverted date
H10-1861-301	003.6	1861	1861/0 overdate
H10-1865-301	003.8	1865	RPD; circulation strike of V-1
H10-1871-301	003.9	1871	MPD; portion of a digit in rock
H10-1872-101	004	1872	DDO
H10-1872S-301	005	1872-S	MPD; 1 in skirt right of ribbon end

Bust Dimes

New FS#	Old FS#	Date/Mint	Brief Description
10-1824-901		1824	Broken wing reverse; relatively common
10-1829-301	001	1829	Curl Base 2
10-1829-901	002	1829	Small/Large 10c
10-1830-301	003	1830	Overdate 30/29

Liberty Seated Dimes—No Stars (1838 only)

New FS#	Old FS#	Date/Mint	Brief Description
10-1838o-501		1838-O	Normal mintmark
10-1838o-502		1838-O	RPM south

Liberty Seated Dimes—Small Stars Obverse, No Drapery, Closed Bud Reverse—1838-1840

New FS#	Old FS#	Date/Mint	Brief Description
10-1838-801	003.27	1838	DDR; all of this type are the DDR

Liberty Seated Dimes—Large Stars Obverse, No Drapery, Closed Bud Reverse—1838-1840

New FS#	Old FS#	Date/Mint	Brief Description
10-1838-401		1838	Cracked obverse die #1
10-1838-402		1838	Cracked obverse die #2
10-1838-403		1838	Cracked obverse die #3
10-1838-802	003.27	1838	Doubled-Die Reverse; same reverse die as 1838-801
10-1838-901		1838	Die flaw rev; large chip between N and M of ONE DIME
10-1840-401		1838	Whiskers at chin; "Whiskers" variety

Liberty Seated Dimes—Large Stars Obverse, Partial Drapery, Closed Bud Reverse—1838-1839

New FS#	Old FS#	Date/Mint	Brief Description
10-1839o-501	003.28	1839-O	RPM; O/O southeast
10-1839o-502		1839-O	Huge O mintmark

Liberty Seated Dimes—Large Stars Obverse, With Drapery, Open Bud Reverse—1840-1853, 1856-1860-S

New FS#	Old FS#	Date/Mint	Brief Description
10-1841-301		1841	Repunched Date; repunched 184
10-1841-302		1841	Repunched Date; repunched 841
10-1841o-301		1841-O	Small O mintmark
10-1841o-302		1841-O	Large O mintmark
10-1841o-901	003.3	1841-O	Transitional reverse; closed bud; Small O mintmark
10-1841o-902		1841-O	Transitional reverse; closed bud; Large O mintmark
10-1843-301		1843	Repunched Date

Liberty Seated Dimes—Arrows Added

New FS#	Old FS#	Date/Mint	Brief Description
10-1853-1301		1853	Repunched Date
10-1854o-501		1854-O	Incomplete mintmark punch, "U" shaped; Breen 3286
10-1856-1101		1856 SD	Small date; Doubled-Die Obverse
10-1856-301		1856	Repunched Date
10-1856o-2301		1856-O	Large O; Repunched Date
10-1872-101	003.4	1872	Doubled-Die Obverse
10-1872-301	003.45	1872	Repunched Date
10-1872-801		1872	New DDR; entire reverse rotated about 175 degrees

Liberty Seated Dimes—No Arrows, Close 3

New FS#	Old FS#	Date/Mint	Brief Description
10-1873-301		1873	Repunched Date; secondary images west of primary images

Liberty Seated Dimes—With Arrows

New FS#	Old FS#	Date/Mint	Brief Description
10-1873-2101	003.5	1873	Doubled-Die Obverse
10-1875-301		1875	MPD; strong 1 in denticles
10-1876CC-101	004	1876-CC	Doubled-Die Obverse; level CC mintmark
10-1876CC-102	004	1876-CC	Doubled-Die Obverse; right C high
10-1876CC-103	004	1876-CC	Doubled-Die Obverse; right C low
10-1876CC-301	003.7	1876-CC	MPD; digits in skirt by shield (#301 listed in *CPG* #3 as P-Mint coin, actually CC-Mint coin)
10-1876CC-901	005	1876-CC	Type II Reverse
10-1887S-501		1887-S	Repunched mintmark; S/S slightly north
10-1888S-501		1888-S	Repunched mintmark; S/S Greer 101

New FS#	Old FS#	Date/Mint	Brief Description
10-1889-801	005.3	1889	DDR
10-1890-301	005.5	1890	MPD
10-1890-302	005.6	1890	MPD; multiple digits in drapery
10-1890S-501		1890-S	Repunched mintmark; Greer 105
10-1890S-502	006	1890-S	Repunched mintmark; wrong photo in *CPG* #3
10-1891-301	1891		MPD; multiple digits in denticles
10-18910-501	008	1891-O	Repunched mintmark; O/Horizontal O
10-189S1-501	007	1891-S	Repunched mintmark; Greer 101

Barber Dimes

New FS#	Old FS#	Date/Mint	Brief Description
10-1892-301	008.3	1892	RPD
10-1892-302	008.4	1892	RPD
10-18920-301	008.5	1892-O	RPD
10-1893S-501	009	1893-S	RPM
10-1895S-301	009.2	1895-S	RPD; secondary image north of primary on 9 and 5
10-1896-301	009.3	1896	RPD; secondary image south on 8, 9, and 6
10-1897-301		1897	RPD
10-1897-302		1897	RPD
10-18990-501		1899-O	RPM
10-19000-501		1900-O	RPM
10-19010-501	010	1901-O	RPM
10-1903-301		1903	RPD
10-19030-301		1903-O	RPD; some think 3/2– we doubt it
10-1904S-501		1904-S	Slanted S mintmark
10-1906-301		1906	RPD
10-1906D-301		1906-D	RPD, RPM
10-1906D-302		1906-D	RPD, RPM; different from above
10-1906D-303		1906-D	RPD, MPD
10-19060-301		1906-O	RPD, MPD
10-1906S-301		1906-S	RPD, RPM; Breen 3552
10-1907-301		1907	RPD
10-1907D-301		1907-D	RPD
10-19070-501		1907-O	RPM
10-1908-301		1908	RPD
10-1908-302		1908	Possible overdate 08/07 low
10-1908-303		1908	RPD; multiple punches
10-1908D-301	010.220	1908-D	RPD; possible overdate
10-1908D-302	010.210	1908-D	RPD
10-1908D-303	010.200	1908-D	Overdate
10-1908D-304	010.225	1908-D	RPD
10-1908D-305	010.230	1908-D	RPD
10-1908D-306	010.235	1908-D	RPD
10-1908D-307	010.240	1908-D	RPD
10-19080-301	010.250	1908-O	RPD; wide right
10-19080-302	010.260	1908-O	RPD
10-1912S-101		1912-S	DDO; obverse letters, date, and ribbon ends

Mercury Dimes

New FS#	Old FS#	Date/Mint	Brief Description
10-1928S-501		1928-S	Large S mintmark
10-1929S-101	010.3	1929-S	Doubled-Die Obverse
10-1931D-101		1931-D	DDO/DDR
10-1931S-101		1931-S	Doubled-Die Obverse

New FS#	Old FS#	Date/Mint	Brief Description
10-1935S-501		1935-S	RPM south (strike doubling on N side of mintmark)
10-1936-101	010.5	1936	Doubled-Die Obverse
10-1936S-110		1936-S	Very likely 1936/192
10-1937-101		1937	Doubled-Die Obverse
10-1937S-101		1937-S	Doubled-Die Obverse
10-1939-101		1939	Doubled-Die Obverse
10-1939D-501		1939-D	D/D south
10-1940S-501		1940-S	RPM west and serifs–S/S/S/S
10-1941-101		1941	Doubled-Die Obverse
10-1941D-101	010.58	1941-D	DDO/DDR, 1-O-V+1-R-II
10-1941S-501	010.6	1941-S	RPM
10-1941S-502		1941-S	Unknown RPM; CPN #13
10-1941S-511	010.65	1941-S	Large S mintmark
10-1941S-801		1941-S	Doubled-Die Reverse; minor
10-1942-101	010.7	1942/1	1942/1 Doubled-Die Obverse
10-1942D-101	010.8	1942/1-D	1942/1-D Doubled-Die Obverse, RPM 4
10-1942D-501		1942-D	1942-D/D RPM 5
10-1943S-501		1943-S	S/S RPM
10-1943S-511		1943-S	Large S, Trumpet Tail S
10-1944D-501		1944-D	RPM
10-1945D-501		1945-D	RPM, D/D northeast
10-1945D-506	010.95	1945-D	D/Horizontal D
10-1945S-503	011	1945-S	S/Horizontal S
10-1945S-511		1945-S	Possible S/D
10-1945S-512		1945-S	Micro S variety

Roosevelt Dimes

New FS#	Old FS#	Date/Mint	Brief Description
10-1946-101	011.4	1946	Doubled-Die Obverse and Doubled-Die Reverse (4-O-V + 3-R-II)
10-1946-102		1946	Doubled-Die Obverse; same obverse die as above, but no DDR
10-1946-103	011.5	1946	Doubled-Die Obverse
10-1946-104		1946	Doubled-Die Obverse
10-1946-801		1946	Doubled-Die Reverse
10-1946-802		1946	DDR; very unusual, strong at only a couple of positions
10-1946D-501		1946-D	D/D south; unlisted
10-1946D-502		1946-D	D/D south
10-1946D-503		1946-D	D/D south
10-1946S-501	011.7	1946-S	RPM and DDR 1-R-II+V; illustrated in CPN 11
10-1946S-502	011.6	1946-S	RPM and DDR 2-R-IV
10-1946S-503		1946-S	Possibly CONECA RPM 13; actually tripled, S/S/S
10-1946S-504		1946-S	Sans serif S; very rare
10-1947-101	011.9	1947	Doubled-Die Obverse; illustrated in CPN 13
10-1947S-501	013	1947-S	S mintmark over D mintmark
10-1947S-502	012	1947-S	S mintmark over D mintmark
10-1947S-503		1947-S	Repunched mintmark; S over S north
10-1947S-504		1947-S	Repunched mintmark; S over S rotated clockwise
10-1947S-801	013.5	1947-S	Doubled-Die Reverse
10-1948-801		1948	Doubled-Die Reverse
10-1950-801		1950 PF	Proof; Doubled-Die Reverse
10-1950D-501		1950-D	New D/S OMM

New FS#	Old FS#	Date/Mint	Brief Description
10-1950D-801	014	1950-D	Doubled-Die Reverse; very strong
10-1950S-501	014.5	1950-S	S over inverted S
10-1953D-501		1953-D	D/Horizontal D MM RPM
10-1954-101		1954 PF	Doubled-Die Obverse
10-1954-801		1954	Unusual Doubled-Die reverse; base of torch and oak stem
10-1954S-501		1954-S	Repunched mintmark
10-1956-101		1956 PF	Doubled-Die Obverse
10-1959D-501	014.8	1959-D	D/Inverted D mintmark
10-1959D-502		1959-D	Repunched mintmark; D/D west
10-1959D-503		1959-D	Repunched mintmark; D/D northwest
10-1960-101		1960 PF	Doubled-Die Obverse
10-1960-102A	015	1960 PF	Doubled-Die Obverse; early die state
10-1960-102B	015	1960 PF	Doubled-Die Obverse; late die state
10-1960-801	015.5	1960 PF	Doubled-Die Reverse
10-1960D-501		1960-D	Repunched mintmark; D/D/D east
10-1961D-801	015.8	1961-D	Doubled-Die Reverse
10-1962D-505		1962-D	D/Horizontal D
10-1963-101	016	1963	Doubled-Die Obverse
10-1963-801	017	1963 PF	Doubled-Die Reverse (listed incorrectly in *CPG* #3 as 5-R-II+V)
10-1963-802	017.5	1963 PF	Doubled-Die Reverse
10-1963-803	018	1963 PF	Doubled-Die Reverse
10-1963-804		1963 PF	Doubled-Die Reverse
10-1963-805		1963	Doubled-Die Reverse
10-1963D-801	018.2	1963-D	Doubled-Die Reverse
10-1964-101	018.4	1964 PF	Doubled-Die Obverse
10-1964-801		1964	Doubled-Die Reverse
10-1964-802	018.3	1964	Doubled-Die Reverse
10-1964D-101	018.45	1964-D	Doubled-Die Obverse
10-1964D-501		1964-D	Repunched mintmark; D/D northeast
10-1964D-502	018.7	1964-D	Misplaced mintmark; D protruding from torch
10-1964D-503		1964-D	Repunched mintmark; D/D south
10-1964D-504		1964-D	Repunched mintmark; D/D south
10-1964D-505		1964-D	Repunched mintmark; D/D south
10-1964D-506		1964-D	Repunched mintmark; D/D south
10-1964D-801	018.5	1964-D	DDR
10-1964D-802		1964-D	DDR
10-1964D-803		1964-D	DDR
10-1967-101	019	1967	DDO
10-1968-101	019.5	1968	DDO
10-1968S-101	020	1968-S PF	DDO
10-1968S-102	020.2	1968-S PF	DDO
10-1968S-501		1968-S PF	No S mintmark
10-1968S-502		1968-S PF	Repunched Mintmark; also a very minor Doubled-Die obverse
10-1968S-801	020.3	1968-S PF	DDR
10-1968S-802		1968-S PF	DDR

New FS#	Old FS#	Date/Mint	Brief Description
10-1969D-501	020.4	1969-D	Repunched mintmark; D/D wide northeast
10-1970-801	020.6	1970	DDR
10-1970D-801		1970-D	DDR
10-1970D-802		1970-D	DDR
10-1975S-501		1975-S PF	Repunched mintmark; S/S north
10-1982-501	021	1982	No "P" mintmark; circulation strike; strong obverse
10-1982-501		1982	No "P" mintmark; circulation strike; weak obverse
10-1983D-501		1983-D	Repunched mintmark; D/D north
10-1985P-501		1985-P	Ghost in neck; similar to a P
10-1986P-501		1986-P	Ghost in field; similar to a P
10-1987P-501		1987-P	Ghost in field; similar to a P
10-2004D-101		2004-D	DDO; doubled ear, rotated

Twenty-Cent Pieces

New FS#	Old FS#	Date/Mint	Brief Description
20-1875S-301		1875-S	MPD; 8 in denticles
20-1875S-302		1875-S	Possible MPD in denticles below 7, RPM

Bust Quarters

New FS#	Old FS#	Date/Mint	Brief Description
25-1831-301		1831	RPD; 1 and 8 south
25-1833-801		1833	DDR
25-1834-901		1834	Recut "OF A" in UNITED STATES OF AMERICA

Liberty Seated Quarters

New FS#	Old FS#	Date/Mint	Brief Description
25-18400-501		1840-O	WD; Large O mintmark
25-18410-101	001	1841-O	Doubled-Die Obverse, CONECA 1-O-III
25-18430-301		1843-O	Repunched Date; 1 and 8 north
25-18430-501	001.5	1843-O	Large O mintmark
25-1845-301		1845	Repunched Date; Large 5/Small 5
25-1847-301	002.3	1847	MPD; 8 protruding from base of rock
25-1847-801	002	1847	RPD, Doubled-Die Reverse, 1-R-II
25-1850-301		1850	RPD; 1 in denticles
25-1853-301		1853	RPD; 5 and 3 evident slightly below the primary digits, slanted

Liberty Seated Quarters—Arrows and Rays

New FS#	Old FS#	Date/Mint	Brief Description
25-1853-1301	003	1853	1853/4 Overdate
25-18530-501		1853-O	O Over Horizontal O
25-18540-501	004	1854-O	Huge O mintmark
25-1856-301		1856	MPD; 1 and 6 punched in gown
25-1856S-501	005	1856-S	Large S / Small S mintmark
25-1857-901	006	1857	Reverse clashed die; clashed with reverse of Flying Eagle cent
25-18570-301	006.2	1857-O	MPD; 1 and 8 in denticles
25-1872-301		1872	RPD; 1 and 8 repunched south of the primary digits
25-1875-301	006.75	1875	MPD; 1 and 7 in denticles
25-1876-301		1876	MPD; top of a 6 in denticles below 6
25-1876-302	006.8	1876	MPD; 1 evident south and west of primary 1 and S and W of primary 8

New FS#	Old FS#	Date/Mint	Brief Description
Liberty Seated Quarters			
25-1876-303	06.85	1876	MPD; 6 in rock
25-1876-304		1876	RPD; triple 6
25-1876-305		1876	MPD; top of 1 and 8 in denticles
25-1876CC-301		1876-CC	RPD; 1, 8, and 7 close south
25-1876S-301	006.88	1876-S	MPD; 7 and 6 in denticles
25-1876S-302		1876-S	MPD; digit in denticles under 8
25-1877CC-301		1877-CC	RPD; 1, 8, and 7 close south
25-1877S-501	007	1877-S	RPM, S/Horizontal S
25-1891-301	007.5	1891	MPD
Barber Quarters			
25-1892-101	007.7	1892	Doubled-Die Obverse; IN GOD WE TRUST
25-1892-301		1892	Tripled-Die Obverse, RPD; very minor TDO, very nice RPD
25-1892-801		1892	Tripled-Die Reverse
25-18920-101	007.8	1892-O	Doubled-Die Obverse; IN GOD WE TRUST
25-18920-301	007.9	1892-O	RPD; very strong south
25-1892S-501		1892-S	RPM; S/S northwest
25-19020-301		1902-O	MPD; digit evident in denticles below O of date
25-1907D-301		1907-D	Doubled-Die Obverse, RPD
25-1907S-501		1907-S	RPM; S/S southeast
25-1908D-301		1908-D	MPD; 8 in denticles between 0 and 8 (likely an 0)
25-1914D-101	007.99	1914-D	Doubled-Die Obverse
25-1916D-501	008	1916-D	D/D, RPM
Standing Liberty Quarters			
25-1918S-101	008.5	1918-S	Overdate Doubled-Die obverse; 1918/7-S
25-1928S-501		1928-S	Inverted S mintmark
25-1928S-502		1928-S	Repunched mintmark
25-1929S-401		1929-S	Very interesting and bold die clash
25-1930S-501		1930-S	Interesting mintmark; likely a small S over large S
Washington Quarters			
25-1932-101		1932	DDO; doubled earlobe
25-1934-101	009	1934	DDO, 1-O-I
25-1934-401		1934	Light Motto
25-1934-402		1934	Medium Motto (common)
25-1934-403		1934	Large Motto (common)
25-1934D-501	009.5	1934-D	Small D; D of 1932
25-1935-101	010	1935	DDO, 1-O-II+V
25-1936-101	011	1936	DDO, 1-O-I
25-1937-101	012	1937	DDO, 1-O-IV
25-1939D-501	012.3	1939-D	D/S (D over S mintmark)
25-1939S-101		1939-S	DDO
25-1940D-101	012.5	1940-D	DDO, 1-O-III
25-1940D-501	012.4	1940-D	RPM; D wide left of primary D
25-1941-101	012.7	1941	Doubled-Die Obverse
25-1941-102	012.9	1941	Doubled-Die Obverse
25-1941-801	013	1941	TDR, 4-R-III+V
25-1941D-801		1941-D	1-R-V; strong on OF AMERICA, weak QUARTER DOLLAR
25-1941S-501		1941-S	Large mintmark; Trumpet Tail style

New FS#	Old FS#	Date/Mint	Brief Description
25-1941S-502		1941-S	S/S, far north; small style mintmark
25-1942-101		1942	Doubled-Die Obverse
25-1942-801	014	1942	Doubled-Die Reverse
25-1942-802	014.3	1942	Doubled-Die Reverse
25-1942-803		1942	Doubled-Die Reverse
25-1942D-101	015	1942-D	Doubled-Die Obverse
25-1942D-801	016	1942-D	Doubled-Die Reverse
25-1943-101	016.5	1943	DDO; strong on motto, weaker on LIB and date
25-1943-102		1943	DDO; strong on LIBERTY, weaker on motto and date
25-1943-103	016.7	1943	DDO; strong on motto, weaker on LIB and date
25-1943D-101		1943-D	DDO; eye, hair curls, initials, lip, chin
25-1943S-101	017	1943-S	Doubled-Die Obverse
25-1943S-501	017.3	1943-S	Trumpet Tail S
25-1943S-502		1943-S	Slightly smaller and slightly different S (Large S is common)
25-1943S-503		1943-S	South, with filled upper loop of primary mintmark
25-1943S-504		1943-S	Knob evident south of primary mintmark
25-1944-101		1944	DDO; light spread on IGWT and minor on date and LIB
25-1944D-101		1944-D	Doubled-Die Obverse– most evident on LIBERTY
25-1944S-101	017.5	1944-S	Doubled-Die Obverse
25-1945-101	018	1945	Doubled-Die Obverse
25-1945S-101		1945-S	Doubled-Die Obverse; IGWT, date, and TY of LIBERTY
25-1945S-102		1945-S	Doubled-Die Obverse; thick on IGWT, Liberty
25-1946-101		1946	Doubled-Die Obverse; IGWT, date, and slightly on LIBERTY
25-1946-801		1946	DDR and DDO; UNITED STATES OF AMERICA, EPU, slightly on QD
25-1946D-501		1946-D	Secondary mintmark weak but evident north of the primary
25-1946S-501		1946-S	S/S north, RPM
25-1947-101		1947	Doubled-Die Obverse; LIBERTY only
25-1947S-501		1947-S	S/S west, RPM
25-1947S-502		1947-S	S/S south
25-1948S-501	018.4	1948-S	S/S/S/S, N and N and very wide northeast
25-1949D-501		1949-D	D/D/D–One D north, another horizontal west
25-1949D-601		1949-D	Possible D/S; several dies reported; only this appears to be D/S
25-1950-801	019	1950	Doubled-Die Reverse; eagle's beak, wings, etc.
25-1950D-801	020	1950-D	Doubled-Die Reverse; talons, feathers, and arrow tips
25-1950D-802		1950-D	DDR; extra thickness on all lettering, especially QUARTER DOLLAR
25-1950D-502		1950-D	D/D, RPM
25-1950D-601	021	1950-D	D/S, OMM
25-1950S-501		1950-S	S/S, north, RPM

New FS#	Old FS#	Date/Mint	Brief Description
25-1950S-601	022	1950-S	S/D, OMM
25-1950S-801		1950-S	Joe Miller
25-1951D-101		1951-D	DDO; nice on LIBERTY, okay on IGWT, weak on date
25-1952-901		1952 PF	"Superbird"; unusual S evident on breast of eagle
25-1952-902		1952 PF	"Superbird," plus recut tail feathers and DDO
25-1952D-101		1952-D	DDO, Class I; nice on all obverse lettering
25-1952D-501		1952-D	Huge D mintmark
25-1952S-501		1952-S	S/S/S, serifs and far north
25-1952S-502		1952-S	S/S, north
25-1953-101		1953 PF	All obverse lettering and date
25-1953-901		1953 PF	Recut tail feathers
25-1953D-801	022.2	1953-D	All reverse lettering, strongest USA and E PLURIBUS UNUM
25-1953D-501		1953-D	Inverted D over D
25-1953D-601		1953-D	OMM, D/S (actually D/D/D/S/S)
25-1956-701		1956 PF	Unusual reverse die gouges
25-1956-701		1956	Reverse die gouge
25-1956-901		1956	Type B reverse on circ strike; intended for Proofs; *rare*
25-1956D-501		1956-D	D over inverted D mintmark
25-1957-901		1957	Type B reverse on circ strike; intended for Proofs; *rare*
25-1957D-901		1957-D	Recut tail feathers
25-1958-901		1958	Type B reverse on circ strike; intended for Proofs; *rare*
25-1959-101	022.45	1959 PF	DDO Strong on IGWT, weaker on other elements
25-1959-901		1959	Type B reverse on circ strike; intended for Proofs; *rare*
25-1959D-501		1959-D	D/D mintmark, interesting as secondary mintmark tilted slightly
25-1960-801	022.5	1960 PF	DDR all reverse elements; small/large design
25-1960-901		1960	Type B reverse on circ strike; intended for Proofs; *rare*
25-1961-101		1961 PF	IGWT, LIBERTY, date, queue; PUP is IGWT
25-1961-901		1961	Type B reverse on circ strike; intended for Proofs; *rare*
25-1961D-501		1961-D	RPM, D/D northeast; secondary is wide northeast
25-1961D-502		1961-D	D/D north
25-1962-101		1962 PF	Strong on all obverse lettering, similar to class VI
25-1962-901		1962	Type B reverse on circ strike; intended for Proofs; *rare*
25-1962D-501		1962-D	Unl RPM D/D strong north, 1/2 letter height
25-1963-101	023	1963	Date, motto, and LIBERTY
25-1963-102		1963	Obverse like 101; reverse on all rim lettering
25-1963-103		1963	Only on 63 of date; strongest on 6
25-1963-801		1963	Doubling evident on C and M of AMERICA, first T of STATES
25-1963-802		1963 PF	Doubling on all reverse lettering, strong spread on AMERICA
25-1963-901		1963	Type B reverse on circ strike; intended for Proofs; *rare*
25-1963D-101		1963-D	DDO 4-0-II+V; all lettering and date, weakest on IGWT
25-1964-101		1964	DDO evident on IN GOD WE TRUST; similar to 63 die 1
25-1964-801		1964	DDR all reverse lettering
25-1964-802	024.5	1964	Evident on QUARTER DOLLAR
25-1964-803		1964	Doubling strongest on STATES OF AMERICA
25-1964-804		1964	DDR evident on UNITED with light doubling
25-1964-901		1964	Type B reverse on circ strike; intended for Proofs; *rare*
25-1964-902		1964	Type C reverse
25-1964D-101		1964-D	Doubling most evident on IN GOD WE TRUST
25-1964D-501		1964-D	D/D east; 1/2 letter width
25-1964D-502		1964-D	D and second D far north protruding from branch
25-1964D-801	025	1964-D	Evident on STATES OF AMERICA, QUARTER DOLLAR
25-1964D-901		1964-D	Type B reverse on circ strike; intended for Proofs; *rare*
25-1964D-902		1964-D	Type C reverse; intended for production beginning in 1965
25-1965-101	026	1965	DDO, very strong, evident on all obverse lettering
25-1965-102		1965	Doubled-Die Obverse; very strong on LIBERTY
25-1965-801		1965	Doubled-Die Reverse; primarily on QUARTER DOLLAR
25-1966-801	026.3	1966	DDR; very rare and very strong on all lettering
25-1967-101	026.5	1967 SMS	Doubled-Die Obverse; evident on all obverse lettering
25-1967-801		1967 SMS	DDR; light on lower branches, leaves, QUARTER DOLLAR
25-1968D-801		1968-D	Doubled-Die Reverse; very strong on all reverse lettering
25-1968S-101		1968-S PF	DDO; evident on all lettering, 1/2 letter width
25-1968S-501		1968-S PF	S/S, north
25-1968S-801	027	1968-S PF	Doubled-Die Reverse; very strong on all lettering
25-1969D-501	027.06	1969-D	D/D slanted west; found in Mint Sets
25-1969D-502		1969-D	D/D slightly west
25-1969S-101	027.08	1969-S PF	Doubled-Die Obverse; very strong on all lettering and date
25-1969S-501	027.1	1969-S PF	Repunched mintmark; S/S/S north and south
25-1970D-101	027.3	1970-D	DDO; evident on all lettering, weaker on LIBERTY
25-1970D-102		1970-D	DDO; evident most on LIBERTY, slightly on date and IGWT
25-1970D-801		1970-D	DDR; evident on all reverse lettering; *strong*
25-1970D-802		1970-D	Doubled-Die Reverse; evident on all reverse lettering
25-1971-801	027.7	1971	Doubled-Die Reverse; very strong on all reverse lettering
25-1971D-801	027.8	1971-D	DDR; very strong on UNITED STATES OF AMERICA

New FS#	Old FS#	Date/Mint	Brief Description
25-1976D-101	028	1976-D	DDO; most on LIBERTY, and in EDS on motto and date
25-1976D-102		1976-D	DDO, 2-0-V CCW; evident on LIBERTY only
25-1979S-501		1979-S PF	Type II mintmark
25-1981S-501		1981-S PF	Type II mintmark
25-1982S-101		1982-S PF	DDO; IGWT, date, and slightly on LIBERTY
25-1989D-501		1989-D	D/D, west
25-1990S-101		1990-S PF	Slight doubling on date and mintmark
25-1995S-101		1995-S PF	DDO on date, mintmark, ribbon, hair, west on LIBERTY and IGWT
25-1996P-701		1996-P	Strange; die abraded through bust (must see photos)
25-2004D-5901		2004-D	Wisconsin quarter, Extra Leaf High (lines pointing up)
25-2004D-5902		2004-D	Wisconsin quarter, Extra Leaf Low (lines pointing down)

Bust Half Dollars

New FS#	Old FS#	Date/Mint	Brief Description
50-1806-301		1806	6 punched over an inverted 6
50-1806-901		1806	STATES/STATAS; an A is evident under the E of STATES
50-1808-301		1808	1808/7 repunched date
50-1812-101		1812	Doubled LIBERTY
50-1812-901		1812	Reverse die clashed; BER of LIBERTY evident
50-1829-301		1829	Curled base 2 of date over a flat based 2

Liberty Seated Half Dollars

New FS#	Old FS#	Date/Mint	Brief Description
50-1840-301		1840	Repunched Date; 4 and 0 of date repunched south; Reverse of '39
50-1840-302		1840	1 and 8 repunched west, 4 and 0 repunched north; small letters
50-1842-301		1842 SD	Repunched Date; 8 42 repunched south
50-1842-801	000.5	1842 SD	UNITED STATES OF AMERICA and eagle doubled
50-18430-301		1843-0	1, 8, and 4 repunched south; 3 repunched north
50-18440-301	001	1844-0	RPD; secondary digits repunched north into rock
50-18450-301	001.5	1845-0	Very strong RPD east; lower secondary 5 very evident
50-18450-302	002	1845-0	Strong RPD; tripled digits, secondary images south
50-18450-303		1845-0	Nice RPD; secondary images west
50-18450-501	002.5	1845-0	RPM O punched over a previously punched horizontal O
50-1846-301	003	1846	6 of date punched correctly over a horizontal 6
50-1847-101		1847	DDO; evident on the shield and LIBERTY
50-1847-301	004	1847	1847/6 overdate
50-1849-301	004.5	1849	RPD; secondary image of lower part of four digits evident west
50-1853-401		1853	Very strong clashed obv die; rays of reverse evident at rock
50-1853-801	004.7	1853	DDR; very strong on UNITED, lighter on HALF

New FS#	Old FS#	Date/Mint	Brief Description
50-1853-802		1853	DDR; best on HALF DOL, AMERICA, and arrows
50-1853-803		1853	DDR; STATES
50-1855-301	005	1855	1855/4 overdate
50-18550-501	006	1855-O	O Over Horizontal O mintmark
50-18560-301		1856-O	RPD; 1 secondary south, 5 and 6 secondary north
50-1858-101		1858	DDO; evident on drapery, skirt, foot, and rock
50-1858-301		1858	RPD; very unusual RPD, right of first 8 and 5
50-1858-302		1858	Misplaced date; 8 protruding from skirt above first 8
50-18500-301		1858-O	MPD; 8 protruding from rock above of second 8
50-18580-901		1858-O	Unusual die clash of reverse; leg of eagle
50-18590-301		1859-O	RPD; 1 secondary image south, and 9 secondary image north
50-19610-401	007	1861-O	Die crack on obverse; Confederate obverse die
50-1865-301		1865	RPD; 1 has secondary image north, 5 has secondary image south
50-1866-301		1866	MPD; 6 (possibly two 6's) in rock above last 6
50-1866-302	007.01	1866	MPD; 6 in denticles after last 6
50-1867-801		1867	DDR; evident on motto, beak, eye, and wings

Liberty Seated Half Dollars—Arrows at Date

New FS#	Old FS#	Date/Mint	Brief Description
50-1873-1101	007.1	1873	DDO; evident on shield, gown, foot, scroll, and lower stars
50-1873-1301		1873	MPD; digit is evident in denticles below arrows
50-1876-301	007.4	1876	RPD; Large/Small Date; small date is likely that of a 20c punch
50-1876-302		1876	RPD; two secondary digits (likely 6) evident west of 7 and 6
50-1876-303	007.3	1876	MPD; a digit is evident in denticles below 7; not WB 103
50-1876-304		1876	Two digits evident in denticles below 8
50-1876-401		1876 PF	Very unusual variety; top of letter C (matching mintmark style) evident punched in Liberty's neck
50-1877-301	007.5	1877	1877/6; 6 is evident on high surface of 7

Barber Half Dollars

New FS#	Old FS#	Date/Mint	Brief Description
50-1892-301	007.7	1892	RPD; very strong with secondary date south
50-1892-801	007.8	1892	DDR; all lettering, arrows, EPU, ribbon, leaves, stars
50-18920-501	007.9	1892	Micro O mintmark; believed to have been a quarter dollar punch
50-1909S-501		1909-S	Inverted S mintmark
50-1911S-501		1911-S	RPM; very strong with secondary image west of primary

New FS#	Old FS#	Date/Mint	Brief Description
Liberty Walking Half Dollars			
50-1916D-501	008	1916-D	RPM; D/D strong southwest, C–RPM
50-1936-101	008.4	1936	DDO; very strong at date; tail of 9 and 3 totally separated
50-1936-102		1936	DDO; evident at date, IGWT, shoe, skirt, rays; C-1-O-II
50-1936D-101		1936-D	DDO; evident on date, shoe, skirt, ground; C-1-O-II
50-1936S-101		1936-S	DDO; evident on date, shoe, skirt, ground; C-1-O-II
50-1939D-101	008.45	1939-D	DDO; evident on date, IGWT, shoe, skirt
50-1939D-501		1939-D	RPM; D/D north; CONECA RPM 1
50-1941D-501		1941-D	RPM; D/D northwest; CONECA RPM 1
50-1941S-501		1941-S	RPM; S/S southwest; listed by Fox as S/Horizontal S
50-1942-101	009	1942	DDO; evident on breast (master die DDO)
50-1942-801	008.5	1942	DDR; evident on AMERICA, HALF DOLLAR, feathers
50-1942D-101		1942-D	DDO; evident on breast (master die DDO)
50-1942D-501	010	1942-D	Formerly believed to be D/S OMM; it is not!
50-1942S-101		1942-S	DDO; evident on breast (master die DDO)
50-1943-101	010.5	1943	DDO; date, IGWT, LIBERTY, skirt, etc.
50-1943D-101	010.5	1943-D	DDO; date, IGWT, LIBERTY, skirt, etc.
50-1943D-501		1943-D	Reported as a D/S; same die as for the 1942-D; *not* D/S!
50-1943S-101	010.5	1943-S	DDO; date, IGWT, LIBERTY, skirt, etc.
50-1944D-901		1944-D	Hand-engraved designer's initials
50-1944S-501	010.6	1944-S	RPM; S/S north
50-1944S-502	010.7	1944-S	RPM; S/S southwest
50-1944S-511		1944-S	Inverted S mintmark
50-1945-901		1945	No designer's initials
50-1946-101		1946	DDO; evident on breast, robe, IGWT
50-1946-801	011.1	1946	DDR; evident on E PLURIBUS UNUM, branches, feathers; C-1-R-III
Franklin Half Dollars			
50-1948-801		1948	DDR; EPU, HALF DOLLAR, AMERICA, clapper
50-1948D-801		1948-D	DDR; EPU, HALF DOLLAR, AMERICA, clapper
50-1949S-501	011.3	1949-S	S/S south; C-RPM (incorrectly listed in *CPG* #3 as 001.3)
50-1950-101		1950 PF	DDO; date, LIBERTY, IN GOD WE TRUST
50-1951S-801	011.5	1951-S	DDR; primarily evident on E PLURIBUS UNUM
50-1953S-501		1953-S	S/S, northwest
50-1954-101		1954 PF	DDO; evident on date, IN GOD WE TRUST, LIBERTY
50-1955-401		1955	Clashed obverse die; "Bugs Bunny"
50-1956-101		1956 PF	DDO; most evident on date, IN GOD WE TRUST
50-1956-801		1956 PF	DDR; evident extra thickness all lettering, spread on EPU
50-1956-802		1956 PF	TY II/TY I DDR; doubled eagle
50-1957-801		1957 PF	DDR; US of A, H D (all), EPU, eagle, right of bell; class II and VI
50-1957D-501		1957-D	D/D; rotated counter-clockwise
50-1959-801		1959	DDR; evident on EPU west (nice separation) and on eagle
50-1960-101	012	1960 PF	DDO; evident on date, TRUST, and LIBERTY
50-1961-801	013	1961 PF	DDR; very strong on EPU, UNITED, and HALF
50-1961-802		1961 PF	DDR; evident on all outer lettering, EPU, eagle's tail feathers
50-1961-803		1961 PF	DDR; evident on all outer lettering, eagle, EPU
50-1962-101		1962 PF	DDO; evident on 2 of date and lightly on lettering
Kennedy Half Dollars			
50-1964-101	013.2	1964 PF	DDO; evident on WE TRUST, RTY, date
50-1964-102		1964	DDO; strong on WE TRUST, LIBERTY and date
50-1964-103		1964 PF	DDO; medium on IGWT, LIBERTY, date, and hair
50-1964-401		1964 PF	Accented Hair variety
50-1964-402		1964 PF	Normal Hair variety (normal type; very common)
50-1964-801		1964	DDR; evident on UNITED STATES OF AMERICA, stars, ribbon, EPU
50-1964D-101	013.4	1964-D	DDO; evident on IGWT, LIBERTY, initials, hair
50-1964D-102			Reserved for future listing
50-1964D-103	013.5	1964-D	TDO; evident on IGWT, RTY, and date, tripled on WE TRUST
50-1964D-104		1964-D	DDO; evident on IN GOD, LI, and 19
50-1964D-105	013.6	1964-D	TDO; evident on IGWT, TY and hair, tripled on WE TRUST
50-1964D-106		1964-D	DDO; evident on WE TRUST, TY and hair
50-1964D-107			Reserved for future listing
50-1964D-108		1964-D	TDO; evident on IGWT, date, initials, RTY
50-1964D-501		1964-D	RPM; D/D south
50-1964D-502		1964-D	RPM; D/D north
50-1964D-503		1964-D	RPM; D/D northeast
50-1965-801		1965 (BS)	DDR; moderate doubling on all outer lettering, stars
50-1966-101	013.8	1966 (BS)	DDO; evident on IN GOD WE TRUST, profile, date

New FS#	Old FS#	Date/Mint	Brief Description
50-1966-102		1966 SMS	DDO; evident on IN GOD WE TRUST, profile, eye
50-1966-103		1966 SMS	DDO; on IGWT, LIBERTY, profile, tripling on WE TRUST
50-1966-104		1966 SMS	DDO; on IN GOD WE TRUST, LIBERTY, date, profile
50-1966-901		1966 SMS	No designer's initials
50-1967-101		1967 SMS	DDO; actually quintupled; evident IGWT, LIBERTY, date
50-1967-102		1967	DDO; evident on IN GOD WE TRUST, LIBERTY, date
50-1967-801		1967	DDR; all reverse lettering, stars, rays; minor DDO
50-1968D-101		1968-D	Tripled-Die Obverse; evident on IGWT, date, and LIBERTY
50-1968S-101	014	1968-S PF	DDO; evident on IN GOD WE TRUST, LIBERTY, date
50-1968S-511		1968-S PF	Inverted S mintmark
50-1968S-801		1968-S PF	Doubled-Die Reverse; all reverse lettering and element
50-1970S-101		1970-S PF	Doubled-Die Obverse; all obverse lettering
50-1971D-101	014.3	1971-D	DDO; evident on LIBERTY, 71, GOD WE TRUST
50-1971D-102		1971-D	DDO; all obverse lettering, best on IGWT; very evident on hair
50-1971S-101		1971-S PF	Doubled-Die Obverse; WE TRUST and date
50-1971S-102	014.5	1971-S PF	DDO; all lettering, date, and upper hair
50-1971S-801		1971-S PF	Doubled-Die Reverse; all reverse lettering, stars
50-1972-101		1972	DDO; IN GOD WE TRUST, Y of LIBERTY, and date
50-1972D-901		1972-D	Missing designer's initials
50-1973D-101	014.8	1973-D	Doubled-Die Obverse; all lettering, date, and hair
50-1974D-101	015	1974-D	DDO; all letters and date, but mostly on WE TRUST
50-1976S-101	016	1976-S	DDO; light spread on WE TRUST; Unc 40% silver
50-1977D-101		1977-D	Doubled-Die Obverse; primarily evident on WE TRUST
50-1979S-501		1979-S PF	Type II mintmark
50-1981S-501		1981-S PF	Type II mintmark
50-1988S-101		1988-S PF	Silver Proof; most lettering, best on WE TRUST, date, and mintmark
50-1992S-101		1992-S PF	Silver Proof; most lettering, best on WE TRUST, date, and mintmark

Liberty Seated Dollars

New FS#	Old FS#	Date/Mint	Brief Description
S1-1865-801		1865	DDR; relatively minor; doubled U of UNITED
S1-1868-301		1868	MPD; top of 6 or 8 evident in denticles below 6
S1-1869-301		1869	RPD; 1 is doubled south of primary 1
S1-1869-302		1869	RPD; base of second 1 is midway up between the 1 and 8
S1-1869-303		1869	MPD; top of a 6 or 9 evident in denticles below 6
S1-1871-301		1871	MPD; top of an 8 evident in denticles below the primary 8

Trade Dollars

New FS#	Old FS#	Date/Mint	Brief Description
T1-1873CC-301	012.3	1873-CC	MPD; top of digit in denticles below between 8 and 7
T1-1873CC-302		1873-CC	MPD; top of digits (an 8 and 7) in denticles below 8 and 7
T1-1875S-501	012.5	1875-S	OMM S/CC; CC mintmark weak, but visible
T1-1875S-502		1875-S	Similar to above; from NGC, Heritage auction 4-25-02
T1-1876-301		1876	RPD; secondary 6 evident within loop of 6
T1-1876CC-801	014	1876-CC	DDR; all reverse elements, especially branch, talons, wing
T1-1876S-101	013	1876-S	DDO; evident on all obverse elements
T1-1877-101		1877	DDO; evident on LIBERTY and wheat fons
T1-1877S-301		1877-S	RPD; final 7 is repunched with 2nd number south of primary
T1-1877S-801	014.5	1877-S	DDR; E PLURIBUS UNUM, ribbon, US of A and top of eagle
T1-1877S-802		1877-S	DDR; lower reverse elements, TRADE DOLLAR, 420 GRAINS
T1-1878S-801	015	1878-S	DDR; evident on all reverse elements; very strong
T1-1878S-802		1878-S	DDR; evident on UNITED STATES and EPU; not dramatic

Morgan Dollars

New FS#	Old FS#	Date/Mint	Brief Description
S1-1878-005		1878 8TF	VAM 5; DDO
S1-1878-009		1878 8TF	VAM 9; first die pairing
S1-1878-014		1878 8TF	VAM 14.11
S1-1878-015		1878 8TF	VAM 15; DDO; doubled LIBERTY
S1-1878-032		1878 7/8	VAM 32; DDR; doubled tail feathers
S1-1878-044	001	1878 7/8	VAM 44; TDO/DDR
S1-1878-115		1878 7TF	VAM 115/199.1; tripled leaves
S1-1878-145		1878 7TF	VAM 145/162; broken M
S1-1878-162		1878 7TF	VAM 162; bottom serifs on N and M of UNUM broken, R of TRUST
S1-1878-166		1878 7TF	VAM 166; spiked P
S1-1878-168		1878 7TF	VAM 168; broken R of TRUST
S1-1878-188		1878 7TF	VAM 188; over-polished L
S1-1878-220		1878 7TF	VAM 220; tripled R of PLURIBUS
S1-1878-901		1878 7TF	Various; Reverse of 1878, flat breast, parallel arrow feathers
S1-1878-902		1878 7TF	Various; Reverse of 1879, round breast, slanted feathers
S1-1878CC-006		1878-CC	DDO; headress and ear; reverse wide, level CC
S1-1878CC-018		1878-CC	DDO; headress and ear; reverse close, uneven CC
S1-1878S-050		1878-S	Tripled-Die Obverse; tripled eyelid
S1-18790-004		1879-O	RPM; O/O/O (formerly O Over Horizontal O)
S1-18790-028		1879-O	RPM; O/O/O (formerly O Over Horizontal O)
S1-1879S-301		1879-S	Reverse of '78; several VAM listings
S1-1880-006		1880	80/79 overdate; "spikes"

New FS#	Old FS#	Date/Mint	Brief Description
S1-1880-007		1880	80/79 overdate; "crossbar"
S1-1880-008		1880	80/79 overdate; "ears"
S1-1880-023		1880	80/79 overdate
S1-1880CC-004		1880-CC	Overdate
S1-1880CC-005		1880-CC	Overdate
S1-1880CC-006		1880-CC	Overdate
S1-1880CC-007		1880-CC	Overdate; Reverse of '78
S1-18800-004		1880-O	Overdate
S1-18800-005		1880-O	Overdate
S1-18800-048		1880-O	"Hangnail" (was VAM 1a)
S1-18800-016		1880-O	Checkmark
S1-18800-017		1880-O	Checkmark
S1-18800-021		1880-O	Checkmark
S1-18810-005		1881-O	O/O; RPM
S1-18810-027		1881-O	DDO
S1-18820-003		1882-O	OMM; O/S; early die state
S1-18820-003		1882-O	OMM; O/S; late die state
		1882-O	OMM; O/S; recused; early die state
S1-18820-004		1882-O	OMM; O/S; recused; late die state
		1882-O	OMM; O/S; broken S; early die state
S1-18820-005		1882-O	OMM; O/S; broken S; late die state
S1-1883-010		1883	DDO
S1-1884-003		1884	Dot
S1-1884-004		1884	Dot
S1-1884-005		1884	DDO
S1-1885-008		1885	Dash variety
S1-1885CC-004		1885-CC	Dash variety
S1-1886-001C		1886	Clashed die
S1-1886-020		1886	RPD
S1-18860-001A		1886-O	Clashed E reverse; clashed die
S1-1887-001B		1887	Clashed E reverse
S1-1887-002		1887	Overdate 7/6
S1-18870-002		1887-O	RPD
S1-18870-003		1887-O	Overdate 7/6
S1-18870-030		1887-O	Clashed dies
S1-18880-001A		1888-O	Clashed E reverse
S1-18880-001B		1888-O	Die break
S1-18880-004		1888-O	DDO; "Hot Lips"
S1-18880-015		1888-O	DDR/RPM
S1-18880-301		1888-O	Oval O
S1-1889-019		1889	Die break
S1-1889-022a		1889	Die break
S1-1889-023a		1889	Clashed die
S1-18890-001a		1889-O	Clashed E reverse
S1-18890-002		1889-O	VAM 2 (?); oval O; various VAMs
S1-18890-017		1889-O	Oval O; included above?
S1-1890CC-004		1890-CC	Tailbar
S1-18900-010		1890-O	Die gouges
S1-18900-020		1890-O	DDO
S1-18910-001a		1891-O	Clashed E reverse
S1-18910-001b		1891-O	Pitted Die
S1-1895S-003		1895-S	RPM; S/S
S1-1895S-004		1895-S	RPM; S/S

New FS#	Old FS#	Date/Mint	Brief Description
S1-1896-020		1896	RPD; formerly listed as VAM 1a
S1-18960-004		1896-O	Micro O
S1-18960-019		1896-O	RPD
S1-18960		1896-O	Formerly listed as VAM 1A
S1-18980-501		1898-O	RPD
S1-18990-004		1899-O	Small O
S1-1900-011		1900	DDR
S1-1900-016		1900	C4/C3 reverse
S1-19000-005		1900-O	Small O
S1-19000-301		1900-O	O/CC
S1-19000-029a		1900-O	Die break
S1-1901-003		1901	DDR
S1-1902-004		1902	DDO
S1-19020-003		1902-O	Small O
S1-1903S-002		1903-S	Small S
S1-1921-301		1921	Wide reeding
S1-1921D-001a		1921-D	Over-polished
S1-1921D-001x		1921-D	Double cud
S1-1921S-001a		1921-S	Die scratch
S1-1921S-001b		1921-S	Die gouges

Peace Dollars

New FS#	Old FS#	Date/Mint	Brief Description
S1-1921-1003		1921	DDR; line through R
S1-1922-001f		1922	Field break
S1-1922-002a		1922	Earring
S1-1922-002c		1922	Extra hair
S1-1922-005a		1922	Scarcheek
S1-1922-012a		1922	Moustache
S1-1922-401		1922	High Relief; design type of 1921
S1-1923-001a		1923	Whisker Jaw
S1-1923-001b1		1923	Extra Hair
S1-1923-001b2		1923	Extra Hair
S1-1923-001c		1923	Tail on O
S1-1923-001d		1923	Whisker Cheek
S1-1923-002		1923	Double Tiara
S1-1923S-001c		1923-S	Pitted reverse
S1-1924-005a		1924	Broken Wing
S1-1925-005		1925	Missing Ray
S1-1926S-004		1926-S	Dot Variety
S1-1927S-101		1927-S	RPM; S/S rotated CCW
S1-1928S-003		1928-S	DDO
S1-1934D-003		1934-D	DDO; Medium D
S1-1934D-004		1934-D	DDO; Small D

Eisenhower Dollars

New FS#	Old FS#	Date/Mint	Brief Description
C1-1971S-103	015.8	1971-S PF	Dramatic DDO on all obverse characters; clad Proof
C1-1971S-106		1971-S PF	DDO, 6-0-I; all obverse |letters and date
C1-1971S-501		1971-S PF	RPM; S/S northwest; 40% silver, Uncirc. "Blue Pack"
C1-1972S-101		1972-S PF	Medium tripling on |IN GOD WE TRUST, LIBERTY, date
C1-1973S-101		1973-S PF	DDO; most evident on IN GOD WE TRUST; 40% silver, Proof

Susan B. Anthony and Sacagawea Dollars

New FS#	Old FS#	Date/Mint	Brief Description
C1-1979P-301	016	1979-P	Near Date variety
C1-1979S-501		1979-S PF	Type II mintmark
C1-1980S-501		1980-S PF	RPM; mintmark repunched northeast of primary S

New FS#	Old FS#	Date/Mint	Brief Description
C1-1981S-501		1981-S PF	Type II mintmark
C1-2000P-901		2000-P	Spikes through breast of eagle

Gold Dollars

New FS#	Old FS#	Date/Mint	Brief Description
G1-1854-1101		1854 Ty 2	DDO/Clashed reverse; strong on obverse lettering, clash
G1-1854-1301		1854 Ty 2	RPD on all four digits
G1-1856S-501		1856-S	RPM, S/S; wide northeast; very strong
G1-1862-101	G-001	1862	DDO; evident on UNITED STATES OF AMERICA, top of crown, beads, hair

Quarter Eagles

New FS#	Old FS#	Date/Mint	Brief Description
G2-1851-301		1851	RPD; evident on 1, 5, and 1
G2-1853-301		1853	RPD; evident on 1 and 8
G2-18540-301		1854-O	MPD; crosslet of 4 in hair curl above 4
G2-1862-301	G-002	1862/1	Overdate, 1862/1
G2-1891-801		1891	DDR; most evident on AMER-ICA, arrow tips, D of 2-1/2 D

$3 Gold

New FS#	Old FS#	Date/Mint	Brief Description
G3-1882-301		1882	RPD; 1882/2

Half Eagles

New FS#	Old FS#	Date/Mint	Brief Description
G5-1802-301		1802	1802/1; strong overdate; fairly common
G5-1819-901		1819	On reverse, 5D over 50, possibly 5D/inverted D
G5-1847-301	003	1847	MPD; top of 7 evident in denticles below 4
G5-1847-302	004	1847	MPD; 1 evident in neck of Liberty
G5-1847-303		1847	RPD; 1 and 8 evident south of primary; evident right of 7
G5-1847-304		1847	MPD; base of 1 evident in bust
G5-1854-101	004.5	1854	DDO; evident on hair and ear; known as "Earring" variety
G5-1881-301	005	1881	1881/0; overdate 1881/1880
G5-1881-302		1881	Repunched date; 1881/881
G5-1881-303		1881	RPD; 1881/1881; secondary date north of primary
G5-1881-304		1881	RPD; 1881/1881; secondary date west of primary
G5-1881-305		1881	RPD; 1881/1881; secondary slightly north and west
G5-1899-301		1899	RPD; evident on 899
G5-1901S-301		1901-S	Overdate; 1901/0-S
G5-1905S-501	006.5	1905-S	S and S; wide east
G5-1906-301		1906	RPD; 6/6
G5-1911S-501		1911-S	Repunched mintmark; S/S, south

Eagles

New FS#	Old FS#	Date/Mint	Brief Description
G10-18460-301		1846-O	RPD and RPM; 1846/6 and O/O north
G10-1853-301	007	1853	1853/2 Overdate; evident within opening of 3
G10-1854S-301		1854-S	MPD; base of 1 evident below and between 1 and 8
G10-1883S-301		1883-S	MPD; 3 evident in denticles below primary 3
G10-1889S-501		1889-S	DDR on STATES OF AMERICA, arrows; strong RPM, S/S
G10-1891CC-501		1891-CC	RPM; secondary second C evident far right of primary

Double Eagles

New FS#	Old FS#	Date/Mint	Brief Description
G20-1852-301		1852	RPD; all digits repunched north
G20-1853-301	G-008	1853	Overdate, 1853/2; evident with 2 inside opening of 3
G20-1857-301		1857	MPD; a digit (likely 1) evident at center right of 5
G20-1859S-101		1859-S	DDO; evident on LIBERTY, hair curl, eye, neck, and profile
G20-1865-301		1865	MPD; digits in denticles; nice
G20-1866-801		1866	DDR; dual hub; small IN over large IN of motto
G20-1066S-1301		1866-S	MPD; digit evident left of primary 1 in denticles
G20-1871S-301		1871-S	MPD; digit in denticles (likely a 7); RPD (1 only)
G20-1873-1101		1873	Open 3; DDO, LIBERTY
G20-1879-801		1879	DDR; most reverse lettering
G20-1883S-301		1883-S	MPD; digit evident in denticles below second 8
G20-1888-801		1888	DDR; strongest on TWENTY DOLLARS and lower ribbon
G20-1896-301		1896	RPD; all digits doubled with secondary images north
G20-1908-801		1908	DDR; evident on eagle's beak, upper lettering
G20-1909-301		1909	Overdate; 1909 over a 1908 date
G20-1909S-501		1909-S	RPM; S/S, southeast
G20-1911D-501		1911-D	RPM; D/D, east (photo from Camire)
G20-1922-801		1922	DDR; evident on motto, lettering, rays, talons
G20-1925-801		1925	DDR; eagle's feathers, rays, IN GOD WE TRUST (NGC)
G20-1926-101		1926	TDO; evident on rays, date, stars, and other elements

Classic Commemoratives

New FS#	Old FS#	Date/Mint	Brief Description
C50-1892-301	C-000.5	1892	Columbian Expo half dollar; RPD, 2/2, north
C50-1892-302		1892	Columbian Expo half dollar; RPD, 2/2, northeast
C50-1892-303		1892	Columbian Expo half dollar; RPD, 89/89, east
C50-1893-301		1893	Columbian Expo half dollar; RPD, 3/3, north
C50-1915S-501		1915-S	Pan-Pac half dollar; RPM, S/S, east; very strong
C50-1925-101	C-001	1925	Stone Mountain half dollar; DDO, 1-O-III
C50-1925-102		1925	Vancouver half dollar; DDO
C50-1933D-101		1933-D	Oregon Trail half dollar; TDO
C50-1935-101		1935	Boone half dollar; DDO (possibly a master die DDO)
C50-1936D-501		1936-D	San Diego half dollar; RPM, D/D, south
C50-1951-801		1951	Carver/Washington half dollar; DDR (possibly a master die DDR)
C50-1953S-801		1953-S	Carver/Washington; DDR (possibly a master die DDR)

CONECA
New Member Application / Renewal Form

Today's Date: _____/_____/______

Membership Type: _____ Regular/Annual Member - $25.00
 _____ Young Numismatist (under 18) - $7.50

Mailing Options: _____ U.S. bulk rate - No extra charge
 _____ First Class or Outside the U.S.A. - $12.50 additional

Total: _____ Amount Due

Name: ____

Address: ______________________________________

City: ______________________State: ______

Zip +4 Code: __________________________

Phone: ________________ Email: __________________________________

Recommended by: *The Cherrypickers' Guide*

Comments/Interests:

____

____

Send application and check/money order (payable to CONECA) to:

CONECA
c/o Mr. Robert Neff, Membership
321 Kingslake Drive
Debary, FL 32713

Your membership is subject to approval by the Membership Committee and
subject to the rules and regulations set forth in the CONECA Constitution and By-Laws.

The error coin shown here sold several years ago. I am looking to replace it and other major errors.

Best Variety
Sportcards & Coins

My 50th Year Dealing With Major Errors
• I have regular coins, too! And major error sports cards.
• Buyer and seller of multiple types of errors on the same coin.

VISA   MasterCard   AMERICAN EXPRESS Cards   DISCOVER NETWORK

In-store debit cards accepted

Questions about coins or bills you have? Contact me!
Visit my web site: Bestvarietycoinerrors.com, or you may contact me at
Bestvariety@hotmail.com (type "cherrypicker" in subject line).
Snail mail is just fine (include a First Class stamp to receive a reply).
Be patient as I am a one-man store.

626-914-2273

Feel confident; I'm an expert in this field.
I am a Life Member of ANA (#2814), CONECA (#51), NASC, and CSNA.

Best Variety, 358 W. Foothill Blvd, Glendora, CA 91741
(North of 210 Freeway. Exit Grand Ave. Go north past Route 66, up to Foothill Blvd.
Turn right and you're almost there.)

Visiting Southern California? Stop in to my custom-built storefront.

THE BEST OF BOTH WORLDS

DGS & DLRC AUCTIONS: A WINNING COMBINATION!

We have the perfect combination to get the most money for your collection. Submit your raw coins to Dominion Grading Service and after they are certified, DLRC Auctions will sell them for you in one of our on-line weekly auctions.

We offer great rates & lightning fast turnaround. In addition, you benefit from our experienced team of numismatists and one of the best online coin auctions in the business.

www.davidlawrence.com | toll free: 800-776-0560 | www.dominiongrading.com

JIM'S COINS & STAMPS

702 N. Midvale Blvd. LL-2
Madison, WI 53705
(608) 233-2118

ERROR AUCTIONS

Six per year for 23 years!

USPS Year subscription $8.00, Sample $2.50, or free download at www.jimscoins.com • We buy errors outright or will auction them for you with no buy-back fee! • We also buy bulk deals of major newly discovered varieties. Email us at jimscoins@sbcglobal.net.

Len Roosmalen  James Essence

ANACS attributes all CHERRYPICKER'S GUIDE Varieties

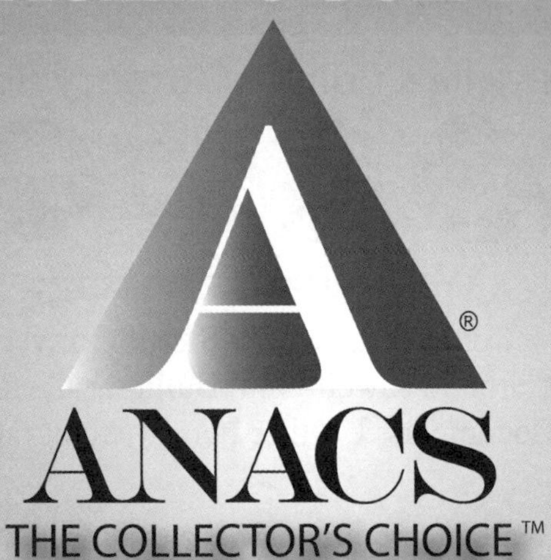

but we don't stop there...

- 3200+ VAM Varieties
- CONECA
- Sheldon
- Breen
- Overton
- And Dozens more.

ANACS-America's Oldest Coin Grading Service. Established 1972.

Call for a free submission kit!

800-888-1861

ANACS
6555 S. Kenton Street, Suite 303
Englewood, CO 80111

CustomerService@ANACS.com
www.anacs.com